Metaphors for Interdependence

Metaphors for Literature

Metaphors for Interdependence

Fazang's Buddhist Metaphysics

NICHOLAOS JONES

OXFORD
UNIVERSITY PRESS

Oxford University Press is a department of the University of Oxford.
It furthers the University's objective of excellence in research, scholarship,
and education by publishing worldwide. Oxford is a registered trade mark of
Oxford University Press in the UK and in certain other countries.

Published in the United States of America by Oxford University Press
198 Madison Avenue, New York, NY 10016, United States of America.

© Nicholaos Jones 2025

All rights reserved. No part of this publication may be reproduced, stored in a retrieval system, transmitted, used for text and data mining, or used for training artificial intelligence, in any form or by any means, without the prior permission in writing of Oxford University Press, or as expressly permitted by law, by license or under terms agreed with the appropriate reprographics rights organization. Inquiries concerning reproduction outside the scope of the above should be sent to the Rights Department, Oxford University Press, at the address above.

You must not circulate this work in any other form
and you must impose this same condition on any acquirer

Library of Congress Control Number: 2025002401

ISBN 9780197807194

DOI: 10.1093/9780197807224.001.0001

Printed by Marquis Book Printing, Canada

for Dorion and Aineias

This is certain, Things, however absolute and entire they seem in themselves, are but Retainers to other parts of Nature, for which they are most taken notice of by us. Their observable Qualities, Actions, and Powers, are owing to something without them; and there is not so complete and perfect a part that we know of Nature, which does not owe the Being it has, and the Excellencies of it, to its Neighbours; and we must not confine our thoughts within the surface of any body, but look a great deal farther, to comprehend perfectly those Qualities that are in it.

— John Locke, *An Essay Concerning Humane Understanding*, 4th edition (London: Awnsham and John Churchil, 1700), IV.vii.11.352

Contents

List of Figures and Tables	xiii
Acknowledgments	xv

1.	**Fazang's Roar**	1
	1.1. Fazang's Biography	1
	1.2. A Lion's Roar	2
	1.2.1. Huayan Interdependence	2
	1.2.2. The LEGO® Model	3
	1.2.3. Fazang as Metaphysician	6
	1.3. A Need for Interpretation	8
	1.3.1. Continuing Influence	8
	1.3.2. Cook's Interpretation	10
	1.4. Goal and Strategy	13
	1.5. Chapter Overviews	16
	1.6. Notes on Usage	18
2.	**Fazang's Vision**	19
	2.1. Rūpāvatī	19
	2.2. Conditionality	20
	2.3. Wages of Conditionality	21
	2.3.1. Evanescence	21
	2.3.2. Duḥkha	22
	2.3.3. Insecurity	23
	2.4. No-Self	24
	2.5. Delusional Cognition	25
	2.5.1. Ignorance and Attachment	25
	2.5.2. Separability	26
	2.5.3. Mutual Reinforcement	27
	2.6. Modes of Experience	28
	2.6.1. Saṃsāra and Nirvāṇa	28
	2.6.2. Revisiting Rūpāvatī	30
	2.7. From Soteriology to Metaphysics	32
	2.7.1. *Saṃsāric* Distortion	32
	2.7.2. *Nirvāṇic* Virtue	32
	2.7.3. Wisdom and Insight	34
3.	**Conceptualizing Causality**	37
	3.1. Conditionality	37
	3.2. Sudhana and Bhīṣmottaranirghoṣa	38

viii CONTENTS

3.3. Fazang's Ontology	40
3.3.1. *Dharmas* and Characteristics	40
3.3.2. Determinacy	42
3.3.3. Dynamic Dispositionality	46
3.4. Real and Nominal	47
3.5. Causality	49
3.5.1. Projecting and Causing	49
3.5.2. *Dharmas* and Powers	51
3.5.3. Inclusion and Identity	53
3.5.4. Emptiness and Existence	59
3.6. An Ontology for Interdependence	62
4. Interpreting Mutuality	64
4.1. Mutuality	64
4.2. Playing Cards	65
4.3. The Standard Interpretation	69
4.3.1. Cosmic Organicism	69
4.3.2. Reimagining Causality	71
4.4. Textual Evidence	74
4.4.1. Completeness	74
4.4.2. Non-Simultaneity	75
4.5. Philosophical Considerations	77
4.5.1. Causal Exclusion	77
4.5.2. Misunderstanding Mutual Inclusion	78
4.5.3. Preserving Causality	79
4.6. An Asymmetry Constraint	80
5. Attending to Aspects	81
5.1. Interpretive Issues	81
5.2. Relativizing Mutuality	82
5.2.1. Aspects	82
5.2.2. The Sarvāstivāda Strategy	83
5.2.3. Vasubandhu's Strategy	84
5.2.4. Fazang's Strategy	85
5.3. Substance and Function	87
5.3.1. The Substance-Function Heuristic	87
5.3.2. Parameterizing Aspects	87
5.4. Correlating Aspects	89
5.4.1. Pairing Aspects	89
5.4.2. Grading Aspects	90
5.5. Inducing Sequentiality	93
5.5.1. Attentional Focus	93
5.5.2. Shifting Focus	94
5.5.3. Mutuality as Sequential	97
5.6. The Role of Mind	101
5.6.1. Modes of Mind	101
5.6.2. The Realm of Mañjuśrī	103

5.6.3. The Realm of Samantabhadra	104
5.6.4. Accessing the Realms	105

6. Indra's Net — 110

6.1. Modeling with Metaphor	110
6.2. Indra's Net	110
6.3. Modeling the Realm of Samantabhadra	112
6.3.1. The Father-Son Model	113
6.3.2. The Meaning of Indra's Net	116
6.3.3. The Aptness of Indra's Net	118
6.3.4. Vairocana's Tower	119
6.4. Contemplating Indra's Net	121
6.4.1. Fazang's Contemplation	121
6.4.2. Competing Interpretations	122
6.5. Sources for Fazang's Contemplation	123
6.5.1. Dushun's Contemplation	124
6.5.2. Buddhist Catoptrics	126
6.5.3. Zhiyan's Contemplation	130
6.6. Conceptualizing Indra's Net	132
6.6.1. The Scope of Fazang's Contemplation	132
6.6.2. Sequencing in Fazang's Contemplation	133
6.6.3. Asymmetry in Fazang's Contemplation	136

7. Counting Coins — 137

7.1. Counting as Contemplation	137
7.2. The Method of Counting	138
7.3. Conceptualizing Counting	141
7.3.1. Counts as Ordered Pairs	141
7.3.2. Gateways	142
7.3.3. Roots and Branches	143
7.3.4. Different Body, Same Body	143
7.4. Counting Coins as Counting Breaths	147
7.4.1. The Literal Interpretation	148
7.4.2. KYTB Coins	149
7.4.3. An Alternative Interpretation	152
7.4.4. Kumārajīva on Counting Breaths	154
7.4.5. Zhiyi on Counting Breaths	155
7.5. Completing Fazang's Metaphor	156
7.5.1. Criteria of Adequacy	157
7.5.2. Counting as Rotational	158
7.5.3. Completion for Different Body	159
7.5.4. Completion for Same Body	161
7.6. Sources for Fazang's Analysis	162
7.6.1. Flower Adornment Sūtra	162
7.6.2. Zhiyan's Contemplation	163
7.6.3. Ŭisang's Contemplation	169

X CONTENTS

7.7.	The Significance of Fazang's Analysis	172
	7.7.1. Developing Indra's Net	172
	7.7.2. Conceptual Insight	174

8. Building Unity — 176

8.1.	From Coins to Buildings	176
8.2.	Competing Architectures	177
	8.2.1. Buddhaghosa's Palace	177
	8.2.2. *Diàntáng* Architecture	178
8.3.	Sources for Fazang's Metaphor	181
	8.3.1. Buildings as Models for Delusion	181
	8.3.2. Buildings as Models for Insight	182
	8.3.3. Buildings as Models of Unity	183
	8.3.4. Zhiyan's Building Metaphor	184
8.4.	Theorizing Six Characteristics	186
8.5.	Identity and Difference	188
	8.5.1. The Characteristic of Identity	188
	8.5.2. The Characteristic of Difference	190
8.6.	Wholeness and Particularity	191
	8.6.1. The Characteristic of Wholeness	192
	8.6.2. Divergence from Abhidharma	193
	8.6.3. The Characteristic of Particularity	196
8.7.	Integration and Disintegration	196
	8.7.1. The Characteristic of Integration	197
	8.7.2. The Characteristic of Disintegration	198
	8.7.3. Divergence from Tiantai	199
8.8.	Justifying Fazang's Theory	201
	8.8.1. Securing Existence	201
	8.8.2. Deriving Six Characteristics	202

9. Fazang's Project — 205

9.1.	Main Conclusions	205
	9.1.1. Conceptualizing Dharmas	205
	9.1.2. Modeling Interdependence	206
9.2.	Interpreting Emptiness	209
	9.2.1. Dependent Arising and Emptiness	209
	9.2.2. Nāgārjuna on Fire and Fuel	212
	9.2.3. Responding to Nāgārjuna	215
	9.2.4. Creeper Vines	217
9.3.	Rethinking Metaphysics	218
	9.3.1. Fundamental Structure	218
	9.3.2. The Presumption of Rigidity	221
	9.3.3. An Analogy from Music Theory	222
	9.3.4. Insights from Jizang	223
	9.3.5. Henology	224

CONTENTS xi

9.4.	Soteriological Justification	227
	9.4.1. Standards of Justification	227
	9.4.2. A Strategy for Fazang	228
	9.4.3. A Preliminary Argument	229
	9.4.4. Contemplating *Dharmas* as Free	231
9.5.	Is Fazang's Metaphysics Syncretistic?	234
	9.5.1. The Syncretic Interpretation	234
	9.5.2. Against Syncretism	234
	9.5.3. Weaving and Crocheting	235
9.6.	Revisiting Soteriology	238
	9.6.1. Tolerance as Soteriological	238
	9.6.2. Overcoming Attachment	239

References	241
Index	259

Figures and Tables

Figures

1.1 LEGO® Lion	5
4.1 Mutually Leaning Playing Cards	66
4.2 Real and Partial Power Playing Cards	67
4.3 Mutual Power Playing Cards, Preliminary View	68
4.4 Mutual Power Playing Cards, Standard View	70
5.1 Queen Includes King	89
5.2 Mutually Leaning Playing Cards, Simplified	92
5.3 Metamorphosis of Baozhi	95
5.4 Mutual Power Playing Cards, Alternative View	99
5.5 Mutual Power Playing Cards, Standard View	100
5.6 Names and Relations for Playing Cards	108
6.1 Glimpsing Indra's Net	111
6.2 Depiction of Simplified Indra's Net (Coarse-Grained)	134
6.3 Depiction of Simplified Indra's Net (Less Coarse-Grained)	135
7.1 Obverse Markings for Kai Yuan Tong Bao Coins	150
7.2 Coin Tree	151
8.1 Kuixing Pavilion (Replica)	179
9.1 Kinds of Fundamental Structure	220
9.2 Planned Pooling	237

Tables

4.1 Non-Simultaneity of Mutual Inclusion	76
5.1 Substance-Function for Identity and Inclusion	88
5.2 Parameterization for Identity and Inclusion	88
5.3 Aspects and Their Gradations	91
5.4 Relationality through Attentional Focus	96

xiv FIGURES AND TABLES

5.5 Potential Conditions for Playing Card Causality 109

6.1 Models for Conceptualizing *Dharmas* 115

7.1 The Structure for Fazang's Metaphor of Counting Coins 138

7.2 First Gateways, Mutual Inclusion, Different Body 160

7.3 Second and Tenth Gateways, Counting Upward, One-Many Inclusion, Different Body 160

7.4 All Gateways, One-Many Inclusion, Same Body 161

9.1 Variability of Scale Degrees 223

Acknowledgments

Fazang first came to my attention some twenty years ago. As a third-year graduate student, I had been assigned as a teaching assistant for Tom Kasulis' *Asian Philosophy* course. In the penultimate week of his course, Tom gave a lecture on Chinese Buddhist philosophy. Fazang made an appearance as the major figure for the Huayan tradition of Chinese Buddhism. I happen to have notes on Tom's lecture (dated May 27, 2003) all these years later. The notes record, in pertinent part, my interpretation of Tom's description for Fazang's distinctive metaphysical vision.

> Causes of all things eventually trace back to a single common cause (which keeps going back). Since things are just interconnected processes, it is arbitrary where to divide things out—we just have one gigantic process that contains everything and is empty (contains no things)—two things in the present are just different ways of looking at the same big process, at different levels of description. It follows that one can understand/know all one needs to know if one really knows one particular thing in excruciating detail.

I'm not sure that I understood any of this. Tom supplemented the abstract description with a discussion about the metaphor of Indra's net. That discussion gave me the sense that I got at least the gist of Fazang's vision. This turned out not to be true, and this book is the result of a decades-long effort to recover the glimmer of insight that Tom bequeathed to me. So I thank Tom Kasulis for exposing me to Fazang's metaphysics as well as for encouraging and supporting my efforts to philosophize beyond the bounds of the Anglo-American canon.

The effort that culminates in this book proceeded through several stages. My initial efforts relied upon extant English-language interpretations of Fazang's thought. I thank Francis Cook, Whalen Lai, and Ming-wood Liu for their scholarly contributions here. They are the giants on whose shoulders I sit in crafting this book. (I also acknowledge a vast body of work by Japanese scholars on Fazang. Limitations of access and linguistic skill prevent me from making much use of their work.)

The second stage of my effort was endeavoring to analyze—in the sense of *analysis* dominant among analytic philosophers—passages, from Fazang's writings, in which Fazang seemed to be giving explanations or making arguments for his metaphysical vision. Here I thank Ben Caplan for encouraging remarks about

xvi ACKNOWLEDGMENTS

one of my first efforts at analysis. I thank Adam Podlaskowski, Bill Melanson, David Merli, and Joshua Smith for their encouragement and conservation over many years. I thank those who have attended my presentations at various conferences, and especially those from the Alabama Philosophical Society, for their curiosity and patience in thinking through how to express Fazang's ideas to audiences trained in an analytic style of philosophy. I also thank my colleagues in the Department of Philosophy at The University of Alabama in Huntsville for supporting and encouraging my efforts to sustain a research program in an area well beyond my dissertation specialization.

Many of my analytic efforts happen to coincide with efforts by Graham Priest to interpret and understand Fazang's metaphysics. I thank Graham for being an exceptionally encouraging colleague. I thank him for helping to bring Fazang's metaphysics to the attention of analytically trained philosophers. I do not always agree with Graham about how to interpret Fazang. But Graham's work is responsible, in no small part, for driving me to clarify the view I think Fazang is presenting and the reasons I think he is presenting it.

The third stage of my effort to understand Fazang's metaphysics—and the stage that culminates with this book—involved connecting Fazang's various arguments and explanations to the metaphors he uses to model his metaphysical vision. My initial strategy here was to try to reverse engineer, from the remarks Fazang makes about his metaphors, how Fazang must have been thinking about the objects of those metaphors (coins, buildings). This led to some progress in understanding Fazang's vision. But, in the course of talking with my spouse, Holly Jones, about some things that still did not quite make sense, I learned about the "new historicist" approach to interpreting literature. This led me to investigate material cultures and theories about mirrors, coins, and building architectures. These investigations helped me to better understand the relation between Fazang's more abstract metaphysical remarks and his various metaphors. I thank Holly for setting me on this new interpretive trajectory. (The result is such that the interpretation of Fazang that I now favor differs significantly from my prior interpretive efforts, and this book should be taken to supersede those earlier interpretations.) I thank Holly also for her care and support; for patient, sometimes heated, and always enjoyable conversation about the ideas and examples in this book; and for contributing her artistic skills to some of the figures for the book.

Between the first draft and final version of this manuscript, I had the good fortune to be able to present some ideas from the book to several audiences. I thank the Cosmopolitan Philosophy group at UC Berkeley and an audience from the University of Kansas for feedback on material from Chapters 4 and 5. I also had the good fortunate to have Bryan Van Norden spend a semester in residence at my university, during which time he provided advice for improving the accessibility of my writing. I thank him for his mentorship.

Finally, I thank several generations of students at The University of Alabama in Huntsville, as well as Alabama taxpayers, for supporting public education in the humanities and thereby empowering the pursuit of this project over the years.

N.J.
Huntsville, Alabama
July 2024

1

Fazang's Roar

1.1. Fazang's Biography

Fazang 法藏 (643–712) is a Buddhist monk from the Tang 唐 era of medieval China (618–907).[1] In 658, full of youthful exuberance, he gave a finger to the Buddha. This probably involved burning incense wrapped around his finger.[2] Whatever the details, Fazang gave his finger in front of the Famen Temple 法門寺.[3] His was an act of religious devotion. The temple housed one of the most famous relics of Tang-era China: a finger bone alleged to have belonged to the body of the historical Buddha.[4] Fazang's self-immolation symbolized his commitment to following the way of the Buddha. He left home one year later, journeying to Mount Taibei 太白山 to study Buddhist literature and Daoist medicine. He studied on the sacred mountain for several years before returning to his family home in the capital city of Chang'an 長安 to care for his ailing parents.[5]

According to the Korean biographer Ch'oe Ch'iwŏn 崔致遠 (857–904), in 663, Fazang witnessed rays of divine light illuminating the courtyard of his family's home.[6] The next morning, after traveling to a nearby Buddhist monastery, he met the monk Zhiyan 智儼 (602–668). Zhiyan embraced Fazang as his student. Yet, for some reason—perhaps to care for his parents, perhaps because he had a wife—Fazang remained as a layperson. By 670, he abandoned his secular life to join the Buddhist community as a monk. He spent much of his religious career as a cosmopolitan priest in the Tang capitals of Chang'an and Shendu 神都.[7]

Fazang achieved renown as an adept shaman, an accomplished engineer, and a prolific writer. He also was a dominant religious influence on Empress Wu Zetian 武則天 (625–705). The Empress relied upon Fazang for authoritative lectures on Buddhist scriptures, esoteric rituals directed toward alleviating

---

[1] The first vowel sound in Fazang's name (in 法 *fǎ*) is similar to the "oh" sound in *John*. The tone begins at mid-range, dips low, and then returns to mid-range. The "z" sound in his name is similar to the "ds" sound in *friends*. The second vowel sound (in 藏 *zàng*) also sounds like "oh" in *John*. The tone begins high and ends low. Ignoring tone, Fazang's name sounds roughly like "fah dsahng."

[2] Benn 1998, 307.

[3] Chen 2007, 58.

[4] Sen 2014.

[5] Chang'an is the modern capital Xi'an 西安 of Shaanxi 陕西 (陝西) province in northwest China.

[6] T50.2054.281b2-8; Chen 2007, 121–2.

[7] Shendu is the modern city Luoyang 洛阳市 in the western region of Henan 河南 province.

Metaphors for Interdependence. Nicholaos Jones, Oxford University Press. © Nicholaos Jones 2025.
DOI: 10.1093/9780197807224.003.0001

2 METAPHORS FOR INTERDEPENDENCE

drought and suppressing enemy armies, and efforts to legitimate her rule as a female monarch. Fazang helped to develop and promulgate the technology of woodblock printing (xylography), and he designed a mirror-lamp to illustrate characteristics of mutual reflectivity.[8]

Fazang's writings range from authoritative commentaries on Buddhist scriptures to systematic treatises that integrate and develop a range of Buddhist teachings. Three of his writings are especially significant.

1. *Commentary on Awakening Mahāyāna Faith*, considered by many to be definitive.[9]
2. *Investigating the Mysteries of the Flower Adornment Sūtra*, an influential commentary on the *Flower Adornment Sūtra* —or, strictly speaking, on a Chinese translation, by the Indian Buddhist monk Buddhabhadra 佛馱 (359–429), of a collection of religious scriptures titled *The Great Expansive Buddha Avataṃsaka Sūtra*.[10]
3. *Treatise on the Divisions within the One Vehicle Doctrine of Huayan*—or, as it is more commonly known, *Treatise on the Five Teachings of Huayan*, a treatise that classifies teachings from various Buddhist traditions and, in its tenth and final chapter, systematically articulates metaphysical doctrines implicit in the *Flower Adornment Sūtra*.[11]

These writings, together with his considerable fame as a popular expositor of Buddhist teaching, secure Fazang's status as a patriarch for the tradition of Buddhism we now refer to as Huayan 華嚴.

1.2. A Lion's Roar

1.2.1. Huayan Interdependence

A central contention of Huayan Buddhism is that everything is included within and identical with everything else. Fazang nicely demonstrates the radically counterintuitive implications of this contention in his *Treatise on the Golden*

---

[8] For additional biographical details, see Fang 1991; Chen 2007; Wickstrom 2017.

[9] Mun dates Fazang's composition of *Commentary on Awakening Mahāyāna Faith* to 695 or 696 (Mun 2002, 421, note 30).

[10] In a letter from January 690, Fazang writes that he is nearly finished composing *Investigating the Mysteries of the Flower Adornment Sūtra*. See Forte 2000, 45–68. For discussion of the title for the *Flower Adornment Sūtra*, see Hamar 2007.

[11] Fazang composed *Treatise on the Five Teachings of Huayan* early in his career, before the age of 38. See Nakamura 1989, 222; Yu 2022, 93, note 78.

Lion.[12] Consider Fazang's remarks about a statue made of gold and shaped as a lion.

> If the eye of the lion encompasses the lion completely, then all is nothing but the eye. If the ear of the lion encompasses the lion completely, then all is nothing but the ear. Each of the parts simultaneously encompasses the others so that all are complete. So each one is mixed with the others. . . .
>
> All the parts of the lion, each and every hair, by means of the gold, encompass the whole lion completely. Each and every part is completely the eye of the lion. The eye is the ear, the ear is the nose, the nose is the tongue, the tongue is the body. Nonetheless, this does not prevent each of them being in its place and completely established. . . .
>
> In every one of the lion's eyes, ears, limbs, and joints, and in each and every hair, there is the golden lion. Furthermore, the golden lion in each and every hair simultaneously enters into any one hair. Consequently, in each and every hair, there are a limitless number of lions. Moreover, each and every hair, which carries this limitless number of lions, also enters into any one hair.[13]

Fazang's remarks liken reality to a golden statue of a lion, the various constituents of reality to the lion's organs, and the fundamental nature of those constituents to the lion's golden substance. For Fazang, just as the lion's eye (or ear, or nose, and so on) encompasses all of the lion's other organs, so too each constituent of reality includes every other. Moreover, just as each part of the lion is completely the lion's eye (or ear, or nose, and so on), so too each constituent of reality is identical with every other.

1.2.2. The LEGO® Model

Fazang's remarks about the statue of the golden lion are counterintuitive. Part of the reason for this is that Fazang's remarks violate a common and natural conception about the structure of reality. This conception—label it the LEGO® model of reality—likens the objects of our everyday experience—chariots, coins, persons—to LEGO® builds.[14] Just as there are basic LEGO® blocks, there are "fundamental concrete objects." Moreover, just as different arrangements of particular

---

[12] For information about the history and doctrinal content of *Treatise on the Golden Lion*, see Girard 2012; Xiong 2024. For an analysis of key concepts, see Jones 2025.

[13] Van Norden 2014, 89–90. See also T45.1880.665a25-b1, b19-23, c19-25.

[14] See Wallace 2011; Paul 2012, 226. For an alternative analysis of the LEGO® model of reality, see Kahn 2017.

4 METAPHORS FOR INTERDEPENDENCE

LEGO® blocks compose different LEGO® builds, different arrangements of fundamental concrete objects compose different everyday objects.

The LEGO® model traces back to a building metaphor from Michel de Montaigne (1533–1592), an influential figure of the late French Renaissance. Montaigne conceptualizes God as an architect (*ce grand architecte*), the earth as the building God constructs (*bastiment qu'il construisoit*), and human efforts to understand this construction as fabrications "forged into poor little human bodies" (*forge en ce pauvre petit corps humain*).[15] He uses this building metaphor in the service of his skepticism, focusing in particular on the different foundations that humans use to build their fabrications. René Descartes (1596–1640), often credited as the founder of modern European philosophy, refines the epistemological aspect of Montaigne's metaphor, contending that some fabricated foundations are firmer than others.[16] But the ontological aspect of Montaigne's metaphor also persists. For example, contemporary metaphysicians characterize specific views as "foundationalist," fundamental objects as "building blocks," and objective dependencies as "building relations."[17]

The LEGO® model supports several inferences about the structure of reality. Four are especially noteworthy. First, reality consists of fundamental "building blocks" of some sort or other, where fundamentality is a matter of not admitting division into smaller blocks. Second, builds—arrangements of fundamental building blocks—are additive, nothing more than the sum of their blocks. Third, blocks and builds sort into kinds, and different kinds have different intrinsic characteristics (such as shape). Fourth, the fundamental blocks are separable from others in the sense that each is completely independent of all others.[18]

Fazang's conception of reality rejects the separability component of the LEGO® model. Consider, by way of illustration, LEGO® set #70123, Lion Legend Beast (Figure 1.1).

This set—the closest LEGO® comes to a golden lion—has 120 distinct blocks, including ten standard 1x2 plates (Part #4528604) and one specialized tail (Part #4183248). According to Brickset.com, Part #4528604—the 1x2 plate—appears in at least 200 other LEGO® sets. Part #4183248—the tail—appears in only two other sets: set #10188, Death Star, where it functions as the neck-like appendage for a Dianoga monster; and set #7582, Royal Summer Palace, where it functions

---

[15] Bachynski 2010, 621, 624. Montaigne's building metaphor descends from the metaphor of a (written) text as a building (see Cowling 1998). So it is fitting that a recent monograph, on a model (or meta-model) in the lineage of Montaigne's building metaphor, bears the title *Writing the Book of the World* (Sider 2012).

[16] See Thagard and Beam 2004; Purdy 2011, 87–92.

[17] Bennett 2017.

[18] For similar claims in the context of value theory, see Oddie 2001. For a scientific application of the LEGO® model of reality, known as the BioBrick approach to synthetic biology, see Canton et al. 2008. For a model that supports similar inferences, based upon the metaphor of reality as a formal language, see Bacon 2020.

Figure 1.1 LEGO® Lion
Image created by the author.

as a canopy bracket. These alternative functions make the Lion Legend Beast's tail piece—Part #4183248 in the LEGO® blocks database—especially salient for clarifying a fundamental contrast between Fazang's conception of reality and the LEGO® model.

According to the LEGO® model of reality, because Part #4183248 is completely independent of all other blocks, the block enacts the same role as the tail in Lion Legend Beast, the neck-like appendage for the Dianoga monster, and the canopy bracket for Royal Summer Palace—the block is akin to an actor who plays the same character in multiple movies. Several options for the role of Part #4183248 are consistent with this requirement. For example, perhaps the role is *appearing as a tail*. This is a reasonable view because having this role explains why Part #4183248 in Lion Legend Beast appears as a tail. Yet it is also mystifying. It entails that Part #4183248 in Royal Summer Palace also appears as a tail—in which case either nothing appears as a canopy bracket in Royal Summer Palace (because tails are not canopy brackets) or appearing as a canopy bracket is, somehow, a way of appearing as a tail.

Perhaps, instead, the role of Part #4183248 is *having a certain shape* (or *occupying a certain spatial region*). This is reasonable because the blocks do not depend upon others for their shape. It also is less mystifying because appearing as a tail and appearing as a canopy bracket might be different ways of having a certain shape. Even so, this more abstract approach does not explain why the same block—Part #4183248—appears as a tail in one build and a canopy bracket in another.

In contrast to the LEGO® model of reality, Fazang's conception of reality entails that Part #4183248 has different roles in different builds—the block is akin to an actor who plays different characters in different movies. For Fazang, fundamental building blocks condition the form of their roles, but they receive their roles from other blocks rather than from themselves. Because Part #4183248 does not depend upon others for its shape, it is limited with respect to the roles it can enact. But, for Fazang, the shape of the block does not suffice to determine the block's role. Instead, Part #4183248 in Lion Legend Beast has the role *appearing as a tail* (and not *appearing as a canopy bracket*) because the other blocks in Lion Legend Beast form a lion. The same part in Royal Summer Palace has the role *appearing as a canopy bracket* (and not *appearing as a tail*) because the other blocks in Royal Summer Palace form a palace.

Prioritizing the role of Part #4183248 in one build is unduly exclusionary. Relegating the various appearances of Part #4183248 to different ways of enacting a common role is unduly abstract. On Fazang's conception, because blocks depend upon others for their roles, fundamental building blocks are inseparable from others. This is why the same block—Part #4183248—appears as a tail in one build and a canopy bracket in another. It is also why, for Fazang, the fundamental building blocks of reality are included within and identical with each other.

1.2.3. Fazang as Metaphysician

Fazang's remarks about the golden lion, and the associated (albeit implicit) contentions about mutual inclusion and mutual identity, are metaphysical. This is because they articulate a view about reality. For Fazang, his metaphysics also serves a broader soteriological purpose. It is metaphysics in the service of soteriology.[19] This is because of the kind of view he takes his remarks to articulate.

---

[19] For similar conceptions of Buddhist metaphysics, see Park 2008, 17–30; Jones 2023b. For a contrary view that interprets Fazang's remarks as instructions for meditative practice (and for this reason *in no way* metaphysical), see Plassen 2023.

Buddhist tradition distinguishes two kinds of view. Some views are points of view (Skt. *dṛṣṭi*; Ch. *jiàn* 見). Points of view are, roughly, interpretations of experience that are partial in some way or other. Partiality marks points of view as obstacles to correct understanding by virtue of lacking insight into reality.[20] Views that lack partiality, by contrast, are views based upon wisdom and insight (Skt. *jñāna-darśana*; Ch. *zhī jiàn* 知見 or *zhì jiàn* 智見). Such views derive from Buddhist teachings, including the written teachings of Buddhist scriptures and the unwritten teachings available through proper meditative practice. They are correctives to partial—and thereby inferior—points of view.

The contrast among kinds of view—points of view on the one hand, and views based upon wisdom and insight on the other hand—is implicit in the *Lotus Sūtra*. The author of this scripture includes, among their reasons for writing, "aspiring to cause all sentient beings to enter into the Buddha's supreme knowledge."[21] Entering into the Buddha's supreme knowledge is coming to have a view based upon wisdom and insight. This involves more than learning how to articulate a correct view about reality and learning how to interpret experience in a way that lacks partiality. It involves, as well, learning the characteristics that differentiate various modes of experience, learning how to rank those modes in terms of their degree of insight into reality, and learning the basis of each mode for the sake of directing meditative and ethical practices toward superior levels of insight.

In his various classifications of Buddhist doctrines and traditions, Fazang presents mutual inclusion and mutual identity as the doctrine that characterizes the most desirable mode of experience with the highest level of insight.[22] From Fazang's perspective, those with wisdom and insight view the constituents of reality as mutually inclusive and mutually identical. This means, in part, that Fazang endorses the doctrine as correct. It means, as well, that sincere efforts to understand the doctrine facilitate entering into the Buddha's supreme knowledge. This is the sense in which Fazang's contentions about mutual inclusion and mutual identity are metaphysics in the service of soteriology.

Some claims in the service of soteriology are merely pragmatic. When Zen masters instruct their students to kill any Buddha they meet on the road, and when they characterize the Buddha as a "dry shit-stick," their proclamations are meant to provoke without regard for correctness. By contrast, Fazang's contentions are philosophical. The reason is that they are "roarings of a lion."

Buddhist tradition imagines a lion's roar as any utterance that promotes progress on the path to awakening while also being defensible in debate.[23] Lions'

---

[20]   See Fuller 2005.

[21]   T9.262.7b18. For an alternative translation, see Kubo and Tsugunari 2007, 31.

[22]   The main source for Fazang's classification scheme is the fourth chapter of his *Treatise on the Five Teachings of Huayan*. See T45.1866.481b5–482a11; Cook 1970, 173–81; Unno et al. 2023, 59–63. For a general discussion of Fazang's scheme, see Liu 1981, 19–29.

[23]   Anālayo 2009, 7. See also Manné 1996, 13.

8 METAPHORS FOR INTERDEPENDENCE

roars are soteriological by virtue of their connection to liberation. They are philosophical by virtue of their connection to defensibility in debate. Fazang supplements his contentions about mutual inclusion and mutual identity with replies to objections and illustrative explanations. The replies to objections indicate Fazang's willingness to defend his contentions against others. The explanations indicate his concern to make the contentions accessible so that they can lead others toward liberation. Fazang's contentions about mutual inclusion and mutual identity are philosophical because they are the roarings of a lion.

1.3. A Need for Interpretation

1.3.1. Continuing Influence

In 705, shortly after taking power from his mother, Emperor Zhongzong of Tang 唐中宗 (r. 705–710) commissioned a portrait of Fazang. He subsequently wrote four eulogies for Fazang. The fourth reads, in part, as follows.

> His names echoing in the imperial palace,
> His reputation circulating among the monastic world.
> The guiding principle for the Brahmanic congregation (i.e., the saṃgha),
> The standard and example for Buddhist followers.[24]

Zhongzong's eulogy indicates something of the esteem Fazang received from his contemporaries. So, too, does the decree issued by Zhongzong's brother and successor, Emperor Ruizong of Tang 唐睿宗 (r. 684–690, 710–712), upon Fazang's death.

> Imperial Commissioner: The late monk Fazang inherited his virtuous karma from the Heavens, and his open intelligence marked a match with the [true] principle. With his eloquence and understanding, his mind was infused with penetrating enlightenment....[25]

A comprehensive history of Fazang's influence upon the trajectory of Buddhism in East Asia has yet to be written.[26] Suffice it to note that, in more recent decades, Fazang's doctrines of mutual inclusion and mutual identity continue to attract interest.

---

[24] Chen 2007, 157.
[25] Chen 2007, 169.
[26] For information about Fazang's immediate disciples, see Ping 2023.

Fazang's doctrines attract interest from contemporary religious leaders. For example, in a speech from December 1962, Martin Luther King, Jr. (1929–1968), an American Christian minister and activist, alludes to a view very much akin to Fazang's doctrine of mutual inclusion.

> The self cannot be self without other selves. I cannot reach fulfillment without thou. Social psychologists tell us that we cannot truly be persons unless we interact with other persons. All life is interrelated. All men are caught in an inescapable network of mutuality, tied in a single garment of destiny.[27]

Fazang's doctrines also inform the teachings of the Vietnamese Zen Buddhist monk Thích Nhất Hạnh (1926–2022). One of Thích Nhất Hạnh's standard teaching slogans is that *to be is to inter-be*. Thích Nhất Hạnh describes his conception of interbeing with a flower contemplation.

> Looking into a flower, we can see that it is full of life. It contains soil, rain, and sunshine. It is also full of clouds, oceans, and minerals. It is even full of space and time. In fact, the whole cosmos is present in this one little flower. If we took out just one of these "non-flower" elements, the flower would not be there. Without the soil's nutrients, the flower could not grow. Without rain and sunshine, the flower would die. And if we removed all the non-flower elements, there would be nothing substantive left that we could call a "flower." So our observation tells us that the flower is full of the whole cosmos, while at the same time it is empty of a separate self-existence. The flower cannot exist by itself alone.[28]

Thích Nhất Hạnh's flower, like the eye of Fazang's golden lion, includes others within itself. Moreover, just as the eye of Fazang's golden lion is identical with the lion's ear, nose, and so on, Thích Nhất Hạnh's flower "inter-is" with soil, rain, and so on.

Fazang's doctrines of mutual inclusion and mutual identity also continue to attract secular attention. For example, the doctrines inform the ecological vision of the American poet Gary Snyder (1930–), and in particular Snyder's efforts to depict hunting and eating as sacred rituals that afford a kind of spiritual

---

[27] King 1986, 122. King would be familiar with Buddhist teachings similar to Fazang's from a well-known friendship with Thích Nhất Hạnh as well as a seminary course covering Mahāyāna Buddhism (see King 1992).

[28] Nhất Hạnh 2017, 11–2. For an exposition of Thích Nhất Hạnh's teaching of interbeing, see Holst 2021.

10 METAPHORS FOR INTERDEPENDENCE

wholeness.[29] The Austrian physicist Fritjof Capra (1939–) finds in Fazang's doctrines parallels with developments in contemporary science that model reality as a realm of interdependence rather than a realm of autonomous and separate individuals.[30] Fazang's doctrines also motivate, and provide historical precedent for, various theories in contemporary analytic metaphysics. These include ontological structuralism, a theory according to which relations are fundamental and related things are derivative; metaphysical coherentism, a theory according to which the myriad things of the world support and depend upon each other; and nonstandard theories of mereology.[31]

1.3.2. Cook's Interpretation

Relatively few English-language monographs devote sustained scholarly attention to Fazang's metaphysics. Several older monographs examine the metaphysics of the Huayan tradition of Chinese Buddhism to which Fazang belongs. Gimello 1976b focuses on the views of Zhiyan, Fazang's teacher. Gregory 1991 focuses on the views of Guifeng Zongmi 圭峰宗密 (780–841), who is responsible for integrating Huayan metaphysics with the Heze 菏澤 school of Chan Buddhism. The only English-language monograph that focuses on Fazang's metaphysics is Cook 1977. The result of this situation is that nearly all contemporary (English-language) discussions of mutual inclusion and mutual identity treat Cook's monograph as authoritative.[32]

Given the influence and attraction that Fazang's doctrines of mutual inclusion and mutual identity continue to have, there is need for a fresh interpretation of those doctrines. Consider, for example, Fazang's contention that everything includes everything else. Cook explains this claim with an example about a wheat seed. According to Cook, one includes others in the way the seed includes the qualities or natures of water, sun, and soil.[33] Cook's example is apt because the seed grows only by internalizing water's moistness, the sun's heat, and soil's nutriment. Cook's example is also misleading. The example does not preclude the

---

[29] See Barnhill 1990.

[30] Capra 1975, 292–7. For a more recent example of Caprian parallelism in relation to Huayan metaphysics, shorn of overtones about "Eastern mysticism," see Fox 2015, 271–2. For a trenchant critique of Capra's parallelism, and of similar efforts by others, see Restivo 1978.

[31] For structuralism, see Priest 2014; Priest 2015. For coherentism, see Bliss and Priest 2017. For mereology, see Cotnoir 2017. I address coherentist interpretations of Fazang's metaphysics in Chapter 6.3.2.

[32] For a general overview of Huayan metaphysics, see Van Norden and Jones 2019. For a review of Huayan metaphysics directed toward contextualizing Zen approaches to ethics, see Park 2008, 161–88. For an examination of the epistemological and ethical implications of Fazang's metaphysics, see Nakasone 2022.

[33] Cook 1977, 68.

possibility of dormant seeds. Yet, for Fazang, seeds that do not grow are seeds in name only. Cook's example also relies upon a process—the seed's internalizing of environmental conditions—that only happens over time. Yet Fazang maintains that each includes all others at every moment.[34] Fortunately, a better explanation of Fazang's inclusion relation is available: one includes another when the one has power to cause the characteristic effect toward which the other is disposed.[35] For Fazang, the wheat seed includes the soil (among other conditions) because, although the soil is disposed to nourish, the seed—and not the soil—has power to cause nourishment.

Consider, also, Fazang's golden lion. Fazang explains that each part of the lion is every other part because each is made of the same golden substance.

> All the parts of the lion, each and every hair, by means of the gold, encompass the whole lion completely. Each and every part is completely the eye of the lion. The eye is the ear, the ear is the nose, the nose is the tongue, the tongue is the body.[36]

Even if the lion's nose and its tongue are made of the same gold, it does not follow that the nose is the tongue. Cook uses the example of his own body, rather than Fazang's lion statue, to address this apparent *non sequitur*.

> In what way can it be said that the nose is identical with my left elbow? . . . Identifying part with part raises difficulty, for the two parts look different, are spatially distinct, and perform different functions. The postulation of identity does not remove these distinctions, and Hua-yen insists that not only are things both identical *and* different, but, paradoxically, that they are identical *because* they are different. In other words, to have the body I now have, I need a nose which is between my eyes and has the office of detecting odors, an elbow which bends in a certain way, allowing me to write and the like, a heart in my chest which pumps blood, and so on. If everything was literally a nose, I would be just one immense nose. . . . Thus each individual is required in its own unique form, with its own unique function, to act as a condition for the whole in question. The identity of the nose and the left elbow consists in their identity as *conditions* for the whole. Therefore, while the two are different, they are the same; in fact, they are identical precisely because they are different.[37]

---

[34] For a similar criticism, see Unno 1978, 164.
[35] I motivate and explain this analysis of inclusion in Chapter 3.5.3.
[36] Van Norden 2014, 89. See also T45.1880.665b19-22.
[37] Cook 1977, 10.

12 METAPHORS FOR INTERDEPENDENCE

Cook's explanation attributes to Fazang a conception of identity according to which one is identical with another if both are simultaneously parts of some common whole.

Cook's explanation has two unfortunate consequences. First, it presents Fazang's doctrine of mutual identity as a rhetorical sleight of hand, baiting readers with a provocative contention about identity and switching that contention with a mundane observation about shared parthood. Second, and relatedly, it drains Fazang's doctrine of its soteriological force. Cook observes, rightly, that Fazang's doctrine is a tool for viewing contraries as harmonized with each other.[38] Yet sick bodies and discordant nations demonstrate that simultaneous parthood in a common whole does not preclude disharmony or obstruction among the whole's parts.

Cook has a strategy for denying that parts of a common whole can be disharmonious. The strategy involves conceptualizing parts as abstractions from a unitary whole while denying that wholes are separate from or prior to their parts.[39] This is an obscure and ineffective way to conceptualize parts of wholes. If parts are abstractions from common wholes, and if wholes are nothing other than their parts, then parts are abstractions from each other. But if, for example, Cook's nose is an abstraction from his elbow, it is not at all clear how his elbow is also an abstraction from his nose. Moreover, even if parts are abstractions from each other, Cook provides no reason to suppose that the abstractions harmonize with each other.

Fortunately, a better explanation of Fazang's identity relation—one that avoids the consequences of Cook's explanation—is available: one is identical with another when the other makes the one enact its characteristic disposition.[40] So, for example, the lion's eye is identical with its ear because the ear is what makes the eye into an organ that sees, and the lion's ear is identical with its eye because the eye is what makes the ear into an organ that hears. For Fazang, the lion's eye and ear harmonize not because they are parts of a common whole, but because each makes the other enact its characteristic dispositionality.[41]

---

[38] Cook 1977, 11.

[39] Cook 1977, 9–10.

[40] I motivate and explain this analysis of identity in Chapter 3.4.3. However, I do not engage with Fazang's contentions about the relation between the lion's organs and its golden substance. Those contentions derive from his approach to conceptualizing the *dharma*-realm of non-obstruction between principle and things (Ch. *lǐ shì wúài fǎjiè* 理事無礙法界). This book focuses on Fazang's approach to conceptualizing the *dharma*-realm of non-obstruction among things (Ch. *shì shì wúài fǎjiè* 事事無礙法界). For more information about these approaches, see Oh 1979, 83–5; Benická 2002, 176–9; Park 2008, 161–9; Hamar 2014a, 155–9; Plassen 2020, 47–50.

[41] I analyze Fazang's approach to part-whole relations in Chapter 8.4–7.

1.4. Goal and Strategy

The primary goal of this book is to provide a rigorous and responsible interpretation of Fazang's doctrines of mutual inclusion and mutual identity. A rigorous interpretation explicates Fazang's technical concepts with explicit definitions and reconstructs technical or obscure aspects of Fazang's explanations. This facilitates having a clear and precise understanding of Fazang's metaphysical claims. Rigorous interpretation is important because Fazang typically does not define or explain the technical terminology that is most central to his metaphysical doctrines. There is a good sociological reason for this. The audience for Fazang's more technical writings is Fazang's fellow monks. Because this audience would be well versed in Buddhist scholarship, Fazang likely presumes that his audience is familiar with his terminology.

A responsible interpretation delves into the details of Fazang's writings. When those writings do not suffice to satisfy demands for rigor, responsible interpretation also grounds itself in texts that were likely accessible and influential to Fazang. When examples from Fazang's writings, or from associated primary texts, are obscure or admit competing interpretations, responsible interpretation also grounds itself in research relevant to the sciences and material cultures with which Fazang was likely familiar. Responsible interpretation is important because Fazang often uses metaphors (Ch. *yù* 喻) to explain his doctrines.[42] It is tempting to suppose that Fazang understands these metaphors in the way we understand them. But this is often not the case, and suppositions to the contrary are persisting sources of confusion about what some of Fazang's more provocative claims mean.

All of this is standard for good scholarship. It reduces the likelihood of misleading examples, and it gives confidence for ascribing the resultant interpretation to Fazang. Taken together, the constraints of rigor and responsibility also facilitate discerning whether Fazang's metaphysics in fact motivates or supports the various contemporary theories that cite Fazang as a precedent.

The primary strategy of this book is to focus interpretive efforts upon the key metaphors Fazang uses to explain his doctrines of mutual inclusion and mutual identity. The book focuses, in particular, upon Fazang's metaphors of Indra's net, counting coins, and the building. Indra's net is, perhaps, the most famous of these metaphors.[43] All three are prominent in the final chapter of *Treatise on the Five Teachings of Huayan*. (I examine Fazang's golden lion metaphor only

---

[42] For precedent on translating 喻 as "metaphor, see Bokenkamp 1989, 212–4. For reasons to translate the character as "metaphor" rather than "comparison" or "model," see Jones 2018a, 1173, note 5.

[43] For evidence that the popularity of Indra's net is a relatively modern phenomenon, see Owens 2022.

14 METAPHORS FOR INTERDEPENDENCE

in passing, because it is absent from this work.) All three are also susceptible to misinterpretation.

Consider, for example, Fazang's metaphor of the building.[44] Fazang claims that the building has the characteristic of integration (Ch. *chéng* 成).

> The characteristic of integration is all dependently arising together.[45]

Fazang clarifies that integration is the characteristic of the building being made by rafters and various other conditions.

> The characteristic of integration explains why the various conditions for the building come to be. Because the rafters and so on complete the building, they are named conditions. If this were not so, both of them would be incomplete. Because they manifest as complete, know that integration is mutual completion.[46]

He also explains an error in denying that the building has the characteristic of integration.

> The building fundamentally depends upon the rafters and various other conditions integrating. Now if they do not make [the building], there is no building. This is annihilationism. Fundamentally, because they are conditions that integrate the building, they are named rafters. Now if they do not make the building, there are no rafters and this is annihilationism.[47]

Rafters are materials that support roofing tiles and other materials. Fazang's contention, in part, is that rafters apart from roofing tiles do not support other roofing materials. Those familiar only with modern conventional buildings should be inclined to reject this contention as incorrect. Because modern conventional architecture uses fasteners—nails, screws, bolts, glue— to connect rafters to roofing materials, it allows rafters to support roofing materials in the absence of roofing tiles.

The same is not true of the Tang-era monastery buildings with which Fazang is likely familiar. Those buildings use sophisticated mortise-and-tenon joinery rather than fasteners to secure rafters and other building materials in their

---

[44] I examine this metaphor more thoroughly in Chapter 8.

[45] T45.1866.507c9.

[46] T45.1866.508b27-9. For alternative translations, see Cook 1977, 86; Elstein 2014, 85; Unno et al. 2023, 206.

[47] T45.1866.508c8-10. For alternative translations, see Cook 1977, 87; Elstein 2014, 85; Unno et al. 2023, 207.

appropriate places. This joinery relies upon the weight of roofing tiles to secure the connection between rafters and roofing materials. Hence, there is a very real, very material sense in which, for Tang-era monastery buildings, rafters apart from roofing tiles do not support other roofing materials.

Making explicit the kind of building Fazang (likely) has in mind forestalls innocent misunderstandings of his metaphor. So, too, with Fazang's other metaphors. Examining the science and material culture that informs Fazang's understanding, and pairing this examination with rigorous and responsible explication of Fazang's technical terminology, facilitates understanding the meaning Fazang likely gives to his metaphors. Because Fazang uses his metaphors to explain what he means by mutual inclusion and mutual identity, this understanding, in turn, reveals the content and significance of Fazang's metaphysical doctrines.

There is a significant commitment implicit in the strategy of interpreting Fazang's metaphysical doctrines by focusing on the metaphors he uses to explain those doctrines. The commitment involves viewing metaphors as something to which meaning must be given.[48] This commitment is neutral on the issue of whether metaphors can be paraphrased without loss of meaning. The commitment arises from acknowledging that metaphors admit competing interpretations.

Consider, for example, the moon as metaphor. The Chinese scholar Qian Zhongshu 錢鍾書 (1910–1998) identifies two interpretations of this metaphor.[49] The first, from the *Flower Adornment Sūtra*, likens the moon to the teachings of the Buddha. Just as the moon's reflections in different rivers are many while the moon remains one, the Buddha's teachings, according to the *Flower Adornment Sūtra*, remain one despite their myriad manifestations.[50] The second interpretation, from the 17th-century novella *A Stone to Sober Up Drunken Men*, likens the moon to the heart of a female courtesan. Just as the moon does not discriminate among the rivers in which it reflects, the courtesan's heart, according to the novella, does not discriminate among the customers she chooses to service. While the first interpretation uses the moon to convey purity, the second uses the moon to convey impurity.

Fazang's metaphors also admit competing interpretations. For some, such as Cook, Fazang's metaphors convey a totalistic commitment to the organic unity of reality, and they facilitate "the new ability to see that everything is wonderful and good."[51] By contrast, on the interpretation I shall develop, Fazang's metaphors convey a flexible commitment to a kind of indeterminacy, and they facilitate the

---

[48] For a similar view of metaphor, see Stewart 1971.
[49] Qian 1998, 126–7.
[50] See T10.279.122c20-3; Cleary 1993, 523; Dharmamitra 2022, 1: 576.
[51] Cook 1977, 89.

16 METAPHORS FOR INTERDEPENDENCE

ability to conceptualize reality without delusion or attachment. Interpreting mutual inclusion and mutual identity as relations that relegate individuals to the status of mere abstractions from some fundamental unity ignores and obscures much of what is insightful and provocative in Fazang's metaphysics.

1.5. Chapter Overviews

Fazang articulates his metaphysics with a sophisticated but technical conceptual repertoire, illustrative but unfamiliar metaphors, and suggestive but obscure explanations. His metaphors serve as aids for understanding his concepts and explanations. Because Fazang's writings presume substantial familiarity with fundamental Buddhist teachings, Chapter 2 contextualizes and motivates Fazang's key metaphysical doctrines with a brief survey of those teachings. The survey focuses on the teachings of evanescence, *duḥkha*, and no-self as well as the distinction between *nirvāṇa* and *saṃsāra*. The survey in Chapter 2 culminates by locating inspiration for Fazang's key metaphysical contentions in the *Flower Adornment Sūtra*.

Fazang's interpretation of Buddhist teaching differs in subtle ways from more familiar interpretations. Fazang also articulates his interpretation with a sophisticated but technical conceptual repertoire. Chapter 3, accordingly, explicates Fazang's basic conceptual framework. The explication defines key technical terminology and illustrates those definitions with examples. The explications provide a rigorous analysis of what Fazang means when he claims that one thing is included within or identical with another.

Standard interpretations of Fazang's metaphysics, including Cook 1977, attribute to Fazang a theory of causality that is causal in name only. They also attribute to Fazang a conception of mutuality that involves holographic, symmetric, and simultaneous relations of dependence. Chapter 4 critiques the standard interpretation. Chapter 5 develops an alternative interpretation. The alternative takes seriously Fazang's use of causal language, and it attributes to Fazang a conception of mutuality that involves aspectual, asymmetric, and sequential relations of dependence. Support for the alternative interpretation derives from careful attention to Fazang's writings. Support derives, as well, from its superiority in preserving standard Buddhist commitments about causality.

Chapter 5 culminates with an analysis of the *dharma*-realm of dependent arising. This realm is the target of Fazang's metaphors. The metaphors of Indra's net, counting coins, and the building are models for the *dharma*-realm of dependent arising. Each model aims to explain what it means for the constituents of this realm to be mutually inclusive and mutually identical. Subsequent chapters examine these metaphors in sequence. Because Fazang's discussions of each metaphor are often brief, cryptic, and prone to innocent misinterpretation, each chapter situates Fazang's metaphors within their intellectual and cultural context, and each chapter addresses potential misinterpretations of the interpretation Fazang (likely) intends for each metaphor.

Chapter 6 examines the metaphor of Indra's net. This metaphor makes a frequent, albeit always limited, appearance in many of Fazang's writings. It models relations among constituents of the *dharma*-realm of dependent arising as relations among bright jewels in a vast and interconnected net. The metaphor seems to originate in the *Flower Adornment Sūtra*. It receives noteworthy attention, among Fazang's predecessors, from his teacher Zhiyan and Zhiyan's teacher, Dushun 杜順 (557–640). Contemporary interpreters typically construe Fazang's metaphor as evidence that he endorses a coherentist metaphysics, wherein nothing is more fundamental than anything else. Chapter 6 reviews the elaborate strategy Fazang uses to analyze Indra's net. The chapter demonstrates that Fazang's interpretation of Indra's net is not a model for metaphysical coherentism.

Chapter 7 examines Fazang's metaphor of counting coins. This metaphor drives nearly the entirety of Fazang's discussion in the third section of the final chapter of *Treatise on the Five Teachings of Huayan*. The nearest ancestor to Fazang's metaphor appears in work by his colleague, and another of Zhiyan's students, Ŭisang 義湘 (625–702). Ŭisang, in turn, seems to adapt his metaphor from earlier metaphors about counting in the *Flower Adornment Sūtra* and work by Zhiyan. Chapter 7 examines in detail Fazang's approach to contemplating the metaphor of counting coins as well as the ways in which Fazang's approach diverges from the approaches of his predecessors. The chapter also connects Fazang's metaphor to Buddhist practices of mindful breathing and incantation, arguing that Fazang most likely intends for the counting of coins to be a surrogate for the counting of breaths.

Chapter 8 examines Fazang's metaphor of the building. This metaphor differs from the metaphors of Indra's net and counting coins by virtue of addressing differences of kind among the constituents of the *dharma*-realm of dependent arising. It also has the oldest ancestry, stretching back to the earliest scriptures of the Buddhist tradition. All of the models for this metaphor use the relation between buildings and their materials to model relations between wholes and their many kinds of parts. Yet Buddhist traditions conceptualize part-whole relations in different ways. Chapter 8, accordingly, examines the ways in which Fazang's conception of part-whole relations differs from those of his predecessors, and it explains the reasons for these divergences. The chapter attends, in particular, to Fazang's theory of six characteristics and the kind of building he likely uses to model relations among the constituents of the *dharma*-realm of dependent arising.

18   METAPHORS FOR INTERDEPENDENCE

Chapter 9 contextualizes Fazang's key metaphysical contentions. The chapter summarizes the results, from previous chapters, about how to interpret Fazang's analyses for the metaphors of Indra's net, counting coins, and the building. The chapter also situates Fazang's metaphysics within the broader tradition of Mahāyāna Buddhism. This involves constructing, on Fazang's behalf, an analysis for a metaphor familiar from that tradition—one concerning the relation between fire and fuel. The chapter further situates Fazang's contentions in relation to the standard conceptual landscape of contemporary analytic metaphysics. The chapter argues that Fazang endorses a heterarchical metaphysics that makes the structure of the world fundamentally perspectival. The chapter also constructs, on Fazang's behalf, a deductive justification for Fazang's key contentions about mutual identity and mutual inclusion.

1.6. Notes on Usage

I provide diacritical marks for all Sanskrit terms, and I typically prefer Sanskrit terms to their Pāli equivalents for the sake of consistency. I provide Hanyu pinyin romanizations (with tone marks) for Chinese characters. These are distinguished from Sanskrit terms by virtue of being accompanied, on their first appearance, with Chinese characters. When I provide Sanskrit equivalents for Chinese terms, I preface the Sanskrit with "Skt." and the Chinese with "Ch." On rare occasions, I mark Pāli terms with "P."

All translations lacking a direct citation to a secondary source are my own. When an English translation is available in an easily accessible source, I typically provide that translation. When a translation is unavailable, or when an existing translation might obscure something of philosophical significance, I provide a translation of my own—and I use notes to explain significant divergences from existing translations. I am indebted, in my translation efforts, to Charles Muller's *Digital Dictionary of Buddhism.*[52]

For translating primary Chinese sources, I rely upon the digitized texts available through the Chinese Buddhist Electronic Text Association, which themselves are based upon either the Taishō Buddhist Canon or the Supplement to the Japanese Edition of the Buddhist Canon. I reference Taishō and Supplement editions by volume number, text serial number, page number, register (a, b, or c), and line number. For example, T45.1866.507b12-13 refers to Taishō Volume 45, Text 1866, Page 508, Register b, Lines 12 through 13.

---

[52] Muller 2022.

2
Fazang's Vision

2.1. Rūpāvatī

The story of Rūpāvatī is set in a capital city undergoing famine.[1] Rūpāvatī—her name denotes one full of beauty—is the protagonist. The story reveals that she is the Buddha in one of his past lives. During a leisurely walk, Rūpāvatī encounters a woman who has just given birth to a baby boy. The woman is starving. Desperate for food, the woman forms an intention to eat her newborn child. Sensing this desperation, Rūpāvatī recommends that the woman eat something from her pantry. The woman replies that her pantry is bare. Rūpāvatī offers to fetch food from her own house. The woman replies that she will die of hunger before Rūpāvatī returns.

Rūpāvatī faces a dilemma. If she takes the woman's son with her when fetching food, the woman will die. If she leaves the boy with his mother when fetching food, the woman will eat the boy. Rūpāvatī resolves the dilemma by slicing her breasts from her own body and calmly feeding them to the starving mother.

The mother in the story of Rūpāvatī illustrates Buddhist teachings about the fundamental characteristics of reality and common phenomenological symptoms of those characteristics. The mother depends upon nourishment for her survival, and without this nourishment she is prone to die or resort to desperate measures. This illustrates the teaching that conditionality, evanescence, and insecurity are fundamental characteristics of reality. Needful of nourishment and beset with desperation, the mother is willing to trade long-term grief—sure to follow from committing filicide—for short-term satiation. This illustrates the teaching that common symptoms of conditionality, evanescence, and insecurity are suffering and distress, pain and dissatisfaction.

The contrast between the starving mother's concern for self-preservation and Rūpāvatī's self-sacrifice illustrates Buddhist teachings about the fundamental source of and cure for suffering. The mother resists her vulnerability. She is willing to trade grief for satiation because she imagines the newborn as food and herself as a hungry body. She thereby resists acknowledging that the newborn is her child and she is his mother. This illustrates the teaching that the source of suffering is

---

[1] For details and discussion about the story of Rūpāvatī, I am indebted to Ohnuma 2000. See also Ohnuma 2004.

Metaphors for Interdependence. Nicholaos Jones, Oxford University Press. © Nicholaos Jones 2025.
DOI: 10.1093/9780197807224.003.0002

20 METAPHORS FOR INTERDEPENDENCE

delusional cognition. By contrast, Rūpāvatī offers her breasts as food because she resists nothing about her situation. She acknowledges the woman as famished and maternal, the newborn as food and child, herself as spectator and participant. Rather than resolve the tragic situation by ignoring some of its characteristics, Rūpāvatī embraces her own vulnerability by acting as mother to woman and child. This illustrates the teaching that the way to cure suffering is to remove delusion.

This chapter surveys Buddhist teachings about the fundamental characteristics of reality, common phenomenological symptoms of these characteristics, causes for the symptoms, and the way to overcome these causes. These teachings form the spine of Buddhist soteriology. The survey of the teachings helps to situate Fazang's metaphysics as a contribution to this soteriology. It helps, in particular, to frame his doctrines of mutual inclusion and mutual identity as efforts to overcome the fundamental causes of suffering.

2.2. Conditionality

Great Sūtra on Nirvāṇa-after-Death reports that, on the verge of death, surrounded by adoring students, Siddhārtha Gautama—the Buddha—made one last pronouncement on the nature of reality.

All conditioned things are of a nature to decay.[2]

A similar pronouncement appears in *Sūtra on the Account of Travels*, translated into Chinese by Buddhayaśas 佛陀耶舍 and Zhu Fonian 竺佛念 in 412–413.

Whatever is conditioned is impermanent, is subject to change, and necessarily ends in cessation.[3]

The phrase "conditioned things" translates the Pāli term *sankhārā* (Ch. *yŏuwéi fǎ* 有爲法 or *xíng* 行), which corresponds to the Sanskrit *samskāra*. The prefix *sam-* means *together*. The root noun *kāra* means *doing* or *making*. Hence, in the most literal sense, a conditioned thing is a fragmental co-happening—something built from others joining together, or something that joins with others to build something else.[4]

Perhaps the most familiar paradigms of conditioned things are biological. Biological organisms are fragmental co-happenings in relation to others and in

---

[2] Walshe 1995, 270.
[3] T1.1.24b19, recited in Ichimura 2015, 138.
[4] See Hsing-kong 1995.

themselves. In relation, they enact the roles of dinner host and guest, eating and being eaten by others. In themselves, they are complex colonies of molecules and mechanisms. Eukaryotic cells are symbiotically evolved collections of mitochondria, ribosomes, and other organelles. Plants and animals are holobionts of microbes and parasites. So, too, with biological mechanisms. In relation, the outputs of biological mechanisms initiate or sustain the operations of other mechanisms, and they require the outputs of other mechanisms to initiate or sustain their own operations. In themselves, mechanisms are nothing but organized entities and activities that—by activating, allowing, inhibiting, making, or preventing each other—accomplish together what none can do on its own.[5]

Conditionality, the nature of conditioned things, is being always and everywhere fragmental. It is an insufficiency for self-sustenance paired with a vulnerability to encroaching others. Conditioned things are simultaneously reaching toward the future and not yet passed, precariously balanced on the edge of their inevitable decline and decay.[6] Our machines break, rust, disintegrate, and disappear. Our crops wither, rot, and scatter to the winds. Our feelings wax and wane with shifts in mood, focus, and context. Our bodies fail, decay, and return once more to dust. Powerless on their own to sustain themselves or repel others, fragmental co-happenings are yet withheld from demise and conquest by equally fragmentary others—even as they themselves return this favor for those others, and even though the favors are bound to fail in time.

2.3. Wages of Conditionality

Buddhism teaches that conditionality is the way of the reality in which we find ourselves. We live among fragmental co-happenings that depend upon others to secure their rise and forestall their inevitable decline. Buddhism presents the wages of conditionality as evanescence, *duḥkha*, and insecurity.

2.3.1. Evanescence

On evanescence, consider a passage from the end of *Sūtra with Mahā Sudassana*.

> Impermanent are compounded things, prone to rise and fall,
> Having risen, they're destroyed, their passing truest bliss.[7]

---

[5] See Gilbert et al. 2012; Salvucci 2016; Heldke 2018; Craver and Darden 2013, 15–20 and 24–5.
[6] See also Mellamphy 1988; Ettlinger 2007.
[7] Walshe 1995, 290.

22 METAPHORS FOR INTERDEPENDENCE

Like the passages from *Great Sūtra on Nirvāṇa-after-Death* and *Sūtra on the Account of Travels*, this passage teaches that all conditioned things are evanescent (Skt. *anitya*; Ch. *wú cháng* 無常). Any conditioned thing built from other things is evanescent, because if those others were to vanish, or grow, or otherwise stop working with each other, the conditioned thing would cease its doings. So, too, with any conditioned thing that participates in building others. Perception reveals nothing but an ongoing succession of rising and falling. No inference demands positing persistence rather than sequential succession. Just as a spreading fire is a sequence of rising and falling flames rather than some one thing that grows and shrinks, Buddhism teaches that even conditioned things that build others are prone to rise and fall.

2.3.2. Duḥkha

Sūtra with Mahā Sudassana characterizes the cessation of conditioned things as blissful. The Sanskrit term for this bliss is *sukha* (Ch. *ānlè* 安樂). *Sukha*, according to *Sūtra on the Not-Born*, is calm, inaccessible to reasoning, clean, everlasting, not born, not arisen, lacking sorrow from loss or separation, free of defilement.[8] The contrast to *sukha* is *duḥkha* (Ch. *kǔ* 苦). Canonical exemplars for this contrast appear in records of the Buddha's first public sermon. According to *Sūtra on Promulgating the True Teaching*,

> Birth is *duḥkha*, aging is *duḥkha*, sickness is *duḥkha*, death is *duḥkha*. Associating with the unpleasant is *duḥkha*. Separation from the pleasant is *duḥkha*. Unmet want is *duḥkha*.[9]

Similarly, according to the *Root Monastic Code of the Mūlasarvāstivādins*, translated into Chinese by Yijing 義淨 (635–718),

> Birth is *duḥkha*, old age is *duḥkha*, disease is *duḥkha*, death is *duḥkha*, separation from what is loved is *duḥkha*, association with what is disliked is *duḥkha*, not getting what one wants is *duḥkha*....[10]

Each exemplar of *duḥkha* is a cause or consequence of evanescence. We are born only because our mothers become pregnant, only because the food she

---

[8] See Ireland 1997, 148–9.
[9] For a slightly different translation, see Bodhi 2000, 1844.
[10] T24.1450.128b4–5, recited in Anālayo 2012, 24. See also Anālayo 2015, 362.

eats becomes blood-born nutrition, only because our lungs replace fluid with air. Our bodies grow and then shrink. Our intellects improve and then fade. Our strength waxes and wanes as we encounter this germ and that toxin. All throughout are moments of pleasure and pain, satisfaction and hunger, ebbing and flowing as their sources approach and recede. Then, as with all living things, death transforms our corpses to dust or food.

Duḥkha is a troublesome term, a frequent source of misinterpretation and misunderstanding. Familiar English equivalents are unsatisfying. *Suffering* connotes ailments such as illnesses, fatigue, anxiety, heartbreak. But *duḥkha* need not be felt as bad or unpleasant. *Pain* is less dramatic, and it includes more ordinary states such as thirst, muscle soreness, boredom, annoyance.[11] But pain varies with tolerance and prescription strength, while *duḥkha* does not. *Dissatisfactory* and *stressful* are better, encompassing tension and loss as well as pain and suffering.[12] But these, too, admit to pharmacological treatment. *Existential suffering*, "the frustration, alienation and despair that result from the realization of our own mortality," moves away from the psychological toward the metaphysical.[13] But this precludes subtler cases and excludes pre-reflective children from experiencing *duḥkha*. So, too, for *distressing*.

Contemporary Buddhist practitioners are fond of saying that, during the Buddha's lifetime, the terms *du* and *kha* had vernacular meanings. *Du* connoted that which is poorly placed, off-axis, uneasy. *Kha* referred to a wheel. So perhaps, speaking in a loose and popular sense, *duḥkha* carries the connotation of *ill-fitting wheel*.[14] This etymology motivates a now-standard analogy of *duḥkha* as akin to riding in an unstable carriage with ill-fitting wheels.

2.3.3. Insecurity

The image of *duḥkha* as an ill-fitting wheel is rich. It brings out the idea that *duḥkha* is unpleasant and unsatisfying, stressful and distressing, with potential to cause pain and suffering. Shifting focus from the impact of ill-fitting wheels upon comfort (inside the carriage) to the impact of such wheels upon safety (outside the carriage), the image also highlights the correlation between *duḥkha* and insecurity. Ill-fitting wheels make their carriages insecure by virtue of harming the carriages' other components and interfering with their proper functioning. Ill-fitting wheels also make passengers insecure by virtue of endangering the

---

[11] See Harvey 2013, 30–1.
[12] See Holder 2006, xiii–xiv; Thanissaro 2008, 2.
[13] See Siderits 2007, 19.
[14] But see Younger 1969, 143, note 15.

24 METAPHORS FOR INTERDEPENDENCE

success of their journey. For the sake of illustrating this correlation and refining the meaning of *duḥkha*, consider the story of the nun Khemā.

Dhammapāla (sixth century), in his *Commentary on the Verses of the Therīs*, tells the story of Khemā's conversion from vain and lustful queen to the Buddha's foremost nun, renowned for her exceptional wisdom.[15] Born with golden skin, intoxicated with knowledge and her own beauty, Khemā's curiosity drives her to visit a nearby monastery known for its beauties. The Buddha, by chance in residence at the monastery, learns of her impending visit. When she arrives, he conjures a young nymph more beautiful than any woman alive. Khemā is awestruck, feeling inadequate and ignorant in the nymph's presence. Then the Buddha causes the nymph to age from youth to mature adulthood, from adulthood to gnarled and broken old age. Confronting life's evanescence and attendant insecurity, Khemā realizes, in that moment, the precarity of her own beauty and the inevitability of her own decline. She achieves insight into the true nature of reality. Perhaps it is no accident that the Sanskrit form of her name, Kṣemā, means *secure*, and that Dhammapāla's story concludes with the complete reversal of her character from insecure to secure.

2.4. No-Self

The correlation between *duḥkha* and insecurity helps to explain the Buddhist tradition's divergence from its Vedic ancestry. Consider, for example, *Bṛhadāraṇyaka Upaniṣad*. This scripture from the Vedic tradition, the oldest of the *Upaniṣads*, proclaims that those who achieve the cessation of *duḥkha*, those who become "calm, composed, cool, patient, and collected," come to know themselves and all things as *ātman*.[16] The scripture continues by characterizing this *ātman*.

> Now, this [*ātman*] is the immense and unborn self, the eater of food and the giver of wealth. A man who knows this finds wealth. And this is the immense and unborn self, unaging, undying, immortal, free from fear—the *brahman*. Brahman, surely, is free from fear, and a man who knows this undoubtedly becomes *brahman* and is free from fear.[17]

The *ātman* self, according to *Bṛhadāraṇyaka Upaniṣad*, lacks exactly those characteristics that, according to *Sūtra on Promulgating the True Teaching*, exemplify

---

[15] See Pruitt 1998, 164–6; Murcott 2006, 77–80; Amatayakul 2023.
[16] *Bṛhadāraṇyaka Upaniṣad* 4.4.23, recited in Olivelle 1998, 127.
[17] *Bṛhadāraṇyaka Upaniṣad* 4.4.24-5, recited in Olivelle 1998, 127.

duḥkha. As eater of food rather than food to be eaten, the *ātman* self is sovereign, subordinate to none. As giver of wealth rather than receiver of wages or charity, it is master, dependent upon and needful of no other. Because the *ātman* self is sovereign and master, it is autonomous and powerful, secure and invulnerable, fearful to others but itself without fear.[18]

The record of the Buddha's second public sermon, *Sūtra on the Characteristic of No-Self*, teaches that sovereign selves are chimeric.[19] Because vulnerability is openness to affecting, and being affected by, others in ways beyond one's control, sovereign selves must be invulnerable selves.[20] The Buddha's insight is that we are fragmental, assemblies of evanescent matters and mentations. Our selves, regardless of whether they persist through change, are thereby vulnerable to their constituents. So our selves, whatever else they are, are not sovereign. This is the Buddhist teaching of no-self (Skt. *anatman*; Ch. *wú wǒ* 無我).[21]

The teaching of no-self extends beyond literal selves to anything built from others. For example, in *Sūtra on the Lute*, the Buddha likens the self to a lute.[22] The likely context for the Buddha's analogy is a view of the self from *Sūtra with Potthapāda*, according to which the self is a physical body that feeds on solid food and that is composed of the four material elements of air, earth, fire, water.[23] Given this context, the lute is akin to the physical body, a composite of many others—including belly, sounding board, arm, head, strings, and plectrum. Just as the lute lacks sovereignty by virtue of its dependence upon component parts, the self lacks sovereignty by virtue of its dependence upon nutrition and its component elements.

2.5. Delusional Cognition

2.5.1. Ignorance and Attachment

Standard Buddhist soteriology identifies delusional cognition as the fundamental source of *duḥkha*. One aspect of delusional cognition is ignorance (Skt. *avidyā*; Ch. *wú míng* 無明). Ignorance is the activity of selectively ignoring

---

[18] See also Geen 2007, 68–70.

[19] See Bodhi 2000, 901–3.

[20] Gilson 2014, 2.

[21] For an analysis of theories of (no-)self and moral responsibility across Indian traditions of Buddhism, see Carpenter 2014.

[22] See Bodhi 2000, 1253–5.

[23] See Walshe 1995, 163. There is Vedic precedent for conceptualizing the (*ātman*) self as a body—as something one grows, over time, from a body that is originally subordinate and mortal. See Kazama 1962, 362–1. Early Vedic thought also tends to view sacrifice (Skt. *yajña*) as a vehicle that imbues bodies with an immortal vitality. See Kazama 1962, 361–0; Smithers 1992, 191–9. For discussion of the shift of focus from sacrifice to renunciation, see Thapar 1994.

26 METAPHORS FOR INTERDEPENDENCE

some characteristics of experience and projecting or imagining others that are unreal.[24] Paradigmatic examples include cognizing memories as evidence for a self that persists through change and cognizing unmet expectations that follow effortful action as evidence that things went wrong. Ignorance, in its many manifestations, has an intimate connection with a second aspect of delusional cognition, namely, attachment (Skt. *upādāna*; Ch. *qǔ* 取). Attachment is the activity of grasping or seizing upon characteristics of experience and imaginings and thereby regarding them as sovereign and enduring.[25] Paradigmatic examples manifest as denying or bargaining after receiving a terminal medical diagnosis, as well as lamenting the wrinkles and pains that accompany bodily aging.

2.5.2. Separability

One of the most fundamental manifestations of ignorance and attachment is the appearance of separability between self and others. Separability, or duality, is not mere difference. It is difference grounded upon independence. Because we cognize ourselves as having characteristics that others lack, we cognize differences between ourselves and others. When ignorance is operative, our cognitions select some of the characteristics that differentiate us from others, ignore the conditionality and vulnerability of these characteristics, and subsequently imagine those characteristics as isolable and independent of others. When attachment is operative, we act as if we have a kind of sovereignty that allows us to control those characteristics at our pleasure. For if the characteristics we selected are indeed separable from others, nothing that happens with others should affect our power over them.

Imagine, for example, Khemā cognizing the difference between her smooth, golden skin and the wrinkled, dull skin of an elderly woman. Prior to her awakening, gripped by ignorance, Khemā ignores the ways in which her skin depends upon auxiliary conditions. She imagines her beauty as unconditioned and enduring. Attachment to this beauty, so imagined, is sure to be a source of distress and dissatisfaction for Khemā as she ages. The Buddha's favor to her, a magical display of a nymph undergoing rapid aging, pierces Khemā's ignorance. The display prompts in Khemā the insight that her beauty is conditioned and ephemeral. The insight reveals to Khemā the error of her attitude toward beauty, and this revelation undermines Khemā's attachment to beauty.

Khemā's insight into the vulnerability of her beauty need not extinguish her ignorance and attachment. For example, Khemā might infer, quite reasonably, that

[24] See also Wayman 1957.
[25] See also Fink 2015.

although beauty is not within her power to control, her attitude toward beauty is. That is, even if Khemā acknowledges that she cannot prevent the loss of her golden skin, she might imagine having complete power over her attitudes toward the value of beauty and the loss of her own beauty.[26] This response narrows the apparent domain of sovereignty for Khemā's *ātman* self. The narrowed domain excludes physical characteristics but includes mental ones—attitudes such as *golden skin is beautiful* and *beauty is desirable*. Even here, ignorance continues to operate. Khemā's attitudes, like her skin, are not entirely voluntary. They are conditioned by and vulnerable to auxiliary conditions such as the inertia of prior attitudes and the weight of cultural norms.

Just as Khemā cannot will her face to blush or her heart to stop beating, she cannot will herself to suddenly believe *golden skin is ugly* or find beauty undesirable. If attachment remains operative, Khemā will interpret failure to exert sovereign control over her attitudes as evidence that her self's domain of sovereignty is something other than attitudes. Perhaps she restricts the domain to assent toward attitudes, allowing attitudes to be conditioned but denying that the giving or withholding of assent is conditioned. Perhaps she restricts the domain to voluntary action, believing that she can exert indirect control over her attitudes by listening to self-esteem recordings, attending therapy sessions, or meditating on a regular basis. Or perhaps she restricts the domain to subjective identity, believing that she is master of who she is in the wider world. The teaching of no-self means that all of Khemā's efforts to locate a domain of sovereign power are doomed to fail.[27] So long as Khemā labors under the illusion that she has complete power over something of her own, the intervention of external conditions is sure to foster stress, dissatisfaction, and other forms of *duḥkha*.

2.5.3. Mutual Reinforcement

The extended example about Khemā illustrates how ignorance and attachment reinforce each other. If not for the Buddha's miraculous power, Khemā might have responded to her skin's gradual aging and loss of luster with a variety of beauty regimens. Attached to imagining her beauty as separable from others, she might have ignored the futility of her efforts and shifted her attention elsewhere. She might have blamed the ineffectiveness of beauty regimens on not having found the right beauty products or not having applied them in the right

---

[26] For a brief history of how Stoic views about sovereign persons develop in a similar manner, restricting domains of sovereign control to attitudes (or assents), see Stacey 2011. Like the early Vedic tradition, the Stoic tradition seems to maintain that a sovereign self is something one must grow over time. See Strange 2004.

[27] For discussion of whether Buddhism accommodates the existence of free will, see Repetti 2017.

28 METAPHORS FOR INTERDEPENDENCE

way—anything other than admitting that the kind of beauty she imagines herself to have, and the kind of power she imagines herself to have over it, are delusions born of ignorance. This is attachment reinforcing her ignorance. Ignorance also reinforces attachment. So long as Khemā imagines that she is sovereign and master over something, she lives under the presumption that some of her efforts cannot be frustrated.

In *Contemplations on Exhausting Delusion and Returning to the Source by Cultivating the Mysteries of Huayan*, Fazang notes a significant consequence of ignorance and attachment reinforcing each other.

Sentient beings' deluded attachments shifting from thought to thought is called suffering [*duḥkha*].[28]

Selective attention and projective imagination foster attachments of various sorts. These attachments encourage more attentional selectivity and imaginative projection. Reinforcing cycles of delusional cognition generate *duḥkha*, which in turn reinforces delusional cognition. Unmet expectations are dissatisfying. Losses are painful. Displeasure and anticipations thereof are stressful. Success, gain, and pleasure, by contrast, confirm their antecedent imaginings. So, too, do resistance to failure, loss, and displeasure.

2.6. Modes of Experience

2.6.1. Saṃsāra and Nirvāṇa

Buddhism teaches that cognizing truth differs from delusional cognition by virtue of being free from ignorance and attachment. This difference supports a distinction between two modes of experience. Buddhist tradition designates the first mode as *saṃsāra* (Ch. *lúnhuí* 輪廻). *Saṃsāric* experiences—or experiences in the mode of *saṃsāra*—arise for those in the grip of ignorance and attachment. For example, in the *saṃsāric* mode, discriminating consciousness (Ch. *yì shí* 意識), afflicted with ignorance, imagines into existence the sovereign self. This imagining fosters a sense of independence from others. If the self is independent of others, it should have a domain of sovereignty within which it has complete power to realize its efforts. Discriminating consciousness, with its sense of independence, thereby generates intentions to fill this domain with the pleasant and empty it of the painful. When discriminating consciousness is laden with attachment, efforts to satisfy these preferences and aversions, regardless of their

---

[28] T45.1876.639a19-20, recited in Cleary 1983, 161.

success, generate *duḥkha* and reinforce the false appearance of independence between discriminating consciousness and others. (The effort-discrimination feedback loop marks *saṃsāra* as cyclical, and the self-reinforcing nature of this feedback marks *saṃsāra* as self-sustaining.)

Buddhism contrasts *saṃsāric* experience with *nirvāṇic* experience. *Nirvāṇa* experience is experience in the mode of *nirvāṇa* (Ch. *nièpán* 涅槃). The term *nirvāṇa* derives from the negative Sanskrit prefix *nir-* and the Sanskrit root *vā* (meaning *to blow*). Its literal sense designates the cessation of blowing, as with natural extinction of fire through lack of supporting and perpetuating causes such as fuel and wind.[29] Fire, in this analogy, is the *saṃsāric* mode of experience. The raging flames of the fire are *duḥkha*; fuel is the body or vitality (Skt. *āyus*) of a sentient being; and wind, the sentient being's ignorance. The body supports the *saṃsāric* mode of experience, just as fuel supports fire. Ignorance, by contrast, exacerbates the *saṃsāric* mode of experience, just as wind fans the fire's flames. Yet just as the fire's flames naturally diminish when wind is absent, *duḥkha* associated with *saṃsāric* experience naturally diminishes when ignorance is absent.

Nirvāṇic experiences arise for those free from ignorance and attachment. The second section of *Chapter on Well-Directed and Clear* compares the insight that extinguishes ignorance to a spike that pierces flesh.

> Suppose a well-directed spike of hill rice or barley were pressed by the hand or foot. It is possible that it would pierce the hand or the foot and draw blood. For what reason? Because the spike is well-directed. So, too, it is possible that a [monk] with a well-directed mind would pierce ignorance, arouse true knowledge, and realize [*nirvāṇa*].[30]

The well-directed mind avoids the mistake of conflating delusion with truth, piercing through ignorance to avoid attachment to the imaginary separation between self and other.

Chapter 21 of the *Flower Adornment Sūtra* grounds the well-directed mind—or the perfection of right mindfulness—upon unconfused practice (Ch. *wú chīluàn hang* 無癡亂行), and it characterizes this as practice in which the mind

> is not scattered and confused and in which it remains steadfastly unmoving, is the most supremely pure, is measurelessly vast, and is free of confusion or delusion.[31]

---

[29] Hwang 2006, 9.
[30] Bodhi 2012, 95–6. See also Harvey 1995, 166.
[31] T10.279.104c6-7, recited in Dharmamitra 2022, 1: 489.

30 METAPHORS FOR INTERDEPENDENCE

Similarly, in *Contemplations on Exhausting Delusion and Returning to the Source by Cultivating the Mysteries of Huayan*, Fazang clarifies that the well-directed mind is a mind that does not flit from thought to thought.

> Because of sentient beings' delusive attachments they do not realize that the essence of karma comes from delusion and thus have no means of escape. Therefore bodhisattvas teach them to practice the twin method of cessation and contemplation, minds not changing for a moment, so cause (karma) and effect (suffering) perish and there is no basis for the production of actions which cause suffering.[32]

Free from ignorance and attachment, the well-directed mind experiences reality in the mode of *nirvāṇa*. These experiences have many of the qualities that the Vedic tradition associates with *ātman*.[33] Because fear requires a sense of separation between subject and object of fear, they are free from fear. Insofar as birth consists of an initial arising of a sovereign "me," *nirvāṇic* experiences are unborn. Because there is no aging or death apart from birth, they also are unaging and undying.[34]

Nirvāṇic experiences have further qualities that differentiate them from *saṃsāric* ones. Because the *nirvāṇic* mode of experience does not experience self apart from others, there is no such separation between that which arises and that from which it arises. Because dependent arising requires a separation between that which arises and that from which it arises, *nirvāṇic* experiences are not dependently arisen. Because vulnerability, like dependent arising, requires a separation between that which is vulnerable and that which renders vulnerable, *nirvāṇic* experiences lack *duḥkha*. Because the absence of ignorance and attachment entails the absence of hindrances and defilements that generate *duḥkha*, *nirvāṇic* experiences are pure and untainted. Because agitation and disturbance arise only in the presence of concerns relating to a sovereign "me," they also are peaceful and calm (Skt. *vūpasanta*).

2.6.2. Revisiting Rūpāvatī

The story of Rūpāvatī is especially helpful for illustrating the distinction between *nirvāṇic* and *saṃsāric* modes of experience and the relation of these modes to delusional cognition. The starving mother relates to her child as

---

[32] T45.1876.639a23-25, recited in Cleary 1983, 161.
[33] See also Harvey 1995, 51–3.
[34] See also Harvey 1995, 189–92.

an eater of food relates to a meal. Beset by ignorance and attachment, she experiences herself and her newborn son in the mode of *saṃsāra*. She ignores the characteristics that make her potential meal someone who is her son and the characteristics that make her a mother. Seizing upon the characteristics that make her son a potential meal and herself one who eats, she regards herself as sovereign over her son's body and so forms the intention to eat the food that would allay her hunger.

By contrast, Rūpāvatī experiences the newborn child and the starving mother in the mode of *nirvāṇa*. She acknowledges the mother's hunger and the child's humanity. She acknowledges the characteristics that make the child something that is food. She also acknowledges these same characteristics in herself. Rather than imagining herself as a sovereign eater of food, she offers herself as food to be eaten. Rather than seizing upon one of mother or child as more deserving of life, she avoids separating herself from their situation and embraces her own vulnerability. Rūpāvatī feeds her breast to the mother so that the mother, in turn, can breastfeed her child. Her response, fearless and serene, models how someone with a well-directed mind, free from ignorance and attachment, puts an end to the thirst and hunger from which *duḥkha* arises.

Fazang likens the difference between *nirvāṇic* experience and *saṃsāric* experience—the difference between Rūpāvatī and the starving mother—to the difference between a tranquil ocean and a tumultuous ocean.

> When delusion ends, the mind is clear and myriad forms equally appear; it is like the ocean, where waves are created by the wind—when the wind stops, the water of the ocean grows still and clear, reflecting all images.[35]

The starving mother's mind is beset with delusion. The mother resists cognizing the newborn baby as her child, and she resists cognizing herself as a mother. Just as a boat traveling upstream generates waves as it resists the river's natural current, and just as a wave rebounding from the shore generates ripples as it moves against the flow of the ocean, the mother generates *duḥkha* as she resists the forms that appear to her. By contrast, Rūpāvatī's mind is still and clear. She flows with the situation. Just as leaves flowing downstream glide gently from one current to the next, and just as the ocean wets every grain of sand that it touches, Rūpāvatī responds to the mother's hunger and the newborn's fragility without resistance.

---

[35] T45.1876.637b22-23, recited in Cleary 1983, 152.

2.7. From Soteriology to Metaphysics

2.7.1. *Saṃsāric* Distortion

For Fazang, the *saṃsāric* mode of experience distorts not only how we cognize ourselves but also how we cognize others. Just as the ignorant cognize the self as separable from others by virtue of being independent of others, they also cognize others as separable from and independent of each other. The realm in which everything is independent is a realm of obstruction (Ch. *zhàng* 障). It is a realm in which all are surrounded by others and yet enclosed within themselves. The denizens of this realm are strong and unyielding (Ch. *gāng* 剛). Each is sovereign unto itself. When one interacts with another, each obstructs (Ch. *ài* 礙) the other. This realm is akin to a table of rolling billiard balls. Interactions are akin to collisions rather than concurrences. They are strikings that alter trajectories without affecting the powers of the interacting parties.

For Fazang, the *saṃsāric* mode of experience also distorts how we engage with others. Attachment fosters intentions to control a sovereign self. It also fosters intentions to dominate others. When the starving mother, from the story of Rūpāvatī, craves to live, she not only cognizes her newborn as food but also forms an intention to take the newborn's life force as her own by consuming that food. Ignorance also fosters intentions to dominate others. Cognizing others as independent means cognizing them as sources of their own power, and so the desire to have the power of another generates intentions to dominate the other. For example, when cognized as independent of others, gold is no mere lump of earth. Instead, it carries its value in itself, and so those who desire wealth form intentions to own more gold (or more items tradable for gold).[36]

2.7.2. *Nirvāṇic* Virtue

Strength and domination are "virtues" for those ensnared within *saṃsāric* experience. Strength preserves oneself against the (imagined) powers of others. Domination subjugates the powers of others to one's own (imagined) domain of control. Fazang contrasts these so-called "virtues" with the virtues of gentleness

---

[36] One indication that cognizing gold as independent of others is delusional is that gold would be worthless if one person were to amass all of it. *Jack Frost*, an animated television special, depicts this through the antagonist Kubla Kraus. When Kubla acquires all of the "real" (gold) coins in the region, the peasants use coins of ice as currency. The peasants, alas, seem to remain mired in delusion. They continue to think of themselves as poor, and they lament that Kubla Kraus owns all of the wealth (Bass and Rankin, Jr. 1979).

(Ch. *róu* 柔) and harmony (Ch. *hé* 和). For Fazang, these are the virtues of those who realize the *nirvāṇic* mode of experience.

> Great wisdom illuminating the real is called honest and sincere. Because great compassion saves things outside oneself, it is called gentle and harmonious. Again, honesty and sincerity concern the constancy of the root nature. Gentleness and harmony concern following and flowing without obstruction. Gentleness means extinguishing afflictions. Harmony means keeping the precepts in accordance with principle. Using these methods of equalizing and harmonizing takes in the lives of all sentient beings. Again, those who are honest and sincere are free from delusion and falsehood. Their words and actions match each other. They accumulate virtue in their heart without regard for fame and profit. They regard gold as lightly as a lump of earth. They regard teachings [of the Buddha] as more precious than jewels. Merely through right action, they equalize the lives of sentient beings and urgently aspire to satisfy self and others. Therefore, this is called the virtue of taking in the lives of sentient beings with gentleness and harmony, honesty and sincerity.[37]

The contrast between strength and gentleness is akin to the contrast between *yin* 陰 and *yang* 陽, or between the flowing water of a river and fixed rocks, in the river, that generate waves by resisting the water. Gentleness extinguishes afflictions by yielding and accommodating. Ethical precepts facilitate correct ways of yielding and accommodating. Harmony enacts these precepts in accordance with principle by coordinating differences in ways that attenuate discord and create optimal outcomes.[38] Rūpāvatī, for example, extinguishes hunger by yielding her body, and this gentleness harmonizes a tragic situation by reconciling the mother's hunger with the newborn's fragility.

Gentleness and harmony are the practical counterparts to the virtues of honesty (Ch. 質 *zhì*) and sincerity (Ch. *zhí* 直). Gentleness and harmony are the impetus for virtuous action. Honesty and sincerity provide direction for this impetus. Honesty confronts self and other as they are rather than as they are imagined to be—as inseparable rather than independent. Sincerity provides insight for discerning efficacious response in light of honest confrontation.[39] Because gentleness and harmony fuel actions that save others from *duḥkha*,

---

[37] T45.1876.639a6-12. For an alternative translation, see Cleary 1983, 160.
[38] See also Ames 2003, 169.
[39] See Ames 2003, 166.

34 METAPHORS FOR INTERDEPENDENCE

compassion is their concern. Because honesty and sincerity direct these actions, wisdom is their concern.

2.7.3. Wisdom and Insight

Fazang's claims about mutual identity and mutual inclusion derive from an effort to conceptualize reality in an honest and sincere manner—that is, in a manner free from ignorance and attachment. This effort differs from the effort merely to experience reality without ignorance or attachment. Some experience is not conceptual. Nonconceptual experience navigates differences without the mediation of concepts. Conceptual experience likewise cognizes differences and distinctions. It does so, however, through the mediation of concepts, discriminating self from other, *this* from *that*. Conceptualizing reality without ignorance or attachment requires cognizing distinctions between *this* and *that* without conceptualizing *this* as separable from *that*. Satisfying these requirements demands wisdom and insight (Skt. *darśana*; Ch. *jiàn*見). Fazang finds this wisdom and insight in the *Flower Adornment Sūtra*.[40]

Chapter 8 of the *Flower Adornment Sūtra* embellishes many of the soteriological teachings that are fundamental to Buddhism. The chapter includes more than one hundred examples of *duḥkha*.[41] Some are quite general: grasping conditions, false views, extreme suffering, absence of real meaning, misery, following feelings. Others are much more specific: the piercing of thorns, an abscess, calling forth adversaries, dwelling in a city, dwelling in a house, sharp blades. The same chapter includes a similarly expansive list for sources of *duḥkha*: craving-based attachment, erroneous awareness, conceptual proliferation, partial assessment, abandoning moral precepts, disharmony; but also great adversaries, powerlessness, neglectfulness, contradictions, owning a house, anger.

Chapter 9 of the *Flower Adornment Sūtra* continues the soteriological elaborations of Chapter 8. It does so by ornamenting the qualities of *nirvāṇic* experience as marks of the Buddha.[42] For example, the chapter characterizes the body of the Buddha as unproduced, becoming measurelessly many, and having no place from which it comes. It also characterizes the Buddha's mind as fearless in action, pure and radiant, free of defiling attachments.

---

[40] For the view that the *Flower Adornment Sūtra* only aims to instruct readers on how to reproduce certain experiences of enlightenment, see Thurman 1980; Obert 2000; Plassen 2012, 214. Even if this view is correct, it does not impugn the claim that Fazang uses the text for metaphysical purposes.

[41] See T10.279.60a15–62a26; Dharmamitra 2022, 1: 273–80.

[42] See T10.279.64b23–c13; Dharmamitra 2022, 1: 291–2.

The *Flower Adornment Sūtra* also makes vivid the virtues that facilitate *nirvāṇic* experience. Chapter 39, for instance, provides (fictional) biographies for an array of bodhisattvas (Ch. *púsà* 菩薩)—those who aim for *nirvāṇa* by endeavoring to help others escape *saṃsāra*. For example the monk Supratiṣṭhita 善住 and Vāsantī-deva 婆珊婆演底主夜神, goddess of night, exemplify the virtues of gentleness and harmony.[43] Chapter 22 illustrates several kinds of generosity (Skt. *dāna*; Ch. *shī* 施) associated with these virtues. For example, the chapter explains the bodhisattva's ultimate giving (Ch. *jiūjìng shī* 究竟施) as a willingness to give up their eyes, ears, nose, tongue, hands, and even feet for the sake of those who lack these organs—and having not a single thought of regret in doing so.[44] (The story of Rūpāvatī illustrates ultimate giving. Rūpāvatī uses her body to alleviate the starving woman's hunger and buy time to fetch food for the woman's newborn baby.)

In addition to its soteriological and ethical instruction, the *Flower Adornment Sūtra* provides instruction in metaphysics—or instruction in how to conceptualize difference and distinction without separation. It does so by invoking the relations of identity (Ch. *jí* 即) and inclusion (Ch. *rù* 入).[45] For example, the 60-scroll version of the scripture, translated by Buddhadhadra 佛馱跋陀羅 (359–429) between 418 and 420, proclaims that each world (Ch. *shì jiè* 世界), or state of existence, is identical with and included within all others.

> Know that one world is identical with measureless, boundless worlds, and measureless, boundless worlds are identical with one world. Know that measureless, boundless worlds enter one world, and one world enters measureless, boundless worlds.[46]

It also proclaims that those with perfect wisdom extend this insight about mutual identity and mutual inclusion to many kinds of conditioned things, including the bodies of sentient beings, eons and thoughts, teachings, sense bases, sense organs, differentiating characteristics, spoken sounds, and the time periods of past, present, and future.[47]

---

[43] See T10.279.336b12-337b15, 369a16-372a2; Cleary 1993, 1186–9, 1284–95; Dharmamitra 2022, 3: 1725–31, 1890–904.

[44] See T10.279.113c1-7; Dharmamitra 2022, 1: 533. For Fazang's remarks on the virtue of ultimate giving (and how bodhisattvas use their bodies as ransom to liberate others), see T45.1876.639a14-16; Cleary 1983, 160. For an analysis of how early Buddhist traditions conceptualize generous action, see Jones 2020.

[45] The character 即 basically means *is*. When Fazang uses 即 in a technical sense, I prefer to translate 即 as denoting a kind of identity because, in Fazang's technical sense, 即 never denotes a relation of predication (as with "Fazang is awesome"). I explicate Fazang's technical sense of 即 in Chapter 3.5.3.

[46] T9.278.450c17-20.

[47] T9.278.607c17-29.

36 METAPHORS FOR INTERDEPENDENCE

The 80-scroll version of the *Flower Adornment Sūtra*, translated near the end of the seventh century by Śikṣānanda 實叉難陀 (652–710) with Fazang's assistance, more explicitly proclaims mutual inclusion among all worlds and all atoms within those worlds.

> Sons of the Buddha, one should realize that the oceans of worlds have ways in which they do not differ that are as numerous as the atoms in an ocean of worlds. For example: . . . In every one of the oceans of worlds, there are no differences in the way all oceans of worlds enter a single atom; and in every one of the oceans of worlds, there is no difference in the way that the sphere of action of all the buddhas, the *bhagavats*, of the three periods of time appears in every atom.[48]

The scripture also connects cognition of mutuality to the virtues of the bodhisattva. For example, the story of the maiden Maitrāyaṇī 慈行童女, from Chapter 39, represents mutuality as a kind of mutual reflectivity among jewels, and it connects cognition of mutuality to the kind of ethical conduct that arises from gentleness and harmony.[49]

The central insight of the *Flower Adornment Sūtra* is that experiencing reality in the *nirvāṇic* mode does not require abandoning conceptual cognition. When one is identical with or included within another, the one and the other are inseparable despite differing from each other. Insofar as ignorance and attachment derive from cognizing separation and not from cognizing difference, it follows that a well-directed mind, free from ignorance and attachment, can cognize the truth about reality by conceptualizing things as mutually identical and mutually inclusive. Fazang's metaphysics is an effort to explain the content of this cognition and thereby vindicate the insight from the *Flower Adornment Sūtra*.

---

[48] T10.279.38c1-2, c11-13, recited in Dharmamitra 2022, 1: 177. See also Cleary 1993, 199–200.
[49] See T10.279.348a26-349b22; Cleary 1993, 1222–6; Dharmamitra 2022, 3: 1786–92.

3

Conceptualizing Causality

3.1. Conditionality

Buddhism teaches that all conditioned things are evanescent and insecure, that ignorance and attachment prompt delusional cognitions of persistence and security, and that overcoming these delusions requires overcoming the tendency to cognize things as separable or independent from each other. Sectarian divisions among Indian Buddhist traditions arise, in part, by virtue of disagreements about how to cognize conditionality without separation. Some traditions maintain that selves and other conditioned things reduce to things that are independent of others, and they conceptualize conditionality and inseparability as a matter of pervasive diachronic causal relations among conditioned things. Other traditions deny that anything is independent of others, conceptualizing conditionality and inseparability as pervasive synchronic interdependence. Monks of the former persuasion typically belong to the Abhidharma tradition of Buddhism.[1] Monks of the latter persuasion, such as Nāgārjuna (2nd–3rd century) and Vasubandhu (4th–5th century), typically belong to the Mahāyāna tradition.[2]

Fazang belongs to the Mahāyāna tradition of Buddhism. He diverges from Indian Mahāyāna traditions by prioritizing the *Flower Adornment Sūtra* as a source of insight into conditionality. The *Flower Adornment Sūtra* teaches that conditioned things differ without separation by virtue of their mutual identity (Ch. *xiāng jí* 相即) and mutual inclusion (Ch. *xiāng rù* 相入).

> Know that one world is identical with measureless, boundless worlds, and measureless, boundless worlds are identical with one world. Know that measureless, boundless worlds enter one world, and one world enters measureless, boundless worlds.[3]

The meaning of this teaching is difficult to decipher. Consider, for example, the relation between the world of feeling (Skt. *kāma-loka*; Ch. *yù jiè* 欲界) and the

---

[1] See Cox 2004. For an overview of Abhidharma metaphysics, see Ronkin 2005.
[2] For an analysis of Nāgārjuna's metaphysics, see Westerhoff 2009. For an analysis of Vasubandhu's, see Gold 2015.
[3] T9.278.450c17-20.

Metaphors for Interdependence. Nicholaos Jones, Oxford University Press. © Nicholaos Jones 2025.
DOI: 10.1093/9780197807224.003.0003

world of form (Skt. *rūpa-loka*; Ch. *sè jiè* 色界). Humans and animals, conditioned by sensual desire, reside in the former. Gods and other deities, free from sensual desire but conditioned by pride and jealousy, reside in the latter. If each world is identical with the other, humans and animals enter the world of form while gods and other deities enter the world of feeling. Yet, if humans and gods reside amid each other, in what sense do the two worlds differ? Conversely, if difference confines humans and gods each to their own world, in what sense does one world enter the other?

This chapter endeavors to address these questions by explaining how Fazang appropriates the Mahāyāna view of conditionality. The goal is to reconstruct a conceptual framework that makes possible a rigorous and responsible interpretation of Fazang's contentions about mutual identity and mutual inclusion. The chapter divides into five parts. The first sketches an example meant to make Fazang's conception of conditionality more intuitive. The second explains how Fazang conceptualizes conditioned things. The third part explains the difference between conceptualizing conditioned things as real and conceptualizing them as nominal. The fourth part explains how Fazang conceptualizes causality, the role of inclusion and identity in this conception, and how Fazang's conception avoids an issue that besets some Mahāyāna approaches to conditionality. The fifth part concludes by explicating the meaning Fazang ascribes to the teaching of mutual identity and mutual inclusion.

3.2. Sudhana and Bhīṣmottaranirghoṣa

For the sake of motivating and lending some modicum of intelligibility to Fazang's conception of mutual identity and mutual inclusion, consider a mundane situation involving the relation between student and teacher. In the final chapter of the *Flower Adornment Sūtra*, the religious pilgrim Sudhana 善財 journeys to visit a spiritual benefactor named Bhīṣmottaranirghoṣa 毘目瞿沙仙 人.[4] Sudhana finds the sage in a forest on a spiritual retreat. Sudhana approaches, pays his respects, and requests spiritual instruction. Bhīṣmottaranirghoṣa rubs Sudhana's head with his right hand.[5] Then, taking Sudhana's right hand into his, Bhīṣmottaranirghoṣa imparts to Sudhana a vision.

> Bhīṣmottaranirghoṣa Rishi then extended his right hand, rubbed the crown of Sudhana's head, and grasped Sudhana's hand, at which point Sudhana immediately saw himself go off and enter worlds of the ten directions as numerous

[4] See T10.279.345a21-346a28; Dharmamitra 2022, 3: 1771–6; Cleary 1993, 1214–7.
[5] For an artistic depiction of this scene, see Mace 2020, Figure 15.

as the atoms in ten buddha *kṣetras*, whereupon he arrived in the abodes of buddhas as numerous as the atoms in ten buddha *kṣetras* in which he saw those buddhas' *kṣetras*, their congregations, those buddhas' major and secondary signs, and their many different kinds of adornments.... [6]

Sudhana's vision—described at much greater length in the *Flower Adornment Sūtra*—imbues him with "the light of the 'universal integration of all regions' *dhāraṇī*." [7]

When the sage Bhīṣmottaranirghoṣa grasps Sudhana's hand, the sage enacts teaching and Sudhana enacts learning. It is natural and tempting to suppose that the sage causes the teaching and Sudhana causes the learning. Yet there is good reason to resist this supposition. When sitting alone in the forest, Bhīṣmottaranirghoṣa is inclined to teach and yet there is no teaching—there is no giving instruction. Similarly, when Sudhana travels alone in search of a spiritual benefactor, he is inclined to learn but there is no learning—there is no receiving instruction. Insofar as causes put inclinations into action, the student causes the sage to teach and the sage causes the student to learn. That is, when the sage enacts teaching and the student enacts learning, the sage enters into the range of Sudhana's causal efficacy and Sudhana enters into the range of the sage's causal efficacy, respectively.

The mutual inclusion between student and sage does not mean that Bhīṣmottaranirghoṣa contributes nothing to teaching and Sudhana contributes nothing to learning. Sudhana causes the sage to teach only because the sage is inclined to teach. Because Bhīṣmottaranirghoṣa has this inclination, he conditions the form of the teaching that Sudhana causes. Similarly, Bhīṣmottaranirghoṣa causes the student to learn only because the student is inclined to learn. Because Sudhana has this inclination, he conditions the form of the learning that Bhīṣmottaranirghoṣa causes.

Fazang deciphers the teachings of mutual identity and mutual inclusion in much the same way that the preceding example deciphers the mutual dependence of student and sage. Yet matters quickly become complicated for examples involving more than two things. For example, if the world of feeling enters into the world of form because the gods put humans into action, is this because each god puts every human into action, because each god puts only some humans into action, or because only some gods put some humans into action? What,

---

[6] T10.279.345c20-5, recited in Dharmamitra 2022, 3: 1774. See also Cleary 1993, 1215–6. A buddha-*kṣetra* is a sphere of activity and influence for a buddha.

[7] T10.279.346a7-8, recited in Dharmamitra 2022, 3: 1775. Cleary translates the quoted phrase as "the light of the mystic formulation of the structure of the universe" (Cleary 1993, 1216). Perhaps worth noting is that Bhīṣmottaranirghoṣa's interaction with Sudhana mirrors the concluding interaction between Govinda and Siddhartha in Hermann Hesse's novel *Siddhartha*. See Hesse 2003, 130–2. I thank Bryan Van Norden for this observation.

40 METAPHORS FOR INTERDEPENDENCE

moreover, is the relation between the gods in the world of form? Do the gods put other gods into action? If so, does each god enter into all other gods or only some other gods? Or is it only that some gods enter into others?

Fazang relies upon a sophisticated battery of technical terms to explain the meaning of mutual identity and mutual inclusion. In doing so, he appropriates two insights about conditionality from Indian traditions of Buddhism. One insight, from Nāgārjuna and the Madhyamaka Mahāyāna tradition, is that conditionality is utterly pervasive: nothing exists without dependence upon another. The other insight, from the Sarvāstivāda Abhidharma tradition but also Vasubandhu, is that one and the same thing can have multiple—even contrary—aspects. Fazang uses these insights to secure the possibility of conceptualizing the realm of conditioned things without ignorance or attachment.[8]

3.3. Fazang's Ontology

3.3.1. *Dharmas* and Characteristics

Following sectarian traditions of Indian Buddhism, Fazang conceptualizes Sudhana and Bhīṣmottaranirghoṣa, humans and animals, gods and other deities as aggregates or composites (Skt. *skandha*; Ch. *yùn* 蘊). Sudhana, for example, is a composite of body and mind. Composites are conditioned things because they depend upon their constituents. Some of these constituents are also composites.

Consider, for example, some remarks from a physician named Samantanetra 普眼長者 in an expanded version of the *Flower Adornment Sūtra*.[9] Before instructing the pilgrim Sudhana about how to cure various bodily illnesses, Samantanetra provides a standard Buddhist analysis of living bodies.[10] Samantanetra resolves the body into a composite of hairs and pores, organs and limbs, fluids and hollows. He resolves these constituents into the great elements: earth, water, fire, air, and empty space. He does not resolve the elements into further constituents. The reason is that the great elements are *dharmas* (Ch. *fǎ* 法).

---

[8] This chapter focuses on Fazang's appropriation of the Madhyamaka insight about conditionality. Chapter 5 focuses on his appropriation of the insight about aspects.

[9] Around 798, Prajña 般若, a dharma preacher from Kashmir, adds details to the conversation between Sudhana and Samantanetra. The details concern then-standard Indian medical knowledge. They are not present in the versions of the *Flower Adornment Sūtra* available to Fazang (see T9.278.707b23–710b6; Cleary 1993, 1240–2; Dharmamitra 2022, 3: 1818–21). However, Fazang certainly would have been familiar with the details relating to the great elements.

[10] See T10.293.711a18–27; Giddings 2017, 96–7.

Dharmas are named from the Sanskrit root *dhr*, meaning that which sustains, supports, upholds, maintains.[11] In addition to the great elements, paradigmatic examples include sensory activity *dharmas* such as "tonguing" and tasting as well as sensory object *dharmas* such as texture and taste. *Dharmas* differ from aggregates or composites such as living bodies and sensory experiences. Aggregates and composites are built from others. Living bodies are built from the great elements. Sensory experiences are built from contacts of sensory activities and sensory objects. *Dharmas*, by contrast, are unbuilt.

Nearly all scholastic traditions of Buddhism conceptualize *dharmas* as having characteristics. A characteristic (Skt. *lakṣaṇa*; Ch. *xiāng* 相) is that which a predicate designates, and something has a characteristic—or, equivalently, a characteristic belongs to (Ch. *shè* 攝) a thing—just in case a predicate designating the characteristic is true of the thing. For example, because earth *dharmas* are solid, earth *dharmas* have the characteristic of solidity. Similarly, because *dharmas* of loving-kindness promote friendship, they have the characteristic of friendliness.

Conceptualizing *dharmas* as having characteristics might suggest that *dharmas* are separable from their characteristics. Buddhist traditions reject this suggestion. The relation between a *dharma* and its characteristics is not the relation between a substance (Skt. *dravya*; Ch. *shí* 實) and its qualities (Skt. *guṇa*; Ch. *dé* 德).[12] Like *dharmas*, substances support and maintain. Substances satisfy this role by virtue of hosting qualities. Substances have qualities in the way that venues have events, and substances are separable from their qualities in the way venues are separable from their events. This separability allows substances to persist through changes in their qualities. By contrast, *dharmas* support and maintain by virtue of being the unbuilt components of composites. *Dharmas* have characteristics in the way that arguments have premises and conclusions, and they are inseparable from their characteristics in the way arguments are inseparable from their premises and conclusions. This inseparability precludes *dharmas* from persisting through changes of characteristics. Changings of characteristics are always changings of *dharmas*.[13]

Commentary on the Great Perfection of Wisdom, attributed to Nāgārjuna by its Chinese translator Kumārajīva 鳩摩羅什 (344–413), divides the characteristics of *dharmas* into specific and general.[14] Specific characteristics (Skt.

---

[11] Fazang ascribes three meanings to *dharma*, the first of which is "that which upholds and maintains" (Ch. *chí* 持) (see T44.1838.63b18-9). For the many meanings and translations of the term *dharma*, see Warder 1971; Carter 1976, 332–4; Wut 2013.

[12] For a review of substance-quality ontologies from (non-Buddhist) Indian traditions of Nyāya, Vaiśeṣika, and Jainism, see Matilal 1977. Matilal notes that Aristotle endorses a similar ontology (Matilal 1977, 99–100).

[13] The inseparability of *dharmas* and their characteristics supports interpreting *dharmas* as property tropes. See also Goodman 2004, 391–5.

[14] T25.1509.293a25; Chödrön 2001, 1742. *Commentary on the Great Perfection of Wisdom* is "one of the most authoritative and influential texts in East Asian Buddhism" (Zaccheti 2021, 1). For this reason, I make frequent appeal to it when explaining Fazang's conceptual framework. For an

42 METAPHORS FOR INTERDEPENDENCE

salakṣaṇa or *svalakṣaṇa*; Ch. *zì xiāng* 自相) are species-inducing. They divide *dharmas* into kinds (Ch. *lèi* 類).[15] *Dharmas* belonging to the same kind have the same specific characteristic. For example, all *dharmas* of earth have solidity as their specific characteristic, and all *dharmas* of fire have heat as their specific characteristic.[16] *Dharmas* belonging to different kinds have different specific characteristics. For example, *dharmas* of consciousness have investigation as their specific characteristic. They differ from *dharmas* of exertion, which have effort as their specific characteristic.[17] Specific characteristics differ from general characteristics (Skt. *sāmānyalakṣaṇa*; Ch. *gòng xiāng* 共相). The reason is that specific characteristics mark differences among kinds, but general characteristics are common to many kinds.[18] The paradigmatic example of a general characteristic is evanescence (Skt. *anitya*; Ch. *wú cháng* 無常). This is a general characteristic because all *dharmas* are prone to rise and fall.

3.3.2. Determinacy

Much of Fazang's metaphysics concerns the relation between *dharmas* and their specific characteristics.[19] *Commentary on the Great Perfection of Wisdom* identifies two such relations. It does so by dividing *dharmas* into fixed or determinate (Skt. *niyata* or *vinayata*; Ch. *dìng* 定 or *jué dìng* 決定) and variable or indeterminate (Skt. *aniyata*; Ch. *bú dìng* 不定). *Dharmas* that are determinate

---

overview of ongoing debates about the authorship of this commentary, see Travagnin 2018. For a distinction between specific and general characteristics in Sarvāstivādin texts, see Cox 2004, 574–6. For an overview of debates about the soteriological significance of the distinction in Abhidharma and Chinese Yogācāra, see Lin 2016.

[15] For an analysis of *kind* (Ch. *lèi* 類) in classical Chinese as a technical equivalent of (mathematical) *class*, see Fung 2020, 224–229.

[16] T25.1509.293a28-9; Chödrön 2001, 1743.

[17] T25.1509.293c4-6; Chödrön 2001, 1746.

[18] Westerhoff also contrasts specific characteristics with general (or common) characteristics (Westerhoff 2009, 21). He characterizes specific characteristics (or qualities) as essence-*svabhāva*. According to Westerhoff, each object has a specific characteristic that is "unique to the object characterized," and each specific characteristic is an essence-*svabhāva* because the object "cannot lose [its specific characteristic] without ceasing to be that very object" (Westerhoff 2009, 21–2). The example he provides from Nāgārjuna only supports conceptualizing essence-*svabhāva* as that which distinguishes kinds of object from each other (Westerhoff 2009, 23). This is also how *Commentary on the Great Perfection of Wisdom* conceptualizes specific characteristics: they mark differences among kinds, but they do not mark differences among members within the same kind. So, too, with Fazang.

[19] *Commentary on the Great Perfection of Wisdom* explains that focusing on the relation between *dharmas* and their specific characteristics (rather than their characteristics more broadly) is necessary for understanding the fundamental nature of *dharmas*. See T25.1509.293c11-3; Chödrön 2001, 1746.

(with respect to their specific characteristics) have their specific characteristics by virtue of the way they themselves are. Schematically, for any x with specific characteristic S_x,

x is determinate (regarding S_x):$=_{df} x$ has S_x, and there is no $y \neq x$ such that x depends upon y for having S_x.

Dharmas that are not determinate are indeterminate. Schematically, for any x with specific characteristic S_x,

x is indeterminate (regarding S_x):$=_{df} x$ has S_x, and there is some $y \neq x$ such that x depends upon y for having S_x.

Indeterminate *dharmas* have their specific characteristics by virtue of their relations to others.[20]

Consider, for the sake of illustrating the determinate/indeterminate distinction, the example of diamond and its firmness from *Commentary on the Great Perfection of Wisdom*.

What some people regard as firm, others regard as not firm. For example, people consider diamond to be firm, but Indra (Śakra) grasps it—like a person holding a staff—and considers it as not firm. Also, because of not knowing the causes and conditions for breaking diamond, it is considered to be firm; but those who know to fasten it atop a tortoiseshell, and use a goat horn to smash it, know that it is not firm.[21]

Diamonds are composites of earth *dharmas*. They arise when earth *dharmas* come to have a particular configuration, and in this configuration diamonds have

---

[20] Because *dharmas* are inseparable from their specific characteristics, categorizing *dharmas* as determinate or indeterminate (with respect to their specific characteristics) is equivalent to categorizing the specific characteristics of *dharmas* as determinate or indeterminate. For an example of the latter categorization, see T25.1509.294b14-c10; Chödrön 2001, 1751–3. Note also that the division between determinate and indeterminate characteristics is similar to the division, in contemporary analytic metaphysics, between intrinsic and extrinsic properties. For an overview of the intrinsic/extrinsic distinction, see Hoffman-Kolss 2021. (I am indebted to Hoffman-Kolss for my gloss on the determinate/indeterminate distinction.)

[21] T25.1509.290b4-8. For an alternative translation, see Chödrön 2001, 1718. Chödrön's translation interprets 堅固 (*jiān gù*; Skt. *sāratā*) as *solidity* rather than *firmness*, and it interprets 金剛 (*jīngāng*; Skt. *vajrā*) as *lightning* rather than *diamond*. Because solidity is a matter of supporting others, Chödrön's translation makes the example unnecessarily confusing. It is not clear how lightning supports anything. It is not clear why lightning would be solid by virtue of being ungraspable. Nor is it clear what it would be to fasten lightning to a curved surface or smash lightning into pieces.

44 METAPHORS FOR INTERDEPENDENCE

the specific characteristic of firmness—where firmness is a matter of piercing others and resisting destruction.[22]

When an ordinary person grasps a diamond, the diamond retains its natural configuration and so retains its firmness. This is why the diamond pierces their skin and does not break. Yet, when Indra grasps a diamond, his strength reconfigures the *dharmas* that compose the diamond and so the diamond does not pierce his skin. Similarly, when someone strikes a diamond with a goat horn on a tortoise shell, the strike reconfigures the *dharmas* that compose the diamond and the diamond shatters. Hence, because the firmness of diamonds depends upon the configuration of the *dharmas* that compose them, diamonds are indeterminate with respect to their firmness.[23]

Diamonds and other composites are paradigmatic examples of indeterminate things. Whether *dharmas*—the unbuilt constituents of composites—are also indeterminate is a matter of debate among various Buddhist traditions. The Chinese traditions of Sanlun 三論 and Tiantai 天台 maintain that *dharmas* are indeterminate.[24] *Commentary on the Great Perfection of Wisdom* offers the example of water as justification. Water has fluidity as its specific characteristic in warm weather. Yet, because water becomes ice in cold weather and thereby takes on the characteristic of hardness, *Commentary on the Great Perfection of Wisdom* infers that water is indeterminate—or, more precisely, that its specific characteristic of fluidity (in warm weather) is indeterminate.[25]

The justification, from *Commentary on the Great Perfection of Wisdom*, for conceptualizing *dharmas* as indeterminate is not decisive. The Indian monk Harivarman 訶梨跋摩 (3rd–4th century), whose views align with the Sautrāntika 經量部 tradition of Abhidharma, offers a typical response. Harivarman contends that the great elements (and other *dharmas*) do not give up their specific characteristics. For example, in the case of water, Harivarman maintains that ice maintains its fluidity even though cold weather alters the way that water manifests this fluidity. For Harivarman, although the specific characteristic of ice manifests as hardness, the ice remains fluid because ice flows—albeit not in the way that warm water flows.[26]

---

[22] *Sūtra on the Questions of Gaganagañja* associates diamond with piercing and firmness with indestructibility. See Han 2020, 242. For ease of exposition, I associate firmness with both piercing and indestructibility.

[23] The point of the diamond example is not that diamond's firmness depends upon people's epistemic attitudes toward it, but that diamond's firmness depends upon its relation to others. When the source text says that someone considers or regards diamond in a certain way, *consider* and *regard* should be interpreted as success verbs.

[24] See Liu 1994, 100–3; Ho 2020; Kantor 2006, 36–41; Ziporyn 2016, 148–50, 159–65.

[25] See T25.1509.294b20-2; Chödrön 2001, 1752.

[26] See T32.1646.264b8-21; Sastri 1978, 88. Harivarman's argument for why ice maintains the characteristic of fluidity is rather dense. The basic idea is that even though ice is solid, it remains water—albeit water in a frozen (and thereby hard) configuration. As anyone familiar with cats in large bowls can attest, solidity is no barrier to fluidity. (For a scientific analysis of cats as fluids, see Fardin 2014.)

Although Fazang tends to align with Mahāyāna traditions such as Sanlun and Tiantai rather than Abihdharma traditions such as Sautrāntika, he maintains—perhaps surprisingly—that *dharmas* are determinate rather than indeterminate (with respect to their specific characteristics). This is explicit in the theory of causality from his *Treatise on the Five Teachings of Huayan*.[27] Fazang remarks that all *dharmas*, insofar as they are causal, are fixed or determinate (Ch. *jué ding* 決定).[28]

Fazang also uses the determinacy of characteristics to explain relations among various aspects of Buddhist teaching and practice. For example, Fazang explains that, despite the distinctions of rank (Ch. *wèi* 位)—or spiritual attainment—among Buddhist practitioners, the ranks themselves interpenetrate without opposing each other—and their sequential order is constant—because the gateways for the various ranks are unmoving (Ch. *bùyí* 不移) and have constant characteristics (Ch. *héng xiāng* 恒相).[29] This appeal to the immobility of ranks and the constancy of their characteristics signals, in effect, a conception of ranks as determinate with respect to their specific characteristics.

Fazang's conception of *dharmas* as determinate (with respect to their specific characteristics) is also implicit in his remark, from the final section of his *Treatise*, that *dharmas* "maintain their own character" (Ch. *zhù zì fǎ* 住自法).[30] This contrasts with the view of the Tiantai master Zhiyi 智顗 (538–597). For Zhiyi, *dharmas* gain their character from their relations to others and, because of this, they are indeterminate with respect to their specific characteristics.[31] Fazang criticizes this kind of view as arising from a fear of sinking into the error of reifying existence.[32] The basis for his criticism is that, if *dharmas* are indeterminate with respect to their specific characteristics, there is no dependent arising.[33] Fazang does not elaborate upon this (surprising) contention. But it is possible to reconstruct an implicit justification from other aspects of Fazang's theory of causality.

---

[27] For Fazang's theory of causality, see T45.1866.502a8-23; Cook 1970, 446–51; Unno et al. 2023, 171–2. For a brief exegesis of the theory, see Nakasone 1980, 109–21. Fazang's theory, or a version thereof, seems to originate in *Compendium of Mahāyāna* (T31.1593.115c1-4), attributed to the Indian Yogācārin Asaṅga (4th century) and translated into Chinese by Paramārtha 真諦 (499–567). Other versions appear in Vasubandhu's *Treatise on the Compendium of Mahāyāna* (T31.1597.329b27-c13), Xuanzang's *Treatise on the Demonstration of Consciousness-Only* (T31.1585.9b7-29), and *Record on Fathoming the Mysteries of Huayan* (T35.1732.66a22-b4) by Zhiyan 智儼 (602–668).

[28] See T45.1866.502a13-16; Cook 1970, 449; Unno et al. 2023, 172.

[29] T45.1866.490a22-7; Cook 1970, 282; Unno et al. 2023, 106.

[30] T45.1866.507c10; Cook 1970, 538; Unno et al. 2023, 201.

[31] See Ziporyn 2010, 504–8; Kantor 2024.

[32] Fazang does not name Zhiyi as a target for his critique. This is likely because Fazang holds Zhiyi in extremely high regard. See T45.1866.481a25-7; Cook 1970, 172; Unno et al. 2023, 59.

[33] See T45.1866.501a8-12; Cook 1970, 430–1; Unno et al. 2023, 166.

46 METAPHORS FOR INTERDEPENDENCE

3.3.3. Dynamic Dispositionality

Fazang's theory of causality conceptualizes *dharmas* as dynamic rather than static. For Fazang, each *dharma* gives rise to some fruit or effect (Skt. *phala*; Ch. *guǒ* 果). This giving rise to an effect is the action or activity (Skt. *kāritra*; Ch. *zuò yòng* 作用) of the *dharma*. The specific characteristics of *dharmas* ground these activities. For example, *dharmas* of consciousness investigate because their specific characteristic is investigation, and *dharmas* of earth support because their specific characteristic is solidity. Moreover, just as *dharmas* are inseparable from their specific characteristics, they are inseparable from their activities.[34] This inseparability means that *dharmas* are doings rather than doers—they are dynamic rather than static.

Because the specific characteristics of *dharmas* ground their activities, each *dharma* gives rise to some specific effect. There is, accordingly, a sense in which *dharmas* are directed or disposed toward the effects to which they give rise. Just as things with dispositions give rise to effects by actualizing their dispositions, *dharmas* give rise to effects by enacting their specific characteristics. Moreover, just as things with dispositions are directed toward their effects by virtue of their dispositionalty, *dharmas* are directed toward their effects by virtue of their specific characteristics.

Following Sarvāstivādins such as Saṃghabhadra 僧伽跋陀羅 (5th century) and Yogācārins such as Xuanzang 玄奘 (602–664), Fazang conceptualizes the dispositional directedness of *dharmas* as *dharmas* inducing or projecting their own effects (Skt. *phalākṣepa* or *svaphalopārjita*; Ch. *yǐn zì guǒ* 引自果).[35] A *dharma* projects an effect when, for some specific characteristic that the *dharma* has, the effect is the enacting of that characteristic. Schematically, for any *dharma* x, any specific characteristic S_x of that *dharma*, and any effect y,

$$x \text{ projects } y :=_{df} x \text{ has } S_x, \text{ and } y \text{ is the enacting of } S_x.$$

Seeds are a standard toy example for the projection relation. Lotus seeds, for instance, have a specific characteristic that differentiates them from other kinds of seed. Because the enacting of this characteristic is a lotus sprout, lotus seeds project lotus sprouts. Fire *dharmas* are a standard technical example of the projection relation. Heat is the specific characteristic of fire *dharmas*, and warmth

---

[34] Gold notes that, according to Vasubandhu, the activities and specific characteristics of *dharmas* are indistinguishable (Gold 2015, 36).

[35] See T45.1866.502a16-8; Cook 1970, 450; Unno et al. 2023, 172. For Saṃghabhadra's view about causality, see his *Treatise Conforming to the Correct Logic* (T29.1562.631c-632b; Dhammajoti 2015, 130). For an overview of Saṃghabhadra's approach, see Cox 1995, 141–5 and Cox 2004, 572–3. For Xuanzang's view, see his *Discourse on the Demonstration of Consciousness-Only* (T31.1585.9b7-29; Cook 1999, 56–7).

is the enacting of heat. So fire *dharmas* project warming. Similarly, friendliness is the specific characteristic of loving-kindness *dharmas*, and friendship is the enacting of friendliness. So loving-kindness *dharmas* project friendship.

By positing that *dharmas* project their own effects, Fazang means, in part, that *dharmas*—or the specific characteristics of *dharmas*—are dispositional. But the qualifier in this posit—about *dharmas* projecting *their own* effects— indicates Fazang also means that *dharmas* do not vary the effects they project when they vary their relations to others. When lotus seeds project lotus sprouts, they are disposed to give rise to lotus sprouts regardless of whether they abide in moist soil or the void of space. Similarly, when water projects fluidity, it is disposed to flow regardless of whether the ambient air is warm or cold. For Fazang, because *dharmas* project their own effects, they are dispositional and their dispositionality is determinate.[36]

Fazang's conception of *dharmas* as dynamic activities with determinate dispositions explains why he conceptualizes *dharmas* as determinate with respect to their specific characteristics. Because *dharmas* are dynamic activities, their specific characteristics ground the effects they project. If *dharmas* were indeterminate with respect to their specific characteristics, these characteristics would vary as their relations to others vary. Hence, because specific characteristics of *dharmas* ground the effects that *dharmas* project, these effects would vary if *dharmas* were indeterminate with respect to their specific characteristics. However, because *dharmas* are determinate with respect to their dispositionality, the effects they project do not vary as *dharmas* vary their relations to others. Therefore, if *dharmas* are dynamic activities with determinate dispositions, *dharmas* must be determinate with respect to their specific characteristics. (Fazang does not offer this argument. But he endorses the premises and the conclusion.)

3.4. Real and Nominal

Because Fazang aligns with the Mahāyāna tradition of Buddhism and yet conceptualizes *dharmas* as determinate with respect to their specific characteristics, his view about the ontological status of *dharmas* might seem to be incoherent. The appearance of incoherence derives from a division, shared across

---

[36] The inseparability of *dharmas* and their activities, together with the determinacy of *dharmas* with respect to the effects they project, supports interpreting *dharmas* as pleiotropic or single-track dispositions. The distinction between pleiotropic and polygenic (multi-track) dispositions originates with Gilbert Ryle. For Ryle, generic or determinable dispositions—polygenic ones—are "dispositions admitting of a wide variety of more or less dissimilar exercises" (Ryle 2009, 43; see also 32, 102, 118).

48 METAPHORS FOR INTERDEPENDENCE

Buddhist traditions, between real existents (Skt. *dravya-sat*; Ch. *shí yǒu* 實有) and nominal existents (Skt. *prajñapti-sat*; Ch. *jiǎ yǒu*假有).

Real existents are self-natured (Skt. *svabhāva*; Ch. *zì xìng* 自性). For example, according to the Saṃghabhadra,

> If, with regard to a thing, a cognition (*buddhi*) is produced without depending on anything else, this thing exists truly—e.g., *rūpa*, *vedanā*, etc. If it depends on other things to produce a cognition, then it exists conceptually/relatively [*prajñaptito'sti*]—e.g., a vase, army, etc.[37]

Being self-natured is a matter of existing without dependence upon others. Schematically,

> x is a real existent:$=_{df}$ there is no $y \neq x$ such that x depends for its existence upon y.

If real existents have specific characteristics, those characteristics must be determinate. Moreover, although Buddhist texts sometimes use the same term—*svabhāva*—for specific characteristics and self-natures, having specific characteristics is consistent with not being a real existent.[38] It is even consistent with having *determinate* specific characteristics—provided that there is some other respect of dependence upon others.

Existents that are not real are nominal. Nominal existents are empty (Skt. *śūnya*; Ch. *kōng* 空) of self-nature. They exist in dependence upon others. Schematically,

> x is a nominal existent:$=_{df}$ there is some $y \neq x$ such that x depends for its existence upon y.

Composites are paradigmatic examples of nominal existents. Chariots, for example, do not exist apart from wheels, carriage, pole, and so on. Similarly, diamonds are nominal existents because they do not exist apart from earth *dharmas*. Whether *dharmas*—the unbuilt parts of composites—are also nominal existents is a matter of debate among various Buddhist traditions.

---

[37] Dhammajoti 2015, 79–80. See also Cox 2004, 568–70.

[38] See Cox 2004, 575; Westerhoff 2009, 21–2; Siderits 2013, 436. Westerhoff resolves the ambiguity of "*svabhāva*" by characterizing real (or primary) existents as things that have substance-*svabhāva* and defining substance-*svabhāva* as a matter of existing without dependence upon others (Westerhoff 2009, 23–4). This disambiguation coheres with the denotation Fazang typically assigns to the characters 自性 (*svabhāva*).

CONCEPTUALIZING CAUSALITY   49

Traditions that align with Abhidharma typically conceptualize *dharmas* as real existents. A typical justification for this view involves a kind of regress argument.[39] Composites lack self-nature because they depend upon their parts. If these parts are also composite, they lack self-nature for the same reason. But, contend the Ābhidharmika, every regress of dependence must terminate in some foundation that lacks dependence. For nominal existents, the regress of dependence terminates with the unbuilt parts of composites because these parts are not composite. This is why, for the Ābhidharmika, *dharmas* are real existents.[40]

Traditions that align with Mahāyāna typically conceptualize *dharmas* as nominal existents. *Commentary on the Great Perfection of Wisdom* offers a typical justification.

If dharmas had a determinate characteristic, they would be real (*aśūnya*). Outside of determinate characteristic, there can be no real dharma.[41]

If *dharmas* are real existents, they do not depend upon others for their existence. Because *dharmas* are inseparable from their specific characteristics, it follows that real *dharmas* do not depend upon others for their specific characteristics. Hence, if *dharmas* are real existents, they are determinate with respect to their specific characteristics. Because *Commentary on the Great Perfection of Wisdom* characterizes *dharmas* as indeterminate with respect to their specific characteristics, it concludes that *dharmas* are nominal existents.

3.5. Causality

3.5.1. Projecting and Causing

Fazang agrees with *Commentary on the Great Perfection of Wisdom* that real existents are determinate with respect to their specific characteristics. But he denies that determinacy of this sort suffices for being real rather than nominal. For Fazang, depending upon others for specific characteristics is not the only way in which something might depend upon others. The reason is that dependence

---

[39] See Westerhoff 2009, 30–1.

[40] A similar regress argument justifies the view that *dharmas* have determinate specific characteristics. Fazang characterizes the *dharmas* as relating to each other "again and again without limit" (Ch. *chóngchóng wújìn* 重重無盡). See T45.1866.505a29; Cook 1970, 499; Unno et al. 2023, 189. This might suggest that Fazang denies that specific characteristics are determinate (by virtue of rejecting the relevant regress argument). But Koh 2019 demonstrates that Fazang's endlessly regressive relation is not the kind that drives regress arguments for determinacy.

[41] T25.1509.294c9-10, recited in Chödrön 2001, 1753.

50 METAPHORS FOR INTERDEPENDENCE

upon others also can be a matter of depending upon others for power to bring about the effect something projects.

For Fazang, projecting an effect is not the same as causing an effect. *Dharmas* project effects in the way that numismatists own coins and ranchers keep horses. Numismatists can own coins without displaying them. Ranchers can keep horses without riding them. So, too, can *dharmas* project effects without causing those effects.[42] This is because *dharmas* give rise to their effects only in the presence of supporting conditions.

Just as sprouts do not arise from seeds alone but also require moist soil for support, and just as no sage teaches alone in the forest, no effect arises from one *dharma* in isolation from others. For example, loving-kindness *dharmas* project friendship. Yet, because loving-kindness *dharmas* arising for an isolated hermit do not result in the hermit having friends, projecting friendship differs from causing friendship. Similarly, firm bricks arise from encounters between earth *dharmas* and water *dharmas*. The specific characteristic of earth *dharmas* is solidity. The specific characteristic of water *dharmas* is fluidity. Insofar as firm bricks are an enacting of solidity rather than fluidity, the earth *dharmas* project the firm bricks and the water *dharmas* provide support. But projecting firm bricks differs from causing firm bricks. Removing all water *dharmas* from a brick results in a heap of dust. Hence, even if the firmness of bricks derives from earth *dharmas* enacting their solidity, earth *dharmas* apart from water *dharmas* do not cause firm bricks.

Because projecting an effect differs from causing an effect, the *dharmas* that project some effect need not be the *dharmas* that cause the effect. Just as someone might display coins that they do not own, and just as someone might ride horses that they do not keep, *dharmas* might cause effects that they do not project. For Fazang, to cause an effect is to put into action whatever it is that projects the effect. Schematically, for any *dharma* x, any (not necessarily distinct) *dharma* z, and any effect y,

x causes $y :=_{df} z$ projects y, and x puts into action z.

For example, if moist soil is what puts lotus seeds into action, then the cause of lotus sprouts is moist soil even though what projects the lotus sprouts is lotus seeds. Again, if the student is what puts into action the sage's activity of teaching

---

[42] The distinction between projecting an effect and causing an effect is similar to a distinction Plato makes, in the *Theaetetus*, between possessing knowledge and having knowledge. For Plato, possessing knowledge is akin to owning a cloak or keeping a bird in a cage, and having knowledge is akin to wearing the cloak or holding the bird in one's hand. See *Theaetetus* 197a5–199b5; Rowe 2015, 78–81.

others, the cause of the teaching is the student even though the sage is the one who projects the teaching.

3.5.2. *Dharmas* and Powers

Fazang uses the distinction between projecting effects and causing effects to distinguish between the specific characteristics of *dharmas* and their powers (Skt. *bala* or *śakti*; Ch. *lì* 力). Specific characteristics divide *dharmas* into kinds. Because *dharmas* are dynamic rather than static, *dharmas* do not merely manifest their specific characteristics. They also give rise to effects. Specific characteristics explain why *dharmas* give rise to some effects rather than others. They do so by grounding the effects that *dharmas* project—that is, by grounding the dispositionality of *dharmas*. Insofar as no effect arises spontaneously, any *dharma* that gives rise to an effect must have some cause that puts the *dharma* into action. Because projecting effects differs from causing effects, specific characteristics do not explain what these causes are. This is why Fazang posits powers.

Powers ground the effects that *dharmas* cause. For Fazang, when a *dharma* has power to cause an effect, the *dharma* causes that effect—it brings about the effect by putting into action whatever projects the effect. Schematically,

x has power:=$_{df}$ there is some $y \neq x$ such that x causes y.

(Sometimes, rather than saying that a *dharma* has power to cause an effect, Fazang says more simply that the *dharma* has power.)

Just as *dharmas* can be determinate or indeterminate with respect to their specific characteristics, they can be determinate or indeterminate with respect to power. *Dharmas* that are determinate with respect to power have power to bring about the effects they project. Schematically,

x is determinate (regarding power):=$_{df}$ x has power, and for any $y \neq x$ such that x projects y, x causes y.

By contrast, *dharmas* that are indeterminate with respect to power lack power to bring about the effects they project. Schematically,

x is indeterminate (regarding power):=$_{df}$ x has power, and there is some $y \neq x$ such that x projects y but x does not cause y.

For the sake of illustration, consider a lotus seed that projects a lotus sprout. If the seed is determinate with respect to power, it puts itself into action. But if the

52 METAPHORS FOR INTERDEPENDENCE

seed is indeterminate with respect to power, whatever puts the seed into action must be something other than the seed itself.

Because *dharmas* manifest their specific characteristics and give rise to effects, there are two ways for *dharmas* to depend upon others. They might depend upon others for their specific characteristics. Or they might depend upon others for power that causes their effects. Because real existents lack dependence upon others, they are determinate with respect to specific characteristics and power. But *dharmas* with determinate specific characteristics need not be real. If *dharmas* are indeterminate with respect to power, they are nominal regardless of whether their specific characteristics are determinate.

Fazang combines the Mahāyāna contention that *dharmas* are nominal existents with the Abhidharma contention that *dharmas* are determinate with respect to their specific characteristics. He does so by maintaining that *dharmas* are indeterminate with respect to power. There is a scriptural basis for this view in Chapter 10 of the *Flower Adornment Sūtra*.

> Dharmas themselves are devoid of any function [Ch. *zuò yòng* 作用] and are also devoid of any essential nature [Ch. *tǐ xìng* 體性].[43]

There is also some precedent for Fazang's view. Vasubandhu, in his *Commentary on the Treasury of Abhidharma* (Chapter 2, Section 50a), claims that each *dharma* is a "reason for existence" (Skt. *kāraṇa-hetu*) for all *dharmas* except itself.[44] Because *dharmas* exist only insofar as they are active and thereby give rise to their characteristic effects, and because *dharmas* give rise to their effects only if something empowers their dispositionality, Vasubandhu's claim is equivalent— in Fazang's conceptual framework—to the claim that each *dharma* empowers all *dharmas* except itself. This, in turn, entails that no *dharma* empowers itself.

Fazang does not rely upon scripture or precedent for his contention that *dharmas* are indeterminate with respect to power. He offers a justification. The justification is that *dharmas*, insofar as they are causal, depend on many conditions (Ch. *dāi zhòng yuan* 待眾緣). According to Fazang, because *dharmas* give rise to the effects that they project, rather than to the effects that their conditions project, they depend upon others for their activity.[45] Because Fazang maintains that *dharmas* depend upon supporting conditions to bring about their effects, he infers that they lack power to bring about their own effects.[46]

Fazang's distinction between projecting effects and causing them, and his associated conception of power, diverges from more familiar approaches to

---

[43] T10.279.66b6, recited in Dharmamitra 2022, 1: 299.
[44] Pruden 1991, 255. See also Kamtekar 2024, 75–8.
[45] See T45.1866.502a17-18.
[46] See T45.1866.502a11-2; Cook 1970, 449; Unno et al. 2023, 172.

CONCEPTUALIZING CAUSALITY   53

causality. For example, the Greek philosopher Aristotle contrasts possessing the power of sight with putting the power of sight to active use.[47] Aristotle's *possessing power* is akin to Fazang's *projecting*, and Aristotle's *putting power to use* is akin to Fazang's *having power*. But Aristotle seems to assume that something puts a power to use only if it possesses that power. That is, he seems to assume that whatever has power to cause an effect also projects that effect. Śāntarakṣita (725–788), an influential Indian interpreter of Nāgārjuna, endorses a similar assumption.[48] By contrast, Fazang allows things to have power to cause an effect even if they do not project the effect.

Fazang's conception of power also differs from Thomas Aquinas' conception of active power. Aquinas (1225–1274), a Roman Catholic monk indebted to Aristotle in many ways, distinguishes between natural inclinations and active powers.[49] For Aquinas, agents have natural inclinations that impel them toward certain effects, and they have active powers that explain why they cause those effects. For example, according to Aquinas, fire has a natural inclination to generate fire, and fire's active power to heat explains why fire causes the burning of flammable objects. Having a natural inclination is akin to projecting an effect. Yet Fazang's conception of power allows that, when an agent is naturally inclined toward some effect, the cause of that effect need not be the agent.

Fazang's conception of power also differs from contemporary, neo-Aristotelian conceptions.[50] These conceptions typically treat powers as dispositions (or capacities) to produce effects, where a disposition projects an effect but causes that effect only in the presence of suitable conditions. For neo-Aristotelians, insofar as fragility disposes pottery to break, pottery projects breaking by virtue of having the power of fragility. By contrast, Fazang's conception of power allows that pottery might project breaking without having the power to cause breaking.

3.5.3. Inclusion and Identity

For Fazang, the existence of effects guarantees both the existence of *dharmas* that project those effects and the existence of *dharmas* that have power to cause the effects. Yet the existence of effects does not guarantee that the power to cause effects resides in the *dharmas* that project those effects. The powers of *dharmas* coincide with the range of their causal efficacy. But, for Fazang, ranges of causal efficacy do not coincide with ranges of projection. Because *dharmas* project their

---

[47] See Aristotle's *Topics* 1.15.106b19-20; Barnes 1991, 177. For more on Aristotle's distinction between possessing power and putting power to use, see Bradshaw 2004, 2–7.
[48] See Fan 2019, 110–1.
[49] See Frost 2022, 19–20, 120–1.
[50] For a survey of contemporary conceptions of power, see Marmodoro 2010.

54   METAPHORS FOR INTERDEPENDENCE

own effects, they are disposed to give rise to effects. Yet, because *dharmas* are indeterminate with respect to power, no *dharma* puts itself into action. That is, because *dharmas* are indeterminate with respect to power, *dharmas* depend upon others to enact their specific characteristics (or activate their dispositionality).

Fazang invokes the relation of inclusion to conceptualize the relation between something that projects an effect and some other that has power to cause the effect. Consider, in the abstract, some effect e. Let p (for *projector*) designate whatever projects e. Let s (for *supporter*) designate the conditions, distinct from p, that support p when e arises. When the power to cause e resides in s (the supporting conditions) rather than p (the projector), Fazang says that p is included within or enters into (Ch. *rù* 入) s, that s contains or takes in (Ch. *shè* 攝) p, and that s receives or encompasses (Ch. *shōu* 收) p.[51] (Entrance is the inverse of containment and reception.) Schematically,

s includes $p := _{df} p$ projects e, s has power to cause e, and $p \neq s$
$\qquad\qquad$ = p is included within / enters into s
$\qquad\qquad$ = s contains / takes in p
$\qquad\qquad$ = s receives / encompasses p.

For example, if moist soil has power to cause lotus sprouts even though what projects those sprouts is lotus seeds, then lotus seeds are included within moist soil—or, equivalently, moist soil includes lotus seeds.

Fazang's inclusion relation helps to articulate Vasubandhu's claim that eyes support seeing but consciousness is what sees. Vasubandhu's reason is that eyes unaccompanied by consciousness do not see.[52] In Fazang's terminology, Vasubandhu's argument is that consciousness includes eyes. That is, Vasubandhu is claiming that eyes project seeing but consciousness has power to cause seeing.

For the sake of further illustrating Fazang's inclusion relation, consider once more the interaction between the sage Bhīṣmottaranirghoṣa and the student Sudhana. The sage projects teaching of others. The student projects learning from others. Sitting alone in the forest, the sage causes no teaching of others. Traveling in search of a teacher, the student causes no learning from others. When the sage and the student converse, teaching and learning arise. Because the sage is powerless to cause teaching of others without a student, the student is the cause of the teaching that arises. Because the student is powerless to cause learning from others on his own, the sage is the cause of the learning that arises.

---

[51] Inclusion, as Fazang conceptualizes it, is an irreflexive relation. A relation **R** is irreflexive if, for any element in the domain of **R**, the element never bears **R** to itself. For example, the numerical relation *greater than* is irreflexive because no number is greater than itself. Inclusion is irreflexive because no *dharma* differs from itself.
[52] See Gold 2015, 70

Hence, when the learning arises, the student enters into the sage and the sage takes in or encompasses the student. Similarly, when the teaching arises, the sage is included within the student and the student contains or receives the sage.[53]

Because Fazang maintains that *dharmas* are indeterminate with respect to power, he also maintains that every *dharma* enters into (or is included within) another.

Indeterminacy Entails Inclusion
When the effects projected by a *dharma* arise, if the *dharma* is indeterminate with respect to power, then the *dharma* enters into another.

When a *dharma* is indeterminate with respect to power, it projects some effect without also causing that effect. Hence, when the effect arises, and because no effect arises spontaneously or without cause, there must be something else that causes the projected effect. But anything with power to cause an effect that it does not project includes (within the range of its causal efficacy) the thing that projects that effect. This establishes *Indeterminacy Entails Inclusion*.

Indeterminacy Entails Inclusion is significant because it helps to explain how Fazang conceptualizes the relations of making and identity. Consider, in the abstract, some effect e. Let p (for *projector*) designate whatever projects e. Let S_p designate the specific characteristic of p by virtue of which p projects e. When p is indeterminate with respect to power, there is some s (for *supporter*), distinct from p, that includes p when e arises. This inclusion relation concerns the relation between p and the power of s: because s includes p, s has power to cause the effect that p projects. But there is also a relation between s and the specific characteristic S_p. This relation is akin to the relation between a painter and a canvas upon which the painter paints.[54]

Suppose that, when a portrait arises from a canvas, the painter has power to cause the portrait. Suppose also that what projects the portrait is the canvas rather than the painter. Then the canvas is indeterminate with respect to power. Because the painter causes the portrait, the painter includes the canvas. (This follows from *Indeterminacy Entails Inclusion*.) Because the painter includes the canvas, the painter brings to fruition whatever specific

---

[53] Pauline theology provides an interesting application for Fazang's inclusion relation. According to Paul, God projects truth and goodness, but the ones who put truth and goodness into action are prophets. Hence, when prophets speak revelation or perform miraculous healing, they receive God within themselves—the prophets are the vehicles that bring to fruition the truth and goodness that God projects, and God enters into the prophets. Similarly, insofar as demons project evil, people contain demons within themselves when they speak lies or harm innocents—that is, liars and villains have power to cause demonic effects. See also Bradshaw 2004, 121–5.

[54] For a discussion of painter-painting metaphors in the history of Buddhism, see Hamar 2014b. For the metaphor in the *Flower Adornment Sūtra*, see T9.278.465c16-466a6; T10.279.102a11-b1; Cleary 1993, 451–2; Dharmamitra 2022, 1: 476–7.

characteristic the canvas has by virtue of which the canvas projects the portrait. The painter does this by putting into action the canvas. There is, accordingly, a sense in which the painter makes the canvas: the painter makes the canvas enact its specific characteristic, and the enacting of this specific characteristic is the portrait.

Just as there is a sense in which painters make the canvases from which portraits arise, Fazang says that when one brings to fruition the specific characteristic of another, the one makes (Ch. *yòng* 用) the other. Schematically, for any *dharma x* with specific characteristic S_x, and for any other *dharma z*,

z makes $x := _{df} x \neq z$, and z brings to fruition S_x.

For example, when moist soil brings to fruition the lotus-seed-hood of a lotus seed, the moist soil makes the lotus seed—that is, the moist soil puts into action the lotus seed by making the seed enact its lotus-seed-hood, and the effect is that a lotus sprout arises from the lotus seed. When a sage brings to fruition the specific characteristic by which a student projects learning-from-others, the sage makes the student—that is, the sage puts into action the student by making the student enact their specific characteristic, and the effect is that the student learns from the sage.

Fazang's identity relation is the inverse of his making relation. For Fazang, when one is identical with (Ch. *jí* 即) another, the other makes the one. Schematically, for any *dharmas x* and *z*,

x is identical with $z := _{df} z$ makes x.

Because Fazang conceptualizes dharmas as determinate with respect to their specific characteristics, his identity relation differs from Zhiyi's. For Zhiyi, because the specific characteristics of *dharmas* are indeterminate, identity is a relation among *dharmas* whereby one is endowed with the characteristics of others.[55] For example, Zhiyi maintains that each of the ten *dharma*-realms is endowed with the characteristics of every other.[56] He also maintains that bamboo has the characteristic of fire.[57] By analogy, the identity of teacher with student means, for Zhiyi, that the teacher is endowed with the characteristic of the student. By contrast, for Fazang, teacher and student maintain their distinct characteristics, and the identity of the teacher with the student means that the student puts the

---

[55] See Hung 2020, 308. Wei Daoru claims that Huayan philosophy "thoroughly eradicates the distinction among things" (Wei 2007, 194). Because Fazang's identity relation preserves determinate distinctions among its relata, Wei's critique is inapt for Fazang.

[56] T33.1716.693c16-8; Liu 1994, 220.

[57] T33.1716.743c28; Hung 2020, 316.

CONCEPTUALIZING CAUSALITY   57

teacher into action by making the teacher enact their specific characteristic. For Fazang, identity involves endowments that enact characteristics and, contrary to Zhiyi, the characteristics so enacted are not endowed by others.

Fazang's identity relation, like his inclusion relation, is not a relation of numerical identity. For Fazang, identity and inclusion are ways to conceptualize certain relations between numerically distinct things. When he focuses on one making another enact its specific characteristic, Fazang speaks of the other being identical with the one. When he focuses on one having power to cause some effect another projects, Fazang speaks of the one including the other.

These different ways of speaking are akin to speaking of Venus as the Morning Star in the morning and the Evening Star in the evening. One speaks of the Morning Star when viewing Venus in the morning. One speaks of the Evening Star when viewing Venus in the evening. So, too, with identity and inclusion. Fazang speaks of identity when focusing on the relation between one *dharma* and the specific character of another. He speaks of inclusion when focusing on the relation between one *dharma* and the effects projected by another. Yet, despite these different ways of speaking, relations of identity always coincide with relations of inclusion.

Inclusion and Identity Coincide
One is identical with another if, and only if, the other includes the one.

Suppose, first, that x is identical with z. Then z makes x: z brings to fruition the specific characteristic of x. Bringing a specific characteristic to fruition is just putting into action what has that specific characteristic. Hence, when x is identical with z, z has power to cause some effect that x projects. Because x projects the effect that z has power to cause, it follows that z includes x. Therefore, when x is identical with z, z includes x.

Suppose, next, that z includes x. Then z has power to cause some effect that x projects. Hence, when z includes x, z puts into action x. Putting into action is just bringing to fruition some specific characteristic of whatever is put into action. Hence, when z includes x, z makes x. Because identity is the inverse of making, it follows that when z includes x, x is identical with z.

Fazang's conception of identity entails that whenever one is identical with another and the other is identical with the one, the one and the other belong to different kinds—they differ in their specific characteristics.

Identity Crosses Kinds
Whatever is identical with another differs in specific characteristics from that other.

58 METAPHORS FOR INTERDEPENDENCE

Suppose, for the sake of argument, that identity need not cross kinds. Suppose, for example, that there are two *dharmas* of earth, *earth-1* and *earth-2*, such that *earth-1* and *earth-2* are mutually identical. Because *earth-1* and *earth-2* belong to the same kind, both project solidity. (Solidity is the specific characteristic of earth *dharmas*.) Because, by supposition, *earth-2* is identical with *earth-1*, *earth-1* brings to fruition solidity. Because bringing a specific characteristic to fruition is just putting into action what has that specific characteristic, *earth-1* puts into action *earth-2*. For the same reason, because *earth-1* has solidity, *earth-1* also puts itself into action. But if *earth-1* puts itself into action, *earth-1* has power to cause whatever effects solidity projects. If *earth-1* has power to cause whatever effects solidity projects, *earth-2* does not include *earth-1*. Because *Inclusion and Identity Coincide*, it follows that *earth-1* is not identical with *earth-2*. This contradicts the original supposition. Hence, there is no mutual identity among things of the same kind. Nor, for the same reason, is there mutual inclusion among things of the same kind. (Because *Inclusion and Identity Coincide* but *Identity Crosses Kinds*, inclusion also crosses kinds.)

Fazang's conception of identity also entails that functional wholes are identical with their constituent parts. Consider, for example, a chariot. Suppose, for the sake of illustration, that the chariot projects transportation-of-others by virtue of its chariot-hood. Suppose also that no chariot part projects the same effect. (Perhaps the pole projects connection-with-horses, the wheels project forward-motion, the framework projects support-of-passenger, and so on.) The chariot serves as transportation for others when the chariot encounters sturdy pole, round wheels, rigid framework, and various other transportation-friendly parts—that is, when the chariot is built from transportation-friendly parts. However, when the chariot is built from transportation-inhibiting parts, the chariot is unfit to transport others. For example, if the pole is rotten, it breaks when the animals pull and so the chariot is unfit for transportation. So, too, with square wheels that do not roll. So the chariot is indeterminate with respect to power. *Indeterminacy Entails Inclusion* thereby entails that the chariot's parts include the chariot.[58] *Inclusion and Identity Coincide* entails, further, that the chariot is identical with its parts.

The same reasoning applies for any functional whole and its constituent parts. Functional wholes are fit for their effects. But this fitness depends upon the wholes being built from function-inducing parts. Replace the parts with function-inhibiting ones and the wholes are unfit for their effects. Because the fitness of functional wholes depends upon the wholes being built from

---

[58] The demonstration that a chariot's parts include the chariot highlights that Fazang's inclusion relation is not mereological. *In the mereological sense of include*, wholes include their (proper) parts by virtue of being built from those parts. For Fazang, however, (proper) parts include their wholes by virtue of building those wholes.

CONCEPTUALIZING CAUSALITY   59

function-inducing parts, functional wholes are indeterminate with respect to power and the wholes themselves are included within their parts. Because *Inclusion and Identity Coincide*, every functional whole is identical with its (function-inducing) parts. This identity is not numerical identity. It is identity in the sense of *being nothing more than* or *not having power apart from*. This is, perhaps, as it should be, given general Buddhist aversions to conceptualizing wholes as real existents rather than mere conventions for designating their parts and what those parts have power to do.

3.5.4. Emptiness and Existence

For Fazang, *dharmas* are determinate and dynamic dispositions that give rise to effects only by virtue of being included within and identical with other *dharmas*. This conception of *dharmas* aligns with central teachings from Abhidharma and Mahāyāna Buddhism. It aligns with Mahāyāna teachings by virtue of conceptualizing *dharmas* as indeterminate with respect to power. This indeterminacy is why, for Fazang, *dharmas* are nominal existents. It also aligns with Abhidharma teachings by virtue of conceptualizing *dharmas* as determinate with respect to their specific characteristics. This determinacy is why, for Fazang, conceptualizations of nominal existents need not be arbitrary or incorrect.

Fazang's innovative conception of *dharmas* demands similarly innovative alterations to what it means for *dharmas* to be empty (of self-nature) or existent. Consider, first, the meaning of *dharmas* being empty. For monks from the Sanlun and Tiantai traditions, *dharmas* are empty by virtue of lacking determinate characteristics. The reason is that emptiness is a matter of depending upon others and, for these monks, *dharmas* depend upon others for their characteristics. Fazang, following Nāgārjuna, agrees that emptiness is a matter of depending upon others. But, for Fazang, *dharmas* depend upon others—and thereby qualify as empty—because they are indeterminate with respect to power.[59]

Consider, next, the meaning of *dharmas* existing (or being existents). Buddhist traditions typically maintain that existing (Skt. *bhāva*; Ch. *yǒu* 有) is a matter of being an object for cognition (Skt. *buddhi*; Ch. *jiào* 覺).

x exists:$=_{df}$ x is an object for cognition.

---

[59] According to Jay Garfield, Huayan maintains that *dharmas* are empty because, "on the Huayan account, since the identity of everything is constituted by everything else, that which constitutes the identity of any one thing is the same as that which constitutes the identity of every other thing" (Garfield 2015, 76). Garfield's explanation is, perhaps, apt as an account of how Sanlun and Tiantai traditions conceptualize the emptiness of *dharmas*. But it is not clear how Garfield's interpretation accommodates Fazang's claim that *dharmas* are determinate with respect to their specific characteristics.

60 METAPHORS FOR INTERDEPENDENCE

This conception is explicit in *Commentary on the Great Perfection of Wisdom* (representing Mahāyāna traditions).

> How do all dharmas have a characteristic of existence (*bhāvalakṣaṇa*)? Among all these dharmas, there are some beautiful (*suvarṇa*) and some ugly (*durvarṇa*), there are some internal (*ādhyātmika*) and some external (*bāhya*). All dharmas, being [a place] of arising for the mind, are said to be existent.[60]

Saṃghabhadra (representing Abhidharma traditions) endorses a similar conception, albeit one restricted to the existence of real existents.

> The characteristic of a real existent is that it serves as an object-domain for generating cognition (覺, *buddhi*).[61]

Saṃghabhadra's definition is restricted to real existents because, in his view, nominal existents exist in name only. For Saṃghabhadra (and other Ābhidharmikas), nominal existents are pieces of language that do not designate objects of cognition. For example, armies are nominal existents because they are built from many soldiers. Yet no army is an object of cognition: the name *army* designates a collection of many soldiers, and although it is convenient to imagine some sort of conjunction or unity among these soldiers, there is no such unity.

Fazang's conception of *dharmas* supports an approach to nominal existents that secures their role as objects of cognition. For Fazang, *dharmas* are objects of cognition because they are determinate with respect to their specific characteristics. This accords with an explanatory principle from *Commentary on the Great Perfection of Wisdom*.

> Each dharma has its own characteristic and it is because of this characteristic that we recognize its existence.[62]

For Fazang, only those with slight wisdom would infer that, because *dharmas* are objects of cognition, they are real existents.[63] Those who endorse such an inference would have some wisdom, namely, the wisdom of conceptualizing *dharmas* as determinate with respect to their specific characteristics. This wisdom explains why *dharmas* are objects of cognition. But such wisdom would be slight unless *dharmas* were also conceptualized as indeterminate with respect

---

[60] T25.1509.293c22-4, recited in Chödrön 2001, 1748.
[61] Dhammajoti 2015, 79.
[62] T25.1509.102c26-7, recited in Chödrön 2001, 300.
[63] See T39.1790.430c16-22.

to power. This further wisdom explains why *dharmas*, as nominal existents, are empty of self-nature.

Fazang's conception of *dharmas* also alleviates the concern that nominal *dharmas* lack existence unless some *dharmas* are real. This concern appears, in *Commentary on the Great Perfection of Wisdom*, as an objection from an anonymous Ābhidharmikan interlocutor.

> *Objection*: Not all *dharmas* are entirely empty [of self-nature]. Why? The causes and conditions give birth to what is empty, but the causes and conditions are not empty. For example, because the ridgepole is the causal condition for unity, there is the house; the house is empty and yet the ridgepole is not empty![64]

The response to the objection is that causes and conditions are indeterminate.[65] But this response is not entirely convincing. If the ridgepole and other building materials are indeterminate with respect to their specific characteristics, it is not at all clear why any of the materials have their particular roles. For example, if a pillar is whatever supports a ridgepole and a ridgepole is whatever supports a roof, it is not clear why a material that supports something else is a ridgepole rather than a pillar. Fazang accommodates the concern in this objection by conceding that *dharmas* are determinate with respect to their specific characteristics. His conception of *dharmas* as indeterminate with respect to power allows him to resist the inference, from this concession, to the real existence of *dharmas*.

Because Fazang maintains that *dharmas* are objects of cognition, and because there is precedent for maintaining that objects of cognition are real existents, there is a risk of misunderstanding Fazang's conception of *dharmas*. Fazang mitigates this risk, and reinforces the compatibility between being an object of cognition and being empty, by characterizing *dharmas* as having the semblance or appearance of existence (Ch. *shì yǒu* 似有).

> Although the appearance of existence manifests in the reply of causes and associated conditions, still these appearances of existence must lack self-nature because all conditions arise lacking self-nature. If not for lacking [self-]nature, there would be no dependence upon conditions. If there were no dependence upon conditions, there would be no appearance of existence. Appearances of existence, when established, must be through many

---

[64] T25.1509.290a8-10. For an alternative translation, see Chödrön 2001, 1717. See also Westerhoff 2009, 36–8.
[65] T25.1509.290a10-6; Chödrön 2001, 1717.

62 METAPHORS FOR INTERDEPENDENCE

conditions. Because they are through many conditions, they must lack self-nature. Therefore, by means of lacking self-nature, appearances of existence are able to be established.[66]

Having an appearance of existence is seeming to be a real existent despite being empty of self-nature. For Fazang, *dharmas* are empty because they are indeterminate with respect to power. *Dharmas* seem to be real existents because it is convenient—or, at least, common—to imagine them as determinate with respect to power. This is convenient because specific characteristics are manifest but power is not, and so it is easy to conflate determinacy with respect to specific characteristics and determinacy with respect to power. For Fazang, avoiding this conflation requires wisdom and insight.

3.6. An Ontology for Interdependence

Fazang's conceptual framework for metaphysics is complex and sophisticated. The framework divides *dharmas* from their characteristics. It divides characteristics of *dharmas* into general and specific, and it divides the specific characteristics of *dharmas* from their power. Specific characteristics of *dharmas* ground their dispositionality and explain why they project effects. Power grounds the causality of *dharmas* and explains why the effects of *dharmas* are caused rather than spontaneous. Fazang's framework also divides *dharmas* into determinate and indeterminate, and the distinction between specific characteristics and power allows the framework to accommodate two senses in which *dharmas* are determinate (or indeterminate): first, with respect to specific characteristics; second, with respect to power.

Fazang combines his conceptual framework with three posits about causality. The first is that *dharmas* are determinate with respect to their specific characteristics. This assuages Ābhidharmikan qualms about endless regresses of dependence among *dharmas*, and it explains why *dharmas* are objects of cognition. It also explains his second posit, namely, that *dharmas* project their own effects—they do not change their dispositions when they change their relations to others. Fazang's third posit is that *dharmas* require others to bring about the effects they project. This accommodates the Mahāyāna insight that *dharmas* are empty of self-nature. It explains why *dharmas* satisfy the meaning of "nominal existent" and why the emptiness (or unreality) of *dharmas* does not preclude

---

[66] T45.1866.499b12-6. For alternative translations, see Cook 1970, 413; Unno et al. 156–7. The translation by Unno and colleagues interprets appearances of existence as false. But this presumes what Fazang denies, namely, that all conceptual cognition is incorrect or erroneous.

CONCEPTUALIZING CAUSALITY   63

their existence. It also yields an ontology in which every *dharma* is conditional by virtue of being included within and identical with another.

Fazang follows the *Flower Adornment Sūtra* by understanding conditionality as mutual inclusion and mutual identity. But, for Fazang, and despite a natural interpretation of "mutual," mutual inclusion does not mean that each *dharma* includes all other *dharmas* and mutual identity does not mean that each *dharma* is identical with all others. Because *Identity Crosses Kinds,* one and another are mutually identical only if the one and the other belong to different kinds. Similarly, because *Inclusion and Identity Coincide,* one includes another only if the one and the other belong to different kinds. Because multiple *dharmas* might belong to the same kind, it follows that mutual inclusion and mutual identity among *dharmas* is compatible with some *dharmas* neither including nor being identical with others (of the same kind).

Given the constraints of Fazang's conceptual framework, Fazang's doctrine of mutual identity must be the contention that, for any kind of *dharma,* all *dharmas* of that kind have their specific characteristics brought to fruition by all *dharmas* of all other kinds. Similarly, his doctrine of mutual inclusion must be the contention that, for any kind of *dharma* and for any effect projected by any *dharma* of that kind, all *dharmas* of that kind lack power to cause that effect and all *dharmas* of all other kinds have power to cause that effect. Because Fazang's posits of causality establish only that, for any kind of *dharma, dharmas* of that kind are identical with and included within *dharmas* of *some* other kind, there is more to Fazang's metaphysics than his theory of causality. The content of this something more is the subject of Chapter 4.

4
Interpreting Mutuality

4.1. Mutuality

Fazang's ontology consists of *dharmas* (Ch. *fǎ* 法) and aggregates. Aggregates are composites of others. *Dharmas* are the unbuilt constituents of aggregates. *Dharmas* are more akin to doings than substances. The reason is that *dharmas* are dynamic and dispositional rather than static or categorical. For Fazang, *dharmas* are also determinate and powerful. *Dharmas* are determinate because their kind-specifying characteristics (Skt. *salakṣaṇa* or *svalakṣaṇa*; Ch. *zì xiāng* 自相) do not vary in relation to others. These characteristics explain why *dharmas* are disposed to do what they do. *Dharmas* are powerful because they give rise to effects and no effect arises without some power responsible for causing it. The powers of *dharmas* explain why *dharmas* actualize their dispositions.

Fazang maintains that *dharmas* are empty of power to actualize their own dispositions. Instead, for Fazang, *dharmas* do what they do only by virtue of entering into (Ch. *rù* 入) the range of power for others. When another includes (Ch. *shè* 攝) a *dharma* in the range of its power, the other invests the *dharma* with power and so the *dharma* actualizes its disposition. Through this investment of power, the other makes (Ch. *yòng* 用) the *dharma* do what it does. *Dharmas* are thereby identical with (Ch. *jí* 即) others, in the sense that *dharmas* enact their doings by virtue of being put into action by others.

For Fazang, the emptiness of *dharmas* is a matter of mutual inclusion (Ch. *xiāng rù* 相入) and mutual identity (Ch. *xiāng jí* 相即). The mutual inclusion of *dharmas* means that, for any kind of existing *dharma*, every *dharma* of that kind includes within its range of power all *dharmas* of all other kinds. The mutual identity of *dharmas* means that, for any kind of existing *dharma*, every *dharma* of that kind makes—or puts into action—all *dharmas* of all other kinds.[1] Fazang's doctrines of mutual inclusion and mutual identity are, in essence, contentions about the powers that *dharmas* have. They derive from a fundamental commitment to each *dharma* having complete power (Ch. *quán lì* 全力) or including all *dharmas* of all other kinds within the range of its causal efficacy. This is a

---

[1] For further explanation of the meaning of Fazang's doctrines of mutual inclusion and mutual identity, refer to Chapter 3.5.3 and Chapter 3.6.

Metaphors for Interdependence. Nicholaos Jones, Oxford University Press. © Nicholaos Jones 2025.
DOI: 10.1093/9780197807224.003.0004

counterintuitive commitment. It entails, for example, that the earth *dharmas* in this book (or on this screen) put into action the air *dharmas* breathed by each of its readers.

According to a standard interpretation of Fazang's doctrines, the realm of *dharmas* is akin to a galaxy of luminous stars, each illuminating all others while simultaneously being illuminated by those others. This interpretation reads Fazang as endorsing a theory of causality whereby every *dharma* simultaneously empowers and is empowered by all others. It also provides a straightforward explanation for why Fazang's doctrines are counterintuitive: his theory of causality is counterintuitive.

The goal of this chapter is to clear the way for an alternative interpretation. The chapter divides into five parts. The first sketches an example meant to make Fazang's conception of mutuality more intuitive. The second documents the standard interpretation as it appears in contemporary English-language scholarship on Fazang's metaphysics. The third part of the chapter presents textual evidence against the standard interpretation. The fourth presents philosophical evidence against the standard interpretation. The chapter concludes with a constraint for a better interpretation of Fazang's doctrines.

4.2. Playing Cards

Standard Buddhist examples for illustrating mutuality involve plants. *Sūtra on Sheaves of Reeds*, for example, uses two sheaves leaning against each other to illustrate interdependence between discriminating consciousness (Skt. *vijñāna*) and name-and-form (Skt. *nāma-rūpa*).[2] Buddhaghosa (5th century), an influential Theravādin monk, uses a similar example, involving three sticks leaning against each other to form a tripod, to illustrate his definition of *mutuality condition* (Skt. *anyamanya-pratyaya*) as that which assists by means of mutual arousing and consolidating.[3] Because plants do not come with labels, these examples do not easily lend themselves to abstract analysis. Playing cards are a convenient alternative.[4]

For the sake of adjusting to contemporary sensibilities, and also for the sake of motivating and lending some modicum of intelligibility to Fazang's conception of mutuality, consider the arrangement of playing cards in Figure 4.1.

---

[2] See Bodhi 2000, 607–9.
[3] See Ñāṇamoli 2010, 553.
[4] For a contemporary use of playing cards to illustrate mutuality, see Frankel 1986. For indications that playing cards originate late in the Tang dynasty, see Wilkinson 1895.

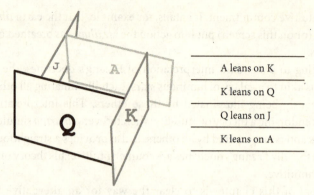

Figure 4.1 Mutually Leaning Playing Cards
Image created by the author.

Figure 4.1 depicts four playing cards: Ace (A), King (K), Queen (Q), and Jack (J). Each card is a different rank. Each card is standing. Each card stands by virtue of leaning upon another card. Ace leans on King, King leans on Queen, Queen leans on Jack, and Jack leans on Ace. Suppose, for the sake of illustration, that each card is akin to a *dharma*, that differences of rank are akin to differences of kind, and that cards with different ranks enact different kinds of standing. Then the mutual leaning of the four cards models mutual dependence among *dharmas* of different kinds.

Fazang's conception of reality, when applied to the playing cards in Figure 4.1, imposes three constraints upon the cards. The first concerns causality.

Causality
For any card x, there is some card y such that x stands only if y has power to cause x to stand.

Causality models Fazang's commitment to the doings of *dharmas* being causal rather than spontaneous. The second constraint concerns efficacy.

Efficacy
For any card x and any card y, if y has power to cause x to stand, then x stands.

Efficacy models Fazang's conception of power as that which puts something into action. The third and final constraint defines what it is for one to have power to put another into action.

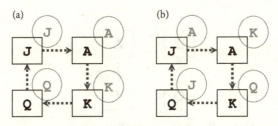

Figure 4.2 Real and Partial Power Playing Cards
Image created by the author.

Power
For any card x and any card y distinct from x, y has power to cause x to stand just in case: if y is not standing, x is not standing.

Power derives from a standard Buddhist formula for dependent arising (P. *paṭicca-samuppāda*; Skt. *pratītya-samutpāda*; Ch. *yuán qǐ* 緣起) according to which one arises in dependence upon another just in case the one does not exist without the other.[5] Insofar as arising in dependence upon another coincides with the other having power to cause the arising, and insofar as cards standing is akin to *dharmas* arising, the formula for dependent arising entails *Power*.

Causality guarantees that, for each card in Figure 4.1, there is some cause for the card's standing. *Efficacy* and *Power*, in turn, forbid some natural and intuitive views about what these causes might be. Figure 4.2 depicts two such views. (Letters in squares represent cards standing, arrows between squares represent leaning relations, and letters in circles attached to squares indicate sources of power for the standing of the cards represented by the attached squares.)

Consider, first, the view that each card is the sole cause of its own standing. (See Figure 4.2a.) This view models a conception of *dharmas* as real existents— as existents empowered to enact their doings regardless of accompanying conditions. On this view, for any cards x and y, y has power to cause x to stand if and only if $y = x$ (y is numerically identical to x). Because Ace is identical to itself, it follows that Ace has power to cause Ace to stand. Because Ace is not numerically identical to King (A ≠ K), it also follows that Ace lacks power to cause King to stand. *Power* thereby entails that King is standing but Ace is not.

---

[5] See Anālayo 2021a.

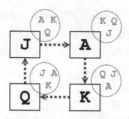

Figure 4.3 Mutual Power Playing Cards, Preliminary View
Image created by the author.

Because Ace is not standing, *Efficacy* entails that nothing has power to cause Ace to stand. This contradicts the prior result that Ace has power to cause Ace to stand. Hence, *Power* and *Efficacy* jointly entail that no card is the sole cause of its own standing.

Perhaps the most natural and intuitive alternative to the first view is the view that one card has power to cause another to stand if and only if the other leans on the one. (See Figure 4.2b.) This view models a conception of *dharmas* as having what Fazang calls "partial power" (Ch. *shǎo lì* 少力).[6] On this view, King has power to cause Ace to stand, Queen has power to cause King to stand, Jack has power to cause Queen to stand, Ace has power to cause Jack to stand, and there are no other sources of power for cards standing. One consequence of this view is that Ace lacks power to cause King to stand. Together with *Power*, this consequence entails that King is standing but Ace is not standing. Because Ace is not standing, *Efficacy* entails that nothing has power to cause Ace to stand. This contradicts the prior result that King has power to cause Ace to stand. Hence, *Power* and *Efficacy* jointly entail that being leaned upon by another is not necessary and sufficient for having power to cause the standing of the other.

Fazang's conception of mutuality supports quite a different view about what causes the four cards to stand. Fazang's doctrine of mutual inclusion is akin to the view that each card has power to cause the standing of all other cards. (See Figure 4.3.)

Some technical terminology helps to articulate a potential condition for this view. Say that a card y belongs to the transitive closure of leaning relations on a card x just in case there is a way to get from y to x by tracing a finite sequence of leaning relations, where the first has y leaning on another and the last has something leaning on x. (For example, Queen belongs to the

---

[6] T45.1866.508a5-6; Cook 1970, 531-2; Elstein 2014, 82, Unno et al. 2023, 203.

transitive closure of leaning relations on Ace because Queen leans on Jack and Jack leans on Ace.)

Given the setup depicted in Figure 4.1, each card belongs to the transitive closure of leaning relations for every card. Hence, the following condition secures a potential analog for mutual inclusion:

Potential Analog for Mutual Inclusion
One card has power to cause another to stand if and only if the one is numerically distinct from the other and the other belongs to the transitive closure of leaning relations for the one.

The numerical distinctness condition ensures that no card has power to cause its own standing. The closure condition ensures that each card has power to cause the standing of all other cards. These conditions yield a view that, while counterintuitive, is consistent with *Power* and *Efficacy*.

The view depicted in Figure 4.3 suffices to illustrate how a commitment to thoroughgoing mutual dependence motivates—and perhaps makes more reasonable—something like Fazang's conception of mutuality. However, the view is not an exact analog for Fazang's doctrine of mutual inclusion. Just what an exact analog might be is a matter requiring interpretation.

4.3. The Standard Interpretation

4.3.1. Cosmic Organicism

What does Fazang mean when he claims that everything is identical with and included within everything else? In a pioneering and widely influential study of Fazang's metaphysics, Francis Cook argues that Fazang endorses a kind of cosmic organicism.

> Thus each individual is at once the cause for the whole and is caused by that whole, and what is called existence is a vast body made up of an infinity of individuals all sustaining and defining each other. The cosmos is, in short, a self-creating, self-maintaining, and self-defining organism.[7]

According to Cook, mutual inclusion means that each *dharma* causes, and is caused by, the totality of *dharmas*. Similarly, mutual identity means that each

---

[7] Cook 1977, 3.

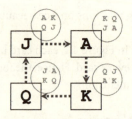

Figure 4.4 Mutual Power Playing Cards, Standard View
Image created by the author.

dharma makes the identity of, and has its identity made by, the totality of *dharmas*. Applied to the example of playing cards, Cook's interpretation yields the view about mutuality depicted in Figure 4.4.

In Figure 4.4, each playing card has power to cause all four cards to stand. (This is why labels for all four cards appear in each of the circles.) For Cook, the same is true for the realm of *dharmas*. Fazang's relations of inclusion and identity, so interpreted, are symmetric.[8] This interpretation entails that the relations are also simultaneous.[9] Cook makes this entailment explicit elsewhere.

> [Each *dharma* is] both the empty result of the conditioning power of the rest of the totality individually and collectively, and is *simultaneously* a real, existent entity exerting causal power on the whole.[10]

Cook also concisely explains what he takes Fazang to mean by claiming that *dharmas* have or lack power.

> To have causal power means that by absorbing into itself the qualities of all other events, a certain event acts as a cause for the whole. . . . Conversely, lacking causal power means that this same event which was previously considered to be the cause from its own point of view is *simultaneously* the

---

[8] A relation R is symmetric if, for any element of the domain of R, whenever one element bears R to another, the other also bears R to the one. For example, the numerical relation *equal to* is symmetric, because $n = m$ whenever $m = n$.

[9] A relation R is simultaneous if, for any element of the domain of R and times t_1 and t_2, one element bears R to other elements at t_1 and the others bear R to the one at t_2 if and only if $t_1 = t_2$. This definition adapts Jammer's definition of simultaneity for events to simultaneity for relations. See Jammer 2006, 10.

[10] Cook 1979, 374, emphasis added.

empty, conditioned result of a host of other events, seen from the standpoint of these others.[11]

According to Cook, Fazang maintains that one includes another whenever the other includes the one. This entails that whatever causes another is simultaneously caused by that other. Because, according to Cook, causes have power and effects lack power, mutual inclusion means that everything simultaneously has power and lacks power. So, for example, if one sun illuminates another whenever the other illuminates the one, the suns must illuminate each other—and be illuminated by each other—at the same time. Similarly, if one card causes another to stand whenever the other causes the one to stand, the one simultaneously has power and—as an empty, conditioned result of the other—lacks power.

Cook expresses some concern that Fazang's doctrine of mutual inclusion, so interpreted, is somewhat unusual.

It must be admitted that the term 'cause' is being used in an unusual manner in these examples, since what is evident is that these are all examples that might better be called interdependency or mutual conditionedness. Yet Fa-tsang and other Hua-yen masters do use the word 'cause,' and the Hua-yen universe is a universe of self-causation.[12]

Fazang uses the term 'cause' in an unusual manner, according to Cook, because causes are typically prior to their effects. Yet Fazang, as Cook interprets him, maintains that causes are simultaneous with their effects.

4.3.2. Reimagining Causality

Scholars who follow Cook's interpretation disagree about what to make of Fazang's supposedly unusual usage of 'cause.' For example, Ming-wood Liu recommends interpreting Fazang's doctrines as contentions about mere conditionality rather than causality.

The elements in the harmonious universe of Fa-tsang interpenetrate and mutually determine each other. That Fa-tsang chooses to regard their relation as a form of causality is largely due to the immense significance Buddhists attribute to the concept, as well as to the fact that the terms 'being', 'emptiness', 'with power', 'without power', 'dependent on conditions' and 'independent

---

[11] Cook 1979, 377, emphasis added.
[12] Cook 1977, 14. See also Cook 1979, 383.

72 METAPHORS FOR INTERDEPENDENCE

of conditions' with which Fa-tsang defines the meaning of interpenetration and mutual determination are derived from his analysis of a number of traditional Buddhist theories on causality. Since in the universe as he depicts it, each dharma can simultaneously be the cause, the condition and the effect of all other dharmas, 'interdependence' or 'mutual conditionality' are perhaps more appropriate designations for their relation than 'causality', for in common understanding, cause and effect is a one way relation and is irreversible.[13]

According to Liu, Fazang uses causal language because he is mimicking prior Buddhist theories about causality, but in fact Fazang denies that there are real causal relations. So interpreted, Fazang's doctrines pertain to causality in name only.

Whalen Lai also follows Cook's interpretation of Fazang's doctrines. Rather than interpreting Fazang as denying real causal relations, Lai interprets Fazang as endorsing a distinctive and unusual kind of causality. Lai names this Dharmadhātu Causation. The name derives from prior scholarship by Takakusu Junjirō (1866–1945). According to Takakusu,

> the causation theory by *Dharma-dhātu* (universe) . . . is the causation by all beings themselves and is the creation of the universe itself, or we can call it the causation by the common action-influence of all beings. . . . [It] is the causation of the universe by itself and nothing more.[14]

Lai notes that Dharmadhātu Causation is an unusual—and mysterious—kind of causality.

> Dharmadhātu Causation is so extravagant in conception that logical language or explanation sometimes cannot depict it as well as analogies, metaphor, or diagrams. . . . It is an endless causation or ontogenesis of the universe in all its parts in a mysteriously concerted manner of mutual influence and penetration. One has to visualize something like a spontaneous, instantaneous, never-ending, self-generating universe to catch a glimpse of Dharmadhātu causation.[15]

Lai takes the mysteriousness of Dharmadhātu Causation to be the reason why Fazang uses metaphors to explain his metaphysical doctrines. He claims that Fazang discovers Dharmadhātu Causation in the *Flower Adornment Sūtra*.[16]

---

[13] Liu 1979, 429.
[14] Takakusu 1956, 118.
[15] Lai 1977, 255–6.
[16] Lai 1977, 257.

He claims, as well, that this discovery leads Fazang to abandon the Buddhist teaching of dependent arising.

> One of the characteristics of Dharmadhātu causation is that it is self-generative, autogenetic. Each of the particular entities initiate[s] its own emanative evolution.... The Absolute is so absolute that it requires no external help to generate causal phenomena. This means, in effect, that the Absolute requires no *pratyaya*, concomitant factors or auxiliary conditions, since it is its own generator. In other words, strictly speaking, the Dharmadhātu Causation is no longer *yuan qi*, dependent coorigination (*pratītyasamutpāda*) but is *xing qi*, self-origination.[17]

If Fazang's relations of inclusion and identity are symmetric and simultaneous, either Fazang denies that there is causality or he denies that causality requires some kind of asymmetry and sequentiality. Cook interprets Fazang as doing both. Liu interprets him as denying causality. Lai interprets him as denying only asymmetric, sequential causation. The result, for Lai, is that Fazang endorses a kind of Abhidharmikan realism in which everything has power to enact its own effects.[18]

Subsequent scholars use a variety of strategies to make Fazang's metaphysics— or, at least, Cook's interpretation of this metaphysics—more intelligible. For example, Alan Fox likens Fazang's universe to a hologram. According to Fox, Fazang's model of causal relation is

> a 'holographic' one, in which at every moment, everything that can be said to be real is, in some sense, simultaneously the cause and effect of everything else that can be said to be real.[19]

Fox does not elaborate on details about how holograms work.[20] Graham Priest, by contrast, uses non-well-founded set theory to construct a rigorous, formal model of a self-generating reality in which relations of inclusion and identity are symmetric and simultaneous.[21] Whether these are apt models for Fazang's doctrines depends, in part, upon whether the standard interpretation of Fazang's metaphysics is correct.

[17] Lai 1977, 258, replacing Wade-Giles romanization with pinyin romanization.
[18] For further discussion of Abhidharmikan realism, refer to the analysis of real existents in Chapter 3.4.
[19] Fox 2013, 181; Fox 2015, 263.
[20] For an analysis of holography with respect to part-whole relations, see Kasulis 2018, 32–4. For discussion of how holograms might model certain aspects of Vasubandhu's metaphysics, see Kaplan 1990. For an interpretation of Fazang's mereology as holographic, refer to Chapter 8.6.
[21] Priest 2014, 175–81; Priest 2018b, 114–24; Priest 2022, 113.

4.4. Textual Evidence

The standard interpretation of Fazang's metaphysics, dominant in the English-speaking world since the 1970s, interprets Fazang's relations of inclusion and identity as symmetric, simultaneous, and causal in name only—or, if not in name only, then in some unusual and extravagant manner. Because Fazang does not explain his technical terminology, the standard interpretation is not unreasonable. There are, however, good textual reasons to abandon it.

4.4.1. Completeness

The first piece of textual evidence against the standard interpretation comes from some of Fazang's remarks about mutual inclusion (Ch. *xiāng rù* 相入).

> Because [one] has complete power, it is able to take in others. Because the others completely lack power, they can enter into [the one]. Understand by contrast others having power and [one] lacking power.[22]

For Fazang, when one has complete power, it takes in others. These others are taken in by the one—they enter into the one—because the others completely lack power. Hence, according to Fazang, when one includes another, the one has complete power and the other completely lacks power.[23]

If the standard interpretation of Fazang is correct, then Fazang's inclusion relation is symmetric and simultaneous. If his inclusion relation is symmetric and simultaneous, then one includes another whenever, and at the same time that, the other includes the one. It follows that, according to the standard interpretation, when one and another are mutually inclusive, each simultaneously has complete power and completely lacks power. This is a straightforward contradiction with Fazang's remark about mutual inclusion. Hence, if the standard interpretation is correct, Fazang's doctrine of mutual inclusion is incoherent.[24]

---

[22] T45.1866.503b16-8. For alternative translations, see Cook 1970, 474–5; Unno et al. 2023, 180.

[23] Wei Daoru offers a similar interpretation: "According to Fazang, among all things originated dependently, if the 'force' exerted by the 'self' of a certain thing is greater than the 'force' exerted by another thing, the first thing has an absolute advantage that draws the latter thing into itself. In other words, if the other thing completely loses its own 'force', it inevitably enters into the 'self' of the first thing, which also means that the two can mutually penetrate" (Wei 2007, 192). Wei's gloss interprets inclusion as a matter of one thing entering into the "self" of another. But this goes beyond Fazang's own declarations, and it risks conflating indeterminacy with respect to power and indeterminacy with respect to specific characteristics. A better interpretation ascribes to Fazang the view that inclusion is a matter of one thing entering into the *range of power* of another (see Chapter 3.5.3).

[24] For an interpretation that reads Fazang's doctrines as intentionally incoherent (or paradoxical), see Wright 1982. Wright admits that he makes "[n]o attempt . . . to avoid, eliminate, or to rationally solve paradoxical elements" in Fazang's writings (Wright 1982, 325).

This is, perhaps, why some commentators interpret Fazang's vision as "verging on a kind of mysticism."[25]

4.4.2. Non-Simultaneity

Perhaps, however, the preceding argument is too quick. Perhaps Fazang means something else by *complete* (Ch. *quán* 全). According to the explication of *inclusion* from Chapter 3, one includes another when the one has power to put the other into action. Hence, when Fazang claims that one has complete power, he likely means that one has power to put all others (of all other kinds) into action *but lacks power to put itself into action*. If completely lacking power only amounts to lacking power to put oneself into action, one having complete power straightforwardly entails that the one simultaneously completely lacks power (to put itself into action).

There is good reason to avoid interpreting Fazang in this manner. (This reason provides the second piece of textual evidence for abandoning the standard interpretation.) Immediately after characterizing the having and lacking of power as complete, Fazang clarifies that having power and lacking power are not simultaneous (Ch. *bú jù* 不俱).

> Because the function of power permeates throughout, mutual inclusion is established. Also, although both havings of power and both lackings of power are not simultaneous, without both there is no mutual inclusion. Because having power and lacking power, and lacking power and having power, are nondual, mutual inclusion is established.[26]

When Fazang claims that "the function of power permeates throughout," he means that each includes all others by virtue of having power. The two havings of power, and the two lackings of power, designate different situations. (See Table 4.1.) In one situation, because one has complete power and others completely lack power, the one includes the others. This is the first having of power and the first lacking of power. In the second situation, because one completely lacks power and others have complete power, the others include the one. This is the second having of power and the second lacking of power.

A plain reading of Fazang's claim about non-simultaneity is that the first situation—with one having power and others lacking power—is not at the

---

[25] Quoting Garfield 2015, 79.
[26] T45.1866.503b19-21. For alternative translations, see Cook 1970, 475; Unno et al. 2023, 180. For a translation of a similar passage by P'yowon 表員 (8th century), see McBride 2012a, 139. (P'yowon is rehearsing Fazang's view.)

76 METAPHORS FOR INTERDEPENDENCE

Table 4.1 Non-Simultaneity of Mutual Inclusion

situation 1	one has power	others lack power	one includes others
situation 2	one lacks power	others have power	others include one

same time as the second situation. Confirmation for this reading appears in *Investigating the Mysteries of the Flower Adornment Sūtra.*

> Therefore, when one upholds many, the one has power and takes in the many. When many depend upon one, the many lack power and lie hidden within the one. Because the one having power necessarily cannot be together with the many having power, the one never fails to take in the many. Because the many lacking power necessarily cannot be together with the one lacking power, the many never fail to enter into the one.[27]

For Fazang, one having power "necessarily cannot be together with" many others having power. This is equivalent to the claim that one having power is not simultaneous with others having power.

The plain reading of Fazang's claim about non-simultaneity explains why Fazang mentions non-duality (Ch. *wú èr* 無二) in his remark about the function of power. If one including others is not simultaneous with the others including the one, one might object that there is no mutual inclusion among the one and the others. Fazang's response is that the two situations—the first with the one having power and others lacking power, the second with the one lacking power and the others having power—are non-dual. The appeal to non-duality is a standard Buddhist strategy for recognizing difference without admitting separation. For example, identity and inclusion are non-dual: the relations are distinct, but there is no identity without inclusion and no inclusion without identity. Similarly, Fazang's two situations are distinct by virtue of not being simultaneous, but one does not obtain without the other obtaining (at some other time). Hence, although the one including others is not simultaneous with the others including the one, there is mutual inclusion between the one and the others because the two situations are non-dual.

The plain reading of Fazang's claim about non-simultaneity is also inconsistent with the standard interpretation of Fazang's metaphysics. If one having power (and others lacking power) is not simultaneous with the one

---

[27] T35.1733.124b8–11. For an alternative translation, see Nakasone 1980, 126–7.

lacking power (and others having power), then the one is not simultaneously a cause that puts others into action and a condition put into action by those others. So Fazang's inclusion relation is not simultaneous. Nor is it symmetric. If the one including others is not simultaneous with the others including the one, there is a situation in which the one includes others but the others do not include the one—and there is a different situation in which others include the one but the one does not include the others. Hence, contrary to the standard interpretation, the one does not include others whenever the others include the one.

4.5. Philosophical Considerations

In addition to the preceding textual evidence against the standard interpretation, there is good philosophical reason to abandon this interpretation. The reason concerns causal exclusion and overdetermination.

4.5.1. Causal Exclusion

According to the standard interpretation, for any *dharma*, each of many others simultaneously has power to put all others into action. For example, if soil, water, and seeds include each other, the standard interpretation entails that soil has complete power to cause sprouts and that water simultaneously has complete power to cause sprouts. Hence, according to the standard interpretation of mutual inclusion, the cause for sprouts is overdetermined.

Buddhist theories of causation typically reject the possibility of causal overdetermination. Consider, for example, an exchange in *Commentary on the Great Perfection of Wisdom*. An anonymous interlocutor ascribes to sovereign selves (Skt. *ātma*) the characteristics of breathing, looking straight ahead and sideways, life, mind, suffering or happiness, affection or aversion, and willing. The respondent agrees that these characteristics occur and yet denies that they are characteristics of a sovereign self.

> But all these characteristics are characteristics of the consciousness (*vijñānalakṣaṇa*)! It is because there is consciousness that there is breathing, looking straight ahead or sideways, life, etc., and when the consciousness leaves the body, all of that disappears.[28]

---

[28] T25.1509.231a1-2, recited in Chödrön 2001, 1188.

According to the respondent, because consciousness (Skt. *vijñāna*; Ch. *shí* 識) suffices for breathing and other activities of a living body, it is consciousness rather than a sovereign self that causes those activities.

One way to reconstruct the preceding argument is to attribute to the respondent a familiar principle about causal exclusion.

Causal Exclusion
If x is a sufficient cause for y, then no z, distinct from x, is simultaneously a cause of y.

The anonymous interlocutor argues that sovereign selves exist because positing such selves is necessary for explaining what causes various activities of living bodies. Assuming that consciousness suffices to cause those activities, *Causal Exclusion* entails that sovereign selves do not cause the same activities. The response thereby undermines the reason the interlocutor gives for supposing that there are sovereign selves.

4.5.2. Misunderstanding Mutual Inclusion

Although Fazang does not explicitly endorse *Causal Exclusion*, he endorses the kind of concern that typically motivates others to endorse it. For example, Jaegwon Kim (1934–2019) famously endorses *Causal Exclusion* when examining the possibility of mental causation. Supposing that, at some particular time, some mental event m suffices to cause a physical event p and that, at the same time, there is also a physical event p^*, distinct from m, that also suffices for p, he asks, "Given that p has a physical cause p^*, what causal work is left for m to contribute"?[29] Kim's answer, and his motivation for endorsing *Causal Exclusion*, is that there is no causal work left for m to contribute because, if both p^* and m suffice for p, then p has too many causes.

Fazang endorses a similar kind of reasoning when considering misunderstandings of mutual inclusion.

If each [of many *dharmas*] only has power and none lack power, then there are excessively many effects because each one brings forth [others]. If each only lacks power and none have power, then there is an excessive absence of effects because when all together are simultaneously without a causal condition, nothing is brought forth.[30]

---

[29] Kim 1998, 37.
[30] T35.1733.124b4-7. For an alternative translation, see Nakasone 1980, 126.

Fazang considers two interpretations of mutual inclusion. In the first, all *dharmas* simultaneously have power. Fazang's reason for rejecting this interpretation is that, if all *dharmas* have power at the same time, each effect has multiple sufficient causes. For Fazang, this is tantamount to there being multiple instances of the same effect, all co-located and co-occurring with each other. Because, for Fazang, this is absurd, he infers that one having power is not simultaneous with others having power. *Causal Exclusion* is the principle that drives this inference. In the second interpretation, all *dharmas* simultaneously lack power. Fazang's reason for rejecting this interpretation is that, if all *dharmas* lack power at the same time, nothing has power to cause effects and so there are no effects. Fazang rejects this as absurd, inferring that others lacking power is not simultaneous with one lacking power. *Causality*—the principle that effects arise only if something has power to cause them—drives this inference.

4.5.3. Preserving Causality

Causality is consistent with the standard interpretation of Fazang's doctrine of mutual inclusion. *Causal Exclusion* is not. If each *dharma* includes all others by virtue of having complete power, then each is a sufficient cause for putting those others into action. If Fazang's inclusion relation is symmetric and simultaneous, all *dharmas* have multiple sufficient causes. *Causal Exclusion*, by contrast, entails that each *dharma* has at most one sufficient cause. This is, perhaps, why advocates of the standard interpretation infer that Fazang speaks of causality in name only. For if having power is *not* a matter of putting into action, no *dharma* has *any* sufficient cause and so there is no violation of *Causal Exclusion*.

Given the choice between attributing a principle like *Causal Exclusion* to Fazang and reading Fazang as speaking of causality in name only, the better choice is to attribute the principle to Fazang. The principle is implicit in writings with which he is likely familiar. Attributing it to Fazang would explain why he denies that inclusion relations are simultaneous. Moreover, Fazang testifies that he is speaking about causality. He claims that existence, emptiness, having power, and lacking power are characteristics of causes.[31] He also insists that his doctrines of mutual identity and mutual inclusion are doctrines "concerning causes" (Ch. *yāo yīn* 約因).[32] A plain reading of Fazang's testimony is inconsistent with the standard interpretation.

---

[31] T45.1866.502a2-5; Cook 1970, 446; Unno et al. 2023, 171.
[32] T45.1866.503a19; Cook 1970, 468; Unno et al. 2023, 178.

4.6. An Asymmetry Constraint

The chief evidence in favor of the standard interpretation is its capacity to secure the coherence of Fazang's doctrines. For suppose, contrary to the standard interpretation, that Fazang endorses an asymmetry constraint on the relations of identity and inclusion. The preceding discussion indicates the likely form of such a constraint.

> *Asymmetry Constraint*
> Any situation in which one is identical with or included within another is not a situation in which the other is identical with or included within the one.

The *Asymmetry Constraint* seems to entail, as an obvious and immediate corollary, that there is no mutual identity and no mutual inclusion. (In the context of the playing cards example, the *Asymmetry Constraint* seems to entail that Figure 4.2a or 4.2b, or some similar variant, correctly depicts causal relations among the cards.) If so, preserving Fazang's doctrines of mutual identity and mutual inclusion requires avoiding this corollary, and avoiding the corollary requires rejecting the *Asymmetry Constraint*. The benefit of the standard interpretation, accordingly, is that it preserves Fazang's doctrines.

The cost of the standard interpretation is rejecting a plain reading of Fazang's claims about simultaneity and causality. (Another cost, perhaps, is making the precise content of Fazang's doctrines somewhat mysterious.) The next chapter develops an alternative interpretation that preserves the coherence of Fazang's doctrines, honors the *Asymmetry Constraint*, and takes Fazang at his word when he claims that his doctrines concern causality and his relations are not simultaneous.

5

Attending to Aspects

5.1. Interpretive Issues

A responsible interpretation of Fazang's doctrines of mutual identity and mutual inclusion should aim to avoid two apparent inconsistencies. The first concerns the relation between having and lacking power. For Fazang, when one includes another, the one has complete power and the other completely lacks power. Mutual inclusion among *dharmas* thereby seems to entail that *dharmas* simultaneously completely have power and completely lack power. Yet nothing that completely has power simultaneously lacks power. The second apparent inconsistency concerns causal overdetermination. For Fazang, mutual inclusion entails that every *dharma* is put into action by many other *dharmas*. Yet the standard Buddhist conception of causality requires that each *dharma* is put into action by at most one other *dharma*.

This chapter develops an interpretation of Fazang's doctrines that preserves the non-simultaneity of power and avoids causal overdetermination.[1] For the sake of convenient reference, label this the *alternative interpretation*. The alternative interpretation reads Fazang as conceptualizing the realm of *dharmas* as akin to an array of twinkling bulbs, where only one bulb shines at any given time and the bulbs take turns illuminating each other.

The chapter divides into six parts. The first explains an insight, from the Sarvāstivāda Abhidharma tradition and the Yogācārin Vasubandhu (4th–5th century), that one and the same thing can have multiple aspects. The second explains how Fazang combines this insight with a substance-function heuristic, indigenous to the Chinese philosophical tradition. It also explains how Fazang uses this combination to secure the coherence of one and the same thing having *contrary* aspects. The third part of the chapter explains how Fazang conceptualizes relations among the aspects of things. The fourth introduces considerations from Buddhist (Yogācārin) epistemology to explain why this conception makes his inclusion relations asymmetric and sequential. The final part of the chapter clarifies the role of mind in Fazang's conception of mutuality, and in particular what Fazang means by claiming that mutual identity and

---

[1] For a similar (albeit more critical) interpretation, see Ziporyn 2013, 230–1.

Metaphors for Interdependence. Nicholaos Jones, Oxford University Press. © Nicholaos Jones 2025.
DOI: 10.1093/9780197807224.003.0005

82 METAPHORS FOR INTERDEPENDENCE

mutual inclusion characterize *dharmas* in the realm of Samantabhadra or the *dharma*-realm of dependent arising.

5.2. Relativizing Mutuality

There are two strategies for preserving the coherence of a doctrine when the doctrine seems to be inconsistent. One is to reinterpret some of the terminology responsible for the apparent inconsistency. The standard interpretation of Fazang's doctrines follows this strategy. Another strategy for preserving coherence is to parameterize—or relativize to implicit parameters—some of the claims responsible for the apparent inconsistency. This is the strategy for this chapter.

The chapter pursues the parameterizing strategy with three tactics. The first is relativizing identity and inclusion relations to aspects of *dharmas*. The second is correlating these aspects with a sequence-inducing factor. The third is using this correlation to secure a coherent conception of mutual identity and mutual inclusion among *dharmas*.[2] This section of the chapter develops the first tactic. The next completes it. Subsequent sections proceed sequentially through the remaining tactics.

5.2.1. Aspects

Motivation for the first tactic—relativization to aspects—derives from the Buddha's first sermon after his awakening, *Sūtra on Promulgating the True Teaching*. The sermon reports that the true teaching consists of four noble truths. These are the truths of *duḥkha*, the cause of *duḥkha*, the cessation of *duḥkha*, and the path leading to the cessation of *duḥkha*.[3] The sermon also reports that the Buddha's knowledge of each truth consists of three phases. The phases are that the truth is, that the truth should be realized, and that the truth has been developed.[4] Because the four noble truths are parts of one true teaching, and because each noble truth has three phases, *Sūtra on Promulgating the True Teaching* reports that the one true teaching has twelve aspects (Skt. *ākāra*; Ch.

---

[2] Some prior scholarship gestures in the direction of a similar interpretive strategy. Jin Park intimates that having power and lacking power are functions of perspective, standpoint, or "referential purpose" (Park 2008, 166). Alan Fox associates Fazang's model of causality with a kind of perspectivalism or standpoint relativity (Fox 2015, 277–8, 284). Neither Park nor Fox explain what they mean by perspectives or standpoints. (For example, are they relative to cognizing subjects or locational in some way?) Nor do Park or Fox ground their interpretation in Fazang's writings or the writings with which he is likely familiar.

[3] See Bodhi 2000, 1844. For a brief overview of *duḥkha*, its causes, and its cessation, refer to Chapter 2.3.2, 2.5.1, and 2.6.1.

[4] See Bodhi 2000, 1845.

háng xiāng 行相). Because each phase is an aspect of the same truth, there are four noble truths rather than twelve. Because each noble truth is an aspect of the same teaching, there is one true teaching rather than four.[5]

The term "aspect" translates the Sanskrit term *ākāra*. The Sanskrit term derives from *ā-kṛ*. This term denotes bringing near or driving together (as with cows or cattle).[6] In its earliest Sanskrit uses, *ākāra* denotes the external appearance of something. For example, *Ṛg Veda* describes chariots in the shape of a city or a mountain, and it characterizes the city and the mountain as the *ākāra* of those chariots.[7]

Early Pāli scriptures use *ākāra* to denote external appearances of things. These appearances are often how facial expressions or behaviors make things look. For example, when *Sūtra on the Great Lion's Roar* reports that non-Buddhists criticize the Buddha's followers for not behaving as if they are satisfied, it characterizes the behaviors as the *ākāra* of the Buddha's followers.[8] Early Pāli scriptures also use *ākāra* more broadly to denote that which gives a thing its appearance or makes (Skt. *ā-kṛ*) something appear the way it appears. This broader conception of *ākāra* is one in which designations for things can differ by virtue of things having different *ākāra*, and in which the same thing can have different appearances by virtue of having different *ākāra*.[9] For example, *Sūtra on Fruits of the Contemplative Life* characterizes purity, excellence, clarity, and brightness as the *ākāra* of a gem.[10]

5.2.2. The Sarvāstivāda Strategy

The Sarvāstivāda Abhidharma tradition invokes the concept of *ākāra* to interpret and systematize Abhidharma doctrine.[11] For doctrinal interpretation, Sarvāstivādins specify a range of application for the concept and a strategy for identifying *ākāra*. They apply the concept to *dharmas* that are mental concomitants (Skt. *caitta* or *cetasika*; Ch. *xīn suǒ* 心所). They identify *ākāra* for these concomitants through a strategy of "*ākāra*-ization."[12] This strategy

---

[5] For further analysis of the use of *ākāra* in *Sūtra on Promulgating the True Teaching*, see Zhao 2016, 10–3. For a similar use of *ākāra* in *Commentary on the Great Perfection of Wisdom*, see T25.1509.137c29-138a19; Chödrön 2001, 513–4.

[6] Zhao 2016, 2.

[7] Zhao 2016, 3; citing *Ṛg Veda* 1.42.9 and 3.21.3.

[8] See Walshe 1995, 156. See also Zhao 2016, 4.

[9] For a similar conception in *Commentary on the Great Perfection of Wisdom*, see T25.1509.227b27-9 and 414a20-2; Chödrön 2001, 1161 and 1993. For a similar conception of *aspect* from contemporary analytic metaphysics, see Baxter 2017 and Turner 2014.

[10] See Walshe 1995, 104. See also Zhao 2016, 5.

[11] Zhao 2016, 37–61.

[12] Zhao 2016, 51–3.

84 METAPHORS FOR INTERDEPENDENCE

endorses two inferences. The first is to infer that a characteristic is an *ākāra* of a mental concomitant if the characteristic assigns the concomitant to a kind.[13] The second is to infer that there are multiple *ākāra* of the same mental concomitant if there are multiple kind-specifying characteristics for the concomitant.

The authoritative commentary for Sarvāstivāda Abhidharma, *Great Compendium of Abhidharma*, exhibits both of these inferential strategies.[14] For example, a specific characteristic of loving-kindness is providing comfort to others, and the commentary asserts that this characteristic is an *ākāra* of loving-kindness.

Loving-kindness has the *ākāra* of providing comfort to others.[15]

The commentary also identifies three specific characteristics of ignorance (Skt. *avidyā*; Ch. *wú míng* 無明) as *ākāra* of ignorance.

Question: So what are the *ākāra* of ignorance? Answer: Not knowing, dark, and foolish are the *ākāra* of ignorance.[16]

5.2.3. Vasubandhu's Strategy

Vasubandhu (4th century), bridging the gap between Sarvāstivāda Abhidharma and Yogācāra Mahāyāna traditions, further develops the Sarvāstivādin conception of *ākāra*. He extends the range of application to include mental concomitants and their accompanied mind (Skt. *citta*; Ch. *zhì duō* 質多). His definition for *ākāra*, in *(Auto-)Commentary on the Treasury of Abhidharma*, makes this extension explicit.

[Chapter 7, Section 13b.] . . . . It is therefore correct to say that "aspect" is a mode of perceiving (*grahaṇa*) objects by the mind and mental states.[17]

For Vasubandhu, both mind and mental concomitants have *ākāra* because both perceive cognitive objects (Skt. *ālambana*; Ch. *suǒ yuan* 所緣) by taking on some form of those objects.

---

[13] *Commentary on the Great Perfection of Wisdom* mentions a similar strategy, reporting that some monks hold that knowledge of aspects pertains to specific characteristics while knowledge of things pertains to general characteristics. See T25.1509.258c29-a1; Chödrön 2001, 1432.

[14] See Zhao 2016, 51–2.

[15] T27.1545.421a18.

[16] T27.1545.196c16-7.

[17] Pruden 1991, 1116.

[Chapter 2, Section 34bd.] . . . The mind and its mental states . . . "have an aspect," because they take form according to their object. . . .[18]

For example, consciousness (Skt. *vijñāna*; Ch. *shí* 識) cognizes objects as blue or yellow, and feeling (Skt. *vedanā*; Ch. *shòu* 受) feels objects as pleasant or painful. Blue and yellow, pleasant and painful are *ākāra*.[19] Hence, whenever consciousness cognizes or feeling feels, they take on some *ākāra*. Because they take on some *ākāra*, they are said to have *ākāra*.

In addition to extending the range of things that can have *ākāra*, Vasubandhu extends the kinds of *ākāra* things can have.[20] For example, *Great Compendium of Abhidharma* attributes to loving-kindness a functional *ākāra*, namely, providing comfort to others. By contrast, Vasubandhu attributes to loving-kindness an *ākāra* that is a content, namely, "happy!" Subsequent interpreters of Vasubandhu infer that, for Vasubandhu, some *ākāra*—the ones indicating function—are modes or ways of appearing. and others—the ones indicating content—are forms of those appearances.[21] Because content-*ākāra* and function-*ākāra* correlate with each other, there is no inconsistency among them. For example, for loving-kindness the content-*ākāra* of "happy!" correlates with the function-*ākāra* of providing comfort to others. The reason is that the presence of one aspect guarantees the presence of the other.

5.2.4. Fazang's Strategy

Fazang does not invoke the concept of *ākāra* (Ch. *háng xiāng* 行相) when discussing the characteristics of existing (Ch. *yǒu* 有), being empty (Ch. *kōng* 空), having power (Ch. *yǒu lì* 有力), and lacking power (Ch. *wú lì* 無力). Instead, he invokes the concept of *meaning* (Ch. *yì* 義).

> Again, because there are the meanings of emptiness and existence, there is the gate of mutual identity. Because there are the meanings of having power and lacking power, there is the gate of mutual inclusion.[22]

Fazang does not explain what he means by phrases such as "the meanings of emptiness and existence" or "the meanings of having power and lacking power." But he likely has in mind a standard usage.

---

[18] Pruden 1991, 205.
[19] See Sangpo 2012, 776–7.
[20] Kellner 2014, 285–6.
[21] Kellner 2014, 286–7.
[22] T45.1866.503a12-3. For alternative translations, see Cook 1970, 467; Unno et al. 2023, 178.

The term "meaning" 義 can designate a content expressed through speech, a thing, a characteristic, or an explanation. In Buddhist writings, it also can designate an attribute of truth or a way in which truth exists and manifests itself. For example, according to Jin Tao, meanings 義, interpreted as *attributes of truth*, are of two types.

> On the one hand, [meanings] are the result of analysis and differentiation, which necessarily entail the use of intellect. On the other hand, they are always claimed to be inseparable and undifferentiated from each other; that is, they are free from intellection. The tie with intellect through differentiation allows truth to be accessible through its attributes, and the denial of differentiation and thus of that tie allows whatever is accessed to be truth—hence the access of truth through intellection![23]

Following this Buddhist usage of "meaning" 義, Fazang most likely uses the term to designate a characteristic that manifests truth. Fazang's meanings are likely characteristics, based upon analysis and differentiation, that make truth manifest while being inseparable and nondual from each other. The term "aspect" 行相 similarly designates a defining activity, a form, or a way that makes truth manifest by explaining how a thing appears. Moreover, just as the Sarvāstivādins and Vasubandhu "*ākāra*-ize" select characteristics of *dharmas*, Fazang "meaning-izes" the characteristics of existing, being empty, having power, and lacking power. So even if, linguistically, Fazang's "meaning" does not mean *aspect*, there is a strong philosophical affinity.

Just as one and the same *dharma* can have multiple aspects, Fazang maintains that each *dharma* has all four meanings of existing, being empty, having power, and lacking power. He follows the Sarvāstivādin strategy of *ākāra*-izing characteristics, and he extends this strategy to apply to general characteristics (Skt. *sāmānyalakṣaṇa*; Ch. *gòng xiāng* 共相). Because one is identical with another only if the one is empty and the other exists, mutual identity among *dharmas* entails that every *dharma* has the meanings of existing and being empty. Because one includes another only if the one has power and the other lacks power, mutual inclusion among *dharmas* entails that every *dharma* also has the meanings of having power and lacking power.

[23] Jin 2013b, 159.

5.3. Substance and Function

5.3.1. The Substance-Function Heuristic

Interpreting the four meanings as aspects of *dharmas* connects Fazang's conceptual framework with prior Buddhist tradition. It also connects his framework with prior Chinese tradition. The four meanings are central to Fazang's conceptual framework in ways that other characteristics, such as being ephemeral or being firm, are not. Fazang marks this centrality by invoking the substance-function (Ch. *tǐ-yòng* 體用) heuristic.

> Each dependently-arisen *dharma* has two meanings. The first meaning is being empty and existing. This is from the perspective of [one's] substance. The second meaning is having power and lacking power. This is from the perspective of power functioning.[24]

The substance-function heuristic pervades Chinese engagements with Buddhism.[25] The paradigmatic application of the heuristic is to the roots and branches of plants. *Substance* (Ch. *tǐ* 體) denotes that which grounds another as it acts. The roots are substance because they hold plants in the ground. *Function* (Ch. *yòng* 用) denotes that which acts. The branches are function because their growth is what plants do. Just as roots are hidden and stationary beneath the soil, substance is hidden and unmoving. Just as branches are manifest and growing above the soil, function is manifest and changing.

5.3.2. Parameterizing Aspects

When explaining his doctrines of mutual identity and mutual inclusion, Fazang uses the substance-function heuristic to organize the meanings of existing, being empty, having power, and lacking power. (See Table 5.1, reading down columns.)

Consider, first, the category of substance. For Fazang, *dharmas* have the characteristic of existing by virtue of being objects of cognition, and objects of cognition appear to be real existents despite lacking reality. Hence, when *dharmas* are objects of cognition, their status as nominal existents is hidden. This is why the meaning of existing pertains to substance.

---

[24] T45.1866.503b8-9. For alternative translations, see Cook 1970, 472; Unno et al. 2023, 179.

[25] For a history of the substance-function heuristic in Chinese traditions, see Muller 2016. For brief overviews of the substance-function heuristic in relation to Fazang's metaphysics, see Jones 2018b, 306–7; Nichols and Jones 2023, 110–3; Ziporyn 2018, 194–204.

88 METAPHORS FOR INTERDEPENDENCE

Table 5.1 Substance-Function for Identity and Inclusion

substance	function
existing	having power
being empty	lacking power

Table 5.2 Parameterization for Identity and Inclusion

another is identical with x	x exists
x is identical with another	x is empty
x includes another	x has power
another includes x	x lacks power

Consider, next, the category of function. For Fazang, being a nominal existent means being empty of power to put oneself into action, and being a real existent means having such power. Because *dharmas* that are objects of cognition appear to be real existents, they do not appear to be empty. So their emptiness is also hidden. This is why the meaning of being empty also pertains to substance. Because having power and lacking power concern the activity of *dharmas*, both meanings pertain to function.

Fazang uses the four meanings as parameters for conceptualizing relations of identity and inclusion. (See Table 5.2, reading left to right across rows.)

Dharmas are that with which others are identical relative to the meaning of existing—that is, others are identical with them insofar as the *dharmas* exist. *Dharmas* are identical with others relative to the meaning of being empty—that is, they are identical with others insofar as they are empty. Similarly, *dharmas* include others relative to the meaning of having power— that is, insofar as the *dharmas* have power. *Dharmas* are included within others relative to the meaning of lacking power—that is, insofar as they lack power.

For the sake of illustrating this tactic for parameterizing the relations of identity and inclusion, consider an excerpt of the playing cards model from Figure 4.2b of Chapter 4. (See Figure 5.1.)

Figure 5.1 Queen Includes King
Image created by the author.

The excerpt depicts King (K) standing and Queen (Q) having power to cause the King's standing. Suppose, for the sake of illustration, that Queen has complete power to cause standing and King completely lacks power to cause standing. Then Queen includes King. The parameterization tactic for relations of inclusion interprets this to mean that, insofar as Queen has power and King lacks power, Queen includes King.

5.4. Correlating Aspects

The results in Table 5.2—the relativization of identity and inclusion relations to four aspects or meanings of *dharmas*—completes the first of Fazang's tactics for conceptualizing mutual identity and mutual inclusion. His second tactic involves correlating the four aspects with a sequence-inducing factor. The correlation proceeds in two stages. The first pairs each substance aspect with a distinct function aspect. The second uses a distinction, separate from and orthogonal to the substance-function distinction, to grade the resulting pairs of aspects. The gradation suffices to induce a sequencing for identity and inclusion relations.

5.4.1. Pairing Aspects

Recall how Fazang uses the substance-function heuristic to organize the aspects or meanings of existing, being empty, having power, and lacking power. (See Table 5.1.) He associates existing and being empty with substance. He associates having power and lacking power with function. The technical meanings of these four aspects secure a pairing of each substance aspect with a distinct function aspect. (See Table 5.1, reading left to right across rows.) Because empty *dharmas* enter into others and whatever enters into another lacks power, Fazang pairs being empty with lacking power. Similarly, because whatever exists appears to be a real existent and real existents have power, Fazang pairs being existent with having power.

90 METAPHORS FOR INTERDEPENDENCE

Fazang's pairings cohere with a distinction, from Sarvāstivāda metaphysics, between conditioning *dharmas* (Skt. *saṃskāra*) and conditioned *dharmas* (Skt. *saṃskṛta*). Dhammajoti summaries the Sarvāstivādin distinction.

> In its aspect of being a dependently co-arisen *(pratītya-samutpāda)* existent, a conditioned *dharma* is said to be *saṃskṛta*—'compounded', 'co-produced', 'conditioned'. In its other aspect of being a causally productive force, it is also called a *saṃskāra*—'conditioning' or 'conditioning force'.[26]

Saṃskāra, as defined in this quotation, designates the existent and powerful aspects of *dharmas*. *Saṃskṛta* names the empty and powerless aspects of the same *dharmas*. In Fazang's conceptual framework, every *dharma* is conditioning and conditioned. Conditioning and being conditioned designate different aspects of *dharmas* rather than different kinds of *dharma*. *Dharmas* condition insofar as they exist and have power. They are conditioned insofar as they are empty and lack power.

5.4.2. Grading Aspects

Fazang does not mark the distinction between his two pairings—existing and having power, being empty and lacking power—with the Sarvāstivādin distinction between conditioning and being conditioned. Instead, he follows a different precedent from the Sarvāstivāda tradition.

For doctrinal systematization, the Sarvāstivādins use gradations to demarcate aspects into kinds.[27] For example, *Great Compendium of Abhidharma* grades aspects of mental concomitants as crude/coarse (Skt. *sthūla*; Ch. *cū* 麁) or subtle (Skt. *sūkṣma*; Ch. *xì* 細) and as keen/sharp (Skt. *tīkṣṇa*; Ch. *lì* 利) or sluggish/dull (Skt. *dhandha*; Ch. *chí dùn* 遲鈍).

> For the affliction of restlessness, the *ākāra* is keen. . . . For the affliction of melancholia, the *ākāra* is obscure and sluggish. . . . The *ākāra* of the feeling of joy is crude or subtle. . . .[28]

These gradations— keen or sluggish, crude or subtle—are contraries. Because they are contraries, they demarcate aspects into kinds. (The aspects, in turn, demarcate mental concomitants into kinds.)

---

[26] Dhammajotti 2015, 534.
[27] Zhao 2016, 53–6.
[28] T27.1545.254c5-7 and 599a3-4.

Table 5.3 Aspects and Their Gradations

aspect	Gradations	
existing	chief	manifest
having power		
being empty	attendant	hidden
lacking power		

Fazang does not use the Sarvāstivādin gradations to demarcate his two pairings—existing and having power, being empty and lacking power—into kinds. Instead, he uses two alternative gradations. (See Table 5.3, reading left to right across rows.)

The first grades aspects as chief (Skt. *pramukha* or *svāmin*; Ch. *shǒu* 首 or *zhǔ* 主) or attendant (Skt. *anuga*; Ch. *bàn* 伴).[29] Chief and attendant are contraries. Chiefs—leaders—are paradigms of individuals who have power and put others into action. Attendants, by contrast, are paradigms of subordinate individuals. They lack the power that chiefs have, and they are put into action when commands from a chief enter into them. Accordingly, Fazang grades the aspects of existing and having power as *chief*, and he grades the aspects of being empty and lacking power as *attendant*. That is, insofar as a *dharma* acts as chief, it exists and has power. Similarly, insofar as a *dharma* acts as attendant, it is empty and lacks power.[30]

For the sake of illustrating Fazang's gradations of chief and attendant, consider the simplified model of playing cards as depicted in Figure 5.2.

Figure 5.2 depicts two playing cards: Queen (Q) and King (K). Each card is standing. The arrows represent that each card leans on the other. The "Q" in the circle attached to the "Q" box represents that Queen—and only Queen—has power to cause Queen to stand. The "Q" in the circle attached to the "K" box represents that Queen—and only Queen—has power to cause King to stand. Hence, according to the model in Figure 5.2, Queen

---

[29] The gradations *chief* and *attendant* are important to Fazang's mystery of Indra's net. See T45.1866.506a12-b10; Cook 1970, 509–12; Unno et al. 2023, 193–4. For discussion of the importance of the chief-attendant relation to Fazang's conception of mutual identity, see Guo 2018, 31, 83, 136–7.

[30] Fazang's association of chief with existing and attendant with emptiness also accommodates a tendency of Tang-era Buddhists to consider existence and emptiness sequentially rather than simultaneously. See Jin 2013a, 123–4.

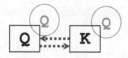

Figure 5.2 Mutually Leaning Playing Cards, Simplified
Image created by the author.

has complete power to cause standing and King completely lacks power to cause standing. The model thereby entails that Queen includes King. (It does not entail that Queen includes Queen, because Fazang's conceptual framework forbids anything from including itself.) Supposing that Queen exists and King is empty, Fazang's gradation tactic interprets *Queen includes King* to mean that, insofar as Queen is chief and King is attendant, Queen includes King.

Fazang's second gradation grades aspects as manifest (Skt. *abhivyakta*; Ch. *xiǎn* 顯) or hidden (Skt. *praticchanna*; Ch. *yǐn* 隱).[31] Manifest and hidden are contraries. They also are associated with the distinction between substance and function. However, as gradations for aspects of *dharmas*, *manifest* and *hidden* are subordinate to the chief-attendant distinction and orthogonal to the substance-function distinction. For example, because emptiness and existence pertain to substance, and because substance is hidden, there is a sense in which both are hidden. Yet there is also a sense in which existing is manifest but emptiness is hidden. This is the sense Fazang has in mind. The reason derives from his conception of existence.

For Fazang, *dharmas* exist because they are objects of cognition, and objects of cognition appear to be real existents. Because this appearing is just what it is to be an object of cognition, the appearing is manifest. Because the appearing indicates existence, Fazang grades the aspect of existing as manifest. Because he pairs existing with having power, he also grades having power as manifest. By contrast, because the source of power for *dharmas* is hidden when they (falsely) appear to be real existents, Fazang grades lacking power as hidden. Because he pairs lacking power with being empty, he also grades being empty as hidden. Hence, with respect to the simplified model of playing cards in Figure 5.2, Fazang's second gradation interprets *Queen includes King* to mean that, insofar as Queen is manifest and King is hidden, Queen includes King.

---

[31] The gradations *manifest* and *hidden* are central to the sixth of Fazang's ten mysteries. See T45.1866.506b22-c9; Cook 1970, 515–6; Unno et al. 2023, 195–6.

5.5. Inducing Sequentiality

Fazang's gradations of chief-attendant and manifest-hidden—and their correlations with the four aspects of existing, being empty, having power, and lacking power—complete the second of Fazang's tactics for conceptualizing mutual identity and mutual inclusion. His third tactic uses the result of the second to induce a sequencing for the relations of identity and inclusion. The sequencing allows for one and the same *dharma* (or group of *dharmas*) to exist and have complete power in one situation while also being empty and completely lacking power in a different situation. The tactic for inducing the sequencing also precludes one and the same *dharma* (or group of *dharmas*) from simultaneously being both chief and attendant.

There are two potential motivations for Fazang's sequencing tactic. The first derives from *Inner Classic of Master Jini*. This work records a dialogue between Master Jini 計倪子 and King Goujian 勾踐 (r. 495–465) of Yue 越.[32] The dialogue concerns ways to strengthen the government, and a potential motivation for Fazang's sequencing tactic appears in one of Master Jini's recommendations. Master Jini advises the king to allow power to shift among ministers in accordance with natural cycles.[33] This advice bears a remote similarity to Fazang's tactic of allowing the power of *dharmas* to shift across situations. But this is quite speculative. A second, more likely motivation for Fazang's sequencing tactic derives from an insight about attention in Buddhist epistemology. The insight concerns attentional focus and the shifting thereof.

5.5.1. Attentional Focus

Buddhist epistemology accommodates the possibility of conceptualizing the same thing under different aspects. It does this by acknowledging shifts of attentional focus/mental engagement (Skt. *manaskāra* or *manasikāra*; Ch. *zuō yì* 作意). Sthiramati 安慧 (6th century), an influential commentator from the Yogācāra tradition, characterizes attentional focus as a bending or turning of mind toward an object.

> [Vasubandhu's *Summary of the Five Heaps*] asks, "What is attention?" and then responds, "The bending of the mind." Bending is that which causes something to bend. Bending of the mind is the condition by which the mind is directed toward an object.

---

[32] See Milburn 2010, 145–60.
[33] See Milburn 2010, 153–4. See also Defoort 1997, 170–1.

94 METAPHORS FOR INTERDEPENDENCE

> Its action is to cause the mind to keep hold of an object. Causing the mind to keep hold of an object means to repeatedly turn the mind toward it.[34]

Attentional focus involves the mind directing its cognitive resources toward one specific target within its cognitive field.[35] For example, when a driver is guiding his chariot through a crowded battlefield toward an enemy target, attentional focus involves the driver bending or turning his mind toward the pathway for reaching the target. Attentional focus prevents the driver's mind from scattering or being distracted by recollections of their breakfast, screams of agony, and sights of birds.

Attentional focus is a skill, and there are practices—contemplative and meditative in nature—that strengthen this skill. These practices often involve directing attention to the breath. For example, Vasubandhu recommends focusing the mind on the breath by counting in-breaths and out-breaths.[36] This counting does not discriminate among distinct inhalations or distinct exhalations. Instead, when attention is focused on the breath, counting breaths involves considering inhalations as belonging to the same kind— and similarly for exhalations. Counting develops skill for attentional focus by challenging the practitioner to keep track of counts. Losing count signals attentional distraction, and practitioners should resume their count from one until they gain the ability to count to ten. They should then proceed to more advanced breath-counting practices to continue developing their skill.

5.5.2. Shifting Focus

Because attentional focus partitions the cognitive field into center and periphery, it induces a sequencing upon the gradations of chief/manifest and attendant/hidden. Consider, as a toy example for how this works, a 17th-century wall painting of the metamorphosis of the monk Baozhi 寶誌 (418–514).[37] (See Figure 5.3.)

---

[34] Engle 2009, 276. For a similar characterization in Sthiramati's commentary on Vasubandhu's *Thirty Verses*, see Kawamura 1964, 51.

[35] Sthiramati's conception of attention coheres with contemporary conceptions. For example, in a review of contemporary scientific research on attention, Jennings characterizes attention as "the prioritization of some mental processes over others, often resulting in the selection of one or more mental processes at the expense of others" (Jennings 2022, 9).

[36] See Pruden 1991, 922. For a more extensive discussion of the relation between Fazang's metaphysics and counting breaths, refer to Chapter 7.4.

[37] For more information about Baozhi, see Berkowitz 1995.

ATTENDING TO ASPECTS 95

Figure 5.3 Metamorphosis of Baozhi
Adapted from Vassil. (2011). La métamorphose du moine Baozhi. Peinture murale provenant d'un temple, Chine du Nord (Shanxi-Hebei), 17ème siècle. Musées Royaux d'Art et d'Histoire (MRAH), Parc du Cinquantenaire, Bruxelles. *Wikimedia Commons.* commons.wikimedia.org/wiki/File:Bruxelles_Baozhi_Shanxi_02_10_2011.jpg. Under a Creative Commons CC0 1.0 Universal Public Domain Dedication (CC0 1.0 DEED).

Relevant details from the image in Figure 5.3 include the metamorphosing Baozhi, a lotus flower—symbolic source for metamorphic birth—opening below him, and two attendants gazing upon the flower.

Contemplating the details in Figure 5.3 requires attentional focus. The natural focus, centered in the painting, is Baozhi. Contemplating Baozhi as central reveals that he is the cause for the opening of the flower and the direction of the attendants' gazes. For if Baozhi were not metamorphosing, the flower would not be opening and the attendants would not be gazing upon the flower. Contemplating Baozhi as central also reveals that the flower and attendants lack power. For when attention focuses upon Baozhi, the role of peripheral elements is hidden and Baozhi appears to be the only one that has power. Hence, insofar as Baozhi is chief or manifest to attentional focus, Baozhi has complete power, the others completely lack power, and Baozhi includes the flower and attendants.

Now shift attentional focus from Baozhi to the lotus flower. Contemplating the flower as central reveals that the flower is the cause for the direction of the attendants' gazes and the metamorphosing of Baozhi. For if the flower were not opening, the attendants would not be gazing upon the flower and Baozhi would not be metamorphosing. Contemplating the flower as central also reveals that the attendants and Baozhi lack power. For when attention focuses on the flower, the role of peripheral elements is hidden and the flower appears to be the only one that has power. Hence, insofar as the flower is chief or manifest to attentional focus, the flower has complete power, the others completely lack power, and the flower includes the attendants and Baozhi. So, too, with each of the attendants. Each attendant, as chief and manifest to attentional focus, has complete power and includes all others, and all of the others completely lack power.

For Fazang, contemplating relations among *dharmas* requires selecting one *dharma*—or, more precisely, one kind of *dharma*—as central to attentional focus. This selection grades the selected *dharma* as chief and manifest. Graded as chief and manifest, the selected *dharma* exists and has complete power. Because other *dharmas*—or, more precisely, other kinds of *dharma*—are peripheral to attentional focus, they are graded as attendant and hidden. Graded as attendant and hidden, these others are empty and completely lack power. (See Table 5.4.)

Table 5.4 Relationality through Attentional Focus

	focal one	peripheral others	relation
gradation	one is chief	others are attendants	one controls others
substance	one exists	others are empty	others are identical with one
function	one has complete power	others completely lack power	one includes others

ATTENDING TO ASPECTS   97

For Fazang, contemplating *dharmas* without ignorance (Skt. *avidyā*; Ch. *wú míng* 無明) or attachment (Skt. *upādāna*; Ch. *qǔ* 取) requires contemplating all potential foci of attention. Because all *dharmas* have the aspects of existing and having power, all *dharmas* are candidates for focal attention. Hence, for Fazang, nothing privileges one focus of attention as correct or denigrates another as incorrect.

5.5.3. Mutuality as Sequential

Because contemplating relations among *dharmas* requires selecting one *dharma* as central to attentional focus, contemplating *dharmas* without ignorance or attachment precludes simultaneously contemplating all *dharmas* as chief or all *dharmas* as attendant. The requirements for correct contemplation are akin to requirements for reading with comprehension. Although the sentences of a printed text exist simultaneously with each other, understanding the text requires reading the sentences in sequence.[38] Similarly, although *dharmas* arise simultaneously with each other, contemplating them correctly requires shifting attentional focus. *Dharmas* are simultaneous because their specific characteristics, by virtue of being determinate, do not depend upon attentional focus. But *dharmas* are dynamic rather than static, and correctly cognizing this dynamism requires contemplating the powers of *dharmas* as sequential.

Fazang summarizes the result of contemplating the substance of *dharmas* without ignorance or attachment.

> Because [one] existing necessitates others lacking [existence], the others are identical with [the one]. Why? Because the others lack self-nature, [the one] makes [them]. Second: Because [one] being empty necessitates others existing, [the one] is identical with the others. Why? Because [the one] lacks self-nature, therefore the others make [it].[39]

Contemplating one as existing involves focusing attention upon the one. This focus grades the one as chief and manifest, and it relegates others to the periphery of attention. The gradation necessitates others lacking existence—being

---

[38] Fazang uses the example of printed text to explain why simultaneity and sequentiality are not contradictory. See T45.1866.482c2-4; Cook 1970, 191; Unno et al. 2023, 66. For a brief history of woodblock printing in China, see Wilkinson 2013, 909–11.
[39] T45.1866.503b10-3. For alternative translations, see Cook 1970, 473; Unno et al. 2023, 179–80.

empty of self-nature and thereby not being real existents—because the others are graded as attendant and hidden. When one exists and others are empty, the one makes the others. So contemplating the one as existing entails that the others are identical with the one. By contrast, contemplating others—individually or collectively—as existing grades them as manifest and chief, and it grades the one as hidden and attendant. This gradation necessitates the one being empty, and it entails that the one is identical with the others. So there is mutual identity between one and others because attention sequentially selects the one or the others as focal.

Fazang summarizes a similar result for contemplating the function of *dharmas* without ignorance or attachment.

> Second: regarding the function of power, because [one] has complete power, it is able to take in others. Because the others completely lack power, they can enter into [the one]. Understand by contrast others having power and [one] lacking power.[40]

Contemplating one as having power involves focusing attention upon the one. This grades the one as chief and manifest, the others as attendant and hidden. This gradation means that the one has complete power and the others completely lack power. So contemplating the one as having power entails that the one includes the others. By contrast, contemplating others as having power grades them as chief and manifest, the one as attendant and hidden. This gradation means that the others have complete power and the one completely lacks power. So contemplating the others as having power entails that the others include the one. Because attention sequentially selects the one or the others as focal, there is mutual inclusion between one and others.

For the sake of illustrating the sequencing of attentional focus and, more generally, for the sake of illustrating the conception of mutual inclusion that this sequencing supports, consider the view about mutuality depicted in Figure 5.4.

Figure 5.4 depicts four models of causality for the playing cards from Figure 4.1 of Chapter 4. In each model, there are four cards—Ace (A), King (K), Queen (Q), Jack (J)—and each card is standing. Each model represents the result of focusing attention on one of the four cards.

For example, Figure 5.4a represents the result of focusing attention on Ace. Focusing attention on Ace grades Ace as chief and manifest, the other cards as attendant and hidden. This gradation means that Ace exists and has power while

---

[40] T45.1866.503b16-8. For alternative translations, see Cook 1970, 474–5; Unno et al. 2023, 180.

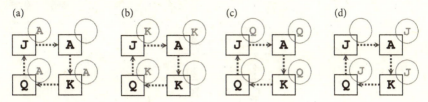

Figure 5.4 Mutual Power Playing Cards, Alternative View
Image created by the author.

the others are empty and lack power. This is why, in Figure 5.4a, Ace has complete power to cause standing and the remaining three cards completely lack power to cause standing. (Figure 5.4a depicts this by showing only "A" in the three circles associated with the squares for K, Q, and J.)

By contrast, Figure 5.4b represents the result of shifting attentional focus to King. This focus grades King as chief and manifest. It means that King exists and has power, the others are empty and lack power. This is why, in Figure 5.4b, King has complete power to cause standing and the other cards completely lack power to cause standing. Similarly, in Figure 5.4c, Queen has complete power to cause standing and the other cards completely lack power to cause standing; and in Figure 5.4d, Jack has complete power to cause standing and the other cards completely lack power to cause standing.

Taken together, the four models in Figure 5.4 represent mutual inclusion among Ace, King, Queen, and Jack. Insofar as Ace is chief and manifest, Ace includes King, Queen, and Jack. Insofar as King is chief and manifest, King includes Queen, Jack, and Ace. Insofar as Queen is chief and manifest, Queen includes Jack, Ace, and King. Insofar as Jack is chief and manifest, Jack includes Ace, King, and Queen. Given Fazang's conceptual framework, this means that each card includes all others.

Because exactly one card is chief and manifest in each model of Figure 5.4, and because some card is chief and manifest in each model, Figure 5.4 illustrates a conception of mutual inclusion in which inclusion relations are asymmetric and sequential. For the sake of contrast, consider a competing model that conceptualizes inclusion relations as symmetric and simultaneous. (See Figure 5.5. This is identical to Figure 4.4 from Chapter 4, and it illustrates the standard interpretation of Fazang's metaphysics.)

There are three noteworthy contrasts between the models in Figure 5.4 and the model in Figure 5.5. First, for the model in Figure 5.5, one card has power to cause another to stand if and only if the one is numerically distinct from the

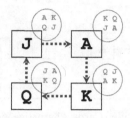

Figure 5.5 Mutual Power Playing Cards, Standard View
Image created by the author.

other and the other belongs to the transitive closure of leaning relations for the one. By contrast, for the models in Figure 5.4, one card has power to cause another to stand if and only if the one is numerically distinct from the other, the other belongs to the transitive closure of leaning relations for the one, and only the one is chief. The difference between these two conditions for having power is that the latter, but not the former, correlates having power with being chief. This correlation is a consequence of the parameter-relativization strategy.

The first contrast between the models in Figure 5.4 and the model in Figure 5.5 explains two further contrasts. The second contrast is that, in Figure 5.5, multiple cards simultaneously have power to cause the standing of some card. By contrast, in each model from Figure 5.4, exactly one card has power to cause the standing of some card. (The visual representation of this difference appears through each circle in Figure 5.4 showing multiple constituents and each circle in Figure 5.5 showing at most one.) This contrast is why the standard interpretation violates *Causal Exclusion* but the alternative interpretation does not.

Causal Exclusion
If x is a sufficient cause for y, then no z, distinct from x, is simultaneously a cause of y.

The reason for the contrast is that the models for Figure 5.4 correlate having power with being chief, and they do so under the assumption that every model has exactly one chief.

The third contrast between the models in Figure 5.4 and the model in Figure 5.5 is that, for the model in Figure 5.5, every card has a cause for its standing. By contrast, for each model in Figure 5.4, some card lacks a cause for its standing. For example, in Figure 5.4a, nothing has power to cause Ace to stand. Similarly, in Figure 5.4b, nothing has power to cause King to stand. (The visual representation of this difference appears through each circle in Figure 5.5 having some constituent and some circles in Figure 5.4 being empty of constituents.)

This contrast might seem to entail that the alternative interpretation of Fazang's doctrines violates *Causality*.

Causality
For any card x, there is some card y such that x stands only if y has power to cause x to stand.

If, for example, nothing in Figure 5.4a has power to cause Ace to stand, why is Ace standing? The answer, according to the alternative interpretation, is that each of King, Queen, and Jack has power to cause Ace to stand. So the interpretation does not violate *Causality*.

The reason each model in Figure 5.4 has some card lacking a cause for its standing is that the models for Figure 5.4 correlate having power with being chief. Because, according to the alternative interpretation, having power is not simultaneous with lacking power, no chief lacks power. Because lacking power is necessary for being included within another, nothing includes any chief. Being chief is a function of attentional focus rather than a function of what something is—that is, chief is a gradation rather than a characteristic. Hence, because there is no privileged attentional focus, the alternative interpretation requires multiple models for causality (one for each of the four cards) such that, in each model, the chief lacks a cause. By contrast, because the standard interpretation does not correlate having power with being chief (or, if it does, it does not do so under the assumption that every model has exactly one chief), the standard interpretation provides exactly one model for causality and, in this model, everything has multiple causes.

5.6. The Role of Mind

5.6.1. Modes of Mind

For Fazang, mutual identity and inclusion among *dharmas* derive from the sequential shifting of attentional focus. Contemplating relations of identity and inclusion among *dharmas* involves sequentially partitioning the realm of *dharmas* into pairings of one and others, focusing attention upon the one in

102 METAPHORS FOR INTERDEPENDENCE

each partition, and then shifting attentional focus to another pairing of one and others.

There are relations of identity and inclusion among *dharmas* because, in every partition of *dharmas* into one and others, the focal one includes and makes the peripheral others. But contemplating relations of identity and inclusion between one *dharma* and others requires focusing attention on the partition in which the one is focal and the others are peripheral. Because attentional focus is limited, there is no way simultaneously to focus attention on all *dharmas*. (Even if there were, such focus would preclude relegating some to peripheral attention and thereby obscure relations of identity and inclusion among *dharmas*.) Because there is no way to contemplate all relations of identity and inclusion simultaneously, the mutuality of identity and inclusion relations cannot be simultaneous.[41]

Although no *dharma* includes and makes another simultaneously with the other including and making it, there is a way to contemplate relations of identity and inclusion sequentially. For any *dharma* that is central to attentional focus, it is possible to shift attention. The shift moves attentional focus to a partition in which the once-focal *dharma* is peripheral and some once-peripheral *dharma* is focal. Because attention can select any *dharma* as focal, it follows that every *dharma* includes and makes all others. This is why *dharmas* are mutually inclusive and mutually identical, and the necessity of shifting attentional focus is why mutuality is sequential rather than simultaneous.

The sequential shifting of attentional focus presumes that there is some source of attention—some mind or discriminating consciousness (Ch. *yì shí* 意識)—that takes the realm of *dharmas* as its object. This is a feature, not a bug.[42] Fazang's doctrines of mutual identity and mutual inclusion are efforts to conceptualize the realm of *dharmas* without ignorance or attachment. For Fazang, conceptual cognition is an activity of mind and so there is no conceptualizing the realm of *dharmas* without some mind doing the conceptualizing. Insofar as there is no mind separate from the realm of *dharmas*, it follows that cognizing *dharmas* as mutually identical and mutually inclusive is not completely correct. Fazang does not contend otherwise. His contention, instead, is that his doctrines are the best one can do *if one's cognition is conceptual*. For Fazang, any cognition of *dharmas* that is free of ignorance, free of attachment, *and conceptual* is a cognition of *dharmas* as mutually identical and mutually inclusive.

---

[41] Brook Ziporyn objects that "the two views [of having power and lacking power] are never simultaneously entertained, and yet Fazang's own discussion . . . is precisely a way of simultaneously entertaining them" (Ziporyn 2003, 509). But just as discussing cause and (subsequent) effect simultaneously does not mean that cause and effect are simultaneous, discussing multiple *dharmas* as powerful does not mean that they are simultaneously powerful.

[42] There are complex and technical connections between Fazang's conception of the realm of *dharmas* and his theory of One Mind (Ch. *yìxīn* 一心). Fazang's theory is beyond the scope of this book. For a brief summary, see Hamar 2023.

5.6.2. The Realm of Mañjuśrī

There are precedents, in the Mahāyāna tradition, for distinguishing between two modes of delusion-free cognition. For example, *Compendium of Mahāyāna*, attributed to the Yogācārin monk Asaṅga (4th century), distinguishes between subsequent nonimaginative cognition (Skt. *pṛṣṭhalabdhanirvikalpakajñāna*) and fundamental nonimaginative cognition (Skt. *mūlanirvikalpakajñāna*). The former allows bodhisattvas to engage in teaching, involves concepts, and is akin to space. The latter is inexpressible, does not involve concepts, and is akin to the appearance of forms in space.[43]

Fazang endorses a similar distinction in his *Commentary on Awakening Mahāyāna Faith*.[44] He accepts that, in some sense, correct cognition of *dharmas* is nonconceptual. For Fazang, perception provides cognition of kind-specifying characteristics, and those who perceive these characteristics without the mediation of concepts—those who cognize *dharmas* only under the name true suchness (Ch. *zhēn rú* 真如), without attaching names to the characteristics or analyzing what puts them into action—experience the realm of Mañjuśrī (Ch. *Wénshū* 文殊), bodhisattva of wisdom. Those who experience this realm—the Buddha, for example—manage to drink water rather than poison, eat plants rather than rocks, and successfully navigate amid other such differences. Perception of this sort does not require conceptual cognition. The reason is that perceiving differences requires neither naming them nor explaining them. Because this cognition is nonconceptual, it is free of ignorance and attachment.

Experiencing the realm of Mañjuśrī is an achievement valuable for its difficulty and rarity. Perhaps such experiences are available during moments of being "in the zone"—while absorbed in gardening, driving familiar and relatively empty roads, playing games with friends. Even these experiences are fleeting and unintentional. They are also relatively rare. A goal of Buddhist practice is to make such experience available with greater ease and longer duration.

More typical is experience laden with conceptual cognition. This kind of experience wonders why things happen, who is responsible for harms, how to achieve goals, and so on. This involves attaching names to things. It also, and more importantly, involves searching for causes. Attaching names to things and locating causes involves conceptual cognition. Here ignorance and attachment induce error. Error, in turn, induces experience in the mode of *saṃsāra* (Ch. *lúnhuí* 輪廻), experience laden with *duḥkha* (Ch. *kǔ* 苦).

---

[43] See Keenan 2003, 95; Spackman 2020, 69–70.
[44] See T44.1846.280c12-20; Vorenkamp 2004, 288–9; Jorgensen et al. 2019, 122.

104 METAPHORS FOR INTERDEPENDENCE

5.6.3. The Realm of Samantabhadra

Fazang maintains that conceptual cognition of *dharmas* need not induce error. For Fazang, those who achieve conceptual cognition without ignorance or attachment experience the realm of Samantabhadra (Ch. *Pǔxián jìngjiè* 普賢境界), bodhisattva of meditation and practice.[45] An example of a barren tree helps to explain the difference between experiencing the realm of Samantabhadra and experiencing the realms of Mañjuśrī and *saṃsāra*.[46] Perceiving the barren tree is experiencing the tree in the realm of Mañjuśrī. Correctly conceptualizing the tree as a barren tree is experiencing the tree in the realm of Samantabhadra. Incorrectly conceptualizing the same tree as a demon is experiencing the tree in the realm of *saṃsāra*. (For the incorrect conceptualization, imagine the tree in dim light, casting shadows that flicker as though the tree is alive.)

Fazang's doctrines of mutual identity and mutual inclusion are, in effect, contentions about how *dharmas* are cognized in the realm of Samantabhadra.[47] Fazang contends that anyone who conceptualizes the realm of *dharmas* without ignorance or attachment does so in accordance with the following six constraints.

1. Conceptualize *dharmas* as inseparable from their kind-specifying characteristics, and conceptualize these characteristics as determinate.
2. Conceptualize *dharmas* as dynamic activities, and conceptualize this activity as a matter of power causing *dharmas* to enact their kind-specifying characteristics.
3. Conceptualize *dharmas* as empty by virtue of lacking power to enact their own kind-specifying characteristics.
4. Use attentional focus to select *dharmas* of one kind as chief, and conceptualize all *dharmas* of this kind as having power to enact the kind-specifying characteristics of all *dharmas* of all other kinds—while conceptualizing all of these other *dharmas* as completely lacking power.

---

[45] Samantabhadra and Mañjuśrī are central characters in the *Flower Adornment Sūtra*. In the final chapter, both accompany the pilgrim Sudhana as he begins his journey. According to Fazang, Mañjuśrī is responsible for sending Sudhana on his journey, and Samantabhadra gives Sudhana a vision that allows him to complete the journey (Lin 2021, 40–1, citing T35.1733.451a9-15).

[46] Fazang uses the example of the barren tree to illustrate his theory of three natures (Skt. *tri-svabhāva*; Ch. *sān xìng* 三性). He associates the realm of Mañjuśrī with the perfect nature (Skt. *pariniṣpanna-svabhāva*; Ch. *zhēnshí xìng* 真實性) of *dharmas*, the realm of Samantabhadra with the other-dependent nature (Skt. *paratantra-svabhāva*; Ch. *yītā xìng* 依他性) of *dharmas*, and the realm of *saṃsāra* with the imaginary nature (Skt. *parikalpita-svabhāva*; Ch. *fēnbié xìng* 分別性) of *dharmas*. See T45.1866.499a11-501c28; Cook 1970, 404–43; Unno et al. 2023, 154–71. For further discussion of Fazang's theory of three natures, see Liu 1982b. For Fazang's tree example, see T45.1866.499b27-8.

[47] See T45.1866.503a19.

ATTENTING TO ASPECTS   105

5. Shift attentional focus to select *dharmas* of some other kind as chief, and conceptualize all *dharmas* of this kind as having power to enact the kind-specifying characteristics of all *dharmas* of all other kinds—while conceptualizing all of these other *dharmas* as completely lacking power.
6. Repeat the shifting of attentional focus for every kind of *dharma*.

Cognition of kind-specifying characteristics is given through perception. But various errors arise when this cognition becomes conceptual.

Some errors concern the basic categories Fazang uses to conceptualize *dharmas*. Conceptualizing *dharmas* as separate from their kind-specifying characteristics induces the error that *dharmas* might persist through change. Conceptualizing these characteristics without uniting them with power induces the error that *dharmas* arise and cease spontaneously (or not at all)—with nothing causing them to enact their kind-specifying characteristics. Conceptualizing *dharmas* as having power to enact their own kind-specifying characteristics induces the error that *dharmas* are real existents. (The models in Figures 4.2a and 4.4—from Chapter 4—commit this error.)

Other errors arise from the way Fazang conceptualizes *dharmas* in relation to each other. Conceptualizing *dharmas* without grading some as chief and others as attendant induces the error that having power does not suffice for causing the enactment of kind-specifying characteristics. (The model in Figure 4.2b—from Chapter 4—commits this error.) Conceptualizing all *dharmas* as chief, or conceptualizing some as simultaneously chief and attendant, induces the error that *dharmas* have multiple sufficient causes. (The model in Figure 4.3—from Chapter 4—commits this error.) Conceptualizing *dharmas* without shifting attention induces the error that some *dharmas* arise and cease spontaneously. Conceptualizing *dharmas* without shifting attention for each kind of *dharma* induces attachment to some *dharmas* as privileged and thereby induces the erroneous view that some are fundamental in a way that others are not.

Taken together, conceptualizing the realm of *dharmas* in accordance with all six constraints avoids the preceding errors and yields a conception of *dharmas* as mutually inclusive and mutually identical.

5.6.4. Accessing the Realms

In *Treatise on the Five Teachings of Huayan*, Fazang explains that whereas experiencing the realm of Mañjuśrī is accessible as the result of cognizing *dharmas* as true suchness, experiencing the realm of Samantabhadra is accessible as the cause of that result.

Perfectly interpenetrating and free, one is identical with all and all are identical with one. But their characteristics are inexpressible. In the *Flower Adornment Sūtra*, this is the interpenetrating meaning of the final result: the ocean of lands [of the Buddhas] on the one hand, and the substance of the ten Buddhas on the other—not to mention Indra's net.... These are inexpressible.... *Treatise on the Ten Stages* says, "Causes are expressible, the result is inexpressible." This is the meaning here.[48]

For Fazang, experiencing the realm of Samantabhadra is the cause of experiencing the realm of Mañjuśrī. The reason is that conceptualizing differences and relations among *dharmas* while free from delusion—cognizing *dharmas* as mutually identical and mutually inclusive—is a vehicle for entering into cognizing *dharmas* as true suchness.

Fazang does not explain his reasoning. A likely explanation is that there is an obstacle to cognizing *dharmas* as true suchness, and conceptualizing *dharmas* as mutually identical and mutually inclusive overcomes this obstacle. Although Fazang does not say what this obstacle is, a likely candidate is available.

Consider the presumption that *dharmas* have or lack power apart from the conceptualizing activity of some mind—that every *dharma* is put into action either by itself, by another, by itself and another, or by neither itself nor another. Mahāyāna traditions teach that all four options are problematic.[49] They are problematic, in part, because perceptions of *dharmas* as true suchness—experiences in the realm of Mañjuśrī—cognize the activities of *dharmas* but do not cognize anything putting *dharmas* into action (or failing to do so). If relations whereby *dharmas* put into action, or fail to put into action, other *dharmas* are inseparable from the conceptualizing activities of mind, then the presumption that *dharmas* have or lack power apart from the conceptualizing activity of some mind is an obstacle to cognizing *dharmas* as true suchness. It is also an obstacle that Fazang's doctrines of mutual identity and mutual inclusion are designed to overcome—provided, of course, that these doctrines are interpreted in accordance with the alternative interpretation rather than the standard one.

On the alternative interpretation of Fazang's doctrines, conceptualizing *dharmas* as mutually identical and mutually inclusive involves conceptualizing *dharmas* as having or lacking power only insofar as they are graded, respectively,

---

[48] T45.1866.503a20-5. For alternative translations, see Cook 1970, 468–9; Unno et al. 2023, 178. The ten Buddhas (Ch. *shí fú* 十佛) are, presumably, the ten kinds of body (Ch. *shēn* 身) accessible to bodhisattvas in the realm of Mañjuśrī, namely, the bodies of sentient beings, lands, karmic reward, *śrāvakas, pratyekabuddhas, bodhisattvas, tathāgatas,* knowledge, reality, and space. According to Jin 2009, the ten Buddhas are an expedient for expressing the doctrine of perfect interpenetration. For a review of Fazang's explanation of the ten bodies, see Lin 2021, 32–9.

[49] See Gold 2007, 144–5; Westerhoff 2009, 99–112; Westerhoff 2018, 110–1.

as chief or attendant. Because grading *dharmas* as chief or attendant is an activity of conceptualizing mind, *dharmas* neither have nor lack power apart from the conceptualizing activity of some mind. Conceptualizing the having or lacking of power as dependent upon the conceptualizing activity of mind thereby undermines the presumption that power belongs to *dharmas* as true suchness. It does not, of course, undermine other delusions. For example, one might privilege some *dharmas* as always chief, never attendant. This supports cognizing some *dharmas* as real existents. Or one might conceptualize all *dharmas* as simultaneously chief and attendant. This supports cognizing *dharmas* as competing with each other to put attendants into action.

Insofar as conceptualizing *dharmas* without delusion requires conceptualizing them as mutually identical and mutually inclusive, one should endorse the following presumption: chief and attendant are mutually dependent. This presumption enshrines an approach to chief and attendant as harmoniously related. Insofar as the conceptualizing mind shifts attention among grading one as chief and others as attendants, the presumption entails that all *dharmas* are interdependent.[50] This entails, in turn, that all *dharmas* are mutually identical and mutually inclusive.

For the sake of illustrating Fazang's view about the relation between the realm of Mañjuśrī and the realm of Samantabhadra, consider once more the example of four playing cards leaning against each other. Perception provides cognition of the setup. The (nonconceptual) content of this cognition is given in the uninterpreted image from Figure 4.1 (in Chapter 4). Perception does not cognize the setup as an arrangement of four cards, each with a different marking, each standing, each leaning against another. This cognition requires conceptualizing some perceptual content as standing cards, discriminating some cards as different from others, naming the different cards—Ace (A), King (K), Queen (Q), Jack (J)—and conceptualizing specific cards as leaning against certain others. Perception also does not provide cognition of the causes for standing. The reason is that several competing cognitions about the causes for standing are available. (See Figures 4.2a, 4.2b, 4.3, 4.4 from Chapter 4, as well as Figures 5.4 and 5.5 from this chapter, for examples.) Because multiple competitors are consistent with the

---

[50] Chengguan 澄觀 (738–839), another influential monk from the Huayan tradition, seems to derive interdependence among *dharmas* from the relation between *dharmas* and principle (see Gregory 1993, 212–3). Priest explicitly endorses this kind of reasoning (Priest 2022, 112). For Fazang, there is good reason to resist any such derivation. If the relation between principle and *dharmas* entails that *dharmas* are interdependent, then *dharmas* in the realm of *saṃsāra*—that is, *dharmas* that manifest as delusional conceptualizations of principle—are interdependent. Yet, for Fazang, those who cognize the realm of *saṃsāra* conceptualize *dharmas* as independent of others. This is consistent with also conceptualizing *dharmas* as manifestations of principle. The likely lesson of this is that, whatever the relation between principle and the realm of *dharmas*, the relevance of that relation to interdependence among *dharmas* is a function of how the mind conceptualizes principle.

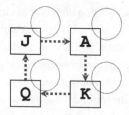

Figure 5.6 Names and Relations for Playing Cards
Image created by the author.

setup given in perception, deciding among these competitors requires inference and argumentation. This is a matter for conceptual cognition.

Figure 5.6 depicts the information available about the image from Figure 4.1 (of Chapter 4) after conceptualizing activity assigns names and relations.

Because the cards in Figure 4.1 have letters on them, the squares in Figure 5.6 contain letters. These letters represent names for the cards, and each card has a different (and determinate!) name. The squares represent that the cards are standing. Because standing is either caused or not, each square in Figure 5.6 is associated with a circle. The circles are empty because assigning names and relations to the cards does not determine what puts into action the standing of the cards.

Given the conceptualization in Figure 5.6, different conditions for causal power support different inferences about the causes for each card's standing. Each condition has the form: for any cards x and y, y has power to cause x to stand if and only if Φ (pronounced 'phi'). Table 5.5 lists several such conditions, the view about the cards associated with each condition, and the figure (from this chapter or Chapter 4) that depicts each such conclusion.

Because the image in Figure 4.1 depicts standing cards and leaning relations even when those relations are not conceptualized, the conditions (from Table 5.5) for Figures 4.2a, 4.2b, 4.3, and 4.4 support the presumption that the playing cards have or lack power apart from the conceptualizing activity of mind. Because being a chief is a gradation imposed by conceptualizing mind, the condition for Figure 5.4 undermines this presumption. This is, incidentally, the reason why the empty circles in Figure 5.4 are a feature, not a bug. Each model in Figure 5.4 contains an empty circle. Every empty circle from Figure 5.4 appears as an empty circle in Figure 5.6. So the models in Figure 5.4 point the way, as it were, toward the model in Figure 5.6. They indicate that there is no putting into action apart from the conceptualizing activity of mind. They also indicate that correctly conceptualizing causality requires shifting attentional focus. Calming the mind, letting it rest from its conceptualizing activity,

Table 5.5 Potential Conditions for Playing Card Causality

condition Φ	for cards with	depicted in
y = x	real existence	Figure 4.2a
x leans on y	partial power	Figure 4.2b
y ≠ x and x belongs to the transitive closure of leaning relations for y	simultaneous partial power	Figure 4.3
x belongs to the transitive closure of leaning relations for y	simultaneous total power	Figure 4.4 / Figure 5.5
y is chief, y ≠ x, and x belongs to the transitive closure of leaning relations for y	sequential total power	Figure 5.4

requires emptying all of the circles—extending the emptiness of one circle from one model in Figure 5.4 to the entirety of the setup. This is the sense in which experiencing the realm of Samantabhadra is the cause for experiencing the realm of Mañjuśrī.

For Fazang, those who experience the realm of Samantabhadra cognize *dharmas* as different and yet also interdependent. *Dharmas* are different by virtue of having different characteristics. They are interdependent by virtue of each being selectable as chief and chiefs including their attendants. This is why Fazang characterizes the realm of *dharmas*, experienced in the realm of Samantabhadra, as the *dharma*-realm of dependent arising (Skt. *dharmadhātu-pratītyasamutpāda*; Ch. *fǎjiè yuánqǐ* 法界緣起).

Dharmas in the realm of Samantabhadra are cognized as distinct by virtue of differing in their specific characteristics. They are cognized as interdependent by virtue of their mutual identity and mutual inclusion. Cognition of interdependence amid distinctness is free from delusion because cognizing mutual relationality among *dharmas* is a matter of shifting attentional focus among correlated aspects of *dharmas*.[51]

---

[51] Fazang's strategy for forestalling conceptual delusion is akin to a strategy that Zhuangzi 莊子 (3rd century BCE) recommends for avoiding attachment to particular ways of speaking or behaving (Ch. *dào* 道). Zhuangzi recommends surveying ways of speaking and behaving from an axis of those ways (Ch. *dào shū* 道樞). This axis is akin to the axis of a spoked wheel. Zhuangzi's idea is that shifting attention to the axis fosters detachment from any particular way of speaking or behaving (see Haiming 2011). Rather than shifting attention from a particular way of speaking and behaving to an axis of those ways, Fazang's strategy involves shifting attention among different aspects of *dharmas*. This is akin to sequentially touching the many spokes of a spoked wheel.

6

Indra's Net

6.1. Modeling with Metaphor

The realm of Samantabhadra (Ch. *Pǔxián jìngjiè* 普賢境界), or the *dharma*-realm of dependent arising (Skt. *dharmadhātu-pratītyasamutpāda*; Ch. *fǎjiè yuánqǐ* 法界緣起), is a realm wherein *dharmas* appear as distinct and yet interdependent, each identical with and included within all others. Fazang's agenda, in the closing sections of *Treatise on the Five Teachings of Huayan*, is to articulate a way for the mind to experience this realm. For Fazang, this means explaining how the mind should cognize *dharmas*, through the mediation of concepts, without succumbing to ignorance or attachment. Some of Fazang's efforts are technical, directed toward explaining what it means to conceptualize *dharmas* as mutually identical and mutually inclusive. Fazang's more accessible efforts, by contrast, are illustrative. These efforts use metaphors to model the *dharma*-realm of dependent arising (as Fazang views it). This modeling is directed toward making vivid Fazang's approach to conceptualizing *dharmas* as mutually identical and mutually inclusive.

This chapter examines Fazang's metaphor of Indra's net. The chapter divides into five parts. The first part introduces Fazang's metaphor. The second examines the metaphor of Indra's net as it appears in the *Flower Adornment Sūtra*, and it explains why this metaphor is superior to alternative metaphors for modeling mutual relationality. The third part of the chapter reviews competing interpretations of Fazang's metaphor. The fourth provides extensive and detailed analyses of how Fazang's predecessors interpret the metaphor. The chapter concludes by using these precedents to explain how Fazang interprets the metaphor, and by explaining how Fazang's interpretation illustrates his views about mutual identity and mutual inclusion.

6.2. Indra's Net

The metaphor of Indra's net likens the *dharma*-realm of dependent arising to a lattice-like array of mirror-like jewels or pearls.

Metaphors for Interdependence. Nicholaos Jones, Oxford University Press. © Nicholaos Jones 2025.
DOI: 10.1093/9780197807224.003.0006

Figure 6.1 Glimpsing Indra's Net
Image created by Holly Jones. Used with permission.

It is like Indra's palace covered by a net of precious pearls. The pearls, because they are bright, penetrate each other in manifesting their reflections. The manifestations of these reflections are reflections that can manifest further reflections. In this way, the manifold is inexhaustible.[1]

Each jewel (pearl) of Indra's net hosts reflections of all others. (See Figure 6.1.)

Because each jewel hosts a subtly different mass of reflections, the jewels differ from each other. These differences model the specific characteristics that mark *dharmas* into different kinds. Because the jewels reflect each other, any mark added to one jewel manifests in the reflections hosted by all other jewels. This relationality models the emptiness of *dharmas*—their indeterminacy with respect to power. Because the reflections in any one jewel arise in dependence upon all other jewels, the array of jewels exhibits thoroughgoing interdependence. This interdependence models the mutual identity (Ch. *xiāng jí* 相即) and mutual inclusion (Ch. *xiāng rù* 相入) of *dharmas*.

---

[1] T45.1871.594c3-5. Worth noting is that Fazang's description for Indra's net closely resembles the description that Wonhyo (617–686) provides. Wonhyo's description also appears in writings by the monks Chengguan 澄觀 (738–839) and Juryō 壽靈 (fl. 757–791). See Plassen 2020, 45.

112 METAPHORS FOR INTERDEPENDENCE

Fazang uses the metaphor of Indra's net to explain how *dharmas* in the realm of Samantabhadra are identical with and included within each other. Consider, for example, his brief remarks about the metaphor in *Treatise on the Five Teachings of Huayan*.

> Perceive [Indra's net] in accordance with wisdom. Select one as chief, and the others are attendants. Insofar as the chief is central, the others surround it as followers. All thereby realize unhindered freedom. . . . Returning to the prior categories of free and unhindered mutual identity and mutual inclusion, know that each takes in every *dharma* of the boundless *dharma*-realm, forming Indra's net.[2]

These remarks highlight several challenges for understanding Fazang's analysis and interpretation of Indra's net. First, why does Fazang use the metaphor of Indra's net to model the *dharma*-realm of dependent arising? Second, how exactly do reflective relations among the jewels of Indra's net model relations of identity and inclusion among *dharmas*? When one jewel hosts the reflections of many other jewels, does Fazang intend this to model one being identical with and included within many others, or does he intend it to model many others being identical with and included within one? Finally, and relatedly, when a jewel acts as chief to others, is it chief by virtue of being the object that is reflected in others, or is it chief by virtue of manifesting reflections of those others?

This chapter provides answers to these questions. The answers, in brief, are as follows: Fazang uses the metaphor of Indra's net because the metaphor appears in the *Flower Adornment Sūtra* and because its model for mutual relationality lacks the limitations of other models from prior Buddhist tradition. One jewel hosting the reflections of many other jewels models *dharmas* of many kinds being identical with and included within *dharmas* of one kind. One jewel acting as chief to others is chief by virtue of manifesting reflections of those others. Subsequent sections of the chapter substantiate these answers.

6.3. Modeling the Realm of Samantabhadra

Fazang uses the metaphor of Indra's net because it appears in the *Flower Adornment Sūtra*. This scripture teaches the mutual identity and mutual

---

[2] T45.1866.506b5-10. For alternative translations, see Cook 1970, 512; Unno et al. 2023, 194. I return to Fazang's conception of jewels (and *dharmas*) as free and unhindered in Chapter 9.4.4.

inclusion of all *dharmas*. But the metaphor is far from a central feature of the *Flower Adornment Sūtra*, appearing only briefly and in passing. So why raise it to prominence? Fazang does not say. A likely reason is that Indra's net is suited to conceptualizing mutuality among *dharmas* in ways that other models are not.

6.3.1. The Father-Son Model

Consider, for the sake of contrast with Indra's net, a model for conceptualizing mutual identity from *Commentary on the Great Perfection of Wisdom*. The model illustrates mutual identity between fathers and sons (Skt. *pitā-putra*; Ch. *fù zǐ* 父子). The context is explaining how the emptiness of *dharmas* is consistent with *dharmas* differing in their specific characteristics.

> Causes and conditions are also empty, because they are indeterminate. Consider, for example, fathers and sons. Because [the son] is born from the father, he is called son. Because the father gives birth [to the son], he is called father.[3]

The specific characteristic of a (biological) father is being the male parent to a child. Fathers lack power to make themselves parents. But when a man has a son, the son makes the man a parent. Hence, fathers of sons are identical with their sons. Similarly, the specific characteristic of a (biological) son is being the male child of their parents. Sons lack power to make themselves sons. But when a male child has a father, the father makes the child a son. Hence, sons are identical with their fathers. Because anything that is identical with another lacks independence, fathers and sons are empty despite differing in their specific characteristics.

The father-son example, as a model of *dharmas* that are empty despite differing in their specific characteristics, seems to be limited in two respects. The example seems to be limited in depth because it depends upon a particular conception of (biological) fathers and sons. Suppose, for example, that being a father and being a son are accidents or descriptions of substances (or persons).[4] Then the mutual identity of fathers and their sons is consistent with the substance of a father or a son having power to enact its own specific characteristic.

---

[3] T25.1509.290a10-2. For an alternative translation, see Chödrön 2001, 1717.

[4] Cohen attributes a similar view to Aristotle, whereby "Socrates the man is a substance, but Socrates the father is not" (Cohen 2013, 238).

114   METAPHORS FOR INTERDEPENDENCE

For example, father and son might be mutually dependent in definition or formula and yet independent in substance.[5]

As a model for the kind of thoroughgoing mutual identity that Fazang ascribes to *dharmas* in the realm of Samantabhadra, the father-son example also seems to be limited in breadth. Even if fathers and their sons are mutually identical despite being empty, nothing in the model relates fathers and sons to neighbors or distant strangers. So the example is consistent with denying that father and sons are identical with all others.

Proper attention to the relation between *dharmas* and their specific characteristics suffices to resolve the apparent limitation in depth. Indian philosophical traditions identify three models for this relation. (See Table 6.1.) The first conceptualizes *dharmas* as substances (Skt. *dharmin*).[6] This model separates the specific characteristics of *dharmas* from their substance. A paradigmatic illustration of this model involves conceptualizing matter as separable from particular forms, so that different forms are capable of inhering in the same matter and the same matter is capable of participating in different forms.

All Buddhist traditions agree that conceptualizing *dharmas* as substances is delusional. The reason is that (conditioned) *dharmas* are ephemeral but substances are not. Because *dharmas* are ephemeral, there is no way for one and the same *dharma* to persist through a change in its specific characteristic. For this reason, Buddhist traditions conceptualize *dharmas* as insubstantial. This conception raises the issue of what it is for a *dharma* to have, or instantiate, a specific characteristic. If *dharmas* are inseparable from their specific characteristics, they are not ontologically prior to their characteristics and so those characteristics do not inhere in *dharmas* in the way that properties inhere in substances. Buddhist traditions typically resolve this issue by conceptualizing *dharmas* as dynamic activities rather than static substrates. Because specific characteristics ground the effects that *dharmas* project, the inseparability of *dharmas* and their specific characteristics guarantees that the projecting of effects is inseparable from *dharmas*. Because projecting effects is characteristic of and inseparable from *dharmas*, *dharmas* are more akin to subjectless dispositions than substantial substrates.

Scholastic Buddhist traditions offer two models for conceptualizing *dharmas* as inseparable from their specific characteristics. The first model, prominent in Abhidharmikan traditions, conceptualizes *dharmas* as real. For Fazang,

---

[5] Westerhoff identifies a similar limitation for the example: "the 'mutual dependence' of father and son that Nāgārjuna postulates is based on two different dependence relations, the son depending existentially on the father, the father notionally on the son" (Westerhoff 2009, 27–8).

[6] For an analysis that conceptualizes *dharmas* as substances, see Hota 1998-9.

INDRA'S NET   115

Table 6.1 Models for Conceptualizing *Dharmas*

dharmas as real and substantial	*dharmas* are separable from their specific characteristics	
dharmas as real and insubstantial	*dharmas* are inseparable from their specific characteristics	specific characteristics and powers are determinate
dharmas as nominal and insubstantial	*dharmas* are inseparable from their specific characteristics	specific characteristics or powers are indeterminate

this means conceptualizing *dharmas* as determinate with respect to both specific characteristics and power.[7] The second model, prominent in Mahāyāna traditions, conceptualizes *dharmas* as nominal. For Fazang, this means conceptualizing *dharmas* as indeterminate with respect to either specific characteristics or power.

Because fathers and sons are mutually identical only if both are empty, only the Mahāyāna model—the model of *dharmas* as inseparable from their specific characteristics and indeterminate with respect to specific characteristics or powers—accommodates the mutual identity of fathers and sons. Because this model avoids the temptation to conceptualize fathers and their sons as mutually dependent in definition or formula but independent in substance, it resolves the apparent limitation of depth for the father-son example in *Commentary on the Great Perfection of Wisdom*, and it does so while preserving the intended interpretation of that example.

The apparent limitation of breadth for the father-son example in *Commentary on the Great Perfection of Wisdom* is more severe than the apparent limitation of depth. Even if being a father is a matter of enacting the role of father in relation to another, someone might enact that role without bearing any particular relation to neighbors or strangers.[8] Hence, even if the example successfully illustrates how the emptiness of *dharmas* is consistent with *dharmas* differing in their specific characteristics, it does not illustrate how all *dharmas* are identical with each other. For the same reason, even if the mutual identity of distinct *dharmas* entails their mutual inclusion (as it

---

[7] For a contemporary analysis of *dharmas* as insubstantial but entirely determinate, see the first chapter in Karunadasa 2019.

[8] Hopkins makes the same point with a different example: "A calf depends on its causes, cow and bull, etc., and the cow and bull as parents depend on their calf though they were not born from the calf. Still, a calf and a pony are not dependent on each other" (Hopkins 1996, 434).

116 METAPHORS FOR INTERDEPENDENCE

does in Fazang's conceptual framework), the example does not illustrate how each empty *dharma* includes all other *dharmas*.

6.3.2. The Meaning of Indra's Net

Illustrating the thoroughgoing interdependence of *dharmas* requires an example other than the father-son example from *Commentary on the Great Perfection of Wisdom*. The *Flower Adornment Sūtra* offers, as a candidate example, the net of Indra.

> [All Buddhas] know that all dharmas without exception arise from conditions. They know all the different world systems without exception. They know all the different phenomena without exception throughout the entire Dharma realm are like the net of Indra.[9]

Two aspects of this passage are noteworthy. The first concerns the symbolic meaning of Indra and his net. The second concerns the basis for associating Indra's net with the thoroughgoing mutual identity and mutual inclusion of *dharmas* in the realm of Samantabhadra.

Consider, first, the symbolic meaning of Indra and his net. Indra—known also by the names Inda (Pāli), Śakra (Sanskrit), and Sakka (Pāli)—is the leading divinity of the early Vedic tradition. The oldest of the Vedic religious scriptures, the *Ṛg Veda*, characterizes Indra as

> He under whose supreme control are horses, all chariots, and the villages and cattle; He who gave being to the sun and morning, who leads the water. . . .[10]

The Vedas trace Indra's sovereign power to his net. For example, *Śvetāśvatara Upaniṣad* 3.1 identifies Indra as "He who, with His net, rules alone by means of his sovereign powers."[11]

The story of Indra and Vritra, from *Ṛg Veda* 1.32, elaborates upon the relation between Indra's instrument of power and his sovereignty.[12] Vritra wears three faces, appearing as a dragon who hoards the waters, a snake who steals the rain clouds, and a demon who hides away the sunlight. He is, in effect, a personification of drought or, perhaps, thick ice—in either case, a formidable force, especially for those who need fresh water to flourish. Indra confronts Vritra

---

[9] T10.279.248c14-6, recited in Dharmamitra 2022, 2: 1240. See also Cleary 1993, 925.
[10] *Ṛg Veda* 2.12.7, recited in Griffith 1889, 351.
[11] See Goudriaan 1978, 215.
[12] See Griffith 1889, 56–9.

because Vritra is hoarding, within his cavern, all the rain clouds, river waters, and sun. Barren of moisture and light, the world has become inhospitable to all living things. Filling his belly with divine nectar (Skt. *soma*), taking into his hand the diamond-like—and so, indestructible—Vajrā (thunderbolt), and riding his golden chariot, Indra leads his army to Vritra's fortress. Battle ensues. Indra emerges victorious, destroying Vritra with the might of his irresistible weapon, releasing the waters and sunlight from their bondage. Indra thereby ascends as the sovereign ruler of the world, assigning to the world's constituents their roles and powers. *Artha Veda* 8.8 subsequently attributes Indra's victory to his powers of deception, alters his weapon from a thunderbolt to a net, and associates this net with magical deception (Skt. *māyā*).[13]

Indian Buddhist traditions invest Indra with a similar role. Consider, for example, the Story of the Nest.[14] Indra, under the name Śakra, banishes the spirits of darkness (Skt. *asuras*) from Mount Sumeru into the ocean. The spirits vow to reclaim their residence in the heavens. Indra, with weapon in hand, battles the spirits of darkness at the border of ocean and land. His army retreats against the onslaught of the spirits. But Indra persists. On the brink of victory, he notices that his offensive efforts are destroying trees that shelter the hatchlings of eagles (Skt. *garuḍa*). Moved by compassion, and risking defeat by exposing himself to the enemy, Indra halts his chariot, offering his life as a sacrifice to preserve the eagles. This disorients his enemy. Thinking Indra's halt signals the impending return of a strengthened army, the spirits flee in terror. Indra thereby secures victory through his compassionate protection.

The Story of the Nest closely resembles the Vedic story of Indra and Vritri. The key difference is that Indra wins through compassionate protection rather than competitive violence. This difference, moreover, invests Indra's net with a different meaning. Several Buddhist scriptures explain the basis for Indra's compassion. For example, *Sūtra on Sakka's Questions* narrates Indra's audience with the Buddha, whereupon Indra learns that release from *saṃsāra* is won by relinquishing clinging (Skt. *upādāna*) rather than battling demonic forces.[15] Similarly, *Sūtra on Four Great Kings* and its sequel depict Indra's transformation from one who is as ensnared in *saṃsāra* and awash in *duḥkha* to one who, despite lacking meditative development, excels in meritorious actions such as giving and virtuous behavior.[16]

According to standard Buddhist teaching, gaining freedom from *saṃsāra* and *duḥkha* requires abandoning delusion in favor of correct view. *Sūtra on the*

---

[13] See Griffith 1896, 343–5.
[14] See Fausböll 1880, 284–7.
[15] See SN 35.118; Bodhi 2000, 1192–3.
[16] See AN 3.37-8, 8.36; Bodhi 2012, 238–9, 1171.

118 METAPHORS FOR INTERDEPENDENCE

Supreme Net, moreover, presents itself as a Supreme Net that embraces all views and, in so embracing them, facilitates proper discernment of correct view.[17] Insofar as Indra's net is a net of this sort, it is not an instrument of magical deception. Instead, in the Buddhist tradition, Indra's net is an instrument that penetrates through delusion to reveal the truth that fosters *nirvāṇa*.

6.3.3. The Aptness of Indra's Net

Consider, next, the basis for associating Indra's net with the thoroughgoing mutual identity and mutual inclusion of *dharmas* in the realm of Samantabhadra. Indra's net is an instrument for revealing truth. Because the truth, in the realm of Samantabhadra, is that all *dharmas* are mutually identical and mutually inclusive, Indra's net is an apt metaphor for illustrating mutual identity and mutual inclusion. Chinese characters for the terms *Indra's net* and *dharma* reinforce the aptness of this metaphor.

Consider, first, two Chinese names for Indra's net. One name, *dì wǎng* 帝網—literally, emperor's net—reinforces the connection between Indra's net and the Supreme Net from *Sūtra on the Supreme Net*. A more specific name, *yīntuóluó wǎng* 因陀羅網—literally, net of the cause that collects everything together—reinforces the connection between Indra's net and the realm of Samantabhadra, a realm within which the mind collects *dharmas* together, without delusion, as mutually identical and mutually inclusive. Indra's coming to be known as Samantabhadra, when the bodhisattva ideal gains influence within the Mahāyāna tradition, further reinforces this connection.[18]

Consider, next, Chinese terminology for *dharmas*, the metaphorical referents for the jewels of Indra's net. The Chinese character for *dharma* is *fǎ* 法. The terms *dharma* and *fǎ* 法 have many similarities in meaning.[19] But the character 法 is especially noteworthy. The left-hand particle of the character is *shuǐ* 水, which denotes a body of water such as a river. The right-hand particle is *qù* 去, which denotes going forth and, in more ancient sources, a beast able to discern truth and eliminate falsity.[20] So the Chinese character for *dharma* connotes *water going forth to reveal the truth*. Indra, according to Vedic legend, is precisely the cause responsible for water flowing forth upon the world. Moreover, after his Buddhist appropriation, Indra also assumes the role of protector of truth. So the notion of a realm of dependently arising *dharmas*—a realm of waters going forth to reveal the truth—affords a strong mythological affinity with Indra's net.

---

[17] See DN 1; Walshe 1995, 90.
[18] See Ho 2018, 150–1.
[19] Wut 2013.
[20] Wut 2013, 79.

The etymological connection between *dharmas* and flowing water also reinforces a tendency, among Chinese Buddhists, to imagine the jewels of Indra's net as mirror-like and to model thoroughgoing interdependence among *dharmas* as reciprocal reflections among these jewels. Shang 商 era oracle-bone inscriptions of the Chinese ideograph for *mirror, jiàn* 鑒, depict two eyes observing themselves while peering into a container of water.[21] Whence the composition of the character 鑒:

> The base of 鑒 is the metal radical; on top of it is the homophone 監, indicating a man lying down and looking into a sacrificial vessel, probably filled with water, and entailing self-scrutiny of a divinatory character.[22]

The Chinese etymology for *mirror* (Ch. *jìng* 鏡) thereby associates mirrors with water and careful examination.[23] Indra's net, according to Vedic legend, is precisely an instrument that liberates water. Moreover, according to Buddhist tradition, the liberating power of Indra's net derives from its role in penetrating delusion to reveal truth. Insofar as Indra's net just is a collection of jewels, those jewels thereby satisfy the conditions that Chinese etymology associates with being mirror-like. Insofar as each mirror, in a network of mirrors, reflects all others, Indra's net is apt for modeling the thoroughgoing mutual identity and mutual inclusion that Fazang ascribes to *dharmas* in the realm of Samantabhadra.

6.3.4. Vairocana's Tower

Although the *Flower Adornment Sūtra* offers the net of Indra as a model for the realm of Samantabhadra, it provides only minimal details for this model. There is a suggestion that relations among the many jewels of Indra's net are akin to relations of dependence among distinct *dharmas*. But the *Flower Adornment Sūtra* does not characterize the relations among the jewels of Indra's net, and it does not specify whether each jewel relates to all other jewels or, instead, only to some of those others. Hence, even if Indra's net is apt for modeling thoroughgoing interdependence among *dharmas* in the realm of Samantabhadra, using the net for this purpose seems to lack textual justification.

Perhaps aware of this difficulty, Fazang, in *Contemplations on Exhausting Delusion and Returning to the Source by Cultivating the Mysteries of Huayan*, likens Indra's net to a different metaphor from the *Flower Adornment Sūtra*.[24]

---

[21] Huang 1995, 76.
[22] Tanner 2018, 225–6.
[23] See also Hall 1935, 182–4.
[24] T45.1876.640c9-10; Cleary 1983, 168.

120 METAPHORS FOR INTERDEPENDENCE

This alternative metaphor justifies contemplating the jewels of Indra's net as mirror-like and relations among those jewels as reflections. It justifies modeling relations of dependence among *dharmas* as reflective relations among the jewels of Indra's net. It also justifies contemplating these relations as thoroughly pervasive, so that each jewel manifests reflections of every other.

The final chapter of the *Flower Adornment Sūtra* introduces Sudhana, a young boy who undertakes a quest for *nirvāṇa*.[25] Nearing the end of his quest, Sudhana encounters Maitreya (Ch. *Mílè* 彌勒 or 弥勒), a bodhisattva destined to become the next Buddha. Sudhana petitions Maitreya for access to a palatial tower containing the adornments of Vairocana.[26] (Vairocana is the *dharmakāya*, the inconceivable reality of which Gautama Buddha is a manifestation.) Maitreya grants the petition. Upon entering Vairocana's tower, Sudhana sees that

> the interior of the palace was as measurelessly vast as empty space. [He saw that] there were *asaṃkhyeyas* of jewels that formed its grounds and there were *asaṃkhyeyas* of palaces, *asaṃkhyeyas* of gateways, *asaṃkhyeyas* of windows, . . . *asaṃkhyeyas* of necklaces strung with the many kinds of jewels, *asaṃkhyeyas* of necklaces made from real pearls, *asaṃkhyeyas* of necklaces made from red-colored real pearls, *asaṃkhyeyas* of lion-pearl necklaces that hung down in place after place. . . . There were countless *asaṃkhyeyas* of adornments such as these that beautified the place.
>
> He also saw within it countless hundreds of thousands of marvelous towers, each of which was adorned as just described. The adorned beauty of them all was as vast as space, yet somehow they did not interfere with each other. Sudhana saw all places in one place and saw all places in just this same way.[27]

The framing of Sudhana's encounter with Maitreya, as occurring near the end of his quest for *nirvāṇa*, indicates that Sudhana's vision purports to reveal truth rather than delusion. Sudhana's vision indicates, as well, that the truth is that each *dharma* depends upon every other. Vairocana's tower is one among countless others, and each tower is akin to a *dharma* (or kind of *dharma*) in the realm of Samantabhadra (or a jewel in Indra's net). Each tower, in Sudhana's vision, reflects—and is reflected by—every other. Because reflections between towers are akin to relations of dependence among *dharmas*, Sudhana's vision models *dharmas* as thoroughly interdependent.

---

[25] See T10.279.332a26-334a9; Cleary 1993, 1173–9; Dharmamitra 2022, 3: 1705–12.

[26] T10.279.434c29-435a1; Dharmamitra 2022, 3: 2208; Cleary 1993, 1489.

[27] T10.279.435a3-25, recited in Dharmamitra 2022, 3: 2209. See also Cleary 1993, 1489–90. Bhikshu Dharmamitra reports that the term "*asaṃkhyeya* (Ch. *āsēngzhǐ* 阿僧祇)" designates a number equal to 10^7.09884336127809E+031 (Dharmamitra 2022, 3: 2421).

Fazang conceptualizes the jewels of Indra's net as akin to the towers of Sudhana's vision.[28] This justifies using Indra's net as a model of thoroughgoing interdependence among *dharmas* in the realm of Samantabhadra. It does not justify Fazang's contention that *dharmas* in the realm of Samantabhadra act as both chief and as attendant, such that each is more fundamental than others when acting as chief but less fundamental than others when acting as attendant. For nothing in Sudhana's vision warrants conceptualizing any tower as more fundamental than any other. Fazang maintains, nonetheless, that it is possible to contemplate Indra's net in a way that illustrates his contention.

6.4. Contemplating Indra's Net

6.4.1. Fazang's Contemplation

In *Contemplations on Exhausting Delusion and Returning to the Source by Cultivating the Mysteries of Huayan*, Fazang offers some relatively elaborate remarks about contemplating Indra's net.

> The . . . contemplation of Indra's net is of chief and attendant manifesting each other. This means that one acting as chief views others acting as attendants; or perhaps one *dharma* acting as chief [views] all [other] *dharmas* acting as attendants; or perhaps one body acting as chief [views] all [other] bodies acting as attendants. So one *dharma*, selected as chief, receives [the other] attendants all together, one after the other without limit. This models the nature of *dharmas* as manifesting reflections one after another, each reality [including all others] within itself without limit, just as compassion and wisdom also multiply one after the other without limit.[29]

Fazang's remarks warrant a brief interpretive digression. It is natural to interpret Fazang as likening the jewels of Indra's net to individual *dharmas*. But Fazang's relations of identity and inclusion are relations among kinds of *dharmas*—and only derivatively relations among individual *dharmas*.[30] Moreover, "Classical Chinese nouns that refer to easily distinguishable and countable objects . . . can also divide their reference into kinds rather than individuals, given an appropriate

---

[28] It is natural to interpret the phrase "Indra's net" as a possessive that ascribes ownership for the array of jewels in the net to an individual named Indra. But the phrase might be an adjectival that individuates one net from other nets—in the way the phrase "Mount Huang (Ch. *Huángshān* 黃山)" individuates from other mountains the mountain named after the legendary emperor Huangdi 黃帝.

[29] T45.1876.640b27-c3. For an alternative translation, see Cleary 1983, 168.

[30] For the relevant analyses of identity and inclusion, refer to Chapter 3.5.3.

122 METAPHORS FOR INTERDEPENDENCE

context."[31] Hence, there is warrant for interpreting Fazang as speaking loosely but meaning to liken a single jewel to a kind of *dharma*. I endorse this interpretation in what follows—but I follow Fazang in speaking loosely. End digression.

In his remarks on Indra's net, Fazang grades each jewel of the net as chief and, alternatively, as attendant. Each jewel, acting as chief, hosts the reflections of all other jewels and thereby includes those others. By analogy, each *dharma*, acting as chief, includes all others—and so those others are identical with that *dharma*. Each jewel, acting as attendant, is also an object reflected in all other jewels and thereby is included within those others. By analogy, each *dharma*, acting as attendant, is included within—and thereby also identical with—all other *dharmas*.

Fazang's contemplation models relations of identity and inclusion among *dharmas* in the realm of Samantabhadra as reflective relations among the jewels of Indra's net. Because identity and inclusion are specific kinds of dependence relation, Fazang's contemplation agrees with Sudhana's vision from the *Flower Adornment Sūtra*. Fazang's contemplation also models the fundamental aspects of each *dharma*. Contemplating jewels as chief models the aspects of *dharmas* whereby they exist and have power. Contemplating jewels as attendants models the aspects of *dharmas* whereby they are empty and lack power. This is consistent with Sudhana's vision. But the distinction between chief and attendant is absent from Sudhana's vision.

6.4.2. Competing Interpretations

Fazang's contemplation of Indra's net goes beyond the text of the *Flower Adornment Sūtra*. It adds to Sudhana's vision a distinction between chief and attendant. It uses this distinction to add a selection function whereby attentional focus shifts from one jewel to another. These additions justify using Indra's net to illustrate the contention that every *dharma* in the realm of Samantabhadra has distinct but correlated aspects. By using the reflections among jewels of Indra's net to model relations among *dharmas* in the realm of Samantabhadra, Fazang's contemplation also specifies that dependence relations among *dharmas* are relations of identity and inclusion. This justifies using Indra's net to model mutual identity and mutual inclusion among *dharmas* as mutual reflectivity among the jewels of Indra's net.

Other approaches to contemplating Indra's net are possible. Some contemplate Indra's net as illustrating a view known as metaphysical coherentism.[32] This is a view according to which everything depends upon everything else,

---

[31] Robins 2000, 165. See also Robins 2000, 167–70
[32] See Priest 2018a, 130–1.

no individual is more fundamental than any other, and so reality itself is non-well-founded in the sense that chains of dependence never end.[33] For example, according to the contemporary environmentalist scholar David Barnhill,

> We are merely one jewel in the endless web of life. From the perspective of Indra's Net, there is no hierarchy among the interdependent things of life.[34]

Coherentist approaches to contemplating Indra's net entail that the jewels of Indra's net are empty of determinate characteristics. Yet, because they reject hierarchical relations (of chief and attendant) among those jewels, coherentist approaches entail that relations among the jewels of Indra's net are symmetric. Coherentist approaches also neglect Fazang's instruction to select different jewels as chief. In doing so, they neglect the existent and powerful aspects of the net's jewels.

Coherentist approaches do not justify using Indra's net as a metaphor for understanding mutual identity and mutual inclusion among *dharmas* in the realm of Samantabhadra. The reason is that, in Fazang's technical framework, the relations of identity and inclusion are asymmetric, and these relations obtain only if some are existent and powerful. Contrary to Fazang's contemplation, coherentist approaches to contemplating Indra's net thereby entail that the jewels of Indra's net are neither mutually identical nor mutually inclusive.[35] Why, then, does Fazang contemplate Indra's net in the way he does?

6.5. Sources for Fazang's Contemplation

Motivations for Fazang's distinctive approach to contemplating Indra's net appear in two works with which Fazang is likely familiar. One is *Ten Mysterious Gates of the Unitary Vehicle of Huayan*. Tradition ascribes this text to Zhiyan 智儼 (602–668), the most important Dharma Master under whom Fazang studied and who entrusted to Fazang the continuation of his teaching.[36] The other is

---

[33] See Bliss and Priest 2018, 7–10.

[34] Barnhill 1990, 21.

[35] The point here is not that coherent interpretations of Indra's net do not accommodate mutual identity or mutual inclusion. The point is that they do not accommodate these relations as Fazang understands them. Certainly other analyses of identity and inclusion are possible. For further critique of coherentist interpretations of Fazang's metaphor, see Jones 2022. See also the critique of the standard interpretation of Fazang's metaphysics in Chapter 4.4-4.5.

[36] See Chen 2007, 121–4. There is some doubt whether the attribution of *Ten Mysterious Gates* to Zhiyan is posthumous. See Park 2018, 72. I follow tradition by ascribing authorship to Zhiyan. Nothing in the analysis to follow turns upon this ascription. No matter the authorship, Fazang is certainly familiar with the work itself.

124   METAPHORS FOR INTERDEPENDENCE

Cessation and Contemplation in the Five Teachings of Huayan. Zhiyan's dharma-teacher, Dushun 杜順 (557–640), often receives credit for authoring this text.[37] Dushun's *Cessation and Contemplation* motivates contemplating Indra's net by shifting attentional focus among jewels. Zhiyan's *Ten Mysterious Gates* introduces the distinction between chief and attendant to characterize jewels as central or peripheral to attention.

6.5.1. Dushun's Contemplation

Consider, first, Dushun's *Cessation and Contemplation in the Five Teachings of Huayan.* This text characterizes Indra's net as "the pearled net of the heavenly emperor." Its contemplation of Indra's net begins with a brief description of the net's composition.

> This imperial net is made entirely of jewels. Because these clear jewels are thoroughly transparent, reflections appear to enter into them repeatedly. They appear within one pearl simultaneously and suddenly. Each one is like this. But nothing goes forth or arrives.[38]

The text proceeds to give instructions for contemplating Indra's net.

> Now temporarily turn toward the southwestern boundary. Select a pearl to examine. This one pearl can suddenly manifest reflections of all pearls. Because this pearl is like this, all the remaining pearls are as well. Just as one pearl simultaneously suddenly manifests every pearl like this, all the others do as well, repeatedly and without limit. One pearl includes within itself the reflections of all pearls repeatedly and without limit. The luminous appearing of the other pearls does not hinder this.[39]

The text then elaborates upon this contemplation.

> Sitting in one pearl is sitting repeatedly in all pearls of the ten directions. Why? Because in one pearl there are all pearls. If every pearl is in one pearl, sitting in one is sitting in all pearls. By the same reasoning, the converse holds for all

---

[37] There is some doubt whether Dushun authors *Cessation and Contemplation,* and there is some evidence that the text appears several decades after Fazang's death. See Ishii 2003; Liefke and Plassen 2016; Plassen 2020. I follow tradition by ascribing authorship to Dushun. Because the text appears in close proximity to Fazang's lifetime, Fazang is likely familiar with its approach to understanding Indra's net even if Dushun is not the author.

[38] T45.1867.513a28-b01. For an alternative translation, see Cleary 1983, 66.

[39] T45.1867.513b1-6. For an alternative translation, see Cleary 1983, 66.

pearls. Since all pearls enter into one pearl without going beyond this one pearl, every pearl enters into one pearl without going beyond this one pearl.[40]

Four aspects of Dushun's contemplation are especially noteworthy. First, Dushun conceptualizes the jewels of Indra's net sometimes as jewels (Ch. *bǎo* 寶), sometimes as pearls (Ch. *zhū* 珠). The differences among jewels and pearls are insignificant. Both are mirror-like, hosting reflections of all others in the net. Dushun thereby makes explicit that each jewel of Indra's net, like each tower in Sudhana's vision, manifests reflections of all others. This justifies modeling dependence relations among *dharmas* as reflective relations among the jewels of Indra's net.

Second, Dushun recommends a sort of perspectivism for contemplating Indra's net. Rather than contemplate the net in its totality, one should—according to Dushun—begin by focusing attention on some arbitrary jewel in the net. Insofar as attention centers this one jewel and relegates other jewels into the periphery, the one jewel manifests reflections of all other jewels but those others do not manifest reflections of the one (or of each other). This justifies contemplating the one jewel as including within itself reflections of all others. Shifting attention to focus, in sequence, on each other jewel similarly justifies contemplating each jewel as manifesting and including within itself reflections of all others. These contemplations are perspectival because each arises from a different attentional focus. The perspective from which one includes another is not the same as the perspective from which the other includes the one. This perspectivism is consistent with ascribing to each jewel two aspects, one whereby it includes others and another whereby it is included within others.

The third noteworthy aspect of Dushun's contemplation of Indra's net is a confession about limitation.

These pearls [that constitute Indra's net] only have reflections taking in and entering each other as appearances. The substance of each differs [from the appearances]. *Dharmas* are not like this, because the whole of their being penetrates completely.[41]

For Dushun, when one jewel (pearl) manifests reflections of many other jewels (pearls), the other jewels are not literally inside the one. What is inside each jewel is reflections of other jewels. These reflections are ways the other jewels appear. Yet the reflections are not the jewels themselves. This indicates that, although the metaphor models mutual dependence among *dharmas*, it does not model

---

[40] T45.1867.513b7-11. For an alternative translation, see Cleary 1983, 66–7.
[41] T45.1867.513c5-6. For an alternative translation, see Cleary 1983, 68.

126 METAPHORS FOR INTERDEPENDENCE

the kind of inclusion whereby *dharmas* include each other. Inclusion relations among the jewels of Indra's net are relations between one jewel and appearances of other jewels. These relations obtain when the appearances are literally inside a jewel—that is, when other jewels appear as reflections within some jewel. By contrast, inclusion relations among *dharmas* are relations between one *dharma* and other *dharmas* rather than relations between one *dharma* and *appearances* of other *dharmas*. For Dushun, the metaphor does not exactly illustrate inclusion relations among *dharmas*.

The fourth noteworthy aspect of Dushun's contemplation is its implicit theory of catoptrics. (Catoptrics is a branch of optics that studies the appearances of objects in mirrors.) Dushun's theory makes two posits. The first is that when one jewel reflects another, the one manifests an appearance of the other. The second is that when one jewel manifests an appearance of another, nothing goes forth from the other or arrives to the one. The first posit signals Dushun's commitment to conceptualizing mirrors (or mirror-like jewels) as receiving appearances projected by others. The second posit signals Dushun's commitment to conceptualizing mirrors as nominal existents rather than real existents. Neither of these commitments is obvious. Motivation for both derives from Buddhist engagements with a competing theory of catoptrics from the (non-Buddhist) Nyāya and Mīmāṃsā traditions.[42]

6.5.2. Buddhist Catoptrics

According to the Naiyāyikas and Mīmāṃsakas, those who encounter a reflection in a mirror are in contact with the object of the reflection.[43] The reason for this contact is a conception of mirrors as inert receivers. This conception posits that when a mirror manifests a reflection of an object, the object projects an appearance of itself into the surrounding environment, the appearance travels from the object to the mirror, and the mirror then receives the appearance.

For the Naiyāyikas and Mīmāṃsakas, because mirrors are inert, they lack power to cause the reflections they manifest. Because any reflection that manifests in a mirror is a transmission from the object reflected to the mirror, the object has power to cause the reflection in the mirror. Because objects reflected both project appearances and have power to cause those appearances to manifest in mirrors, objects reflected are real existents. Because the reflections that manifest in mirrors are transmissions from the objects reflected in mirrors, the

---

[42] The Nyāya and Mīmāṃsā theory of catoptrics is a realist theory. For similar theories in the medieval philosophical tradition of Western Europe, see Lička 2019.

[43] See Ratié 2017, 209.

Naiyāyikas and Mīmāṃsakas infer that encountering a reflection in a mirror is being in contact with the object reflected: the contact is mediated by the transmission of an appearance from the object to the mirror.

For the sake of contrasting the Nyāya and Mīmāṃsā theory of catoptrics with Dushun's theory, consider a mirror that manifests a reflection of the Buddha's face. For the Naiyāyikas and Mīmāṃsakas, the cause of the reflection is the Buddha's face. The Buddha's face projects an appearance of itself, this appearance goes forth from the face to the mirror, and the mirror manifests a reflection of the Buddha's face when the appearance arrives at the mirror. But this is not how Dushun analyzes the cause of the reflection in the mirror.

Dushun claims that when a mirror manifests a reflection of an object, nothing goes forth or arrives. For example, according to Dushun's catoptrics, when a mirror manifests a reflection of the Buddha's face, the face projects an appearance and the mirror hosts this appearance as a reflection of the face in the mirror. Because nothing goes forth or arrives, the cause of the appearance in the mirror is the mirror rather than the face. Because objects reflected in a mirror project their appearances but the mirror has power to cause those appearances, the objects reflected are nominal existents and mirrors include the objects they reflect (in Fazang's technical sense of inclusion).

Dushun's *Cessation and Contemplation* provides some support for his implicit theory of catoptrics with a thought experiment. The experiment is meant to demonstrate that the many jewels of Indra's net are, in some sense, identical with each other. Dushun instructs the reader to imagine placing a colored dot on one pearl, and then to (imaginatively) observe that this dot immediately appears within every other pearl.[44] According to Dushun's further elaboration, this observation should support the following reasoning. First, because the dotted pearl makes a dot in every other pearl, it makes a dot in the reflections of these other pearls and these dotted reflections manifest in the dotted pearl. Second, because the dotted pearl changes how the other pearls appear in the dotted pearl, the dotted pearl makes whatever reflections it hosts. Finally, because the dotted pearl makes the reflections it hosts, the objects reflected in the dotted pearl are identical with the dotted pearl.[45]

Precedent for Dushun's theory of catoptrics appears in prior Buddhist writings.[46] Central to Dushun's theory is the contention that nothing goes forth

---

[44] T45.1867.513b26. Dushun's thought experiment calls to mind a remark, in *Dhāraṇī for Adorning the Bodhi Site*, that installing one written *dhāraṇī* (incantation) within a *stūpa* immediately spreads the *dhāraṇī* to hundreds and thousands of other *stūpas*. See Copp 2014, 36–7, citing T19.1008.672c. See also Shen 2012, 223–5.

[45] See Cleary 1983, 67–8.

[46] See Wayman 1974, Ratié 2017.

128   METAPHORS FOR INTERDEPENDENCE

or arrives when one jewel manifests the reflection of another. The same contention appears in *Noble Sūtra on the Rice Stalk*.

> There is nothing whatsoever that transmigrates from this world to another
> world. There is (only) the appearance of the fruit of karma, because of the
> non-deficiency of causes and conditions. It is, monks, like the reflection of a
> face seen in a well-polished mirror. No face transmigrates into the mirror, but
> there is the appearance of a face because of the non-deficiency of causes and
> conditions.[47]

Explaining the Heart of Dependent Arising makes a similar claim.[48]

Also central to Dushun's theory of catoptrics is the contention that when a
mirror manifests a reflection of an object, the cause of the reflection is the mirror
even though the object projects the appearance that manifests in the mirror as
that reflection. This contention conceptualizes the reflections in mirrors as unreal appearances of their hosts. Nāgārjuna (2nd–3rd century) invokes this conception in his *Precious Garland*.

Nāgārjuna likens the aggregates (Skt. *skandhas*) that constitute a person
to a mirror, and he likens the self of the person to a face that appears in the
mirror.

> 31. Just as through the medium of a mirror one sees the reflex[ion] of one's own
> face, though it is in fact nothing real,
>   32. even so one perceives the personality through the medium of the groups
> [*skandhas*], though, in truth, it is nothing real, but like the reflex[ion] of the
> face.[49]

Nāgārjuna's contention is that just as a face does not cause the reflection
of the face that manifests in a mirror, the self does not cause the aggregates
that manifest as a person. This contravenes the theory of the Naiyāyikas
and Mīmāṃsakas, which entails instead that there are reflections of faces in
mirrors only if there are faces that cause those reflections—and so, by analogy,
there are aggregates manifesting as a person only if there is a self causing that
manifestation.

Vasubandhu (4th–5th century) provides support for the Buddhist theory of
catoptrics, and against the competing theory of the Naiyāyikas and Mīmāṃsakas,
in his *(Auto-)Commentary on the Treasury of Abhidharma*.

---

[47] Reat 1993, 64.
[48] Wayman 1974, 259.
[49] Tucci 1934, 315.

INDRA'S NET   129

[Chapter 3, Section 12b.] ... It is by reason of two causes that a reflection arises, by reason of the mirror and of the object. The principal of these two causes is the cause upon which it takes its support in order to arise, namely the mirror.[50]

The causes of reflections are their hosts, according to Vasubandhu, because hosts support (Skt. *āśraya*) their reflections. For example, although the organs of living bodies arise by virtue of food and the four great elements (air, earth, fire, water), the cause of the organs is the elements rather than the food, because the elements support the organs while the food merely conditions the state of the organs.[51] By analogy, the cause of a reflection is its host rather than the object reflected, because the host supports the reflection while the object reflected merely conditions the form of the reflection.[52]

Because each jewel of Indra's net includes appearances of all other jewels, Dushun infers that each jewel includes all other jewels. Because reflections of jewels being in a jewel do not model this technical kind of inclusion, Dushun concludes that Indra's net is not an exact model for mutual inclusion among *dharmas*. However, rather than reject Indra's net as an inapt metaphor for understanding relations among *dharmas* in the realm of Samantabhadra, Dushun frames his contemplation of the metaphor as a skillful means (Skt. *upāya*; Ch. *fāng biàn* 方便) that facilitates the quest for *nirvāṇa*.[53]

Dushun's framing of the metaphor of Indra's net as a skillful means is equivalent, in modern parlance, to conceding that the metaphor has a negative analogy.[54] The negative analogy of a metaphor includes any property of the metaphor that does not belong to the target of the metaphor. For Dushun, the way

---

[50] Pruden 1991, 385.

[51] See Pruden 1991, 441.

[52] Vasubandhu uses the theory that hosts of reflections are causes of their reflections to argue that reflections are illusory. See Pruden 1991, 284–5; Ratié 2017, 208–9. For contemporary engagement with arguments similar to Vasubandhu's, see Steenhagen 2017. *Commentary on the Great Perfection of Wisdom* seems to reject this theory.

The reflection in the mirror is not produced by the mirror (*ādarśa*), nor by the face (*vaktra*), nor by the person holding the mirror (*ādarśadhara*), nor by itself (*svataḥ*); but it is not without causes and conditions (*hetupratyaya*). (T25.1509.104b18-9, recited in Chödrön 2001, 308.)

If reflections have causes but these causes are neither their host nor the objects reflected, it is tempting to suppose that the cause of a reflection is the entirety of the situation in which the reflection arises. This seems to be the supposition that coherentist interpretations of Indra's net make. It is not one that Fazang makes. He maintains, instead, that each jewel of Indra's net is a sufficient cause for its reflections. Although Fazang uses much of the technical terminology from *Commentary on the Great Perfection of Wisdom*, he does not always endorse the same metaphysics.

[53] T45.1867.513c4-513c5; Cleary 1983, 68.

[54] Chengguan's remark on metaphors confirms the equivalence: "To raise a metaphor when it is conceded that it cannot be likened to anything is to use a partial metaphor temporarily to convey the mysterious meaning, to cause those of developed perceptivity to see the great by way of the small, to forget words on comprehending the message" (T45.1883.676c22-4, recited in Cleary 1983, 94).

130 METAPHORS FOR INTERDEPENDENCE

mirrors include reflections is a negative analogy for the way *dharmas* include other *dharmas*.

6.5.3. Zhiyan's Contemplation

The contemplation of Indra's net in Dushun's *Cessation and Contemplation* differs from Fazang's contemplation in two significant ways. First, although Dushun's approach contemplates each jewel of Indra's net from different perspectives, it does not explain what is involved in shifting perspectives. Second, although Dushun's approach frames Indra's net as a metaphor for the realm of Samantabhadra, it denies that relations among the jewels of Indra's net correctly model relations among *dharmas* in the realm of Samantabhadra.

Both of these differences are absent in the approach to contemplating Indra's net that appears in Zhiyan's *Ten Mysterious Gates*. Zhiyan's approach begins by specifying the salient characteristics of Indra's net.

> When discussing Indra's net, we explain the net of the palace of Indra as a metaphor. Explaining the net of the palace of Indra as a metaphor requires first knowing what this net of Indra's and its appearances are like. It is like many mirrors mutually illuminating each other, their reflections appearing in one mirror. Because the reflection of this one reappears in the reflections of many, every reflection reappears in many reflections. That is, the repeatedly appearing reflections become one endlessly, going forth and returning endlessly.[55]

After connecting Indra's net to some passages from the *Flower Adornment Sūtra*, Zhiyan provides additional instructions for contemplating the metaphor:

> By following distinctions in awareness, we select one as chief, and so the remaining act as attendants. Likewise, with Indra's net we select one pearl as chief and the many others appear within it. Because one pearl is like this, the reflections of all pearls are also thus.[56]

Three aspects of Zhiyan's approach are especially noteworthy. The first is his perspectivism. Zhiyan recommends contemplating Indra's net by first selecting one jewel as chief, the others as attendants.[57] This is similar to the procedure in Dushun's *Cessation and Contemplation*, which recommends first centering

---

[55] T45.1868.516b8-12. For an alternative translation, see Cleary 1983, 135–6.
[56] T45.1868.516b26-8. For an alternative translation, see Cleary 1983, 136.
[57] T45.1868.516b27-8; Cleary 1983, 136–7.

attention upon one jewel and relegating the others to the periphery of attention. Zhiyan characterizes the centering of attention upon one jewel as selecting the one as chief. He also characterizes this selection function as a matter "following distinctions in awareness" (Ch. *suí zhì chā bié* 隨智差別).

Zhiyan briefly elaborates on the meaning of "following distinctions in awareness" by comparing the distinction between chief and attendant to the distinction between cause and effect.[58] According to Zhiyan, one bodhisattva, acting as chief, testifies to the truth and thereby causes other bodhisattvas to realize the truth; but the same bodhisattva, acting as attendant, realizes the truth as an effect of testimony from other bodhisattvas. Zhiyan conceptualizes causes as prior in sequence to their effects (Ch. *yīn guǒ xiān hòu cì dì* 因果先後次第).[59] Because being a chief correlates with being a cause, following distinctions in awareness to select one jewel of Indra's net as chief is a matter of focusing attention on the aspect of that jewel whereby it acts as a cause. Similarly, because being an attendant correlates with being an effect, other jewels of Indra's net being attendants is a matter of those jewels acting as effects. Hence, contemplating Indra's net with Zhiyan's approach involves conceptualizing each jewel of the net as having two aspects, one whereby it acts as a cause, another whereby it acts as an effect. This is precisely the approach that Fazang takes when contemplating each jewel of Indra's net as being chief (with aspects of existing and having power) and being attendant (with aspects of being empty and lacking power).

The second noteworthy aspect of Zhiyan's approach to contemplating Indra's net is its favorable view of the metaphor. Near the end of *Ten Mysterious Gates*, Zhiyan frames metaphors as tools that "reveal correct teaching and produce understanding" (Ch. *xiǎn fǎ zhǔ xiè* 顯法主解).[60] He cites, as an example of such a metaphor, Sudhana's vision of jeweled towers in the final chapter of the *Flower Adornment Sūtra*. Parallels between this network of towers and Indra's net indicate that, contrary to Dushun's attitude in *Cessation and Contemplation*, Zhiyan affirms that Indra's net correctly models relations among *dharmas* in the realm of Samantabhadra.

Even though Zhiyan presents Indra's net as an apt metaphor for the realm of Samantabhadra, there is no indication that he rejects Dushun's distinction between jewels and their reflections. Dushun uses this distinction to argue that, because only reflections appear in the jewels of Indra's net, Indra's net does not model relations of inclusion among jewels. Zhiyan acknowledges that each jewel of Indra's net includes reflections of all other jewels. He also acknowledges that no jewel is in any other jewel. Yet, for Zhiyan, relations among the jewels are

---

[58] T45.1868.516b28-c4; Cleary 1983, 136–7.
[59] T45.1868.516c3.
[60] T45.1868.518c10-1; Cleary 1983, 146.

132 METAPHORS FOR INTERDEPENDENCE

irrelevant to whether Indra's net models relations among *dharmas*. This is because, for Zhiyan, relations of inclusion among *dharmas* are akin to relations among the reflections of jewels in Indra's net.

Zhiyan motivates his alternative interpretation of Indra's net by appealing to a contrast between substance (Ch. *tǐ* 體) and function (Ch. *yòng* 用). This is the third noteworthy aspect of Zhiyan's approach. Substance corresponds to that which is fundamental, a source of existence and power. Function corresponds to that which is derivative, a manifestation or development of some source. Substance and function are inseparable, or nondual, because there are no manifestations without sources and no sources without manifestations.[61] For example, with respect to a tree, the substance is the root system, the function is the trunk and branches, and these are nondual because the tree's roots always and only develop together with its trunk and branches.

For Zhiyan, jewels are the substance of Indra's net, and reflections of those jewels in each other are the function. Because the reflections in one jewel appear in the reflections of all other jewels, each jewel of Indra's net has its reflection manifest in the reflections of all other jewels. Zhiyan takes this to mean that Indra's net models relations among *dharmas* in the domain of function.[62] In the domain of function, *dharmas* in the realm of Samantabhadra are akin to reflections of jewels from Indra's net. Because the reflection of each jewel is in the reflection of all other jewels, Zhiyan concludes that the function of Indra's net models the mutual inclusion of *dharmas* in the realm of Samantabhadra.

6.6. Conceptualizing Indra's Net

6.6.1. The Scope of Fazang's Contemplation

Zhiyan's approach to contemplating Indra's net motivates Fazang's contention that Indra's net is an apt model for *dharmas* in the realm of Samantabhadra. Zhiyan's distinction between chief and attendant—which itself derives from Dushun's distinction between centered and peripheral attention—motivates ascribing different aspect to the jewels of Indra's net. These aspects model the aspects that Fazang ascribes to *dharmas*, namely, the aspects of existing with power and of being empty without power.

Zhiyan's restriction of Indra's net to a metaphor in the domain of function also explains Fazang's admission, in his *Record of Freely Wandering Mind in the*

---

[61] For more on the substance-function contrast, see Chapter 5.3.1 and Muller 2016.
[62] T45.1868.515c3, 517b25-8; Cleary 1983, 132, 141.

Dharma-Realm of Huayan, that Indra's net is only a partially reliable model for the realm of Samantabhadra.

> *Dharmas* can be considered through the example of the metaphor [of Indra's net]. But *dharmas* are not really the same [as the jewels in the metaphor]. The metaphor is not representative. I say this because only one component of the metaphor resembles *dharmas*. In the metaphor, the jewels reflect all around, but their substances do not enter into each other.[63]

This admission is quite similar to Dushun's reason for claiming, in *Cessation and Contemplation*, that Indra's net is merely a skillful means for understanding relations among *dharmas* in the realm of Samantabhadra.[64] Fazang demurs from this assessment by restricting the scope of Indra's net. For Fazang, as for Zhiyan, the function of Indra's net—but not the substance of the net—models relations among *dharmas*.

Like Zhiyan, Fazang does not make explicit exactly how the function of Indra's net models mutual identity and mutual inclusion among *dharmas* in the realm of Samantabhadra. These missing details, however, are straightforward consequences of the Buddhist theory of catoptrics and Fazang's conceptual framework. The Buddhist theory of catoptrics entails that, when one jewel reflects another, the one causes the reflection of the other to manifest while the other conditions the form of this reflection. In Fazang's conceptual framework, this means that the one has power (to cause the reflection) and the other lacks power (despite projecting the reflection). Because one *dharma* includes another only if the one has power and the other lacks power, the relations among jewels within Indra's net model the aspects that *dharmas* have when they include each other (in Fazang's technical sense of *inclusion*.) Because one has power only if it exists and lacks power only if it is empty, and because one is identical with another only if the one is empty and the other exists, the same relations among jewels also model the aspects that *dharmas* have when they are identical with each other (in Fazang's technical sense of *identity*).

6.6.2. Sequencing in Fazang's Contemplation

Like both Dushun and Zhiyan, Fazang does not make explicit why contemplating Indra's net requires sequentially selecting each jewel as chief. Nor does he explain why the jewel selected as chief should be conceptualized

---

[63] T45.1877.647b28-9. For an alternative translation, see Liu 1981, 29.
[64] See T45.1867.513c5-6.

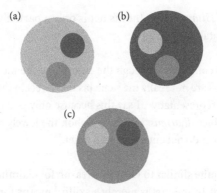

Figure 6.2 Depiction of Simplified Indra's Net (Coarse-Grained)
Image created by the author.

as existing with power while the other jewels, relegated to the periphery as attendants, should be conceptualized as empty and powerless. These missing details, however, are consequences—albeit less straightforward ones—of the Buddhist theory of catoptrics and Fazang's conceptual framework. Sequentially selecting each jewel of Indra's net as chief—that is, sequentially centering each jewel as the focus of attention—is necessary to the correct contemplation of Indra's net because some selection function is required to avoid causal overdetermination for the reflections that manifest in the jewels of Indra's net.

For a vivid demonstration of this requirement, consider a simplified model of Indra's net that consists of exactly three jewels A, B, and C. Figure 6.2 depicts these jewels as three circles, each with a slightly different shading, and it depicts the reflections of two jewels in one jewel as smaller versions of the other two circles.

The depiction in Figure 6.2 is coarse-grained. It neglects the reflections of reflections that appear within each jewel. For example, the circle for A includes smaller versions of the circles for B and C. But in the smaller version of the circle for B, the depiction omits the smaller versions of the circles for A and C; and in the smaller version of the circle for C, it omits the smaller versions of the circles for A and B.

Figure 6.3 corrects this oversight by depicting the reflections of reflections that appear in each jewel. But even Figure 6.3 is coarse-grained (albeit less so than Figure 6.2). It omits the smaller versions of the even smaller circles that appear in each of the smaller circles—that is, it does not depict reflections of reflections of reflections.

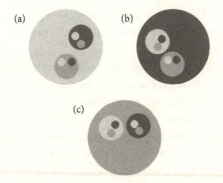

Figure 6.3 Depiction of Simplified Indra's Net (Less Coarse-Grained)
Image created by the author.

Although the depictions of (the simplified versions of) Indra's net in Figure 6.2 and Figure 6.3 are coarse-grained, they suffice to illustrate the concern about causal overdetermination. Consider the reflection depicted in the circle for A in Figure 6.2. Figure 6.3 depicts this same reflection in the circles for B and C: in each of the circles for B and C, it appears in the circle that depicts the reflection of A. Because each of A, B, and C hosts the same reflection, the Buddhist theory of catoptrics entails that each of A, B, and C suffices, by itself, as a cause for the reflection. Hence, when applied to mutually reflecting objects, the Buddhist theory of catoptrics seems to entail that all reflections of such objects have multiple sufficient causes. This entailment, if correct, violates *Causal Exclusion*—the principle that nothing has more than one sufficient cause.[65]

Mutual reflectivity among the jewels of Indra's net, together with the Buddhist theory of catoptrics and *Causal Exclusion*, creates an *aporia*. Three statements suffice to articulate the *aporia*.

1. Each jewel of Indra's net hosts every reflection that manifests within Indra's net.
2. Hosts of reflections are sufficient causes for those reflections.
3. There is at most one sufficient cause for any reflection that manifests within Indra's net.

The first statement is a corollary to mutual reflectivity among the jewels of Indra's net. The second is a corollary to the Buddhist theory of catoptrics. The third is

---

[65] For discussion of *Causal Exclusion*, refer to Chapter 4.5.1. For evidence that Fazang endorses *Causal Exclusion*, refer to Chapter 4.5.2.

136 METAPHORS FOR INTERDEPENDENCE

a corollary to *Causal Exclusion*. The first two statements jointly entail that there are multiple sufficient causes for the reflections that manifest within Indra's net. The third denies this.

There are two potential strategies for resolving the *aporia* about causal over-determination for Indra's net without rejecting *Causal Exclusion*. Both target the statement that hosts of reflections are sufficient causes for those reflections. The first strategy is to infer that the reflections within the net lack causes. The second is to introduce some function that selects exactly one jewel of the net as sufficient cause for the net's reflections while also allowing for any selection to be correct. For Fazang, the first strategy is not viable because whatever arises has some cause and the reflections within Indra's net certainly arise. Hence, for Fazang, the only way to avoid the *aporia* about causal overdetermination for Indra's net is to introduce a specific kind of selection function. This is precisely what Dushun does, and this is also the reason why Zhiyan speaks of jewels as chiefs and attendants.

6.6.3. Asymmetry in Fazang's Contemplation

How exactly does a selection function resolve the *aporia*? Fazang's conceptual framework provides the answer. This answer also explains why jewels selected as chief should be conceptualized as existing with power and why other jewels, relegated to the periphery as attendants, should be conceptualized as empty and powerless.

When selecting some jewel of Indra's net as chief, the selection should attend to the aspects of the jewel whereby it exists and has power. The reason is that, when attending to the selected jewel as having power, it is correct to conceptualize the selected jewel as causing the reflections that manifest within the net. The selection also should relegate other jewels within the net to peripheral attention, attending to their aspects of being empty and lacking power. The reason is that, when attending to the other jewels as lacking power, it is incorrect to conceptualize them as causing reflections—and this is so even though the other jewels host reflections.

This way of directing attention to different jewels within Indra's net guarantees that, for any selection, correct cognition of Indra's net cognizes exactly one sufficient cause for the reflections that manifest within the net. Because attention can select any jewel as chief, this way of directing attention also guarantees that, for any given jewel within Indra's net, correct cognition cognizes that jewel as a sufficient cause for the reflections that manifest within the net. Because attention always selects only one jewel as chief, it follows that correct cognition of Indra's net preserves *Causal Exclusion* while cognizing every jewel as a sufficient cause for the reflections that manifest within the net.

7

Counting Coins

7.1. Counting as Contemplation

The metaphor of Indra's net is Fazang's most effective vehicle for contemplating the thoroughgoing relationality among *dharmas* within the realm of Samantabhadra. The metaphor likens *dharmas* to mirror-like jewels, and it likens relations of inclusion and identity to reflective relations among the jewels. For Fazang, there are four requirements for correctly contemplating Indra's net. The first is selecting one jewel as chief and central to attentional focus while relegating other jewels to peripheral attention and marking them as attendants. The second requirement is conceptualizing the chief jewel as existing with power. The third is conceptualizing the attendants as empty and without power. The fourth is repeatedly shifting attentional focus to mark different jewels as chief and their companions as attendants.

Fazang's analysis for the metaphor of Indra's net focuses on the relations whereby attendants are included within and identical with their chief. Fazang's analysis does not address sequential shifts of attentional focus. For analyzing attentional shifts, Fazang prefers the metaphor of counting ten coins (Ch. *shǔ shí qián* 數十錢). This metaphor uses counting as a method for contemplating mutual but asymmetric relations of inclusion and identity among *dharmas*. But Fazang's analysis of the metaphor is dense and highly technical, and there is no obvious sense to be made of how coins—or even counts of coins—model relations of identity and inclusion among *dharmas*. Nor is there any obvious sense to be made of how they model these relations as mutual but also asymmetric.

This chapter examines Fazang's metaphor of counting coins. The chapter divides into six parts. The first introduces Fazang's metaphor. It also motivates three groups of challenges for understanding the metaphor. Each of three subsequent parts of the chapter addresses one of these groups. The fifth part of the chapter provides extensive and detailed analyses for precedents to Fazang's metaphor, and it explains the novelties and improvements in Fazang's analysis of the metaphor. The chapter concludes by examining the significance of Fazang's analysis for contemplating the realm of Samantabhadra. The overall gist of the

Metaphors for Interdependence. Nicholaos Jones, Oxford University Press. © Nicholaos Jones 2025.
DOI: 10.1093/9780197807224.003.0007

138 METAPHORS FOR INTERDEPENDENCE

Table 7.1 The Structure for Fazang's Metaphor of Counting Coins

different body	inclusion	many in one
		one in many
	identity	many identical with one
		one identical with many
same body	inclusion	many in one
		one in many
	identity	many identical with one
		one identical with many

chapter is that Fazang's metaphor offers a set of instructions for contemplating interdependence that far exceeds the instructions associated with the metaphor of Indra's net.

7.2. The Method of Counting

Fazang introduces the metaphor of counting ten coins as a vehicle for showing how to contemplate the mutual inclusion and mutual identity of *dharmas* in the realm of Samantabhadra. Because the number ten symbolizes inexhaustibility, Fazang restricts his metaphor to counts that involve numbers between one and ten (inclusive).[1] This is a skillful means, and Fazang allows for increase and decrease in the numbers counted.[2] Yet even with this skillful restriction, Fazang's metaphor is extremely complex.

Unlike Fazang's metaphor of Indra's net, his metaphor of counting coins does not lend itself to a concise summary. One reason for this is the complex structure of the metaphor. (See Table 7.1.)

Fazang's metaphor divides into two parts. The first part involves counting with respect to different body (Skt. *anyatva*; Ch. *yì tǐ* 異體). The second involves counting with respect to same body (Skt. *ekatva*; Ch. *tóng tǐ* 同體). Each of these parts contains two analyses, one for mutual inclusion (Ch. *xiāng rù* 相入) and another for mutual identity (Ch. *xiāng jí* 相即). Each of these analyses has two counting directions. Fazang counts upward to analyze many being included

---

[1] T45.1866.508b1-2; Cook 1970, 471; Unno et al. 2023, 179.
[2] T45.1866.504c2-5; Cook 1970, 492; Unno et al. 2023, 185–6.

within and identical with one. He counts downward to analyze one being included within and identical with many.

Another reason why Fazang's metaphor eludes concise summary is that Fazang himself presents the metaphor only in the context of his analysis for the metaphor. This analysis is extremely dense and highly technical. Consider, for example, Fazang's analysis of mutual inclusion with respect to different body.

> First, counting upward has ten gateways. In the first, one is the root for counting. Why? Because conditions come to be. Going so far as ten, one includes ten. Why? Without one, ten would not come to be. Because one has all the power, it takes in ten. But ten is not one. The remaining nine gateways are also like this. Each one has ten [within itself]. Know this in accordance with [the first] example.
>
> [Second,] counting downward also has ten gateways. In the first, ten takes in one. Why? Because conditions come to be. That is to say, without ten, one would not come to be. Because one entirely lacks power, it returns to ten. But one is not ten. The remaining cases are like this.
>
> Therefore, both root and branch are in each gateway. Consider each of the remaining coins in accordance with the preceding examples.[3]

Fazang analyzes one including ten in relation to counting upward, and he analyzes ten including one in relation to counting downward. This indicates that counting upward is Fazang's method for contemplating many as included within and identical with one, and it indicates that counting downward is his method for contemplating one as included within and identical with many. Because one including ten and ten including one entails that one and ten are mutually inclusive, Fazang's analysis also indicates that changing the directionality of counting (from upward to downward) is Fazang's method for contemplating the mutuality of inclusion and identity relations.

Despite these indicators, Fazang's analysis is extremely dense. Although Fazang mentions nine other gateways for counting upward with respect to different body and nine other gateways for counting downward, he analyzes only the first gateway for each direction. Although Fazang analyzes the relation between "one" and "ten," he leaves analyses of other relations—for example, between "one" and "two"—as exercises for the reader. Moreover, Fazang does not specify the objects for counting. He does not explain why different counts model

---

[3] T45.1866.503b24–c3. For alternative translations, see Cook 1970, 476–8; Unno et al. 2023, 180–1.

140 METAPHORS FOR INTERDEPENDENCE

different instances of inclusion or identity. Nor does he explain how to go about counting.

Fazang's analysis is also highly technical. Fazang invokes his technical notion of inclusion as well as the associated notions of having power and lacking power. He mentions, but does not explain, the concept of a gateway for counting. He mentions, but does not explain, a distinction between roots and branches for counting within gateways. He also situates these technicalities within a broader—and largely unanalyzed—distinction between counting with respect to different body and counting with respect to same body.

The structural and analytic complexities of Fazang's metaphor highlight several challenges for understanding how the metaphor is a method for contemplating inclusion and identity relations among *dharmas* in the realm of Samantabhadra. The challenges divide into three groups. The first group concerns counting. What is a count in Fazang's method of counting? What is a gateway for counting? What is the difference between a root for counting and a branch for counting? What is the difference between counting with respect to different body and counting with respect to same body? The second group of challenges concerns the objects of counting. What gets counted in Fazang's counts? Why do relations among objects counted model relations of inclusion and identity among *dharmas*? The third group of challenges concerns the completion of Fazang's metaphor. Within each gateway for counting, how does the counting proceed beyond Fazang's explicit instructions? For each direction and body of counting, how does the counting proceed from the first gateway to the remaining nine gateways?

This chapter provides answers to all of these questions. The answers divide into three groups. For questions about counting, the answers are as follows: Counts are ordered pairs, such as *one-two* and *one-three*. A gateway for counting is a collection of counts in which one member in each count is always the same while the other member varies. A root for counting within a gateway is the member of each count, within the gateway, that is contemplated as existing or having power. The branches for counting within a gateway, by contrast, are the members of counts that are contemplated as empty or lacking power. When counting with respect to different body, the members of counts are individual numbers; when counting with respect to same body, one member is an individual number and the other is a whole that has ten distinct numbers as its parts. For questions about objects of counting, the answers are as follows: The objects of counting are breaths rather than coins. Relations among breaths model relations of inclusion and identity only by convention, because Fazang relies upon a tradition that uses breathing-based meditation as a vehicle for contemplating inclusion and identity relations. For questions about the completion of Fazang's metaphor, the answers are too lengthy for a brief summary—but those with irrepressible curiosity might glance ahead to Table 7.2.

7.3. Conceptualizing Counting

Fazang's metaphor of counting coins invokes a distinction between counting upward and counting downward. It associates different counts with different gateways. It distinguishes, within gateways, between roots and branches for counting. It also distinguishes between counting with respect to different body and counting with respect to same body. Fazang's analysis for his metaphor does not explain any of this. This section remedies Fazang's omissions.

7.3.1. Counts as Ordered Pairs

The natural way to interpret Fazang's distinction between counting upward and counting downward involves considering counts as individual numbers. So interpreted, counting upward from one means counting *one, two, three, ..., nine, ten*; and counting downward to one means counting *ten, nine, ..., two, one*. But this interpretation does not fit the use to which Fazang puts his metaphor. For example, Fazang's analysis of the first gateway for counting upward with respect to different body indicates that counting upward from one involves considering one in relation to two, then considering one in relation to three, and so on through considering one in relation to ten. The reason is that considering one in relation to two is Fazang's method for contemplating one as including two, and considering one in relation to ten is his method for contemplating one as including ten.

A better way to interpret Fazang's distinction between counting upward and counting downward involves considering counts as pairs of numbers. But this requires some subtlety. Fazang uses his counts to contemplate relations of inclusion and identity. Because these relations are irreflexive, interpreting Fazang's counts as pairs requires restricting counts to pairs of distinct numbers—for example, allowing *one-two* but forbidding *one-one*. Because the relations are asymmetric, interpreting Fazang's counts as pairs also requires restricting the counts to ordered pairs, so that *one-two* is distinct from *two-one*. So interpreted, counting *one-two, one-three, ..., one-nine, one-ten* is a way of counting upward; and counting *ten-one, nine-one, ..., three-one, two-one* is a way of counting downward.

Interpreting Fazang's counts as ordered pairs of distinct numbers coheres with the use to which Fazang puts his metaphor of counting coins. For example,

142 METAPHORS FOR INTERDEPENDENCE

if the ordered pair *one-ten* represents *one includes ten* and the ordered pair *ten-one* represents *ten includes one*, the interpretation secures the distinction between one including another and the other including the one. The interpretation also helps to make sense of what Fazang intends by a gateway for counting and what he means by the distinction between roots and branches for counting.

7.3.2. Gateways

Although Fazang does not explain what he means by *gateway for counting*, his meaning is straightforward. The term *gateway* (Ch. *mén* 門) can designate an entrance, or vehicle for entering, into a way of doing something. Paradigmatic examples of gateways include doorways into temples, rafts for crossing streams, and teachings for overcoming obstacles. Doorways, rafts, and teachings are vehicles for changing those who use them.[4] Rafts, for example, take travelers from one shore to another. Because gateways are vehicles for changing their users, methods or disciplines for particular practices also can be gateways.

Fazang's gateways for counting are vehicles or methods for the practice of counting. Each gateway provides instructions for how to count. The instructions specify how to start counting and how to construct each successive count from its predecessor. For example, if Fazang's counts are ordered pairs of distinct numbers, the first gateway for counting upward might specify to begin at *one-two* and proceed in sequence as *one-three, one-four, . . ., one-ten*. By analogy, the second gateway for counting upward might specify to begin at *two-three* and proceed in sequence as *two-four, two-five, two-six. . . .* So interpreted, each gateway for upward counting follows a common pattern.

Interpreting Fazang's counts as ordered pairs of distinct numbers explains two remarks Fazang makes about gateways. When analyzing counting upward with respect to different body, Fazang remarks that there are ten gateways and that each gateway includes ten within itself. If Fazang's counts are ordered pairs of distinct numbers, the ten gateways are ten different instantiations of a common pattern for counting. There are ten within each gateway, because counting through a gateway involves counting with ten numbers: the number for the gateway is a repeating member of each count, and the remaining nine numbers are the members paired to that repeating number.

---

[4] For a similar interpretation of *gateway*, in relation to Laozi 老子 and Zhuangzi 莊子, see Dor 2013.

7.3.3. Roots and Branches

When concluding his analysis for counting with respect to different body, Fazang mentions that root and branch are in each gateway. He remarks that the first gateway for counting upward with respect to different body focuses on one as the root (Ch. *běn* 本) for counting, and he notes that the counting in this gateway goes so far as ten. Fazang does not mention the branches (Ch. *mò* 末) for this root. But elsewhere he specifies that branches depend upon their roots.[5] Because Fazang's first gateway for counting upward with respect to different body is a vehicle for contemplating one as including ten, and because one includes another only if the other depends upon the one, Fazang likely means for ten to be a branch that has one as its root.

Interpreting Fazang's counts as ordered pairs of distinct numbers explains Fazang's analysis for the first gateway of counting with respect to different body. For example, when counting upward, Fazang claims that one includes ten. If Fazang's counts are ordered pairs of distinct numbers, Fazang associates this claim with the count *one-ten*. The root of this count is *one*. The branch is *ten*. Just as roots are sources of power for trees while branches merely condition the form of trees, Fazang maintains, by analogy, that the root for a count has power for the count while the branch merely conditions the form of the count. Because, according to Fazang's conceptual framework, one including another means the one has power and the other lacks power, Fazang associates *one-ten* with the claim that the one (in the *one-ten* count of the first gateway) includes the ten.[6]

7.3.4. Different Body, Same Body

Interpreting Fazang's counts as ordered pairs of distinct numbers explains many aspects of Fazang's analysis for counting with respect to different body. But Fazang also analyzes counting with respect to same body. Accommodating the claims he makes for this analysis requires a slight adjustment to the interpretation of Fazang's counts. Motivating this adjustment requires a somewhat lengthy detour through Fazang's distinction between different body and same body.

---

[5] See T45.1866.482c7-8; Cook 1970, 191–2; Unno et al. 2023, 67. The root-branch contrast is similar to the contrast between substance (Ch. *tǐ* 體) and function (Ch. *yòng* 用). Just as substance and function are inseparable by virtue of function depending upon substance, Fazang conceptualizes root and branches as inseparable by virtue of branches depending upon their root. For more on the root-branch contrast in Chinese philosophical traditions, see Wang et al. 2020, 295–306. For more on the substance-function contrast, see Muller 2016.

[6] For details and further discussion of Fazang's conceptions of having power and lacking power, refer to Chapter 3.5.2 and Chapter 4.4.

144 METAPHORS FOR INTERDEPENDENCE

Fazang comments on the distinction between different body and same body in his *Treatise on the Five Teachings of Huayan*.

> This [metaphor of counting coins] has two parts. The first is different body. The second is same body. The reason for these two gateways is that every gateway for dependent arising has two meanings. The first meaning is not being mutually dependent. This designates one's having limbs. For example, in the cause there is no need for conditions and so on. The second meaning is being mutually dependent. For example, needing conditions and so on. The former is same body. The latter is different body.[7]

These remarks are obscure and border on paradox. If a cause has no need for conditions, the cause does not depend upon conditions. If causes act as roots and conditions act as branches, causes have their own limbs in the way tree roots have their own branches. Yet roots and their branches are nondual. There are no tree roots without branches, and there are no tree branches without roots. So if causes act as roots and conditions act as branches, causes need conditions. Hence, if causes do not need conditions because causes act as roots and conditions act as branches, it seems to follow that causes do not need conditions only if causes need conditions.

Fazang's *Essay on the Three Treasures* provides more elaborate and less apparently paradoxical remarks on the distinction between different body and same body.

> First, gateways that consider conditions as differing from each other are different body. Second, gateways that consider conditions as responding to each other are same body.[8]

Fazang explains that considering conditions as differing from each other (Ch. *hùyì* 互異) means conceptualizing them as not joined together.

> First, dependent arising has gateways for differing from each other. These designate that, within the limitless and great [*dharma*-realm of] dependent arising, all conditions face each other as substance and distinct function. Because limbs are not mixed or combined, this is called different.[9]

---

[7] T45.1866.503b2-6. For alternative translations, see Cook 1970, 471–2; Unno et al. 2023, 179. Cook translates 德 as *qualities* rather than *limbs*. If 德 translates the Sanskrit term *aṅga*, either translation is possible—as is the translation of 德 as *constituent part*. I prefer *limbs* for its suggestive connection to the root-branch contrast, and because conceptualizing conditions as limbs of their associated causes is more sensible than conceptualizing them as qualities of their causes.

[8] T45.1874.620a5-6.

[9] T45.1874.620a10-2. For an alternative translation, see Liu 1979, 406. Cook interprets *different body* as *dharmas* producing their effects only by working in cooperation with others (Cook 1977, 67). This ignores Fazang's remarks about lack of mixture or combination.

COUNTING COINS 145

For Fazang, many conditions differ from each other when, for any condition that relates to many others, it relates to each of those others separately rather than to all of them joined together. This corresponds to a definition of difference (Ch. *yì* 異) from the *Mozi* 墨子, according to which things are different when they are not joined together.[10]

Fazang's explanation for mutual difference indicates that counting with respect to different body involves counts that relate one root to several distinct and separate others. This means, for example, that the first gateway for counting upward with respect to different body is a matter of separately considering *one* in relation to each of *two*, *three*, and so on. Each count in this gateway relates the root count to an individual branch. Because each count relates a root to an individual branch, the counts do not mix or combine the branches and so the counting is with respect to different body.

When a limb is included within a root one, the one acts as substance that has complete power while the limb acts as function that completely lacks power. When the limb is the root for a count and the one is included within this limb, the limb acts as substance that has complete power while the one acts as function that completely lacks power. This is why Fazang characterizes mutual inclusion with respect to different body as each one facing another as both substance and function.

Fazang also explains that considering conditions as responding to each other (Ch. *hù yìng* 互應) means conceptualizing them as parts of a unified whole (Ch. *yītǐ* 一體).

> There are gateways for all conditions responding to each other. These designate that, because among the multitude of conditions one condition responds to many conditions, and each takes part in those many as one of the given whole, therefore this one has each of the many. In this way, although all of these many follow the root one, because the many conditions respond, these many are one. Because, in this way, the root takes part in one body without distinction, these gateways are called same body.[11]

For Fazang, many conditions respond to each other when each condition relates to a unified whole that has the others as its parts. This corresponds to a definition

---

[10] See Johnston 2010, 453; Fung 2020, 215.

[11] T45.1874.620b10-4. For an alternative translation, see Liu 1979, 411. Cook interprets *same body* as *dharmas* being similar to each other by virtue of functioning as causes (Cook 1977, 63). This ignores Fazang's remarks about mutual responsiveness.

146   METAPHORS FOR INTERDEPENDENCE

of sameness (Ch. *tóng* 同) from the *Mozi*, according to which things are the same when they are common parts of a whole.[12]

Fazang's explanation for mutual responsiveness indicates that counting with respect to same body involves counts that relate one to some whole (Ch. *quán* 全). Fazang characterizes this whole as "all ten together" and "ten ... considered to be one." Consider, for example, Fazang's analysis for mutual inclusion with respect to same body.

> The first [analysis] has two aspects. The first is one including many. The second is many including one. One including many has ten distinct gateways. [Consider] the first as one. Why? Because conditions come to be, one is the root count. One includes all ten together. Why? Because this one's own nature is one. Then because one makes two, two is considered to be one. Because one makes each part of ten, ten is considered to be one. Therefore, this one includes within itself the one that is ten. But one is not ten, because this is not yet the gateway for identity. Because the first is like this, the remaining two, three, four, five—each of the remaining nine gateways—are also like this. Know each in accordance with the example.
>
> The second [analysis] also has ten gateways. [Consider] the first as ten. Why? Because conditions come to be, ten includes one. Why? Because ten considered to be one makes one. That is, because the first one—the one that is one of ten— is separate from ten, one is not the first one. So this one is one included within ten. But ten is not one. The remaining nine, eight, seven—and so on down to the first—are like this. Know each in accordance with the example.[13]

Fazang's remarks on counting with respect to different body indicate that counting upward (or downward) with respect to different body involves ten gateways and that each gateway has ten within itself. By contrast, his remarks on counting with respect to same body indicate that counting upward (or downward) with respect to same body only involves ten gateways. For counting with respect to same body, no gateway has ten within itself. Instead, counting with respect to same body involves considering one in relation to "ten ... considered to be one."

For Fazang, counting with respect to same body involves considering one in relation to some whole that is "all ten together." This whole has ten individuals as its parts.[14] But considering one in relation to the whole is not considering one

---

[12] See Johnston 2010, 453; Fung 2020, 214. A standard definition of sameness, in the Mohist sense, involves water, vinegar, salt, plums, and fish harmonizing with each other as soup. See He 2019, 121.

[13] T45.1866.504b8-21. For alternative translations, see Cook 1970, 488–9; Unno et al. 2023, 184–5.

[14] For an interpretation that treats "all ten together" as a whole with *nine* parts, see Jones 2018a, 1163. This alternative interpretation makes for a wild (implausible) proliferation of wholes: for any collection of N dharmas ($N > 2$), it allows for N wholes that differ by only one part. I hereby retract the alternative interpretation as a misunderstanding of what Fazang means by *same body*.

in relation to each separate and distinct part. Because one relates to many in this way, it relates to the ten without distinction and thereby relates to them as "same body." When one is included within the whole ("all ten together"), the whole acts as root that has complete power and the one is completely without power by virtue of following the whole. When the whole is included within one, the one acts as root that has complete power and the whole completely lacks power by virtue of following the one. This is the sense in which, for Fazang, mutual inclusion with respect to same body is the whole and each of its parts responding to each other.

Because counting with respect to same body involves considering one in relation to a whole that has many as its parts, the counts for counting with respect to same body cannot be ordered pairs of distinct numbers. For example, let *all* represent the whole that has the numbers *one* through *ten* as its parts. Then the first gateway for counting upward with respect to same body coincides with the count *one-all*, the second coincides with the count *two-all*, and so on. Similarly, the first gateway for counting downward with respect to same body coincides with the count *all-one*, the second coincides with *all-two*, and so on. Because no individual number has other numbers as parts, *all* is not an individual number. Hence, the counts for counting with respect to same body are not ordered pairs of distinct numbers. Instead, they are ordered pairs in which one member of the pair is a number and the other member is "all ten together."

7.4. Counting Coins as Counting Breaths

Counting with ordered pairs—such as *one-two* or *one-all*—is Fazang's method for contemplating inclusion and identity relations. Counting upward—for example, from *one-two* to *one-three*—is his method for contemplating many as included within and identical with one. Counting downward—for example, from *three-one* to *two-one*—is his method for contemplating one as included within and identical with many. Changing the directionality of a counting sequence (from upward to downward) is Fazang's method for contemplating the mutuality of inclusion and identity relations. Changing the repeating elements within a sequence of counts—for example, from the (partial) sequence *one-two, one-three, one-four*, . . . to the (partial) sequence *ten-two, ten-three, ten-four*—is his method for preserving the asymmetry of inclusion and identity relations. But even when these elements for Fazang's method of counting are made explicit, there remains the issue of just what Fazang's method is counting.

The standard approach to Fazang's metaphor opts for a literal interpretation whereby Fazang's method involves the counting of coins. But Fazang's analysis for the metaphor of counting coins does not mention coins, and it does not

148　METAPHORS FOR INTERDEPENDENCE

model relations among *dharmas* as relations among coins. Instead, Fazang's analysis considers relations among distinct but unspecified objects, each of which is named for a number between one and ten (or for all ten together). These objects, whatever they are, model relations among *dharmas*. Fazang claims that the objects include each other and that they are identical with each other. He characterizes them under the aspects of being existent, being empty, having power, and lacking power. He also designates them as root, branch, having substance, and lacking substance. There is no obvious sense in which the objects satisfy these relations or have these characteristics. Fazang merely asserts that they do. Understanding Fazang's analysis, accordingly, requires some interpretive creativity.

7.4.1. The Literal Interpretation

Some commentators interpret the objects counted in Fazang's metaphor as coins. Cook, for example, endorses this interpretation without argument.

> The ten coins are an analogy for the totality of existence, and the relationship between any one coin and the remaining coins is a model for the relationship between any thing and the infinity of all other objects which constitute existence.[15]

Liu endorses a similar interpretation, remarking that "the ten coins together stand[ing] for the totality of dharmas while each coin stands for each dharma of the totality is very obvious." Yet Liu also admits that, so interpreted, "many of [Fazang's] arguments appear to be highly dubious."[16]

Liu attempts to supplement Fazang's analysis with a narrative about why distinct coins depend upon each other.

> Suppose that a certain community issues coins and stipulates that they have monetary value only when used in groups of ten. Then each coin strictly speaking is not a coin, for alone it cannot be used to exchange goods; yet when it is grouped together with nine other coins, it becomes a coin, for then it assumes all the characteristics of a form of currency. The same is true of the nine other coins, which are associated with this one piece of coin to form a monetary unit. In this way, ten coins are dependent on each other and have their nature defined by each other.[17]

---

[15] Cook 1977, 64.
[16] Liu 1979, 408.
[17] Liu 1982a, 66. See also Liu 1979, 408.

COUNTING COINS   149

Liu provides no motivation for interpreting the objects counted in Fazang's metaphor as coins. Moreover, Liu's supplement to Fazang's analysis does not illustrate mutual dependence.

Consider, for example, two collections of ten coins. The first consists of one penny, three quarters (each worth $0.25), four dimes (each worth $0.10), and two nickels (each worth $0.05). The second consists of the same penny, four quarters, and five nickels. Suppose each collection is worth $1.26. Then the penny has the same value ($0.01) in both collections.[18] Because there are no dimes in the second collection, the value of the penny does not depend upon the dimes in the first collection. Hence, even if the penny has monetary value only when used with nine other coins, its value does not depend upon any particular nine coins.

7.4.2. KYTB Coins

The standard interpretation of Fazang's metaphor founders upon a lack of motivation and an inaptness for illustrating mutual dependence. But it is worth considering whether more careful attention to the coinage of Fazang's era might rescue the standard interpretation. It does not. Explaining why helps to loosen the temptation to suppose that, because Fazang's metaphor is a metaphor of counting coins, his method of counting involves counting coins.

The main currency of the Tang Dynasty 唐朝 (618–907) is the Kai Yuan Tong Bao (KYTB) coin.[19] KYTB coins have the characters 開元通寶 (*kāi yuán tōng bǎo*) imprinted upon the four cardinal directions of their obverse (see Figure 7.1).

The balance of historical evidence seems to indicate that Tang Dynasty coins would have been made by the method of sand casting (Ch. *fānshāfǎ* 翻砂法).[20] The technique begins by reinforcing fine sand with an organic binder of some sort. The sand mixture is poured into a rectangular, wooden box. Then many mother coins (Ch. *mǔ qián* 母钱)—made individually or as copies of one ancestor coin (Ch. *zǔ qián* 祖錢)—are pressed into the surface of the

---

[18] Rather than stipulating the value of quarters, dimes, and nickels, a more complicated example would provide disjunctive conditions for these values. One such condition might be: a quarter is worth $0.25 *either* when used with one penny, two other quarters, four dimes, and two nickels *or* when used with one penny, three other quarters, and five nickels. I leave these more complicated details aside. They do not affect the main point of the example, which is that belonging to a group of ten coins does not require belonging to a group of ten specific coins.
[19] See Wilkinson 2013, 567. P'yowon 表員 (8th century) explicitly identifies Kai Yuan Tong Bao coins as the sort of coins to which Fazang's coin metaphor refers (X8.237.419c11-2). See McBride 2012a, 137, note 140.
[20] See Cao 2018, 190–2.

150   METAPHORS FOR INTERDEPENDENCE

Figure 7.1 Obverse Markings for Kai Yuan Tong Bao Coins. The proper reading order for the characters is top-bottom-right-left.
Image created by the author.

sand. Pressing a second mold box onto the top of the coins makes an impression for both sides of the mother coins. Channels are made down the center of the mold and between the coin impressions. This process is repeated to make a set of two-sided molds. When the molds are fixed together and set alongside each other, pouring a molten alloy into the molds yields a set of coin trees (Ch. *qiánshù* 钱树). Each tree is a set of coins connected to each other as in Figure 7.2. (Some money, it seems, really does grow on trees!) The coins are ready for circulation after being separated from each other and having their sides sanded.

There are some parallels between sand-casted KYTB coins and *dharmas* in the realm of Samantabhadra. Sand-casted coins naturally arise as connected with each other, each coming to be together with others. The subsequent appearance of the coins as separate from each other is derivative, and this appearance conceals the prior unity of the coins from those who do not understand how the coins come to be. Each master coin—be it an ancestor coin or a mother coin—is, in a very literal sense, the root of many other coins, and the many cast coins are the branches of their master. Moreover, because, during the sand-casting process, molten alloy flows into a mold impression for one KYTB coin only if it flows into the mold impressions for all coins, no coin arises from the casting

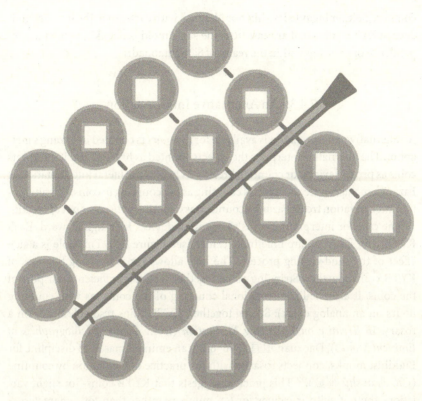

Figure 7.2 Coin Tree
Image created by the author.

process unless all coins arise from the process. Hence, each sand-casted coin arises in dependence upon every other.

Despite these parallels, sand-casted KYTB coins are not apt models for *dharmas* in the realm of Samantabhadra. The coins depend upon each other only by virtue of participating in a common casting process. This kind of indirect dependence is not how Fazang envisions mutual dependence among *dharmas*. Because the coins project monetary value, and because each coin, once cast, has monetary value by virtue of its markings rather than by virtue of its relation to others, the coins depend upon each other without thereby making or including each other (in Fazang's technical senses of *make* and *include*).[21] Because the

---

[21] For a detailed interpretation of Fazang's conceptions of inclusion and making (and identity), refer to Chapter 3.5.3.

152   METAPHORS FOR INTERDEPENDENCE

coins are neither included within nor identical with each other, the interdependence of KYTB coins that are cast from the same mold is not akin to the interdependence of *dharmas* within the realm of Samantabhadra.

7.4.3. An Alternative Interpretation

An alternative interpretation is available for the objects counted in Fazang's metaphor. The alternative interprets the objects counted as breaths, and it interprets coins as proxy devices for counting breaths. Whereas the literal interpretation of Fazang's metaphor treats Fazang's counting as the counting *of* coins, this alternative interpretation treats Fazang's counting as counting *with* coins but *of* breaths.

The case for interpreting coins as counting devices is straightforward. Each KYTB coin has a square hole in its center (see Figure 7.1). This hole is a side effect of the sand-casting process. The hole allows ropes to string bunches of KYTB coins together. Stringing coins together facilitates efficient transport of the coins. It also facilitates rotational counting of the coins (as with counting hours on an analog clock). Strung together, KYTB coins resemble beads on a rosary. In *Treatise on Practicing Meditation* (from *Continued Biographies of Eminent Monks*), Daoxuan 道宣 (596–667), an eminent master of discipline for Buddhist monks, connects rosaries with the practice of meditation by counting (Ch. *chán shǔ* 禪數).[22] This practice suggests that KYTB coins—or slight variations thereof, with markings for ten numbers rather than four characters— would make good devices for counting.

The case for interpreting the objects counted in Fazang's metaphor as breaths is less direct. There is strong precedent, in nearly all Buddhist traditions, for meditating upon breaths in order to induce *nirvāṇic* experience.[23] For example, in his *Commentary on the Treasury of Abhidharma*, the Indian Yogācārin Vasubandhu (4th to 5th century) examines mindfulness of breathing (Skt. *ānāpānasmṛti*). Vasubandhu discusses counting (Skt. *gaṇanā*) as the first of six breathing practices, explaining the basics of the technique as well as differences between the technique's correct and faulty enactments.

> [Chapter 6, Section 12.] Counting. One fixes the mind on in-breathing and out-breathing, without effort or contention; one lets the body and mind be as they are; and one counts from one to ten only in the mind. One does not count to less than ten, nor to more than ten, for fear of contention and of mental distraction.[24]

---

[22] T50.2060.597a25; Chen 2002, 340.
[23] See Dhammajoti 2008; Qing 2016.
[24] Pruden 1991, 922.

Treatise on Foundations of Yogic Practice, a 5th century compendium attributed to the future Buddha Maitreya 彌勒菩薩 or the Indian Yogācārin Asaṅga (4th century), divides the breath-based practice of counting numbers (Ch. *suàn shù* 算數) into four kinds.

> The first is counting one as one. The second is counting two as one. The third is counting "with the grain." The fourth is counting "against the grain."[25]

The first kind of breathing practice counts inhalations and exhalations separately. The second counts each pair of inhalation-exhalation as one. The third and fourth, counting "with the grain" (Skt. *anuloma-gaṇanā*; Ch. *shùn suàn shù* 順算數) and counting "against the grain" (Skt. *pratiloma-gaṇanā*; Ch. *nì suàn shù* 逆算數), are akin to Fazang's counting upward and counting downward.

For those who master counting "with the grain" and "against the grain," *Treatise on Foundations of Yogic Practice* recommends advanced counting (Skt. *gaṇanā-viśeṣa*; Ch. *shèng jìn suàn shù* 勝進算數).

> What is the meaning of "advanced counting"? Some take as their basis counting one as one. Some take as their basis counting two as one, uniting two as one and then counting. If they take as their basis counting one as one, they count by combining two inhalations and exhalations into one. If they take as their basis counting two as one, they count by combining four inhalations and exhalations into one. In this way, they gradually count up to ten. In this way, they successively and gradually improve to using one hundred as one for their counting. By counting one hundred as one, they gradually count up to ten. In this way, they diligently improve counting breaths mindfully up to using one hundred numbers as one.[26]

Although advanced counting differs in specific detail from Fazang's method of counting, both methods involve counting sequentially from one to ten, and both shift from considering distinct objects as separate to considering distinct objects as united together into wholes. This is similar to the shift of counting in Fazang's metaphor of counting coins. Counting with respect to different body relates one to each of several others. Counting with respect to same body then shifts to relate one to "all ten together." These parallels support interpreting the objects counted in Fazang's metaphor as breaths.

[25] T30.1579.431a22-3.
[26] T30.1579.431b12-20.

7.4.4. Kumārajīva on Counting Breaths

Additional support for interpreting the objects counted in Fazang's metaphor as breaths derives from the alignment between the abilities required for conceptualizing *dharmas* as mutually inclusive and the abilities developed by counting breaths. For Fazang, conceptualizing relations of inclusion among *dharmas* requires focusing attention on some *dharmas* while relegating others to peripheral attention. Kumārajīva 鳩摩羅什 (344–413), in *Sūtra on the Concentration of Sitting Meditation*, explains how counting breaths develops this kind of attentional focus. He explains, in particular, how counting breaths develops the ability to focus on one number as central while ignoring other thoughts.

> Counting the breath is quick and easy to turn away. To illustrate, when one releases cattle, since they are hard to lose, keeping them is an easy business. When one releases monkeys, however, since they are easy to lose, keeping them is a difficult task. The matter is the same here. When counting the breath, the mind cannot think of other things even for a moment. Once the mind thinks of other things, it will lose the number. For this reason, when one first [attempts to] sever thoughts, one should count the breath.[27]

For Fazang, conceptualizing relations of inclusion among *dharmas* also requires an ability to contemplate *dharmas* as unreal by virtue of being put into action by others. Kumārajīva explains how counting breaths develops this kind of discernment.

> Also, wind arises near the navel and appears to keep going. Breath goes out of the mouth and nose. Once it goes out, it ceases, just like the wind in bellows that ceases when the bellows are opened. If [the air] is drawn in by means of the mouth and nose, wind enters [the body]; this [wind] arises anew based on causes and conditions. It is just like a fan that produces wind when it meets with various conditions.
>
> At that time, one knows that inhalation and exhalation depend on causes and conditions and are delusive and unreal; they are impermanent [and not free from] arising and ceasing. One should contemplate in the following way: exhalation is drawn in by the mouth and nose as causes and conditions. The causes and conditions of inhalation are brought about by the movement of mind. A deluded person, however, does not know this and thinks that it is his own breath.[28]

---

[27] T15.614.275a3-6, recited in Yamabe and Sueki 2009, 27–8.
[28] T15.614.275a17-23, recited in Yamabe and Sueki 2009, 28.

COUNTING COINS 155

For Kumārajīva, counting breaths develops the abilities to contemplate exhaled air as put into action by the mouth and nose, inhaled air as put into action by the movement of mind and navel. These are just the sort of abilities required for contemplating *dharmas* as mutually inclusive.

7.4.5. Zhiyi on Counting Breaths

Further support for interpreting the objects counted in Fazang's metaphor as breaths derives from an examination of mindful breathing by Zhiyi 智顗 (538–597), founder of Tiantai 天台 Buddhism. In his *Six Wondrous Dharma Gates*, Zhiyi presents counting as the first of six gateways to *nirvāṇa*. Counting, for Zhiyi, is counting breaths. This involves regulating and harmonizing the breath, proceeding slowly from "one" up to "ten," focusing the mind on the counting itself. With practice, the mind gains control over its attention, diminishing its tendency to scatter "like a monkey in a tree." When the mind becomes calm and its control becomes effortless, a practitioner is able to proceed to more refined techniques for cultivating stillness and peacefulness.

According to Zhiyi, contemplating counting as an activity of mind facilitates the realization that, because all *dharmas* arise from the mind, they are all empty.

> Take for example when one first begins to study contemplation of the mind. One realizes that all of the worldly and supramundane methods for "enumeration" all come forth entirely from the mind and that, apart from the mind, there does not exist even one single additional dharma. This being the case, then, in enumerating all dharmas, in every case it is an instance of enumeration done in concert with the mind.[29]

The perfection of this contemplation, moreover, allows the practitioner to contemplate discrete objects as interdependent.

> Now [as for the perfect contemplation], the practitioner contemplates any single manifestation of mind and yet perceives all manifestations of mind as well as all dharmas. He contemplates but a single dharma and yet perceives all dharmas as manifestations of mind. He contemplates bodhi and yet perceives all instances of affliction and birth-and-death. He contemplates affliction and birth-and-death and yet perceives all instances of bodhi and nirvāṇa. He contemplates but a single buddha and yet perceives all beings as well as all

---

[29] T46.1917.553c25-c29, recited in Dharmamitra 2009, 109.

156 METAPHORS FOR INTERDEPENDENCE

buddhas. He contemplates but a single being and yet perceives all buddhas as well as all beings.

In every case, everything manifests like reflections which do not abide either inwardly or outwardly and which are neither singular nor differentiated. Throughout the ten directions, everything is [recognized as] inconceivable and ineffable. The original nature is naturally so. There is no one who could create such circumstances.[30]

In *Great Cessation and Contemplation*, Zhiyi notes specifically that counting breaths facilitates the realization that even something as small as the pore of a hair includes within itself something as great as the Buddha.

Therefore the *Sūtra on Petitioning Avalokiteśvara* [請觀世音菩薩消伏毒害陀羅尼呪經] says, "If you concentrate your mind by counting your breaths, you can see a Buddha in the pore of a hair, dwell in the Śūraṅgama [Samādhi], and attain the state of non-retrogression." By means of counting your breaths you can open the gate of liberation....[31]

Zhiyi maintains that counting breaths yields insight into interdependence. So, too, does Fazang—provided that Fazang's coins are proxies for counting breaths.

Zhiyi's description of the method of counting also strongly resembles the method Fazang pursues when analyzing the metaphor of counting ten coins. Both count sequentially from one to ten. Both conceptualize the objects counted as models for *dharmas*. Both consider counting as a vehicle for cognizing *dharmas* without ignorance or attachment. That the objects counted by Yogācārins and Zhiyi are breaths rather than material objects further supports interpreting the objects counted in Fazang's metaphor as breaths rather than coins.

7.5. Completing Fazang's Metaphor

So much for Fazang's method of counting and the interpretation of what gets counted. Fazang's metaphor also suffers from lack of completion. For each kind of counting (with respect to same body and with respect to different body), Fazang analyzes only two gateways of counting. But each kind of counting has ten gateways. Moreover, for counting with respect to different body, Fazang analyzes only part of the first gateway for each counting direction (upward and

---

[30] T46.1917.554a25-b1, recited in Dharmamitra 2009, 115.
[31] T46.1911.93a3-5, recited in Swanson 2018, 1197.

downward). But each gateway for counting with respect to different body has nine parts.

7.5.1. Criteria of Adequacy

There are many ways to complete Fazang's metaphor for counting coins. For example, the Japanese monk Hōtan Sōshun 鳳潭僧濬 (1659–1738) discusses four competing completions.[32] Hōtan's criticisms of various alternatives indicate that he (implicitly) endorses four criteria of adequacy for a correct completion.

1. In each gateway, every number should be part of some count.
2. In each gateway, every count should be unique.
3. The sequence of counts in one gateway should differ from the sequence in all other gateways.
4. The sequence of counts in one gateway should not change direction: if the gateway involves counting upward, the sequence of counts should always increase; if the gateway involves counting downward, the sequence should always decrease.

All of Hōtan's criteria are reasonable. Requiring that every number be part of some count in every gateway ensures that Fazang's metaphor is complete. Requiring uniqueness for each count within a gateway ensures that the completion is simple. Requiring uniqueness for sequencing across gateways ensures that the gateways are not mixed up or confused with each other. Requiring sequencing within gateways to be unidirectional ensures that counting within a gateway is either always progressive or always regressive.

Hōtan's fourth criterion is ambiguous. According to Hōtan, the sequence of counts *two-nine, two-ten, two-one* involves a change of direction: the sequence *two-nine, two-ten* is counting upward (because ten is greater than nine), but the sequence *two-ten, two-one* is counting downward (because one is less than ten). This indicates that, for Hōtan, directions for counting are linear—counting upward is akin to adding on a number line, and counting downward is akin to subtracting. But there are other ways to count *in the same direction*. For example, on an analog clock, counting hours in a clockwise direction is always progressive, but counting hours progressively (on a 12-hour clock) allows counting from twelve to one. If counting upward is akin to adding on a numbered circle (such as a clockface), counting upward does not require counting to a larger number.

---

[32] See T73.2344.447b6-450c1. For details about Hōtan's discussion, I am indebted to Koh 2024.

158   METAPHORS FOR INTERDEPENDENCE

Hōtan's four criteria also seem to be incomplete. Hōtan's criteria allow gateways to include counts of the form *one-one*, *two-two*, and so on. These counts would model one thing including, or being identical with, itself. Yet, for Fazang, relations of inclusion and identity are irreflexive: nothing includes itself, and nothing is identical with itself. This motivates a fifth criterion of adequacy.

5. Every count should contain two distinct elements.

All of the completions that Hōtan considers, including his own, violate this constraint. But a correct completion of Fazang's metaphor should honor the constraint.

7.5.2. Counting as Rotational

Criteria of adequacy help to guide efforts to complete the missing components of Fazang's metaphor. But such efforts also require a decision about how to interpret what it takes to count sequentially in a particular direction. There are two interpretive options. If counting is linear, then counting in a particular direction is akin to the following markings on a ruler, and so counting from one to another is counting upward only if the one is less than the other. By contrast, if counting is rotational, then counting in a particular direction is akin to following the hours on an analog clock, and so counting from (say) ten to one can qualify as counting upward even though one is less than ten.

There are two reasons to prefer completions of Fazang's metaphor that interpret counting in a particular direction as rotational rather than linear. The first reason—albeit a speculative one—concerns horology, or the measuring and keeping of time. During the Tang Dynasty, one method for marking time divides the day into watches (Ch. *gēng* 更). Because each watch is one-tenth of one day, this method of timekeeping counts ten watches, and it counts the first watch as the immediate successor to the tenth.[33] Fazang's metaphor also involves ten counts. Hence, insofar as counting, in Fazang's metaphor, is akin to keeping time, there is some reason to interpret counting in a particular direction as rotational.

The second reason to interpret counting directions as rotational rather than linear concerns elegance. If counting directions are linear, Hōtan's criteria of adequacy require discontinuous sequences of counting. For example, Hōtan's completion for the third gateway of upward counting includes the sequence

---

[33] See Wilkinson 2013, 536–7.

three-one, three-two, three-four, three-five.[34] This induces a discontinuity in the move from "two" to "four."

There is a way to avoid Hōtan's discontinuities if counting in a particular direction is rotational. For example, in the second gateway for counting upward with respect to different body, the trick is to begin the sequence at *two-three*. Because the sequence of counts within a gateway should not change direction, the count should proceed *two-four, two-five*, and so on until *two-ten*. Supposing that directions for counting are rotational, the immediately following count would be *two-one*. This completes the gateway without discontinuity. Each count in the sequence is unique. Moreover, even though *two-two* does not appear as a count, each number appears in some count because *two* appears as the first member of the ordered pair that is each count. Similarly, in the second gateway for counting downward with respect to different body, the trick is to begin the sequence at *two-one*, proceed backwards (rotationally) to *two-ten*, and end at *two-three*. This honors all five criteria of adequacy for completing Fazang's metaphor.

7.5.3. Completion for Different Body

Table 7.2 depicts a completion for Fazang's first gateways for mutual inclusion with respect to different body.

Every number, between one and ten, appears in some count for each gateway. Every count within each gateway is unique. The sequences for counting are distinct. The sequence always increases when counting upward, and it always decreases when counting downward. The numbers in each count are distinct. Hence, Table 7.2 satisfies the criteria of adequacy for completing Fazang's first gateways for mutual inclusion with respect to different body.

Table 7.3 depicts completions for Fazang's second and tenth gateways of counting upward with respect to different body for one including many.

Table 7.3 satisfies the criteria of adequacy for completing Fazang's metaphor. The reasons are the same as the reasons for Table 7.2. But there are two noteworthy aspects of Table 7.3. The first is that the final two counts in the second gateway proceed from *ten* to *one*. Provided that counting upward is rotational rather than linear, this does not violate Hōtan's criteria of adequacy. The second noteworthy aspect of Table 7.3 is that the first count in the tenth gateway for counting upward is identical to the first count in the first gateway for counting downward (see Table 7.2). Because this count does not appear elsewhere in either gateway, and because the successive counts in the second gateway differ

---

[34] Koh 2024, 189, Diagram 3-4.

160   METAPHORS FOR INTERDEPENDENCE

Table 7.2 First Gateways, Mutual Inclusion, Different Body

First Gateway		First Gateway	
Counting Upward	One-Many Inclusions	Counting Downward	Many-One Inclusions
one-two	1 includes 2	*ten-one*	10 includes 1
one-three	1 includes 3	*nine-one*	9 includes 1
one-four	1 includes 4	*eight-one*	8 includes 1
one-five	1 includes 5	*seven-one*	7 includes 1
one-six	1 includes 6	*six-one*	6 includes 1
one-seven	1 includes 7	*five-one*	5 includes 1
one-eight	1 includes 8	*four-one*	4 includes 1
one-nine	1 includes 9	*three-one*	3 includes 1
one-ten	1 includes 10	*two-one*	2 includes 1

Table 7.3 Second and Tenth Gateways, Counting Upward, One-Many Inclusion, Different Body

Second Gateway		Tenth Gateway	
Counting Upward	One-Many Inclusions	Counting Upward	One-Many Inclusions
two-three	2 includes 3	*ten-one*	10 includes 1
two-four	2 includes 4	*ten-two*	10 includes 2
two-five	2 includes 5	*ten-three*	10 includes 3
two-six	2 includes 6	*ten-four*	10 includes 4
two-seven	2 includes 7	*ten-dive*	10 includes 5
two-eight	2 includes 8	*ten-six*	10 includes 6
two-nine	2 includes 9	*ten-seven*	10 includes 7
two-ten	2 includes 10	*ten-eight*	10 includes 8
two-one	2 includes 1	*ten-nine*	10 includes 9

COUNTING COINS 161

from the successive counts in the tenth gateway, there is no violation of Hōtan's criteria.

Completing the remaining gateways of counting with respect to different body for mutual inclusion involves judicious substitutions of numbers in various counts. Completing the gateways of counting with respect to different body for mutual identity involves replacing "includes" with "makes." These are straightforward exercises. More interesting is the completion of Fazang's metaphor for counting with respect to same body.

7.5.4. Completion for Same Body

Table 7.4 depicts a completion for Fazang's ten gateways with respect to same body and one-many inclusion. (The square brackets are meant to designate all ten—one through ten—being together or considered as one.)

Every number, between one and ten, appears in some count for these gateways. For example, in the first gateway, one is the root for the count, and the remaining nine numbers belong to the "all" of the branch. Every count is unique. The counts across gateways are progressive. The elements in each count are distinct. Hence, Table 7.4 satisfies the criteria of adequacy for completing Fazang's metaphor for one-many inclusion with respect to same body.

Completing Fazang's gateways of counting with respect to same body for many-one inclusion involves inverting the terms in the columns for counts and

Table 7.4 All Gateways, One-Many Inclusion, Same Body

Gateway	Count	Inclusion
1	*one-all*	1 includes [all]
2	*two-all*	2 includes [all]
3	*three-all*	3 includes [all]
4	*four-all*	4 includes [all]
5	*five-all*	5 includes [all]
6	*six-all*	6 includes [all]
7	*seven-all*	7 includes [all]
8	*eight-all*	8 includes [all]
9	*nine-all*	9 includes [all]
10	*ten-all*	10 includes [all]

162   METAPHORS FOR INTERDEPENDENCE

inclusion relations. Completing the gateways of counting with respect to same body for identity relations involves replacing "includes" with "makes." These are straightforward exercises.

7.6. Sources for Fazang's Analysis

Motivations for Fazang's approach to contemplating the metaphor of counting coins appear in three works with which Fazang was likely familiar. The first is the *Flower Adornment Sūtra*. This is the root scripture for many doctrines in the Huayan tradition. The second is *Ten Mysterious Gates of the Unitary Vehicle of Huayan*. Tradition ascribes this work to Fazang's teacher Zhiyan 智儼 (602–668). The third is *Diagram of the Dharmadhātu of the One Vehicle of Hwaŏm*. This work was written in 668 by Ŭisang 義湘 (625–702), a monk from Silla (Korea) studying as Fazang's elder colleague under Zhiyan.

7.6.1. Flower Adornment Sūtra

The (80-scroll version of the) *Flower Adornment Sūtra* introduces the metaphor of the method of counting to explain the teaching that all things are empty by virtue of depending upon others.

> Though *nirvāṇa* cannot be seized upon, when spoken of, it is of two kinds. So too it is with all *dharmas*, for it is through discriminations that differences exist.
>
> Just as it is in reliance on those things which are counted that there exists that which is able to keep their count. Their respective natures are entirely non-existent. Just so does one completely understand dharmas.
>
> This is analogous to the method of counting that increases from one to the measureless. The method of counting is devoid of any essential nature. It is by resort to intelligence that such distinctions are made.[35]

These verses merit some brief commentary.

Discrimination (Ch. *fēn bié* 分別) refers to the activity of discriminating consciousness (Skt. *vijñāna*; Ch. *yì shí* 意識). This activity separates "external" objects of conscious experience from the "internal" contents of conscious experience. *Dharmas* exclude each other insofar as discriminating consciousness separates them from each other. But exclusion is not intrinsic to *dharmas*, and their separation ceases when discriminating consciousness ceases. Because

[35] T10.279.101b13-8, recited in Dharmamitra 2022, 1: 474. See also Cleary 1993, 448.

COUNTING COINS 163

grasping (or seizing) essentially involves discriminating consciousness, *nirvāṇa* cannot be grasped.

Discriminating consciousness is that which grasps and also that which counts. *Dharmas*, when discriminated one from another, appear as discrete and separate. These appearances render *dharmas* countable. Because *dharmas* are countable, each appears to be independent from others—and so each appears to be a real existent. But these appearances are deceptive. No *dharma* is independent of others. *Dharmas* are empty. The *Flower Adornment Sūtra* offers the method of counting as a metaphor for understanding this insight.

The *Flower Adornment Sūtra* provides no specifics about the method of counting. But there is some reason to suppose that the scripture means to refer to a meditation technique (Skt. *dhyāna*) for cultivating *nirvāṇic* experience. For example, *Sūtra on Perfect Enlightenment* mentions a similar method of counting.

> Son of good family, any beings who would cultivate *dhyāna* should first use the method of counting so as to become thoroughly aware of the number of the thoughts that arise, continue, and disappear in their minds. In this way if they extend [this practice] in everything [they do], discriminating the number of thoughts in the midst of the four modes of activity, then there will be none that are not known. They will gradually advance more and more until they are aware of everything, including even a drop of rain, in hundreds and thousands of worlds just as if their eyes were looking at something they held in hand.[36]

Sūtra on Perfect Enlightenment is an apocryphal text likely originating in early eighth-century China. But, whatever its provenance, it suggests that counting "from one to the measureless" refers to a meditative practice.

7.6.2. Zhiyan's Contemplation

In *Ten Mysterious Gates of the Unitary Vehicle of Huayan*, Zhiyan clarifies his views about interdependence within the *dharma*-realm of dependent arising—the realm of Samantabhadra—with a metaphor of counting to ten.

Zhiyan introduces the metaphor by citing a verse from a different (60-scroll) version of the *Flower Adornment Sūtra*.

> It is like the teaching of counting to ten, increasing by ones to arrive at the limitless. All are understood to be the root count, differentiated and discriminated [from each other] by wisdom.[37]

---

[36] Gregory 2005, 105.
[37] T45.1868.514b14-5. For an alternative translation, see Cleary 1983, 127.

164   METAPHORS FOR INTERDEPENDENCE

Zhiyan immediately distinguishes between two aspects or approaches to contemplating this metaphor. The first involves counting with respect to different body; the second, with respect to same body.[38] His analysis for both approaches resembles Fazang's analysis. But there are important differences. Fazang introduces various concepts—*gateway*, *making*, *root* and *branch*, *having power* and *lacking power*—that are absent from Zhiyan's analysis. The specifics for Fazang's analysis, and in particular his explanation for one-many and many-one inclusion relations, also differ from Zhiyan's analysis.

Zhiyan first explains the mutual inclusion of one and many with respect to different body.

> Counting from one to ten is going up. Counting backwards from ten to one is going down. Regarding one, because one is the cause of coming to be, in one there is ten. So one comes to be. Without ten, one does not come to be, because it lacks the characteristic of being the cause of coming to be. Because in one there is ten, one comes to be; and two, three, four, and so on all come to be. If one abides in its own nature, ten does not come to be; and if ten does not come to be, one does not come to be either.[39]

Like Fazang, Zhiyan begins with the example of one including ten. For Fazang, one includes ten because there is no ten without one. Yet, for Zhiyan, one includes ten because there is no one without ten. Fazang's explanation *inverts* Zhiyan's explanation. Zhiyan's reasoning seems to presume that when one includes another, the one is put into action (or comes to be) by virtue of the other. Fazang's technical analysis of inclusion rejects—and in fact inverts—this presumption. For Fazang, when one includes another, the one has complete power and the other completely lacks power—and so the other is put into action by the one. Because the other is inseparable from its activity, Fazang explains that one includes another because there is no other without the one. Hence, while Zhiyan's analysis for mutual inclusion likely inspires Fazang's own, Fazang's more sophisticated technical framework yields a slightly different analysis.

---

[38] Seok argues that the distinction between different body and same body is Fazang's innovation (Seok 2005). But, according to Chang, Jizang 吉藏 (549–623) is the first to make the distinction explicit. Chang provides evidence that Jizang's distinction derives from debates, among interpreters of *Treatise on Accomplishing Reality* by the Sarvāstivādin Harivarman (4th century), about the relation between conventional truth and ultimate truth. According to these masters, the two truths are one with respect to same body by virtue of being truthful, and the two truths are different with respect to different body by virtue of one being conventional and the other being ultimate. See Chang 2012, 28–9.

[39] T45.1868.514b23-8. For an alternative translation, see Cleary 1983, 127.

COUNTING COINS 165

Although Fazang's analysis of mutual inclusion differs from Zhiyan's analysis, his analysis of mutual identity does not. This is surprising and somewhat confusing. It is confusing because of Fazang's abstract analysis for mutual identity. Fazang presents the abstract analysis before presenting the metaphor of counting coins.

> Because [one] existing necessitates others lacking [existence], the others are identical with [the one]. Why? Because the others lack self-nature, [the one] makes [them]. Second: Because [one] being empty necessitates others existing, [the one] is identical with the others. Why? Because [the one] lacks self-nature, therefore the others make [it].[40]

According to this analysis, when one exists and another is empty, the other is identical with the one; and when one is empty but another exists, the one is identical with the other.

Fazang's analysis of identity in his metaphor of counting coins should follow the pattern of his abstract analysis for mutual identity. For example, he should explain one being identical with ten (with respect to different body) by considering ten as the root and one as the branch: as root, ten exists; as branch, one is empty; and one is identical with ten because branches are identical with their roots. Similarly, he should explain ten being identical with one (with respect to different body) by considering one as the root and ten as the branch: ten is identical to one because one exists but ten is empty.

Yet Fazang's analysis of identity in his metaphor does not follow the pattern for his abstract analysis of mutual identity. Consider his analysis of mutual identity (with respect to different body) for the first of his ten gateways.

> The first direction has ten gateways. [Consider] the first as one. Why? Because conditions come to be, one is identical with ten. Why? Without one, there is no ten. Since one has substance, all of the remaining are empty. Therefore, this one is identical with ten. Thus, going upwards so far as ten, know each in accordance with this first example.
>
> Speaking of the downward [direction], there are also ten gateways. [Consider] the first as ten. Why? Because conditions come to be, ten is identical with one. Why? Without ten, there is no one. Since one lacks substance, all of the remaining exist. Therefore, these ten are identical with one. Thus, going downwards so far as the first, know each in accordance with this first example.[41]

---

[40] T45.1866.503b10-3. For alternative translations, see Cook 1970, 473; Unno et al. 2023, 179–80.
[41] T45.1866.503c26-504a5. For alternative translations, see Cook 1970, 481–2; Unno et al. 2023, 182.

166   METAPHORS FOR INTERDEPENDENCE

Fazang explains that one is identical with ten because one has substance (Ch. *tǐ* 體), and he explains that ten is identical with one because one lacks substance. When one has substance, Fazang infers that it exists. When one lacks substance, Fazang infers that it is empty. Hence, Fazang's *metaphorical* explanation *inverts* his more abstract explanation. In his metaphorical explanation, X is identical with Y because X exists and Y is empty. In his abstract explanation, X is identical with Y because X is empty and Y exists. Fazang's metaphorical explanation does not cohere with his technical framework, and it does not cohere with the relation he takes to hold between inclusion and identity.

Given his technical framework, and given the relations between inclusion and identity, Fazang should have written, in the first gateway for counting upward, *ten is identical with one*; and in the first gateway for counting downward, he should have written *one is identical with ten*. Zhiyan is the likely reason why Fazang does not write these claims.

Here is Zhiyan's explanation for the mutual identity of one and many with respect to different body.

> It is the same as the former going up and going down [for mutual inclusion]. Just as one is identical with ten because [one] is the cause of coming to be, if one is not ten, then ten does not come to be. Following the above downward yields the same conclusion. Ten is identical with one because [ten] is the cause of coming to be. If ten is not one, one does not come to be.[42]

For Zhiyan, one is identical with ten because one is the cause of coming to be and ten depends upon one. This is equivalent, in Fazang's conceptual framework, to one existing and ten being empty. Zhiyan follows the same pattern for explaining why ten is identical with one. For Zhiyan, X is identical with Y because X exists and Y is empty. This is precisely the pattern Fazang follows in *his* metaphorical explanation of identity with respect to different body. But it is an inversion of the pattern he endorses in his more abstract—and more technically sound— explanation of mutual identity. Fazang's imitation of Zhiyan's analysis for mutual identity is surprising because Fazang does *not* follow Zhiyan's analysis for mutual inclusion.

Fazang's analysis of mutual identity with respect to same body is also surprising—and more confusing than his analysis with respect to different body. Here is Fazang's analysis.

> The second [analysis with respect to same body] has two aspects. The first is one being identical with ten. This has ten distinct gateways. [Consider] the first

---

[42] T45.1868.514c7-9. For an alternative translation, see Cleary 1983, 128.

as one. Why? Because conditions come to be, one is identical with ten. Why? Because this one of the ten is the first one. Because it lacks a distinct self-nature, therefore ten is identical with one. The remaining nine gateways are also like this. Know each in accordance with the example.

The second aspect is ten identical with one. This also has ten distinct gateways. [Consider] the first as ten. Why? Because conditions come to be, ten is identical with one. Why? Because that first one is identical with ten, and because [ten considered as one] is not itself [the first] one, the first one is identical with ten. Know the remaining nine gateways in accordance with this example.[43]

According to this analysis, when one is the root count, one is identical with ten; and when ten is the root, ten is identical with one. This conforms to Zhiyan's pattern for analyzing mutual identity—a pattern in which roots are identical with their branches. But Fazang changes tack midway through each gateway. The analysis that *begins* at one being identical with ten *ends* at ten being identical to one. The analysis that *begins* at ten being identical with one *ends* at one being identical with ten. The ending of each analysis coheres with Fazang's *abstract* analysis for mutual identity: for example, ten is identical with one because ten is empty of self-nature. The beginning of each analysis aligns with *Zhiyan's* analysis: for example, ten is identical with one because ten exists. These shifts might indicate that Fazang is fundamentally confused about how to explain relations of identity with his metaphor. A more charitable interpretation is that Fazang uses the character for identity (Ch. *jí* 即) in a way that is ambiguous: there is Fazang's technical precisification, whereby "X 即 Y" is true when X is empty and Y exists; and there is a Zhiyan-style precisification, whereby "X 即 Y" is true when X exists and Y is empty.

If Fazang uses the character for identity (Ch. *jí* 即) in a way that is ambiguous, his metaphorical analysis for mutual identity pays homage to Zhiyan's analysis, and his more abstract analysis indicates a more refined (and systematic) understanding. Other comparisons between Fazang and Zhiyan exhibit similar evidence of Fazang's more refined understanding. For example, when an anonymous interlocutor asks about the difference between ten being in one and ten being identical with one, Zhiyan offers a subtle reply.

[Ten is in one because] apart from one there is no ten, and yet ten is not one. [Ten is identical with one because] apart from one there is no ten, and ten itself is one, because ten is the cause of one coming to be.[44]

---

[43] T45.1866.504b24-c2. For alternative translations, see Cook 1970, 490–1; Unno et al. 2023, 185.
[44] T45.1868.514c18-20. For an alternative translation, see Cleary 1983, 128.

168 METAPHORS FOR INTERDEPENDENCE

Fazang's analysis supports a clearer and more refined answer: ten is in one, because one has power but ten lacks power; ten is identical with one, because one exists (or has substance) but ten is empty. This indicates that although Zhiyan's analysis of counting with respect to different body motivates Fazang's analysis, Fazang's analysis improves upon Zhiyan's by invoking a more sophisticated conceptual framework.

Despite Fazang's improvements to Zhiyan's conceptual framework, Fazang is clearly indebted to Zhiyan's analyses. This is evident in Fazang's metaphorical analyses for mutual identity. It is also evident in Fazang's distinction between different body and same body. Zhiyan explains the difference between different body and same body by contrasting two different senses in which one is said to include many.

> Speaking of one including ten through different [body] means that, from the perspective of the remaining nine, the one includes ten. Speaking of one including ten through [same body] means that, because one is inseparable from the nine it includes, one includes ten.[45]

Zhiyan clarifies that considering the remaining nine (Ch. *hòu jiǔ* 後九) to be inseparably (Ch. *jí* 即) one means "the nine are in themselves a body and yet this one [body] is not nine."[46] He declares, accordingly, that using the method of counting to contemplate numbers with respect to same body reveals, of the numbers one through ten, that each mutually includes and is mutually identical with a unified body (Ch. *yītǐ* 一體) that has the remaining nine as parts. This is a clear precedent for Fazang's own use of the distinction between different body and same body.

Overall, Zhiyan's analysis for the method of counting motivates several features of Fazang's analysis. Zhiyan introduces the distinction between counting upward and counting downward. He introduces the difference between counting to understand mutual inclusion and counting to understand mutual identity. He introduces the distinction between counting with respect to different body and counting with respect to same body. Much of the reasoning in Zhiyan's analysis also appears in Fazang's analysis.

Three differences between the analyses by Zhiyan and Fazang are salient. The first is that Fazang uses various concepts that are absent from Zhiyan's analysis. For example, Fazang, but not Zhiyan, considers multiple gateways for each direction of counting. Fazang, but not Zhiyan, also invokes various distinctions—such as *root* and *branch*, *having power* and *lacking power*—to explain relations

---

[45] T45.1868.515a20-2. For an alternative translation, see Cleary 1983, 130.
[46] T45.1868.515a23-4. For an alternative translation, see Cleary 1983, 130.

among the objects counted in each direction. The most likely explanation for this difference is that Fazang uses a conceptual framework that is more sophisticated than Zhiyan's. The second salient difference is that Fazang endorses an abstract analysis of inclusion and identity that diverges from Zhiyan's analysis. For example, when one is root and another is its branch, Fazang infers that the one includes the other but Zhiyan infers that the other includes the one. Here again, the most likely explanation is that Fazang's conceptual framework is more sophisticated than Zhiyan's. The third salient distinction is that Fazang mentions coins in relation to the method of counting but Zhiyan does not. A likely explanation for this difference—and an explanation that complements the explanation for the first salient difference—is that there is a further source of motivation for Fazang's analysis.

7.6.3. Ŭisang's Contemplation

In *Diagram of the Dharmadhātu of the One Vehicle of Hwaŏm*, Zhiyan's student, Ŭisang, refines the method of counting to ten into a method of counting ten coins (Ch. *shǔ shí qián fǎ* 數十錢法). *Diagram of the Dharmadhātu* consists of a 210-character poem and an extensive auto-commentary.[47] The method of counting ten coins appears in the auto-commentary as a tool for contemplating the *dharma*-realm of dependent arising.[48] Ŭisang divides the method into two parts.

> Those who wish to contemplate the method of the incantation of the true nature of dependent arising should first understand the method of counting ten coins—that is, [counting from] one coin up to ten coins. The reason for speaking of ten is the desire to manifest the uncountable. This method has two parts. The first is one in ten, ten in one. The second is one identical with ten, ten identical with one.[49]

Like Zhiyan and Fazang, Ŭisang maintains that the method of counting is a vehicle for contemplating mutual inclusion and mutual identity. Like Zhiyan and Fazang, Ŭisang also distinguishes between counting upward and counting downward. Unlike Zhiyan and Fazang, Ŭisang is explicit that the method of counting ten coins is suitable for advanced practitioners who wish to contemplate the true

[47] For a review of debates regarding the authorship of *Diagram of the Dharmadhātu*, see Plassen 2007.

[48] See McBride 2012b, 159, 168.

[49] For an alternative translation, see McBride 2012b, 168. I rely upon McBride 2012b as an authoritative Chinese-language edition of Ŭisang's work.

170   METAPHORS FOR INTERDEPENDENCE

nature of dependent arising. Moreover, unlike Zhiyan, but like Fazang, Ŭisang invokes a distinction among different gateways for counting as well as the distinction between root and branch.

Consider, for the sake of contrast with the analyses by Zhiyan and Fazang, Ŭisang's contemplation of mutual inclusion using the first gateway for the method of counting ten coins.[50]

> The first gateway [of the method of counting ten coins] has two [directions]. The first is going upward. The second is going downward.
>
> Speaking of going upward, there are ten distinct gateways. [Consider] the first as one. Why? Because conditions come to be, one is the root for counting up to ten and so one includes ten. Why? Without one, ten does not come to be. Yet ten is not one. Because the remaining gateways are like this, know them in accordance with the example.
>
> Speaking of going downward, there are also ten gateways. [Consider] the first as ten. Why? Because conditions come to be. Going so far as ten, ten includes one. Why? Without ten, one does not come to be. Yet one is not ten. The remaining are also like this.[51]

Apart from the mention of gateways and an ambiguity about whether Ŭisang conceptualizes ten with respect to different body or same body, Ŭisang's reasoning strongly resembles Fazang's.[52] Unlike Zhiyan and Fazang, Ŭisang specifies that his method of counting involves real coins.

> The above method of counting coins depends throughout upon considering real coins, manifesting the other-dependence of the causes and conditions of dependently arising coins.[53]

Ŭisang's analysis also includes a brief postscript that interprets coins as markers for counting gateways.

> Conceiving transformations such as these, both should be considered together to know that in each and every coin, all ten gateways are complete. Just as coins

---

[50] For Ŭisang's contemplation of mutual identity, see McBride 2012b, 172.

[51] For an alternative translation, see McBride 2012b, 168–9.

[52] P'yowon interprets the ambiguity in Ŭisang's analysis as evidence that Ŭisang (inappropriately) ignores Zhiyan's distinction between different body and same body (X8.237.420a7-12; see also McBride 2012a, 142–3, notes 152–3). Contemporary commentators infer, from Ŭisang's omission of this distinction, that Zhiyan is not the author of *Ten Mysterious Gates*. (For extensive references, see McBride 2012b, 78–9, note 151.) An alternative explanation is that Ŭisang's concern is more practical than scholastic. Motivation for this alternative is that Ŭisang characterizes the method of counting as an incantation rather than a contemplation.

[53] For an alternative translation, see McBride 2012b, 176.

that are both root and branch encompass all ten gateways completely, understand the remaining eight coins in accordance with the example.[54]

The two coins to which Ŭisang refers correspond to the two cases he considers in
his contemplation of mutual inclusion. In the first case, one is root, ten is branch,
and one includes ten. This is the first of ten gateways for counting upward. In the
second case, one is branch, ten is root, and ten includes one. This is the first of
ten gateways for counting downward. Hence, for Ŭisang, coins are markers for
counting gateways rather than objects counted within gateways.

For Ŭisang, coins are devices for tracking attentional focus. This confirms the
contention that, in Fazang's metaphor of counting coins, the relata for relations
of inclusion and identity are not coins. It also provides a clue about Ŭisang's motivation for transforming Zhiyan's method of counting into a method of counting
coins. Ŭisang characterizes his method of counting coins as an incantation (Skt.
dhāraṇī; Ch. tuóluóní 陀羅尼) of the true nature of dependent arising rather
than a contemplation of the *dharma*-realm of dependent arising. Incantations
are skillful means for sustaining or bearing something in mind.[55] They can take
form as chants or recitations that confer special powers. Typical powers include
working miracles, recollecting past lives, and gaining release from defilement.[56]
For Ŭisang, the incantation associated with the method of counting coins
confers special power of the latter sort, namely, release from delusional cognition of *dharmas*.

Insofar as Ŭisang's method of counting coins is an incantation, its similarities
to Fazang's metaphor of counting coins provides further reason to interpret
Fazang's metaphor as a meditative vehicle. The content of incantations is secondary to their performance.[57] This explains Fazang's lack of attention to the
details of the objects counted. If Fazang's metaphor is a meditative vehicle, and if
his analysis for the metaphor is an incantation that enacts this vehicle, the content of the analysis is secondary to its performance.

Interpreting Fazang's analysis for the metaphor of counting coins as an incantation coheres with evidence that Fazang participated in a variety of incantatory practices.[58] It also supports a conjecture about why Fazang's metaphor and
Ŭisang's incantation involve counting coins rather than numbers or breaths.

Medieval Chinese Buddhists did more than teach and interpret. They
also participated in a variety of material practices. For example, they wrote
incantations on paper or silk, wrapping the inscribed sheets on knotted

[54] McBride 2012b, 169.
[55] Ujike 1983, 558.
[56] McBride 2005, 90.
[57] Copp 2014, 4–5.
[58] See Chen 2007, 269–73.

172 METAPHORS FOR INTERDEPENDENCE

incantation cords (Skt. *pratisarā*; Ch. *zhòu suǒ* 咒索) and wearing the enchanted cords around their waists. During the Song Dynasty 宋朝 (960–1279), under the influence of Daoist traditions, they also began circulating numismatic charms, imprinted with symbols of Buddhism, for use in various rituals.[59] According to Fang and Thierry,

> Every element on [Chinese numismatic charms], including every character, every phrase, every object, every plant, and every animal, produces a precise sense, based on form, about a physical or therapeutic property, about a historical reference, about a literary allusion, about the iconography, and ultimately about any relationship between this object and its nature, through symbols, metaphors, riddles and homophones.[60]

Fazang's metaphor and Ŭisang's incantation are, perhaps, partial anticipations of later practices relating to numismatic charms.

7.7. The Significance of Fazang's Analysis

The precedents for Fazang's metaphor of counting coins motivate Fazang's focus on the method of counting, various aspects of his reasoning and conceptual framework, as well as the association he makes between counting and coins. The *Flower Adornment Sūtra* motivates contemplating the realm of Samantabhadra by counting numbers. Zhiyan introduces the distinction between different body and same body. He also introduces the distinction between counting upward and counting downward. Ŭisang, in turn, makes explicit that the method of counting is a practice for advanced practitioners. He also introduces the association between counting and coins. Fazang improves upon these precedents by invoking distinctions—for example, between having power and lacking power—that are absent from those sources. His analysis is also more thorough, systematic, and comprehensive than anything that appears in his sources. But the significance of Fazang's analysis extends beyond these improvements.

7.7.1. Developing Indra's Net

When considered in relation to Fazang's analysis for the metaphor of Indra's net, Fazang's analysis for the metaphor of counting coins is

---

[59] Geng 2016, 84.
[60] Fang and Thierry 2016, 12–3.

somewhat inferior. The metaphor of Indra's net is more vivid, and Fazang's analysis for that metaphor is more principled. Because the jewels of Indra's net manifest reflections and because these reflections enter into each other, the jewels are vivid analogues for the mutual identity and mutual inclusion of *dharmas* in the realm of Samantabhadra. Fazang makes explicit no such analogues in his metaphor of counting coins. The Buddhist theory of reflection also provides principled support for Fazang's analysis of identity and inclusion relations among the jewels of Indra's net. By contrast, Fazang's assertions about such relations in the metaphor of counting coins are brute and unprincipled.

Despite these differences between the metaphors of Indra's net and counting coins, Fazang's metaphor of counting coins develops his metaphor of Indra's net in three significant ways. The first development concerns the introduction of gateways. Contemplating the metaphor of Indra's net involves selecting one jewel as central to attentional focus and relegating all others to peripheral attention. Completing the contemplation requires shifting attentional focus from one jewel to another. There is nothing in the metaphor that marks these attentional shifts. Contemplating the metaphor of counting coins also involves selecting one (breath) as central to attentional focus, relegating others to peripheral attention, and then shifting attentional focus to another. The metaphor of counting coins differs from the metaphor of Indra's net by introducing gateways to mark these attentional shifts. Because each gateway is a vehicle for guiding contemplation, counting from one gateway to another is akin to shifting attentional focus from one *dharma* to another.

The second significant development in Fazang's metaphor of counting coins concerns the distinction between different body and same body. Contemplating the metaphor of Indra's net involves considering one jewel in relation to all other jewels. There is an ambiguity in this contemplation. Sometimes one relates to many others by virtue of relating to each of those others as distinct individuals and not the whole that they all compose. For example, someone can be friends with each person on a team without being friends with the team itself. By contrast, sometimes one relates to many others by virtue of relating to some whole to which all belong despite not relating to other parts of that whole as distinct individuals. For example, someone can be loyal to a country without being loyal to each citizen of that country.

It is not clear whether considering one jewel of Indra's net in relation to all other jewels is a matter of considering the one in relation to each other jewel as an individual or, instead, a matter of considering the one in relation to the whole mass of jewels. Fazang's metaphor of counting coins avoids this ambiguity by dividing contemplation of the metaphor into two parts. The first part, concerning

174   METAPHORS FOR INTERDEPENDENCE

different body, considers one (breath) in relation to each of nine others. The second part, concerning same body, considers one in relation to the whole that is "all ten together."

The third significant development in Fazang's metaphor of counting coins concerns directionality. Contemplating the metaphor of Indra's net involves considering jewels under multiple aspects. Considering jewels as chief involves attending to the aspects of existing and having power. Considering jewels as attendant involves attending to the aspects of being empty and lacking power. There is nothing in the metaphor that marks the shift from considering one pair of aspects to considering the other pair. Contemplating the metaphor of counting coins also involves considering the objects contemplated (breaths) under multiple aspects. Considering objects counted as root or substance involves attending to the aspects of existing and having power. Considering objects counted as branch or function involves attending to the aspects of being empty and lacking power. The metaphor of counting coins differs from the metaphor of Indra's net by introducing, to the contemplation with respect to different body, the distinction between counting upward and counting downward. This distinction marks the shift from considering one as existing with power to considering the same one as empty and without power.

7.7.2. Conceptual Insight

From an interpretive perspective, the significance of Fazang's analysis for the metaphor of counting coins resides with neither the vividness of its metaphor nor the justification for the analysis. The significance resides, instead, with the insight that the analysis offers into Fazang's conceptual framework. Fazang's analysis for the metaphor of counting coins is his most detailed analysis for any metaphor about the realm of Samantabhadra.

The details of Fazang's analysis—or, at least, the details for his analysis of mutual inclusion—confirm and illustrate much of the conceptual framework attributed to Fazang in Chapter 3 and Chapter 5. The details also illustrate something that his analysis of Indra's net does not, namely, how cognizing the realm of Samantabhadra involves shifting attentional focus among various gateways for contemplation.

Fazang's analysis for the metaphor of counting coins illustrates that cognizing mutuality among *dharmas* within the realm of Samantabhadra requires three abilities. The first is the ability to shift among gateways without attachment to one as more fundamental (or correct) than others. The second is the ability to shift between the gradations of chief and attendant without attachment to one gradation as more apt (or correct) than the other. The third is the ability to cognize the many *dharmas* relegated to peripheral attention as relating to whatever is central to attentional focus as both discrete individuals (with respect to different body) and as parts of a unified whole (with respect to same body).

8
Building Unity

8.1. From Coins to Buildings

Latent within Fazang's analyses for the metaphors of Indra's net and counting coins is a commitment to the existence of wholes (Ch. *quán* 全). For Fazang, *dharmas* relate to each other as individuals, each sovereign over and vulnerable to particular others. These are relations with respect to different body (Ch. *yì tǐ* 異體). Yet Fazang also acknowledges relations with respect to same body (Ch. *tóng tǐ* 同體).[1] These are relations whereby one *dharma* as chief relates to all other *dharmas* together as attendants. For Fazang, the togetherness of the attendants derives from their mutual responsiveness (Ch. *hù yìng* 互應), and this responsiveness means that the chief and attendants are parts of a unified whole (Ch. *yītǐ* 一體).

Fazang's analysis of same-body relations presumes that there are wholes, composed of many *dharmas*, in the realm of Samantabhadra. This is evident, for example, in his remark that "chief and attendants together form one whole."[2] When one (chief) *dharma* relates to many (attendant) others and these others are mutually responsive, Fazang's analysis of same-body relations entails that the one and the others compose a whole. For example, when one is mutually responsive with nine others, the one belongs to a whole that has itself and the nine others as parts. Because this is true for each of the ten, there is exactly one whole, this whole has exactly ten parts, and gateways for contemplating this whole differ only with respect to which part is considered to be its chief (or root).

Fazang concludes his *Treatise on the Five Teachings of Huayan* with a metaphor that explains his conception of wholes. The metaphor likens *dharmas* to different kinds of material—rafters, roofing tiles, pillars, and so on. It likens wholes to a building that the various materials compose. Fazang's central contention, in his analysis for the metaphor of the building, is that each part of a whole (or kind thereof) by itself makes the whole. This contention derives from Fazang's conception of interdependence. But it contravenes a more natural assumption, namely, that rafters, roofing tiles, pillars, and so on make the building only by virtue of cooperating with each other.

[1] For more extensive discussion of *different body* and *same body*, refer to Chapter 7.3.4.
[2] T45.1866.484a22. For alternative translations, see Cook 1970, 209; Unno et al. 2023, 74.

Metaphors for Interdependence. Nicholaos Jones, Oxford University Press. © Nicholaos Jones 2025.
DOI: 10.1093/9780197807224.003.0008

This chapter reconstructs Fazang's analysis for his building metaphor and contextualizes his approach to that analysis. The goal is to articulate a way of conceptualizing buildings that supports Fazang's analysis while also being independently plausible. The chapter divides into seven parts. The first part contrasts a familiar style of building architecture with a style more familiar to Fazang. The second reviews ancestors to Fazang's building metaphor. The third part of the chapter introduces Fazang's theory about part-whole relations—his so-called theory of six characteristics. Three subsequent parts of the chapter examine pairs of these characteristics for the sake of clarifying and making precise Fazang's conception of wholes. The chapter concludes by reconstructing a justification for Fazang's theory of six characteristics. The reconstruction relies upon Fazang's conception of interdependence in the realm of Samantabhadra.

8.2. Competing Architectures

A natural assumption about buildings is that various materials make a building only by virtue of cooperating with each other. This assumption derives from a particular conception of how building materials compose buildings. Fazang rejects this conception. The likely reason is his familiarity with a distinctive style of architecture.

8.2.1. Buddhaghosa's Palace

The influential Theravādin monk Buddhaghosa (5th century) offers a paradigmatic example for the conception of buildings as composites of cooperating parts. He does so in a metaphor that likens contact (Skt. *sparśa*; P. *phassa*)—or the coming together of sense organ, sense object, and sense consciousness—to a pillar in a palace.

> [Contact] is like a pillar in a palace being the firm support to the rest of the structure; and just as beams, cross-beams, wing-supports, roof-rafters, cross-rafters, and neck-pieces are fastened to the pillar, are fixed on the pillar, so also is [contact] a firm support to the simultaneous and associated events. It is like the pillar, the rest of the psychic events is [sic] like the other structure material.[3]

When fasteners fix the upper structure of a palace to the palace's pillars, the materials of the upper structure fall if the pillars fall, but the pillars remain upright

---

[3] Guenther 1957, 48.

178 METAPHORS FOR INTERDEPENDENCE

even if the fasteners and materials of the upper structure fall. For Buddhaghosa, "a state that assists in the mode of foundation and support is a *support condition* [Skt. *niśraya-pratyaya*], as the earth is for trees, as canvas is for paintings, and so on."[4] Hence, because the pillars assist the materials of the upper structure in the mode of support or foundation, they are support conditions for those materials. But the materials of the upper structure are not support conditions for the pillars.

Imagine, for the sake of further illustration, that the upper structure of Buddhaghosa's palace consists of a roofing truss and roofing tiles. Suppose that the roofing truss is made from beams running the length and width of the palace, rafters sloping upward from those beams, and a ridgepole at the peak of the palace's roof. Suppose, further, that fasteners fix the roofing tiles to the outer surface of the roofing truss. Then the pillars are support conditions for both the roofing truss and the roofing tiles, and the roofing truss is a support condition for the roofing tiles. But the roofing tiles are not support conditions for the roofing truss, and neither tiles nor truss are support conditions for the pillars.

Because, in this extension of Buddhghosa's metaphor, the roofing truss supports the roofing tiles but not the pillars, the truss' support of the tiles depends upon something the truss does not support. Hence, the roofing truss does not by itself support the tiles. Because the truss supports the tiles only in cooperation with the pillars, it assists the palace in the mode of support only in cooperation with the pillars. Insofar as the palace in Buddhaghosa's metaphor is a whole that has pillars and other building materials as parts, and insofar as Buddhaghosa's support relation models the relation whereby *dharmas* of one kind make *dharmas* of other kinds, this conception of how building materials compose buildings entails that some wholes contain *dharmas* that do not, as a kind, by themselves make the whole.

8.2.2. *Diàntáng* Architecture

The central contention in Fazang's analysis of his building metaphor—that each part of a whole (or kind thereof) by itself makes the whole—derives from a competing conception of how building materials compose buildings. The architectural design of Buddhist temples from the Sui 隋 and Tang 唐 eras supports this competing conception. These temples are *diàntáng* 殿堂 (palace-hall) constructions.[5]

---

[4] Ñāṇamoli 2010, 553.
[5] See Fu 2017, 254–8. See also Needham 1971, 91–104; Ledderose 2000, 107–11; Steinhardt 2002, 7–8; Sun 2011, 4.

BUILDING UNITY 179

The main parts for a *diàntáng* construction are the body and the roof. A network of columnar pillars (Ch. *zhù wǎng* 柱網) forms the bay of the body. Thick tie-beams fix the columns together and support the wooden roofing truss. The roofing truss—composed of further tie-beams running the width of the building, purlins running the length of the building, a ridgepole at the peak, and rafters sloping in between—supports heavy clay roofing tiles. Wooden *dǒugǒng* 斗拱 (cap-and-block) brackets connect the roofing truss to the pillars.

Several features of *diàntáng*-style architecture are visible in a miniature replica of the Kuixing Pavilion 奎星阁 at the China Three Gorges Museum (Ch. 重庆中国三峡博物馆) in Chongqing 重庆. (See Figure 8.1.)

The top area of Figure 8.1 displays tie-beams, purlins, and rafters as well as wooden replicas for clay roofing tiles. The bottom area displays *dǒugǒng* brackets. These particular brackets elevate the roofing structure atop the uppermost terrace of the pavilion. One of the supporting columns for the pavilion is visible in the bottom center of the image.

Diàntáng buildings are remarkably stable against earthquakes. The key to their stability is joinery. Fasteners do not hold together the materials of

Figure 8.1 Kuixing Pavilion (Replica)
Photograph by the author.

180 METAPHORS FOR INTERDEPENDENCE

diàntáng buildings. Instead, mortise-and-tenon joints, pressed together by the weight of the roofing tiles, connect tie-beams, purlins, rafters, and ridgepole into the roofing truss. Similar joints, pressed together by the weight of tiles and truss, connect the many small, interlaced components that make the *dǒugǒng* brackets.[6] The weight of the roofing materials and brackets, in turn, presses the pillars of the body into a series of floating joints that connect the pillars to a flattened area on the ground. Because the floating joints and mortise-and-tenon joinery allow the pillars to auto-deform and the upper sections of the building to slide independently, the materials of *diàntáng* buildings have the capacity to cancel horizontal thrusts and absorb energy from internal friction or rotation.[7]

In *diàntáng* buildings, materials of each kind are support conditions for materials of every other kind. Pillars support brackets, both pillars and brackets support the roofing truss, and materials of all three kinds—pillars, brackets, truss—support the roofing tiles. This much is similar to Buddhaghosa's palace metaphor. Yet, because materials in *diàntáng* buildings hold together by virtue of their weight rather than by virtue of fasteners, all of these support relations are mutual. Roofing tiles press tie-beams, purlins, rafters, and ridgepole into mortise-and-tenon joints, and these materials thereby form the roofing truss. The tiles and the roofing truss press purlins and beams into brackets, thereby forming the upper structure of the building. The materials of this structure push the brackets onto the tops of the pillars, and the entire structure presses the pillars into joinery on the ground of the building. Because the materials of the truss would fall without the weight of the roofing tiles, and because the roofing tiles would fall without the materials of the truss, truss and tiles are inseparable. So the roofing truss supports the roofing tiles, and the tiles also support the truss. For similar reasons, tiles and brackets support each other, tiles and pillars support each other, and in general materials of each kind support materials of every other kind.

Insofar as the support relation models the relation whereby *dharmas* of one kind make *dharmas* of other kinds, *diàntáng* buildings are examples of wholes in which each part (or kind thereof) by itself makes all other parts. Because one kind of material supporting all other kinds suffices for the composition of the building, *diàntáng* buildings are also examples of wholes in which each part (or kind thereof) by itself makes the whole. Fazang's central contention—that each part of a whole (or kind thereof) by itself makes the whole—is, in effect,

---

[6] For diagrams of mortise-and-tenon joinery and the components of *dǒugǒng* brackets, respectively, see Figure 763 and Figure 744 in Needham 1971, 98, 109. Fans of the TV series *Ashes of Love* (Ch. *Xiāng mì chén chén jìn rú shuāng* 香蜜沉沉烬如霜) can see a digital rendering of a *dǒugǒng* bracket in Season 1, Episode 40, at 36:15 (Liu and Zhang 2018).

[7] Que et al. 2017, 210–4.

the contention that wholes in the realm of Samantabhadra are akin to *diàntáng* buildings.

8.3. Sources for Fazang's Metaphor

Unlike the metaphors of Indra's net and counting coins, Fazang's metaphor of the building does not appear in the *Flower Adornment Sūtra*. Nonetheless, like Fazang's other metaphors, his metaphor of the building belongs to a family of metaphors from the Buddhist tradition.

8.3.1. Buildings as Models for Delusion

Some metaphors from the Buddhist tradition invoke buildings to explain the teaching of no-self (Skt. *anatman*; Ch. *wú wǒ* 無我). Consider, for example, *Greater Sūtra on the Simile of the Elephant's Footprint.*

> Just as when a space is enclosed by timber and creepers, grass, and clay, it comes to be termed 'house,' so too, when a space is enclosed by bones and sinews, flesh and skin, it comes to be termed 'material form'.[8]

Nearly the same metaphor appears in the Chinese version of the scripture.

> Just as when a space is enclosed by timber, clay, and reeds it comes to be termed a "house," so too, venerable friends, it is with this body: know that when a space is enclosed by sinews, bones, skin, flesh, and blood it comes to be termed a "body."[9]

Houses and physical bodies are composites of many parts. Composites, and physical bodies in particular, are targets for attachment. Attachment to composites fosters the delusion that there is an unchanging self that is sovereign over and yet not vulnerable to the composite. *Greater Sūtra on the Simile of the Elephant's Footprint* forestalls this attachment by likening bodies to houses. Just as houses are empty of self, so, too, is a person's physical body empty of self.

Other building metaphors from the Buddhist tradition associate buildings and their materials with the symptoms and conditions of *saṃsāric* experience. *Sūtra*

---

[8] Ñāṇamoli and Bodhi 1995, 283.
[9] MĀ 3.31; T1.26.466c29-467a2, recited in Bingenheimer et al. 2013, 232.

182 METAPHORS FOR INTERDEPENDENCE

on the Perception of Impermanence likens ignorance about the nature of the self to the ridgepole of a building, and it likens greed for existence (Skt. *bhavarāga*), greed for sensual pleasure (Skt. *kāmarāga*), and greed toward materiality (Skt. *rūparāga*) to the rafters that support the ridgepole.[10] The third chapter of the *Lotus Sūtra* likens characteristics of *saṃsāric* experience to materials within a burning house, and it likens cessation of *saṃsāra* to escape from the house.[11] Both of these metaphors conceptualize buildings as denizens of a realm laden with ignorance and attachment—the realm of the imaginary (Skt. *parikalpita*; Ch. *suǒ zhí* 所執). This seems to entail that buildings are not apt models for the realm of Samantabhadra.

Fazang is certainly familiar with precedents, internal to the Buddhist tradition, that associate buildings with the imaginary. For example, when commenting upon the parable of the burning house, the Chinese monk Daosheng 道生 (360–434), himself an eminent student of the esteemed translator Kumārajīva 鳩摩羅什 (344–413), likens the house to a refuge of those who take delusion as truth, and he likens various building materials—walls, pillars, beams, ridgepoles—to afflictions such as delusion, false view, ignorance, and self-love.[12] Similarly, the Dharmaguptaka (Ch. *Fǎzàng bù* 法藏部) school's *Treatise on Abhidharma [Preached by] Śāriputra*, translated into Chinese by the monks Dharmayaśas 曇摩耶舍 and Dharmagupta 曇摩崛多 between 407 and 414, likens the illusory self to a building.[13] According to Daosheng and the Dharmaguptaka, buildings are illusions that appear to those beset with ignorance and attachment.

8.3.2. Buildings as Models for Insight

Despite the precedents for associating buildings with the realm of imaginary, there is a competing precedent that associates buildings with a realm that is free from ignorance and attachment. Consider, for example, *Questions of King Milinda*. In the thirteenth chapter of the first book, Nāgasena 那先, a Buddhist sage, and King Menander 彌蘭陀王 (P. Miliṇda), an Indo-Greek ruler of an empire in the northwestern Indian subcontinent, discuss right concentration (Skt. *samyaksamādhi*; P. *sammā-samādhi*). The king asks Nāgasena to define the nature of concentration. Nāgasena obliges with a building metaphor.

Leading, O king, for all good qualities have [right] concentration as their chief; they incline to it, lead up towards it. . . . As the rafters of a house incline and lead

[10] See Bodhi 2000, 961–2.
[11] See Kubo and Yayama 2007, 56–60.
[12] See Kim 1990, 206–7.
[13] T28.1548.626c11-18.

up to the ridge-pole and the ridge-pole is the highest point of the roof. So too all good qualities incline and lead up to [right] concentration....[14]

The Chinese parallel, *Sūtra on the Monk Nāgasena*, invokes a similar metaphor.

Nāgasena said, "Among all skills, mental unification alone is foremost. All skills ensue for a person who is able to unify the mind."

Nāgasena said, "It is similar to a flight of steps to an upper story which should have something as its support, so all skills adhere to mental unification."[15]

Nāgasena likens building materials to qualities that facilitate the attainment of *nirvāṇa*. Just as a ridgepole brings together rafters to support a roof, and just as runners support steps as they rise to higher floors, right concentration centers consciousness and its concomitants upon a single object.[16]

Nāgasena's metaphor is consistent with his view, elsewhere in *Questions of King Milinda*, that wholes are imaginary delusions. But the metaphor at least provides precedent for associating building materials with that which facilitates freedom from ignorance and attachment. This is precisely what Fazang does with his metaphor of the building, likening different kinds of building material to *dharmas* of various kinds within the realm of Samantabhadra.

8.3.3. Buildings as Models of Unity

There is also precedent, internal to the Buddhist tradition, for supposing that building materials of various kinds unite into a building. Consider, for example, Nāgārjuna's *Twelve Gate Treatise*.[17] Nāgārjuna's first gate concerns the emptiness of causal conditions. He contrasts internal causal conditions—conditions such as ignorance, consciousness, and attachment—with external causal conditions. To illustrate the concept *external causal condition*, he provides an example about a building.

For example, when managing a building location, foundation, pillars, rafters, mud, grass, skilled labor, and so on unite. This is why a building arises.[18]

---

[14] Pesala 2001, 41–2.
[15] T32.1670B.718b18-20, recited in Anālayo 2021b, 142.
[16] See also Ñāṇamoli 2010, 81–2.
[17] The *Twelve Gate Treatise* is a pivotal text for the tradition of Chinese Madhyamaka. Fazang identifies Nāgārjuna as the author (T42.1826.212c10). For contemporary debate about whether Nāgārjuna is the author, see Cheng 1982, 27–33.
[18] T30.1568.160a2-3. For an alternative translation, see Cheng 1982, 55.

184   METAPHORS FOR INTERDEPENDENCE

Nāgārjuna proceeds to argue that nothing arising from causal conditions is real.[19] On the one hand, because arising from causal conditions precludes being self-natured, that which arises from causal conditions cannot be real by virtue of being self-natured. On the other hand, because that which arises does not have the specific characteristics of that from which it arises, that which arises from causal conditions cannot be real by virtue of being other-natured.

These arguments are consistent with the view, in *Commentary on the Great Perfection of Wisdom*, that wholes are imaginary delusions. But the context makes clear that Nāgārjuna equates being imaginary with being empty of self-nature. For Nāgārjuna, buildings are empty of self-nature because they are unities (Skt. *saṃgraha*, *samagra*; Ch. *hé hé* 和合) of their various materials; and buildings are imaginary because they are empty of self-nature.

Given Fazang's conception of the realm of Samantabhadra, according to which *dharmas* are empty of self-nature and yet not imaginary, Nāgārjuna's arguments do not preclude supposing that building materials (or parts of other kinds) sometimes unite into nonimaginary wholes.[20] Such wholes would be empty of self-nature. But they would be apparent existents rather than imaginary ones. This conception of wholes aligns with precedent, from indigenous Chinese traditions, for denying that wholes are mere reifications of the imagination. For example, according to the *Zhuangzi* 莊子,

> Now you can point to the hundred parts of a horse's body and never come up with a horse, and yet the horse is right there, tethered in front of you; it is precisely through establishing the hundred parts that we call it 'horse.'[21]

The same conception of wholes—as empty of self-nature but appearing to exist—is one that Fazang adopts in his building metaphor.

8.3.4. Zhiyan's Building Metaphor

Whatever the precedents for Fazang's metaphor of the building, Fazang likely inherits the metaphor from his mentor, Zhiyan智儼 (602–668). In *Ten Mysterious Gates of the Unitary Vehicle of Huayan*, Zhiyan conceptualizes building materials as mutually identical.

---

[19] See Cheng 1982, 55–6.
[20] For Fazang's conception of *dharmas* as empty, refer to Chapter 3.4 and Chapter 3.5.3.
[21] Ziporyn 2020, 214. See also Qian 1998, 290–2.

Question: Why is it that, if one does not complete ten, ten also does not come to be?

Answer: It is just like if pillars were not a building, the building would not come to be. When there is a building, there also are pillars. That is, because the pillars are identical with the building, the building's existence returns the pillars' existence. Because one is identical with ten and ten is identical with one, one's coming to be returns ten's coming to be.[22]

Zhiyan's building metaphor occurs in the context of explaining the mutual identity of one and many with respect to different body. Zhiyan's explanation models *dharmas* of various kinds as distinct numbers ranging from one through ten. This is an explanation of mutual identity with respect to different body—a matter of one being mutually identical with each of the remaining nine (two, three, four, and so on).[23] By analogy, when Zhiyan claims that the pillars are identical with the building, he means that the pillars are identical with all other kinds of materials within the building. Because whatever holds for the pillars also holds for each other kind of building material, and because Zhiyan likens *dharmas* of different kinds to different kinds of building material, Zhiyan's building metaphor models *dharmas* of each kind as identical with *dharmas* of all other kinds.

Like Zhiyan, Fazang uses his metaphor of the building to model the mutual identity of *dharmas* with respect to different body. Fazang also uses his metaphor of the building to model the mutual identity of *dharmas* with respect to same body. Mutual identity with respect to same body is a matter of one and many others composing a whole and this whole being unified by virtue of its constituents responding to each other (Ch. *hù yìng* 互應). Rather than relating one to each of many others, mutual identity with respect to same body relates one to a unified whole composed by the one and many others.[24]

This use of the building metaphor seems to be an innovation by Fazang. Like Zhiyan, Fazang likens *dharmas* of different kinds to different kinds of building material. Fazang's innovation is to liken unified wholes composed of many kinds of *dharma* to a building composed of many kinds of building material. This innovation allows Fazang to use the building metaphor to explain how to conceptualize wholes without ignorance or attachment—and so how to conceptualize wholes as denizens of the realm of Samantabhadra.

---

[22] T45.1868.514c9-12. For an alternative translation, see Cleary 1983, 128.

[23] See T45.1868.514b23-8. For further discussion of Zhiyan's conception of *different body*, refer to Chapter 7.6.2.

[24] For Fazang's conception of *same body*, refer to Chapter 7.3.4.

8.4. Theorizing Six Characteristics

Fazang explains how to conceptualize wholes without ignorance or attachment by using the building metaphor to illustrate his theory of six characteristics (Ch. *liù xiāng* 六相). Whereas specific characteristics (Skt. *salakṣaṇa* or *svalakṣaṇa*; Ch. *zì xiāng* 自相) demarcate *dharmas* into distinct kinds (Ch. *lèi* 類) and general characteristics (Skt. *sāmānyalakṣaṇa*; Ch. *gòng xiāng* 共相) are common to *dharmas* of many kinds, Fazang's six characteristics purport to be characteristics of wholes (Ch. *zǒng* 總) in the realm of Samantabhadra. Fazang conceptualizes these wholes as arising when many *dharmas* unite by responding to each other. His theory of six characteristics ascribes to these unified wholes the characteristics of wholeness (Ch. *zǒng* 總), particularity (Ch. *bié* 別), identity (Ch. *tóng* 同), difference (Ch. *yì* 異), integration (Ch. *chéng* 成), and disintegration (Ch. *huài* 壞).[25]

Fazang offers a preliminary account of the meaning for the six characteristics in the fourth and final section of the tenth chapter of his *Treatise on the Five Teachings of Huayan*.

> First, the presentation of the names for the characteristics of wholeness, particularity, identity, difference, integration, and disintegration. The characteristic of wholeness is one building having the power of many. The characteristic of particularity is the many powers not being one. Particulars depend upon their contrast with the whole to complete the whole. The characteristic of identity is the many parts not opposing each other to complete one whole. The characteristic of difference is the many parts all differing from each other. The characteristic of integration is all dependently arising together. The characteristic of disintegration is each of the many always maintaining its own character and not moving from itself.[26]

Fazang's preliminary account of the meaning for the six characteristics is terse and somewhat cryptic. Although he offers some scattered remarks on the six

---

[25] There are no standard English equivalents for Fazang's terms. According to Hino, the Sanskrit equivalents are *aṅga, upāṅga, salakṣana, vilakṣana, samvarta, vivarta* (Hino 1953, 410–1). Each term receives a variety of English-language translations. See Chang 1971, 168; Cleary 1983, 40; Cleary 1993, 41; Cook 1970, 527; Cook 1977, 76; Cook 1979, 378; Elstein 2014, 81; Hsien 1980, 71; Koh 2015, 7; Liu 1979; Liu 2003, 257; McBride 2012a, 115; Unno et al. 2023, 201. I follow Elstein's translation because he has the most consistent preference for the dominant translation choice (see also Jones 2019, 471–2).

[26] T45.1866.507c5-10. For alternative translations, see Cook 1977, 76–7; Unno et al. 2023, 201. In Fazang's gloss for the meaning of wholeness, Cook translates the character 德 (*dé*) as "quality." Unno and colleagues translate it as "virtue." I prefer "power" because this conveys the sense in which wholes depend upon parts for their functionality. In Fazang's gloss for the meaning of identity, Cook translates the character 義 (*yì*) as "concepts." Unno and colleagues translate it as "significances." I prefer "parts" because 義 can designate reasons, parts of wholes are reasons for wholes, and these reasons are the "significances" to which Fazang is referring.

characteristics in other works, these remarks also tend to be cryptic.[27] He likely inherits his theory of six characteristics from his mentor because the closing poem of Fazang's analysis for the building metaphor likely derives from a lost treatise on the six characteristics by Zhiyan.[28]

According to Fazang's *Biographies and Records of the Flower Adornment Sūtra*, Zhiyan taught the six characteristics after being directed to study them by another monk.[29] Fazang, in his *Investigating the Mysteries of the Flower Adornment Sūtra*, identifies *Sūtra on the Ten Grounds* as a source for Zhiyan's study of the six characteristics.[30] That scripture appears as Chapter 26 of the *Flower Adornment Sūtra*.

[The bodhisattva who dwells on the Ground of Joyfulness] makes a great vow in which he vows to explain in accordance with their reality all of the bodhisattva practices, so vast, so immeasurable, indestructible, unalloyed in their purity, inclusive of all the pāramitās, vows to explain the purifying cultivation of the grounds, their general characteristics, their specific characteristics, their common characteristics, their differentiating characteristics, the characteristics conducing to success in them, and the characteristics leading to ruination, vowing too to teach these matters to everyone, thus influencing them thereby to take on these practices and bring forth increasing resolve.[31]

The meaning of the six characteristics, as mentioned in the *Flower Adornment Sūtra*, is open to many interpretations.[32]

Because Zhiyan's treatise on the six characteristics is lost, and because the *Flower Adornment Sūtra* mentions but does not explain the six characteristics that Fazang ascribes to wholes, no precedent is available for clarifying Fazang's theory of six characteristics. Subsequent sections of this chapter, accordingly, examine Fazang's six characteristics in pairs. The goal is to explicate each pair of characteristics in a way that coheres with Fazang's analysis while making Fazang's intended meaning clearer and more precise. Because Fazang's discussion of the

---

[27] See Liu 1979, 446.

[28] See Kiyotaka 1977, 396–8; Liu 1979, 445–6.

[29] T51.2073.163c14-8. See also Gimello 1976b, 166–7.

[30] T35.1733.148c29-149a3.

[31] T9.278.545b25-c3, recited in Dharmamitra 2022, 2: 889. See also Cleary 1993, 705. The six kinds of characteristics in Dharmamitra's translation correspond to Zhiyan's six characteristics as follows: general = wholeness; specific = particularity; common = identity; differentiating = difference; success-conducive = integration; ruin-inducing = disintegration.

[32] See Kim 2007, 945; Park 2016, 5. The six characteristics also appear in Bodhiruci's translation of Vasubhandu's *Treatise on the Ten Stages* (T26.1522.125a1-2) and in Huiyuan's 慧遠 (523–592) *Chapters on the Meaning of Mahāyāna* (T44.1851.524a1-b16). Fazang identifies Vasubhandu's *Treatise* as the source for his own list (T35.1733.148c29-149a3). But Fazang does not retain Vasubhandu's meanings for the terms (Che 2013).

188 METAPHORS FOR INTERDEPENDENCE

first pair of characteristics—namely, wholeness and particularity—relies upon contentions about part-whole relations that he does not address until his discussion of identity and difference, the examination that follows rearranges Fazang's order for examining the six characteristics.

8.5. Identity and Difference

Fazang prefaces his discussion of the six characteristics with a reminder that all dependently arising *dharmas* interpenetrate.[33] Because Fazang's theory of the six characteristics and his analysis of the building metaphor are meant to explain how to conceptualize wholes in the realm of Samantabhadra, this is a reminder that his analysis proceeds under the assumption that all *dharmas*—that is, all of the basic constituents of wholes—are mutually identical and mutually inclusive. His discussion for the characteristic of identity makes explicit this assumption, and his discussion for the characteristic of difference forestalls a potential confusion about the characteristic of identity.

8.5.1. The Characteristic of Identity

Fazang's analysis for the characteristic of identity is challenging to understand because, implicit in his discussion, there is a background distinction between unified wholes and mere aggregates. In mere aggregates, the arrangement of parts makes no difference to the existence or efficacy of the aggregate. Mathematical sets are good examples of mere aggregates. For instance, even though the sets {1,2,3} and {3,2,1} differ in the ordering of their elements, the sameness of their elements makes them the same set. By contrast, in unified wholes, the arrangement of parts makes a difference to the existence or efficacy of the whole. For Fazang, buildings are examples of unified wholes. For instance, sheaves of reeds compose a hut when they lean against each other, but arraying the same sheaves alongside each other—or separating them across a vast distance—does not compose a hut.[34]

There are two common strategies for explaining why many things compose a unified whole rather than a mere aggregate. The first—label it the *common cause strategy*—locates unity in some cause external to the many. This strategy

---

[33] T45.1866.507c19-20.
[34] *Sūtra on Sheaves of Reed* uses two sheaves of reed to explain mutual dependence (see Bodhi 2000, 607–9). For a similar example in the Chinese translation of this scripture, involving three sheaves of reeds rather than two, see Choong 2010, 178.

conceptualizes the source of unity among many as akin to a movie camera that focuses and frames the various objects of a movie scene without itself being part of the scene.[35] The second—label it the *pervasive connector strategy*—locates the unity of many in some relation that one of the many bears to the others. This strategy conceptualizes the source of unity among parts as akin to the mortar of a brick wall, transforming the bricks from a mere heap into a wall by touching every brick and being part of the resulting wall.[36] Fazang's analysis for the characteristic of identity signals that he endorses the pervasive connector strategy.

When discussing the characteristic of identity in the context of the building metaphor, Fazang claims that identity is the characteristic of rafters and other materials harmonizing together (Ch. *hé tóng* 和同) to make the building by virtue of not opposing (Ch. *xiāng wéi* 相違) each other.

> The characteristic of identity is the rafters and various other conditions harmonizing together to make the building. Because they do not oppose, all are named conditions for the building. Because they do not make different things, this is named the characteristic of identity.[37]

When paraphrasing the characteristic in the poem that concludes his *Treatise on the Five Teachings of Huayan*, he claims that identity is the characteristic whereby many kinds (Ch. *duō lèi* 多類) are the same (Ch. *tóng* 同) as each other in completing a whole.[38]

Fazang's meaning is not that the different parts of a whole are the same as each other by virtue of each being a part of the whole.[39] There is no barrier to materials from one building combining with materials from another to compose a new building. Parts from different wholes can combine with each other. Yet Fazang insists that if materials oppose each other and do not harmonize together, then they cannot combine with each other.[40] Hence, harmonizing together to make a whole—or being the same as each other in completing the whole—is something more than merely sharing parthood in that whole.

A better interpretation is that, when Fazang claims that the rafters and various other conditions harmonize together to make the building, and when he claims

---

[35] See Shoppa 2016, 799. For a more metaphysical example of the common cause strategy, see Vallicella 2002, 28–9. Fazang's analysis of same-body relations pairs naturally with the common cause strategy.

[36] For other examples of the pervasive connector strategy, see Findlay and Thagard 2012.

[37] T45.1866.508b7-9. For alternative translations, see Cook 1977, 85; Elstein 2014, 84; Unno et al. 2023, 205.

[38] T45.1866.509a1.

[39] Cook offers a contrary interpretation, according to which wholes have the characteristic of identity because each of their parts is a part of the same whole (Cook 1977, 85).

[40] T45.1866.508b13-4.

190   METAPHORS FOR INTERDEPENDENCE

that many kinds are the same as each other in completing a whole, he means that each kind of material for the building transforms the entire collection of materials from a mere aggregate into a unified whole. Because the building and its materials are models for wholes and parts in the realm of Samantabhadra, the building materials are mutually identical and mutually inclusive. This mutual relationality is why the building materials harmonize together and do not oppose each other. The same mutuality qualifies each kind of building material as a pervasive connector—a part of the building that unifies the many parts by relating to every other part. Each of the rafters, pillars, and other building materials completes the building by making the building a unified whole, and each makes the building a unified whole because each makes and includes all other building materials (in Fazang's technical sense of *make* and *include*).

8.5.2. The Characteristic of Difference

Fazang's characteristic of identity is, in effect, the characteristic of wholes whereby *dharmas* of any one kind within the whole make and include *dharmas* of every other kind within the same whole. This characteristic explains why wholes in the realm of Samantabhadra are unities. Because Fazang explains the unity of unified wholes by appealing to the mutual identity of their parts, those who only partially grasp his meaning might infer that he means to claim that the parts of unified wholes are *numerically* identical to each other. Fazang allays this potential confusion by explaining the characteristic of difference.[41]

When discussing the characteristic of difference in the context of the building metaphor, Fazang claims that difference is the characteristic of rafters and other building materials being different in kind from each other.

> The characteristic of difference is the rafters and various other conditions differing from each other in accordance with their own forms and kinds.[42]

When paraphrasing the characteristic in the poem that concludes his *Treatise on the Five Teachings of Huayan*, Fazang claims that difference is the difference between each part of a whole and others that manifests in identity.[43]

---

[41] Cook also interprets Fazang's explanation of difference as a way to forestall confusion. According to Cook, Fazang's remarks about difference "should dispel any mistaken understanding of the idea of identity as removing the differences between things . . ." (Cook 1977, 86).

[42] T45.1866.508b16-7. For alternative translations, see Cook 1977, 85; Elstein 2014, 84; Unno et al. 2023, 205.

[43] T45.1866.509a1.

For Fazang, rafters and other materials do not compose a unified building by virtue of some carpenter or architect fashioning them into a building. Because arrangements are not building materials, rafters and other materials also do not compose a unified building by virtue of their arrangement. Instead, for Fazang, rafters and other materials compose a unified building because each of the materials relates to the others in a unity-inducing manner. The unity-inducing relations, for Fazang, are identity and inclusion (in Fazang's technical senses).

Fazang's introductory explanation of difference specifies that the relations of identity and inclusion are irreflexive by kind. This means that the unity-inducing relation between one and many is not a relation that the one bears to anything of the same kind as itself.[44] An immediate consequence of this specification is that the many building materials compose a unified building only if there are multiple kinds of building material. Hence, difference is the characteristic of wholes having *dharmas* of multiple kinds as parts. Because harmony requires difference, having the characteristic of difference allows wholes to have the characteristic of identity.

8.6. Wholeness and Particularity

Fazang begins his analysis of the building metaphor—and the presentation for his theory of six characteristics—with the characteristics of wholeness and particularity. These are especially important characteristics because they concern the relation between wholes and their parts. Fazang's analysis for these characteristics is challenging to understand because there is, implicit in his presentation, a background distinction between additive and holographic parts of wholes. When a part of a whole is additive, the part is insufficient for the whole. Grains in a heap of sand are good examples of additive parts. No grain of sand by itself suffices for a heap. By contrast, when a part of a whole is holographic, the part by itself suffices for the whole. Sectors of holograms are good examples of holographic parts. Each sector of a hologram contains information sufficient for the entire holographic image. For Fazang, the parts of unified wholes are holographic.[45] This is a consequence of unified wholes having the characteristic of wholeness.

---

[44] For discussion of why Fazang's relations of identity and inclusion are irreflexive by kind, refer to the derivations of *Inclusion and Identity Coincide* and *Identity Crosses Kinds* in Chapter 3.5.3.

[45] See also Kasulis 2009, 226–7; Fox 2013, 185.

8.6.1. The Characteristic of Wholeness

When introducing the characteristic of wholeness, Fazang claims that it is the characteristic of rafters being the building. He elaborates that he means, by this claim, that the rafters by themselves make the building.

> The rafters are the building. Why? Because the rafters by themselves entirely make the building.[46]

Recall that, for Fazang, one makes (Ch. *zuō* 作) another when the one puts into action the other, and this is equivalent to the other being identical with (Ch. *jí* 即) the one.[47] The activity of the building is not only the building-like activity of some whole but also the unification of the parts of that whole. Because the rafters are part of the building, and because the rafters by themselves make and include the other materials of the building, the pervasive connector strategy for explaining unity entails the rafters by themselves put into action the building's unification of its parts. (This follows from the interpretation of Fazang's remarks about the characteristic of identity.) Because the rafters by themselves make and include the building's other materials, and because the building's activity is just the activity of its many materials, it also follows that the rafters put into action the building's materials and thereby put the building itself into action. Hence, the rafters by themselves entirely make the building because they suffice for putting into action both the building-like activity of the building and the building's unification of its parts.

Fazang's characteristic of wholeness is, in effect, the characteristic of wholes whereby *dharmas* of any one kind within the whole by themselves put the whole into action.[48] This is why, in his concluding paraphrase for the characteristic of wholeness, Fazang claims that wholeness is the characteristic whereby one is endowed with (Ch. *jù* 具) many.[49] The one is some unified whole. The many are the many kinds of *dharmas* that are parts of this whole. When wholes have the characteristic of wholeness, each of their parts (or kinds thereof) puts the whole into action. They do so by inducing unification among the whole's many parts. The activity of unification thereby completes (Ch. *jù* 具) the many parts by

---

[46] T45.1866.507c21-2. For alternative translations, see Cook 1977, 78; Elstein 2014, 82; Unno et al. 2023, 202.

[47] For discussion of Fazang's conceptions of *making* and *identity*, refer to Chapter 3.5.3. Note that the relation of identity (Ch. *jí* 即) is not the same as the characteristic of identity (Ch. *tóng* 同).

[48] Cook provides a similar, albeit less technical, interpretation, focusing on the rafters of Fazang's building: "When the rafter becomes a rafter through its integration into the building, the combined powers of the total number of conditions which are called 'building' are taken on by the rafter, which then has the total power to create the building" (Cook 1977, 80).

[49] T45.1866.508c24.

transforming them into a unified whole. This completion of the many parts by the one whole is just what it is for the one to be endowed with many.

8.6.2. Divergence from Abhidharma

Fazang's analysis for the characteristic of wholeness entails that the parts of unified wholes are holographic rather than additive. Because any whole with the characteristic of wholeness is such that each of its parts puts the whole into action, each part of such a whole by itself makes the whole. When one by itself makes another, the one suffices for the other. For example, in standard Abrahamic theology, God by itself makes the world. Similarly, according to Wang Bi 王弼 (226–249), the featureless and ineffable Dao 道 makes the myriad things of the world.[50] In both of these cases, the one that does the making suffices for the one that is made. Because parts that suffice for their wholes are holographic, and because unified wholes have the characteristic of wholeness, it follows that unified wholes have holographic parts.

This consequence of Fazang's analysis for the characteristic of wholeness sets Fazang against precedent, internal to the Buddhist tradition, for conceptualizing parts of unified wholes as additive. For example, in *Path of Purification*, Buddhaghosa conceptualizes parts of wholes as additive. He uses an example of a tripod to explain the sense in which parts of wholes are mutuality conditions (Skt. *anyamanya-pratyaya*).

A state that assists by means of mutual arousing and consolidating is a *mutuality condition*, as the three sticks of a tripod give each other consolidating support.[51]

The sticks of a tripod give each other consolidating support because one falls whenever any falls and all are upright whenever one is upright.[52] The sticks also happen to be additive parts of the tripod. No stick by itself suffices for a tripod.

When clarifying the meaning of *mutuality condition*, Buddhaghosa offers an example that allows additive parts to compose unified wholes.

A man born blind and a [man unable to walk] wanted to go somewhere. The blind man said to the [immobile man], "Look, I can do what should be done by

[50] Hong 2019, 220–1.
[51] Ñāṇamoli 2010, 553.
[52] See also Ñāṇamoli 2010, 618. Tanaka demonstrates that Abhidharma Buddhist traditions conceptualize mutuality conditions as arising simultaneously with and being inseparable from each other. See Tanaka 1985, 94–7.

legs, but I have no eyes with which to see what is rough and smooth." The [immobile man] said, "Look, I can do what should be done by eyes, but I have no legs with which to go and come." The blind man was delighted, and he made the [immobile man] climb up on his shoulder. Sitting on the blind man's shoulder the [immobile man] spoke thus, "Leave the left, take the right; leave the right, take the left."

Herein, the blind man has no efficient power; he is impotent; he cannot travel by his own efficient power, by his own strength. And the [immobile man] has no efficient power; he is impotent; he cannot travel by his own efficient power, by his own strength. But there is nothing to prevent their going when they support each other.[53]

When the blind man sits atop the immobile man, the men compose an efficient traveler. Because the men compose the efficient traveler only when the immobile man sits atop the shoulders of the blind man, the efficient traveler is a unified whole. Yet, according to Buddhaghosa, because the blind man lacks vision and the immobile man lacks mobility, each man is an additive part of the efficient traveler. Buddhaghosa's example of the efficient traveler thereby seems to demonstrate that additive parts are able to compose unified wholes.

Fazang does not discuss the example of the efficient traveler. However, when elaborating upon his analysis for the characteristic of wholeness, he signals that he rejects the possibility of unified wholes having additive parts.

If each of the rafters and various other conditions does not complete the whole but instead has only part of the power, then each condition has partial power. This is only many conditions with partial power and they do not complete one whole building.[54]

When a part of a whole has only partial power (Ch. *shǎo lì* 少力), it does not by itself suffice for the whole. Just as Night makes Day only by cooperating with Darkness (according to Hesiodic theogony), and just as Ahura Mazdā (Ohrmazd) makes the world only by cooperating with Ahriman (according to Zoroastrian cosmogony), parts with partial power make their wholes only by cooperating with other parts of the same whole.

---

[53] Ñāṇamoli 2010, 619. For an analogous contemporary example and a similar analysis of unity, see Birch 2019. For an analysis of Buddhaghosa's example in relation to contemporary analytic mereology, see Jones 2021, 181–6.

[54] T45.1866.508a7-9. For alternative translations, see Cook 1977, 80; Elstein 2014, 82; Unno et al. 2023, 203.

Buddhaghosa's efficient traveler is an example of a whole that seems to have partially powered parts. If the men in Buddhaghosa's example are additive parts, each man contributes a small part of the power to form the efficient traveler. The blind man contributes to the efficient traveler only the mobility component. The immobile man contributes only the navigation component. Because the efficient traveler requires both components, Buddhaghosa infers that the men make the efficient traveler only by cooperating with each other.

Fazang rejects Buddhaghosa's inference. If the men in Buddhaghosa's example are additive parts, Fazang denies that they compose a unified whole. If Buddhaghosa's efficient traveler is a unified whole, he denies that each man contributes only partial power—and thereby denies that the men are additive parts. These denials follow directly from Fazang's analysis for the characteristic of wholeness. The same analysis also explains the error in Buddhaghosa's reasoning.

For Fazang, the men in Buddhaghosa's example are mutuality conditions because each makes and includes the other. The pervasive connector strategy for explaining the unity of wholes entails that, when one makes and includes many others, the one induces unity with and among the others. Because wholes with unity-inducing parts of this sort have the characteristic of wholeness, and because wholes with this characteristic are unified wholes, Fazang can agree that Buddhaghosa's efficient traveler is a unified whole. But these same reasons entail that Buddhaghosa's men do not each contribute only a small part of the power to form the efficient traveler. The blind man contributes the mobility component of the efficient traveler by virtue of his capacity to move—he projects moving. Yet, because the blind man is identical with and included within the immobile man, the blind man moves only because the immobile man has power to cause his moving. Similarly, although the immobile man contributes the capacity to see (or projects seeing), he sees only because the blind man has the power to cause his seeing.

Because Buddhaghosa's men make and include each other, each contributes to the mobility and navigation of the efficient traveler. If each were to contribute to one component of the efficient traveler but not the other, each would need to put into action their own capacity. But then each would be a real existent. This is a welcome result for Buddhaghosa because Buddhaghosa belongs to a Buddhist tradition that conceptualizes *dharmas* as real existents. Because Fazang denies that there are real existents, the same result signifies (to Fazang) a fatal error in Buddhaghosa's analysis.[55]

---

[55] For further discussion of the relation between Fazang's conception of unified wholes and a conception akin to Buddhaghosa's, see Jones 2019, 486–8.

8.6.3. The Characteristic of Particularity

The preceding digression about Buddhaghosa's and Fazang's competing conceptions of mutuality conditions demonstrates a potential source of confusion about the characteristic of wholeness. The potential source of confusion is the idea that parts of unified wholes are real existents. Because Fazang explains the characteristic of wholeness by examining how each part of a whole by itself suffices for the whole, another potential confusion is that each part of a whole just *is* that whole. Fazang allays this potential confusion by explaining the characteristic of particularity.

When discussing the characteristic of particularity in the context of the building metaphor, Fazang claims that particularity is the characteristic of building materials of various kinds differing from the building.

> The characteristic of particularity is the rafters and various other conditions being different from the whole.[56]

When paraphrasing the characteristic in the poem that concludes his *Treatise on the Five Teachings of Huayan*, Fazang claims that particularity is the characteristic of many and one not being the same.[57] Rafters and other conditions for the building are akin to *dharmas* of various kinds that are parts of some whole. The rafters and other conditions are the many. The whole—that is, the building—is the one. Being different (or not the same) refers to the relation of numerical distinctness. Hence, particularity is the characteristic of wholes being (numerically) distinct from their constituent *dharmas*.

For Fazang, wholes have the characteristic of particularity because they have the characteristic of wholeness. When a whole has the characteristic of wholeness, each of its parts by itself puts the whole into action. Putting a whole into action is inducing unification among the whole's many kinds of parts. If a whole were numerically identical to one of the parts that puts it into action, the whole would have no other parts and so there would be nothing in need of unification. Hence, when a whole has the characteristic of wholeness, it must be numerically distinct from its constituent parts.

8.7. Integration and Disintegration

When wholes have the characteristic of wholeness, they are put into action by each of their parts. Because a part of a whole puts the whole into action by virtue

---

[56] T45.1866.508a23. For alternative translations, see Cook 1977, 83; Elstein 2014, 83; Unno et al. 2023, 204.
[57] T45.1866.508c24.

of making and including the whole's other parts, wholes have the characteristic of wholeness by virtue of having the characteristic of identity. But when one makes or includes another, the one has power to cause whatever effects the other projects; and when one has power to cause whatever effects the other projects, the other conditions the form of the effect that the one causes. Hence, when wholes have the characteristics of wholeness and identity, one of their parts puts the whole into action by virtue of all of their other parts conditioning the forms of the effects that the one causes. Because the parts of a whole have the whole itself (or the activity thereof) as their effect, it follows that when wholes have the characteristics of wholeness and identity, each of their parts conditions the form of the whole. Fazang identifies this consequence as the characteristic of integration.

8.7.1. The Characteristic of Integration

When introducing the characteristic of integration, Fazang claims that it is the characteristic of the rafters and materials being conditions for the building.

> The characteristic of integration explains why the various conditions for the building come to be. Because the rafters and so on complete the building, they are named conditions. If this were not so, both of them would be incomplete. Because the building manifests as complete, know that integration is mutual completion.[58]

Dharmas come to be through their activity. The activity of a *dharma* is a matter of the *dharma* projecting an effect and some cause putting the *dharma* into action by having power to cause the projected effect. Hence, *dharmas* are complete—they come to be through their activity—only by virtue of projecting their effects and being put into action by something with power to cause those effects.

Because the *dharmas* that compose a unified whole are identical with and included within each other, every *dharma* is put into action by something with power to cause whatever effect the *dharma* projects. But the activity of these *dharmas* are complete only if the *dharmas* also project their own effects. Because

---

[58] T45.1866.508b27-9. For alternative translations, see Cook 1977, 86; Elstein 2014, 85; Unno et al. 2023, 206.

198   METAPHORS FOR INTERDEPENDENCE

any *dharma* that projects an effect conditions the form of that effect, it follows that the activities of *dharmas* are complete only if they condition the form of their effects—or, in brief, only if they are conditions. Hence, the *dharmas* that compose a unified whole are complete only if each conditions the form of its own effects and puts into action the effects that others condition.

Fazang's characteristic of integration is, in effect, the characteristic of wholes whereby *dharmas* of any one kind within the whole both condition the form of their own effects and put into action the effects conditioned by *dharmas* of all other kinds.[59] The first of these roles is why Fazang claims that the various materials of the building are named conditions. The combination of this role with the second role is why he claims that integration is mutual completion. It is also why he claims, in his concluding paraphrase of the characteristics, that integration is the subtle principle (Ch. *lǐ miào* 理妙) of the dependent arising of one and many.[60] The subtle principle is the mutual identity and mutual inclusion of everything within the realm of Samantabhadra. Mutual identity and mutual inclusion require that *dharmas* not only condition the form of their own effects but also bring about the effects that others condition. This is just what the characteristic of integration is.

8.7.2. The Characteristic of Disintegration

Because integration means that parts of wholes condition the form of their own effects and bring about the effects that other parts condition, each part of a whole gives rise to its effect by virtue of integrating its dispositionality with the powers of other parts. The dispositionality of each part determines the effect that the part projects. The powers of other parts put this dispositionality into action. But just as horses put chariots into action by changing the state of the chariot from stationary to mobile, it is tempting to infer that parts of wholes put other parts into action by changing their characteristics.

The temptation to infer that parts of wholes put other parts into action by changing their characteristics is ingrained in folk physics. For example, when fire melts ice, it is tempting to infer that fire puts the ice into action by changing the characteristic of ice from solid to fluid. The temptation also finds expression in popular culture. Consider, for example, the animated series *He-Man and the*

---

[59] In prior work, I interpret integration as the characteristic whereby one part of a whole makes the whole only if some other part of the same whole also makes the whole (Jones 2019, 485). I hereby retract this interpretation as insufficiently attentive to Fazang's pervasive connector strategy for explaining the unity of wholes. It also has the unfortunate consequence of making the characteristic of integration effectively equivalent to the characteristic of wholeness.

[60] T45.1866.509a2.

Masters of the Universe.[61] When forces of evil threaten the kingdom of Prince Adam (the protagonist of the series), Prince Adam uses a magical sword to become He-Man: the Power of Grayskull enters into the prince and transforms his character from meek and slender prince to confident and muscular hero.

When the roofing tiles of a building seal the joints of materials in the building's roofing structure, folk theories of physics and magic make it tempting to infer that the roofing tiles change the characteristics of the materials in the roofing structure. Fazang forestalls this temptation by explaining the characteristic of disintegration.

When discussing the characteristic of disintegration in the context of the building metaphor, Fazang claims that disintegration is the characteristic of rafters and other conditions maintaining their own character.

> The characteristic of disintegration is the rafters and various other conditions maintaining their own character and not making [the building].[62]

His concluding paraphrase of this characteristic is nearly identical.[63]

The key phrase in Fazang's discussion of disintegration is "maintaining its own character" (Ch. *zhù zì fǎ* 住自法). The notion of maintaining—or abiding, or dwelling (Ch. *zhù* 住)—also appears in a discussion of the relation between ignorance (Ch. *wú míng* 無明) and *dharma*-nature (Ch. *fǎ xìng* 法性) by the Tiantai 天台 scholar Zhanran Jingxi 湛然荊溪 (711–782). According to Zhanran, because *dharma*-nature is identical with ignorance, *dharma*-nature does not dwell; and because ignorance is identical with *dharma*-nature, ignorance does not dwell.[64] For Zhanran, when one is identical with another, the one does not dwell. By contrast, for Fazang, when one is identical with another, or when one has its specific characteristic brought to fruition by another by virtue of integrating its dispositionality with the power of the other, the one does dwell—that is, the one maintains its own character.

8.7.3. Divergence from Tiantai

Zhanran's conception of mutual identity derives from the teachings of an earlier master from the Tiantai tradition, Zhiyi 智顗 (538–597). According to Zhiyi (and Zhanran), *dharmas* are indeterminate with respect to their specific characteristics by virtue of gaining their character from their relations to others. Just

---

[61] Scheimer 1983-1985.
[62] T45.1866.508c12-3. For alternative translations, see Cook 1977, 87; Elstein 2014, 85; Unno et al. 2023, 207.
[63] T45.1866.509a2.
[64] T33.1717.920a28-9. See also Hung 2020, 318.

as humans create the five oceans—Arctic, Atlantic, Indian, Pacific, Southern—by imposing artificial boundaries upon an undifferentiated body of water, Zhiyi maintains that humans create *dharmas* by imposing distinctions upon that which lacks distinction.[65] Just as one ocean gains its boundaries only in relation to other oceans, Zhiyi maintains that *dharmas* gain their (individuating) character only in relation to other *dharmas*. This is why, for the Tiantai masters, *dharmas* that are identical with others do not dwell. If *dharmas* gain their character only in relation to other *dharmas*, *dharmas* change their character when those others change, and so *dharmas* do not maintain their own character.

Fazang's conception of mutual identity differs from the Tiantai conception. Like Zhiyi and Zhanran, Fazang maintains that all *dharmas* are empty. For Fazang, however, *dharmas* are determinate with respect to their specific characteristics, and they are empty by virtue of lacking power to put themselves into action—that is, by virtue of gaining causal efficacy from their relations to others.

In his discussion of disintegration, Fazang offers a terse—and perhaps circular—justification for why *dharmas* are determinate with respect to their specific characteristics.

> If [the rafters and various other conditions] that make the building do not maintain their own character, the building is incomplete. Why? Because if they do not maintain their character in making the building, the building is incomplete.[66]

For the sake of clarifying Fazang's reasoning, suppose that pillars have a character that grounds their support for brackets, roofing truss, and roofing tiles. Suppose also, for the sake of argument, that the pillars do not maintain their character in making the building. Then the pillars do not support brackets, roofing truss, and roofing tiles. But if the brackets, roofing truss, and roofing tiles are not supported, they remain resting on the ground rather than elevated in the air. Hence, if the character of the pillars is indeterminate, the other materials lack significant elevation from the ground—and so the building is incomplete.

The alternative to pillars and other building materials having indeterminate characters is having determinate characters. Because having a determinate character is equivalent to maintaining one's character, the characteristic of disintegration is, in effect, the characteristic of having a determinate character.[67]

---

[65] Kang 2024, 1213–14. See also Ziporyn 2010, 504–8.

[66] T45.1866.508c15-7. For alternative translations, see Cook 1977, 87; Elstein 2014, 85; Unno et al. 2023, 207.

[67] In prior work, I interpret the characteristic of disintegration as the characteristic whereby parts of wholes do not cooperate with each other in composing wholes (Jones 2019, 485). I hereby retract this interpretation. It derives from an incomplete understanding of what Fazang means by parts maintaining their character.

Because Fazang denies that there are real existents, having a determinate character is not equivalent to being real. Instead, for Fazang, having a determinate character (and so maintaining one's character) means having specific characteristics that are determinate—or having specific characteristics that do not depend upon relations to others.

For Fazang, conceptualizing the specific characteristics of *dharmas* (or building materials) as determinate is consistent with denying that *dharmas* are real existents. The reason is that, for Fazang, *dharmas* are akin to dispositions in action. The specific characteristics of *dharmas* ground the directionality or dispositionality of *dharmas*. But what puts *dharmas* into action is other *dharmas*. (This is why *dharmas* have the characteristic of integration.) Hence, even though *dharmas* do not depend upon others for their specific characteristics, they depend upon others for power to enact those characteristics. This is why, for Fazang, *dharmas* with intrinsic specific characteristics—or *dharmas* that maintain their own character—are not real existents.

8.8. Justifying Fazang's Theory

8.8.1. Securing Existence

So much for explaining the details of Fazang's theory of six characteristics. Fazang's theory grounds a conception of wholes that diverges from other conceptions in prior Buddhist traditions. In doing so, his theory presumes that wholes exist in the realm of Samantabhadra. This presumption is contentious, especially in the context of Buddhist metaphysics. Paul Williams explains why.

> The relationship of putative wholes to parts . . . is central to a great deal of Buddhist ontology. If it could be shown that it makes sense to include in one's ontology wholes (as such, or particular examples) as well as parts then Buddhist ontology would have problems.[68]

For example, Abhidharmika traditions of Buddhism typically endorse a metaphysics in which wholes are mere illusions imagined upon arrangements of *dharmas*.[69] Similarly, Mādhyamikas seem to conceptualize wholes as collectively constituted fictions, and Yogācārins seem to conceptualize wholes as mere logical constructions.[70]

[68] Williams 2000, 441.
[69] See Jones 2021, 176–80.
[70] See, respectively, Garfield 2006, 304 and Kapstein 1988, 33.

Fazang, for his part, should have no objection to conceptualizing wholes as imaginary constructions. His only objection would be to using the imaginary status of wholes to exclude wholes from his ontology. The basis for this objection is a distinction between two kinds of nominal existent. Fazang denies that *dharmas* are real existents. His reason is that *dharmas* lack self-nature. He denies that wholes are real existents for the same reason. Fazang also affirms that *dharmas* are nominal existents because they are objects for cognition and it is convenient to imagine these objects as entirely determinate even though they are not. For the same reason, he affirms that wholes are nominal existents. Insofar as *dharmas* belong to the ontology for the realm of Samantabhadra, wholes belong to the same ontology.[71]

When Buddhists from other traditions exclude wholes from their ontology, they typically do so by assuming that nominal existents are existents in name only. They assume, in other words, that nominal existents are imaginary in the way that sons of barren women and flowers growing in the sky are imaginary. Sky flowers and sons of barren women belong to the realm of *saṃsāra*.[72] They are imaginary because cognizing them is conceptual. They belong to the realm of *saṃsāra* because cognitions of these objects are laden with error—to conceptualize flowers growing in the sky or sons of barren women is to conceptualize in a way that is incorrect.

For Fazang, wholes in the realm of Samantabhadra are not like this. Wholes in the realm of Samantabhadra are imaginary because every cognition of a whole is a conceptual cognition. Yet cognitions of wholes need not be incorrect. Fazang's theory of six characteristics is a strategy for conceptualizing wholes without error. Fazang does not demonstrate the success of this strategy. But the tactic for the demonstration is relatively straightforward: first, show that each of the six characteristics follows from contentions that are free from error; then, infer that conceptualizing wholes as having the six characteristics means conceptualizing wholes without error.

8.8.2. Deriving Six Characteristics

Fazang maintains that any error-free conception of reality should endorse two contentions. The first is a standard Buddhist teaching, namely, the teaching of dependent arising (Skt. *pratītyasamutpāda*; Ch. *yuánqǐ* 緣起). The second derives from teachings about interdependence from the *Flower Adornment*

---

[71] For further discussion of the distinction between real existents and nominal existents, refer to Chapter 3.4.

[72] For further discussion of the distinction between the realm of *saṃsāra* and the realm of Samantabhadra, refer to Chapter 5.6.3.

Sūtra. Because, for Fazang, these teachings are free from error, anything that follows from them is a truth about the realm of Samantabhadra.

Consider, first, the teaching of dependent arising. This teaching has three key components. The first is that whatever arises always arises in dependence upon causes and conditions (Skt. *hetu-pratyaya*; Ch. *yīn yuán* 因緣). The second is that causes differ in kind from their conditions. The third is that both causes and conditions differ from their effects.

Because wholes arise in dependence upon causes and conditions, and because parts of wholes are the causes and conditions of wholes, the first and second components of the teaching of dependent arising jointly entail that wholes have *dharmas* of multiple kinds as parts. This means that wholes have the characteristic of difference. Because wholes arise in dependence upon their parts and these parts are *dharmas*, the first and third components of the teaching of dependent arising jointly entail that wholes differ from their constituent *dharmas*. This means that wholes have the characteristic of particularity. Hence, conceptualizing wholes as having the characteristics of difference and particularity is free from error.

Consider, next, teachings about interdependence from the *Flower Adornment Sūtra*. For Fazang, the *Flower Adornment Sūtra* teaches that *dharmas* in the realm of Samantabhadra are interdependent by virtue of making and including each other. Because the fundamental parts of wholes in the realm of Samantabhadra are *dharmas*, it follows that within any whole, *dharmas* of each kind by themselves make and include *dharmas* of all other kinds. This means that wholes have the characteristic of identity. Because one brings about the effects that others project when the one makes the others, and because bringing about effects of others entails that the others condition the form of those effects, any whole with the characteristic of identity must have the characteristic of integration. Hence, conceptualizing wholes as having the characteristics of identity and integration is also free from error.

The teachings of dependent arising and mutual identity do not quite suffice to secure correctness for the remaining characteristics of wholeness and disintegration. But they do so when supplemented with two auxiliary assumptions. The first concerns the completeness of wholes. Fazang claims that wholes are incomplete if their parts do not maintain their character in making wholes. The reason for Fazang's claim likely derives from his theory of causality and his conception of *dharmas* as dynamic activities with determinate dispositions.[73] But whatever its justification, Fazang's claim, together with the existence of wholes in the realm of Samantabhadra, entails that parts of wholes maintain their own character. This means that wholes have the characteristic of disintegration.

---

[73] For further discussion on Fazang's conception of *dharmas*, refer to Chapter 3.3.

Fazang's second auxiliary assumption concerns the source of unity for wholes. Fazang endorses a pervasive connector strategy for explaining the unity of wholes. The reason why Fazang endorses this strategy likely derives from his conception of *same body*. This conception locates the cause of each whole—the chief for each whole's parts—as itself part of the whole. The pervasive connector strategy honors this conception; the alternative, common cause strategy does not. But whatever its justification, Fazang's strategy entails that when one (kind of) part for a whole makes the other parts of the whole, the one acts as a pervasive connector for the parts of the whole and thereby unifies the parts into a whole. Because wholes have the characteristic of identity, the pervasive connector strategy for explaining the unity of wholes entails that for any whole, *dharmas* of each kind within the whole by themselves make the whole. This means that wholes have the characteristic of wholeness.

The teachings of dependent arising and mutual identity secure correctness for four of Fazang's six characteristics of wholes—difference, particularity, identity, and integration. Two plausible auxiliary assumptions secure the remaining characteristics of wholeness and disintegration. One of these assumptions likely derives from Fazang's theory of causality. The other, concerning the source of unity for wholes, likely derives from his conception of *same body*. If these assumptions are correct, Fazang's theory of six characteristics yields a conception of wholes that is free from ignorance and attachment.

9

Fazang's Project

9.1. Main Conclusions

This chapter serves four purposes. The first is to summarize the main conclusions from the preceding chapters. The summaries focus, in particular, on how to interpret Fazang's metaphors of Indra's net, counting coins, and the building as well as how each metaphor models different aspects of Fazang's systematic metaphysics. The second purpose is to situate Fazang's key contentions within the broader tradition of Mahāyāna Buddhism. The third purpose of the chapter is to connect the more systematic aspects of Fazang's metaphysics to contemporary metaphysical debates. The fourth is to make explicit some ways in which Fazang's metaphysics is more than a mixture of doctrines from other Buddhist traditions—and also more than just a metaphysics.

9.1.1. Conceptualizing Dharmas

Fazang's central metaphysical contentions concern mutual identity and mutual inclusion. These contentions pertain to the *dharma*-realm of dependent arising (Skt. *dharmadhātu-pratītyasamutpāda*; Ch. *fǎjiè yuánqǐ* 法界緣起), a realm accessible to conceptual cognition and free from the obstacles of ignorance and attachment. The basic constituents of this realm are *dharmas*. Free from ignorance and attachment, the cognizing mind conceptualizes *dharmas* as ephemeral activities rather than persisting substances, and it conceptualizes these activities as dynamic enactings of characteristics (Skt. *lakṣaṇa*; Ch. *xiāng* 相). More specifically, the cognizing mind conceptualizes each *dharma* as an enacting of a characteristic specific to the kind of *dharma* it is—that is, as an enacting of some specific characteristic (Skt. *salakṣaṇa* or *svalakṣaṇa*; Ch. *zì xiāng* 自相). So conceptualized, the arising of a *dharma* just is the enacting of the specific characteristic for the *dharma*.

By virtue of their specific characteristics, *dharmas* project their own effects (Skt. *phalākṣepa* or *svaphalopārjita*; Ch. *yǐn zì guǒ* 引自果). Free from ignorance and attachment, the cognizing mind conceptualizes the effects projected by *dharmas* as arising by virtue of some power (Skt. *bala* or *śakti*; Ch. *lì* 力)

Metaphors for Interdependence. Nicholaos Jones, Oxford University Press. © Nicholaos Jones 2025.
DOI: 10.1093/9780197807224.003.0009

206 METAPHORS FOR INTERDEPENDENCE

that brings to fruition the specific characteristics of those *dharmas*. This avoids the error of conceptualizing effects as arising spontaneously. Free from ignorance and attachment, the cognizing mind also conceptualizes *dharmas* as lacking power to bring to fruition their own specific characteristics. It thereby conceptualizes *dharmas* as empty (Skt. *śūnya*; Ch. *kōng* 空), their existence as nominal (Skt. *prajñapti-sat*; Ch. *jiǎ yǒu* 假有), and their powerfulness as indeterminate (Skt. *aniyata*; Ch. *bú dìng* 不定). This avoids the errors of conceptualizing *dharmas* as self-natured (Skt. *svabhāva*; Ch. *zì xìng* 自性), their existence as real (Skt. *dravya-sat*; Ch. *shí yǒu* 實有), or their powerfulness as determinate (Skt. *niyata* or *vinayata*; Ch. *dìng* 定 or *jué dìng* 決定).

For reasons that he does not make explicit, Fazang maintains that conceptualizing *dharmas* as empty requires conceptualizing them as mutually identical (Ch. *xiāng jí* 相即). Insofar as *dharmas* are mutually identical, each brings to fruition the specific characteristics of all others. Fazang also maintains that conceptualizing the effects projected by *dharmas* as arising by virtue of some power requires conceptualizing *dharmas* as mutually inclusive (Ch. *xiāng rù* 相入). Insofar as *dharmas* are mutually inclusive, each puts into action all others. Because putting a *dharma* into action just is bringing to fruition the specific characteristic of that *dharma*, mutual inclusion among *dharmas* coincides with their mutual identity.

9.1.2. Modeling Interdependence

Fazang invokes the metaphor of Indra's net to model the relations of mutual identity and mutual inclusion among *dharmas* in the *dharma*-realm of dependent arising. This metaphor likens *dharmas* to mirrored jewels, and it likens differences in the specific characteristics of *dharmas* to differences in the reflections hosted by these jewels. Each reflection is inseparable from its jewel. This models *dharmas* as enactings of their characteristics rather than substances that are separable from their characteristics. Each jewel includes the reflections of all other jewels. This models the indeterminacy of *dharmas* with respect to power. Each jewel also supports reflections that appear in all other jewels. This models all *dharmas* making (Ch. *yòng* 用) each other. For Fazang, this making is a priority relation whereby the maker, as fundamental or chief (Skt. *pramukha* or *svāmin*; Ch. *shǒu* 首 or *zhǔ* 主), puts into action that which is made, the derivative or attendant (Skt. *anuga*; Ch. *bàn* 伴). Because one is identical with another when the other makes the one, and because one includes another when the one puts into action the other, the mutual reflectivity of jewels thereby models the mutual identity and mutual inclusion of *dharmas*.

Fazang also invokes the metaphor of Indra's net to model the perspectivity of mutual identity and mutual inclusion. Because each jewel includes the reflections of all other jewels and supports the reflections that appear in all other jewels, and because jewels are inseparable from their reflections, each jewel by itself supports all other jewels. This models the fundamentality of *dharmas* whereby each *dharma* by itself makes all others. For Fazang, the supporting relation, like the making relation, is a priority relation. Because priority relations are asymmetric, cognizing one jewel as by itself supporting all other jewels involves focusing attention to center one jewel and relegate all others to the periphery. Attentional selection models gateways (Ch. *mén* 門) for cognizing some *dharmas* as fundamental or chief and other *dharmas* as derivative or attendant. Even so, because each attentional selection is equally correct, nothing privileges one jewel as the natural or objective chief. This models a kind of equality among gateways for cognizing *dharmas* and a kind of aspectualism whereby every *dharma* is both fundamental and derivative.

While Fazang uses Indra's net as a vehicle for contemplating how *dharmas* relate to each other, he uses coin counting as a vehicle for contemplating the vastness and nuances of those relations. The metaphor of counting coins uses counts to mark differences among gateways for cognizing *dharmas*, and it likens counting coins to contemplating identity and inclusion relations among *dharmas*. The objects of counting in Fazang's metaphor are likely breaths—the coins are vehicles that guide counting rather than the objects counted. Relations among these objects admit two analyses. One is distributive; the other, collective. For the distributive analysis, one object relates to each of many others separately. This analysis is a vehicle for contemplating relations of identity and inclusion among *dharmas* with respect to different body (Ch. *yì tǐ* 異體). For the collective analysis, one object relates to all considered collectively. This analysis is a vehicle for contemplating relations of identity and inclusion among *dharmas* with respect to same body (Ch. *tóng tǐ* 同體). The two analyses add nuance for modeling the mutual identity and mutual inclusion among *dharmas* in the *dharma*-realm of dependent arising. The counting of ten coins models the vastness of these relations.

Fazang invokes the building metaphor to model relations of composition and parthood among mutually identical and mutually inclusive *dharmas*. Both of these relations are mereological. Composition is the relation whereby many *dharmas* together compose a unified whole (Ch. *yītǐ* 一體). Parthood is the relation whereby some *dharma* belongs to a unified whole. The building metaphor likens different kinds of building material—rafters, pillars, tiles, and so on—to *dharmas* of different kinds, and it likens a building composed of different kinds of material to a unified whole composed of different kinds of *dharmas*. The building in Fazang's metaphor is likely an instance of *diàntáng* 殿堂 (palace-hall) architecture, with materials that connect to each other by mortise-and-tenon joinery rather than special fasteners. This joinery style ensures that joined materials are mutuality conditions such that one supports another only if the other supports the one. It also allows Fazang to liken support relations among materials of different kinds to making relations among *dharmas* of different kinds.

Some scholars maintain that Fazang uses his analysis of part-whole relations to derive his doctrines of mutual identity and mutual inclusion. Peter Gregory provides the gist of the relevant derivation.

> Since the whole is nothing but the interrelation of its parts, each phenomenon can therefore be regarded as determining the character of all other phenomena as well as having its own character determined by all other phenomena.[1]

Gregory's inference is invalid. Suppose, for example, that a puzzle is nothing more than its pieces. Then the picture on the puzzle is nothing more than the interrelation of the images on the pieces. But it does not follow that any piece determines the image on any other. Gregory's inference is also inapt. Even if Fazang agrees that a whole is nothing more than the interrelation of its parts, he maintains that the parts of wholes (the *dharmas*) are determinate with respect to their specific characteristics. Because this determinacy means that no part of a whole determines the character of any other, Gregory's reasoning does not cohere with Fazang's metaphysics.

Rather than deriving his doctrines of mutual identity and mutual inclusion from his analysis of wholes, Fazang assumes, in his building metaphor, that the building's various materials are mutually identical and mutually inclusive. This allows him to use the building to model the six characteristics that he attributes to unified wholes. Two of these characteristics, particularity and difference, are relatively unremarkable. Particularity (Ch. *bié* 別) is the characteristic whereby wholes are numerically distinct from their constituent parts. Difference (Ch. *yì* 異) is the characteristic whereby wholes have many different kinds of parts as constituents. The two most counterintuitive characteristics are wholeness and identity. Wholeness (Ch. *zǒng* 總) is the characteristic whereby, for any whole and any kind of part within that whole, parts of that kind by themselves suffice to make the whole. Identity (Ch. *tóng* 同) is the characteristic whereby, for any whole and any kind of part within that whole, parts of one kind by themselves make parts of all other kinds.

Because the characteristics of wholeness and identity derive from Fazang's assumption that the parts of wholes are mutually identical and mutually inclusive, they mark what is most distinctive about Fazang's metaphysics. The remaining

---

[1] Gregory 1993, 210. See also Cook 1977, 77; Jiang 2001, 471.

two characteristics, integration and disintegration, mark further distinctive corollaries to this metaphysics. Integration (Ch. *chéng* 成) is the characteristic whereby parts of one kind condition the form of the effects they project while also bringing about the effects that parts of other kinds project. Disintegration (Ch. *huài* 壞) is the characteristic whereby, for any kind of part within a whole, parts of that kind do not change their specific characteristics when put into action by parts of other kinds.

9.2. Interpreting Emptiness

Fazang's contentions about mutual identity and mutual inclusion, and his theory of six characteristics, are efforts to conceptualize reality in a way that accords with the doctrine of emptiness (Skt. *śūnyatā*; Ch. *kōng* 空) from the Mahāyāna tradition of Buddhism. For Fazang, the doctrine of emptiness teaches that reality is a realm of dependent arising (Skt. *pratītyasamutpāda*; Ch. *yuánqǐ* 緣起) and that the denizens of this realm are nominal existents. Because the doctrine of emptiness derives from writings by the Indian monk Nāgārjuna (2nd–3rd century), some scholars maintain that Fazang's metaphysics is a restatement of Nāgārjuna's doctrine. For example, according to Francis Cook, Nāgārjuna presents the negative aspects of emptiness by virtue of deconstructing and devaluing the view that *dharmas* are real, and Fazang presents the positive aspects by virtue of affirming relationality among that which is nominal.[2] There is some truth to this way of situating Fazang in relation to Nāgārjuna. But the differences between Fazang's view and Nāgārjuna's are more than a matter of aesthetic or valuational emphasis.

9.2.1. Dependent Arising and Emptiness

Conceptualizing reality as a realm of dependent arising derives from the earliest Buddhist teachings. Early Pāli discourses define dependent arising with a standard formula.

> When this exists, that comes to be; with the arising of this, that arises. When this does not exist, that does not come to be; with the cessation of this, that ceases.[3]

---

[2] Cook 1977, 47–8.
[3] MN 79, SN 12.21, SN 12.37; recited in Ñāṇamoli and Bodhi 1995, 655; Bodhi 2000, 552; Bodhi 2000, 575.

210 METAPHORS FOR INTERDEPENDENCE

Early Chinese translations of these discourses define dependent arising with a similar formula.

> Depending upon this, there is that; with this arising, that arises . . . with this ceasing, that ceases; this not being, that is not.[4]
>
> Because this exists, that exists; because this arises, that arises. . . . And again, when this does not exist, that does not exist; when this ceases, that ceases.[5]

When one arises in dependence upon another, the one does not exist without the other. For example, a house arises in dependence upon timber, mud, and reeds because there is no house without timber, mud, and reeds enclosing an empty space.

> Depending upon timber, mud, and reeds covering and wrapping empty space, there arises that which is named 'house.'[6]

There is no house without timber, mud, and reeds because empty space becomes a house only when the timber, mud, and reeds provide a locus or context for the house arising.[7]

Both Nāgārjuna and Fazang endorse the standard conception of dependent arising. Both interpret dependent arising as teaching that everything is empty of self-nature. Both also agree that emptiness entails that there are no real existents. Nāgārjuna further articulates the meaning of emptiness in the dedicatory verse that opens his *Fundamentals of the Middle Way*. The Sanskrit version of this verse (translated into English) is the most familiar to contemporary scholars.

> I salute the Fully Enlightened One, the best of orators, who taught the doctrine of dependent origination, according to which there is neither cessation nor origination, neither annihilation nor the eternal, neither singularity nor plurality, neither the coming nor the going [of any dharma, for the purpose of nirvāṇa characterized by] the auspicious cessation of hypostatization.[8]

---

[4] EĀ 42.3; T2.125.776a24-7.

[5] SĀ 335; T2.99.92c20-1, 22–3, recited in Choong 2010, 63.

[6] MĀ 3.31; T1.26.466c29-467a1. For an alternative translation, see Bingenheimer et al. 2013, 232. See also MN 28, translated in Ñāṇamoli and Bodhi 1995, 283.

[7] See also Macy 1991, 52–3.

[8] Siderits and Katsura 2013, 13.

The version from the 4th-century commentary of Piṅgala (Blue Eyes) 青目, translated into Chinese by Kumārajīva (334–413) as *Middle Treatise*, is quite similar.

> Neither arising nor ceasing, neither permanence nor annihilation, neither identity nor difference, neither coming nor going can explain dependent arising and skillfully remove all hypostatization. I bow in obeisance to the Buddha, whose teaching is the greatest of all.[9]

For Nāgārjuna, any effort to conceptualize reality succumbs to the error of hypostatization (Skt. *prapañca*; Ch. *xì lún* 戲論). This is the error of supposing that speech or conceptualization marks characteristics of real existents, and it is an error because there are no real existents. Fazang agrees with Nāgārjuna that hypostatization is an error. Yet, because Fazang maintains that conceptual cognition of the realm of Samantabhadra is free from delusion, he denies that all efforts to conceptualize reality succumb to the error of hypostatization. This divergence from Nāgārjuna is more substantial than a difference of aesthetic or valuational emphasis.

For evidence that Fazang's metaphysics is a positive restatement of Nāgārjuna's doctrine of emptiness, Cook cites a suggestive passage from Fazang's *Treatise on the Five Teachings of Huayan*.

> *Question*: What is the difference between the six meanings and the eight negations spoken [by Nāgārjuna]?
> *Answer*: The eight negations concern prohibition, the six meanings concern appearance. Moreover, the eight negations concern opposing delusion to manifest principle. The six meanings concern manifesting principle to extinguish delusion. These are [complimentary like] the left and right ears.[10]

The eight negations are the eight denials from the opening dedication of Nāgārjuna's *Fundamentals of the Middle Way*. The six meanings are the six general characteristics that Fazang ascribes to causes.[11] These include instantaneous cessation (Skt. *kṣaṇa-bhaṅga*; Ch. *chànà miè* 剎那滅), or ceasing to exist at the moment of their arising; projecting their own effects; simultaneous existence

---

[9] T30.1564.1b14-7. For an alternative translation, see Bocking 1984, 1. For additional discussion of the relation between Sanskrit and Chinese versions of Nāgārjuna's dedicatory verse, see Hsu 2007, 69–77.

[10] T45.1866.502c4-6. For alternative translations, see Cook 1970, 461–2; Unno et al. 2023, 175–6. Cook translates the last phrase as "two sides of the same coin."

[11] T45.1866.502a8-23; Cook 1970, 446–51; Unno et al. 2023, 171–2.

212 METAPHORS FOR INTERDEPENDENCE

(Skt. *saha-bhū*; Ch. *jù yǒu* 俱有), or being inseparable from the effects they project; and needing many conditions (Skt. *pratyayâpekṣa*; Ch. *dāi zhòng yuán* 待眾緣), or giving rise to effects only in the presence of suitable conditions.

Cook interprets Nāgārjuna as emphasizing that objects lack independence, and he interprets Fazang as emphasizing "the active, creative force which any object exerts on all other objects."[12] But a plain interpretation of Nāgārjuna's dedicatory verse entails that, from Nāgārjuna's perspective, Fazang's six meanings qualify as erroneous. For example, the meaning of instantaneous cessation affirms arising and ceasing, but Nāgārjuna's first two negations deny arising and ceasing.[13] Hence, even if Cook is correct about Fazang's emphasis, he is incorrect in claiming that this is just a more positive valuation of Nāgārjuna's doctrine of emptiness.

Fazang himself is more cognizant of the difference between his own view and Nāgārjuna's doctrine of emptiness. Fazang interprets Nāgārjuna's doctrine as directed toward those who are attached to real existence. The eight negations, so interpreted, are skillful means for opposing this attachment. Fazang interprets his own view as directed toward those who are attached to emptiness. Fazang's target includes those who interpret Nāgārjuna as endorsing a sort of nihilism according to which nothing exists. His six meanings concern appearances (Skt. *vijñapti*). For Fazang, cognizing these appearances without succumbing to delusional imagining involves shifting attention among the aspects whereby they are existent and empty, powerful and powerless—that is, it involves skillfully coming to and going from different aspects without attachment. Fazang's insight is that conceptualizing emptiness as mutual identity and mutual inclusion, rather than as brute inexistence, is a skillful means for cognizing the realm of nominal existents without ignorance or attachment.[14]

9.2.2. Nāgārjuna on Fire and Fuel

For the sake of illustrating how Fazang's approach to the doctrine of emptiness differs from Nāgārjuna's approach, consider a metaphor about fire and fuel from Chapter 10 of Nāgārjuna's *Fundamentals of the Middle Way*.

> 8. If fire depends on fuel and fuel depends on fire, which of the two is arisen first, fuel or the fire that is dependent upon that?

---

[12] Cook 1977, 48.
[13] See also Cheng 1982, 428–9.
[14] P'yowon 表員 offers a similar interpretation. For P'yowon, Nāgārjuna's eight negations accommodate quiescence and Fazang's six meanings accomplish the teaching of Samantabhadra (see McBride 2012a, 119).

FAZANG'S PROJECT 213

9. If fire is dependent on fuel, then there is the establishing of an already established fire. If so then also fuel would come to be without relation to fire.

10. If an entity x is established in dependence [on something else y], and in dependence on that very entity x there is established that y on which x's establishment depends, then what is dependent on what?

11. The entity that is established in dependence [on something else], how does it, before being established, depend [on that]? But if it is not something established that is dependent [on something else], it is not right to say that it depends [on something else].[15]

Nāgārjuna's metaphor targets an anonymous interlocutor who maintains that one of fire and fuel is self-natured despite each arising in dependence upon the other.[16]

Because the metaphor presumes a now-defunct conception of fire, transpose Nāgārjuna's reasoning to a more familiar example. Rather than fire and fuel, imagine the anonymous interlocutor as claiming that although a sage and their student are mutually dependent, one of them is self-natured. Then Nāgārjuna's critique invokes two (implicit) suppositions. The first is that anything that establishes, or brings about, another is prior to that other. For example, if sage establishes student, the sage must arise prior to the student. Nāgārjuna's second (implicit) supposition is that nothing prior to another arises in dependence upon that other. For example, if sage is prior to student, then the sage does not arise in dependence upon the student.

Both of Nāgārjuna's suppositions are plausible for those who, like the anonymous interlocutor, maintain that one of sage and student is self-natured. Suppose, for example, that the sage is self-natured and the student is not. Then, because the student is one who can learn, the student arises only by virtue of the sage first establishing the student as one who can receive teaching. Or suppose, instead, that the student is self-natured and the sage is not. Then, because the sage is one who can teach, the sage arises only by virtue of the student first establishing the sage as one who can give learning. In both cases, the one who does the establishing, by virtue of being self-natured, is prior to the one who is established. This is Nāgārjuna's first supposition. Similar considerations motivate the second supposition. If the sage establishes the student as one who can receive teaching, there is no student prior to the sage and so the sage must arise without dependence upon the student.

Nāgārjuna's first supposition entails that sage and student are mutually dependent only if each is prior to the other. The second entails that if each of sage

---

[15] Siderits and Katsura 2013, 114–6.
[16] Garfield 1995, 191–2; Siderits and Katsura 2013, 114.

214   METAPHORS FOR INTERDEPENDENCE

and student is prior to the other, neither arises in dependence upon the other. The suppositions thereby jointly entail that sage and student are mutually dependent only if neither arises in dependence upon another. But this is just to say that sage and student do not arise in dependence upon each other—and, in general, that there is no mutual dependence. Because endorsing one of sage or student as self-natured supports both of Nāgārjuna's suppositions, it follows that Nāgārjuna's anonymous interlocutor should either deny that sage and student—or fire and fuel—are self-natured or else concede that they are not interdependent.[17]

Although Nāgārjuna's argument about fire and fuel targets the view that some things are self-natured, it also applies to a view, like Fazang's, that maintains that things are empty but also mutually identical. For Fazang, relations of identity (and inclusion) are asymmetric. When one is identical with (or included within) another, the other is not identical with (or included within) the one. Because identity relations are asymmetric, they are priority relations. When one is identical with another, the other is prior to the one. So Fazang's conceptual framework commits him to endorsing an analog to the first supposition from Nāgārjuna's argument. The analog is this: anything with which another is identical is prior to that other. Conjoining this analog with Nāgārjuna's second supposition—that nothing prior to another arises in dependence upon that other—entails that mutual identity requires mutual independence.

Suppose, for example, that sage and student are mutually identical. The analog supposition entails that student is prior to sage and sage is prior to student. Nāgārjuna's second supposition entails, further, that student does not arise in dependence upon sage and sage does not arise in dependence upon student. Hence, if sage and student are mutually identical, neither arises in dependence upon the other. This result generalizes.

1. All *dharmas* are mutually identical.
2. If one is identical with another, the other is prior to the one.
3. Nothing prior to another arises in dependence upon that other.
4. Therefore, no *dharma* arises in dependence upon another.

The first premise of this argument is Fazang's doctrine of mutual identity. The second premise is the analog to Nāgārjuna's first supposition. The third is Nāgārjuna's second supposition. The conclusion is a deductive consequence of the three premises. Because Fazang maintains that cognizing *dharmas* as mutually identical is a correct way to cognize *dharmas* as dependently arising, this is a disastrous result for his metaphysics.

---

[17] Nāgārjuna prefers the first option because he accepts that fire and fuel are mutually dependent. See Garfield 1995, 193.

9.2.3. Responding to Nāgārjuna

Fazang does not directly address this sort of challenge to his metaphysics. His brief remarks about Nāgārjuna's eight negations also provide no clear guidance for how to reconcile mutual dependence with mutual identity. Fortunately, Fazang's answer to a question about mutual identity indicates his likely response. The relevant question appears in the final chapter of *Treatise on the Five Teachings of Huayan*.

> *Question*: With respect to same body, when one gateway is identical with and takes in the whole without limit, does this manifest simultaneously or one after another?
>
> *Answer*: One gateway simultaneously clearly manifesting the whole belongs to the subtle category. Hidden and reflected mutually manifesting again and again belongs to the category of [the realm of] Indra. There are also the meanings of sameness and difference, many and few, existence and nonexistence, start and finish. Hence, *dharma* gateways are freely endowed with the whole without limit. Accordingly, choosing one to act as chief, the others act as attendants.[18]

This question-answer pair addresses the topic of "all *dharmas* freely identified with each other" (Ch. *zhū fǎ xiāng jí zì zai* 諸法相即自在).[19] Fazang conceptualizes mutual identity among *dharmas* through gateways. Each gateway is a vehicle for cognizing the relation between *dharmas* of one kind and *dharmas* of all other kinds, and there is a unique gateway for each kind of *dharma*. For Fazang, mutual identity is a matter of there being a gateway, for each kind of *dharma*, in which *dharmas* of that kind are mutually identical with *dharmas* of all other kinds. Cognizing this identity through the concept *same body* is then a matter of cognizing, within each gateway, each group of *dharmas* as a unified whole.

The question from the anonymous interlocutor asks for clarification about how—or, better, when—to cognize various groups of *dharmas* as wholes. Suppose, for the sake of illustration, that there are three kinds of *dharmas*. Label these kinds, respectively, A, B, and C. Then mutual identity involves three gateways. Each cognizes one kind of *dharma* in relation to some whole that is all *dharmas* together. In the first, A is mutually identical with this whole. In the second, B is mutually identical with the whole. In the third, C is mutually identical with the same whole. Label this whole W. So mutual identity among A, B, and C is, in part, a matter of A relating to W and B relating to W.

---

[18] T45.1866.505b14-9. For alternative translations, see Cook 1970, 501–2; Unno et al. 2023, 189–90.
[19] T45.1866.505a27.

216   METAPHORS FOR INTERDEPENDENCE

Part of what Fazang's anonymous interlocutor is asking is whether these relations are simultaneous or sequential. Cognizing the relations as simultaneous requires cognizing B as both unified with C (because, in relation to A, both B and C are parts of W that do not make W) and not unified with C (because, in relation to C, B makes W but C does not). By contrast, cognizing the relations as sequential seems to entail that *dharmas* of one kind are mutually identical with *dharmas* of a second only insofar as no *dharmas* of some third kind are mutually identical with *dharmas* of the second kind. Both options are problematic. The former seems to require a conceptual impossibility. The latter seems to entail that gateways obstruct each other.

Rather than choose among problematic options, Fazang answers the anonymous interlocutor's question by maintaining that neither option is problematic. Fazang agrees that the first option—cognizing the various gateways simultaneously—is a conceptual impossibility. He adds that simultaneous cognition of multiple gateways is subtle (Ch. *wēi xì* 微細). Subtle cognition, for Fazang, is cognition within the realm of Mañjuśrī, cognition that is inexpressible and inconceivable. Because simultaneous cognition of the various gateways is cognition of *dharmas* as such apart from conceptualization, the conceptual impossibility of the first option is not problematic.

For the second option of cognizing the various gateways sequentially, Fazang denies that the gateways obstruct each other. Sequential cognition of multiple gateways belongs to the realm of Indra—or, in more familiar terminology, to the realm of Samantabhadra. Because this cognition is conceptual, Fazang maintains that the gateways do not obstruct each other. His likely justification is that gateways obstruct each other only if differences among the gateways are real rather than conceptual (or nominal), but cognizing the gateways as real involves cognizing each gateway as having some time during which it grounds mutual identity and other gateways do not. Insofar as cognition of this sort invests each gateway with a determinate characteristic, such cognition is delusional. Because cognition in the realm of Samantabhadra is free from delusion, it follows that differences among the gateways are merely conceptual and so the gateways do not obstruct each other. This is the sense in which mutual identity among *dharmas* in the realm of Samantabhadra is free (Ch. *zì zai* 自在).

Although Fazang's answer to the anonymous interlocutor does not address the topic of priority relations among mutually identical and interdependently arising *dharmas*, Fazang's strategy for answering motivates a twofold response to the concern that mutual identity requires mutual independence. Recall the two suppositions that drive this concern. The first is that anything with which another is identical is prior to that other. The second is that nothing prior to another arises in dependence upon that other. For mutual identity among *dharmas* in the realm of Mañjuśrī, the first supposition is incorrect. *Dharmas* in the realm of Mañjuśrī are mutually identical. But there are no distinctions among prior and subsequent in this realm. The reason is that those distinctions are conceptual but cognition in the realm of Mañjuśrī is nonconceptual. Fazang makes a similar observation elsewhere in *Treatise on the Five Teachings of Huayan*, albeit regarding relations of causality rather than relations of identity.

Cause and result being equal, there is no distinction of prior and subsequent.[20]

For mutual identity among *dharmas* in the realm of Samantabhadra, the second supposition—that nothing prior to another arises in dependence upon that other—is incorrect. Just as differences among gateways in the realm of Samantabhadra are conceptual rather than real, so, too, are distinctions among prior and subsequent. If distinctions among prior and subsequent were real, the prior would be established independently of the subsequent. But if these distinctions are merely conceptual, correctly cognizing one as prior for one gateway does not preclude correctly cognizing the same one as subsequent and dependent for other gateways.

9.2.4. Creeper Vines

For the sake of illustrating this twofold response to the concern that mutual identity requires mutual independence, consider, on Fazang's behalf, a metaphor about creeper vines.[21] Let correct cognition of *dharmas* be akin to the removal of a creeper vine, and let various gateways for cognizing *dharmas* in this realm be akin to different sections of the vine. Suppose, for the sake of simplicity, that the vine divides into three sections: root, middle, tip. Suppose also that there are three tactics for removing the vine: cut the roots, pull the middle, yank the tip. Because enacting any one tactic suffices to remove the vine, each of the three strategies is equally effective even though selecting one tactic means neglecting the others.

Moreover, as anyone practiced at weeding gardens surely knows, enacting one tactic rather than another is possible regardless of whether one attends to the different sections as sections. Those who remove the vine while "in the zone" are akin to those who correctly cognize *dharmas* in the realm of Mañjuśrī. Just as there is no distinction among root, middle, and tip for such gardeners, there is no distinction among prior and subsequent for such cognizers. By contrast,

---

[20] T45.1866.505c7. For alternative translations, see Cook 1970, 504; Unno et al. 2023, 191.

[21] Inspiration for the metaphor of the creeper vine, and for the subsequent analysis, derive from Chapter 17.28–42 of Buddhaghosa's *Path of Purification*. See Ñāṇamoli 2010, 540–1.

218 METAPHORS FOR INTERDEPENDENCE

those who remove the vine by attending to one section rather than another are akin to those who cognize *dharmas* in the realm of Samantabhadra. Just as any of the three tactics is equally effective for weeding, any gateway for cognizing *dharmas* is equally correct.

Furthermore, just as focusing on one section as the target for weeding (and relegating other sections to peripheral attention) does not make it ineffective for others to focus on a different section as the target, cognizing one kind of *dharma* as chief does not make it incorrect for others to cognize *dharmas* of the same kind as attendant. The different weeding tactics do not obstruct each other. Nor, for Fazang, do the different ways of cognizing *dharmas* as chief or attendant, prior or subsequent.

9.3. Rethinking Metaphysics

So much for situating Fazang's key contentions within the broader tradition of Mahāyāna Buddhism. This section revisits the LEGO® model of reality, from Chapter 1, for the sake of connecting Fazang's metaphysical vision with contemporary analytic metaphysics. The connections concern two domains of metaphysical inquiry—inquiry into fundamental structure, and inquiry into ontology. Inquiry into fundamental structure investigates relations of grounding or priority among things, ranking some as more fundamental (or more "real") than others and using this ranking to explain the sense in which some things derive from others. Inquiry into ontology, by contrast, investigates what exists, or what there is, or what kinds of things make up reality. Taken together, these domains dominate inquiries in contemporary analytic metaphysics. Fazang's vision motivates re-envisioning the standard notion of fundamental structure, and it motivates reconsidering whether ontology is a primary task of metaphysics.

9.3.1. Fundamental Structure

The LEGO® model of reality aims to explain what analytic metaphysicians refer to as the fundamental structure of the world. L.A. Paul, a contemporary philosopher working in the analytic tradition, articulates a standard account of what *fundamental structure* means.

I take fundamentality to be metaphysical priority, where "metaphysical priority" is best understood in the traditional sense, such that the metaphysically prior is that in which everything else consists. The fundamental structure [of the world] concerns the fundamental constituents of the world, the constituents from which everything else is constructed, and the fundamental categorical structure. The fundamental categorical structure is determined by the fundamental kinds or natures of the world, i.e., by the fundamental categories. The fundamental constituents are the constituents of these categories.[22]

In the LEGO° model, the fundamental categories are akin to bricks of various kinds, the fundamental constituents are akin to individual bricks, and fundamental constituents being metaphysically prior to all others is akin to individual bricks being the fundamental parts for all LEGO° builds.

Several historically influential accounts of fundamental structure approximate the LEGO° model. For example, Plato's *Timaeus* posits isosceles and scalene right-angled triangles as the fundamental constituents, four kinds of element—earth, air, fire, water—composed as regular solids from these triangles, and more complex bodies composed from these elements.[23] The Vaiśeṣika tradition from ancient India posits partless substances as the fundamentalia and a recursive hierarchy of substantial wholes inhering in conjunctions of other substances.[24] The Sarvāstivāda tradition of Indian Buddhism posits partless *dharmas* as the fundamentalia and a recursive hierarchy of nominal wholes designated to collections of these *dharmas*.[25] More recently, Paul Oppenheim and Hilary Putnam posit elementary particles as the fundamentalia and a recursive hierarchy of composite things— molecules, cells, multicellular living things, and social groups—built atop these particles.[26]

Despite their differences, the accounts from Oppenheim and Putnam, Plato's *Timaeus*, and the Vaiśeṣika and Sarvāstivāda traditions agree that the world has a fundamental structure, that asymmetric relations of metaphysical priority fix this structure, and that the fundamentalia are a foundation for the world's fundamental structure. These agreements mark the accounts as varieties of Foundationalism. Denying each of the agreements in sequence also generates three competing views. Infinitism is the view that, although the world has a fundamental structure fixed by asymmetric relations of metaphysical priority, the fundamental structure lacks a foundation.[27] Coherentism is the view that, although the world has a fundamental structure fixed by relations of metaphysical priority, these relations are not asymmetric.[28] Flatworldism is the view that the

---

[22] Paul 2012, 221.
[23] Di Giacomo 2021.
[24] Kronen and Tuttle 2011, 297–8.
[25] Williams 1981, 237–9.
[26] Oppenheim and Putnam 1958, 9–11.
[27] See Morganti 2014.
[28] See Thompson 2016.

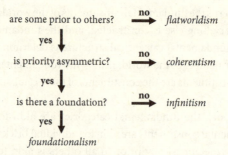

Figure 9.1 Kinds of Fundamental Structure
Image created by the author.

world lacks a fundamental structure—that there are no relations of metaphysical priority among the world's constituents.[29]

Foundationalism, Infinitism, Coherentism, and Flatworldism exhaust the extant conceptual space, within contemporary analytic metaphysics, for accounts of the fundamental structure of a pluralistic world. Three questions suffice to carve this conceptual space: Are some constituents of the world metaphysically prior to others? Are relations of metaphysical priority asymmetric? Does the world have a foundation? (See Figure 9.1.)

There is good reason to suppose that Fazang's metaphysics should fit within this conceptual space. Abhidharma Buddhist views belong to the category of Foundationalism. Some Madhyamaka Buddhist views seem to belong to the category of Flatworldism. If some Buddhist views fit within the contemporary analytic conceptual space for accounts of fundamental structure, it seems that Fazang's view should as well.

Despite this expectation, Fazang's view does not fit within the contemporary analytic conceptual space for accounts of fundamental structure. Fazang's relations of identity and inclusion are relations of metaphysical priority. So his view is not Flatworldism. Some argue that, because Fazang endorses thoroughgoing interdependence among *dharmas*, his view is a kind of Coherentism.[30] Yet Fazang's relations of identity and inclusion are asymmetric. One *dharma* is identical with another only insofar as the other acts as chief and the one acts as attendant. Insofar as a *dharma* acts as chief, it does not also act as attendant; and insofar as a *dharma* acts as attendant, it does not act as chief. Hence, when one *dharma*, acting as attendant, is identical with another *dharma*, the other is not

---

[29] See Bennett 2017, 214; Duncan et al. 2018.
[30] See Bliss and Priest 2017, 71–2; Priest 2018a, 130–1.

identical with the one. So Fazang's view is not Coherentism. Fazang's view is also not Infinitism, because any *dharma*, insofar as it acts as chief, is metaphysically prior to others and metaphysically subsequent to none. Nor is Fazang's view Foundationalism, because every *dharma* is identical with—and so metaphysically subsequent to—other *dharmas*.

9.3.2. The Presumption of Rigidity

Why does Fazang's metaphysics not fit within the contemporary analytic conceptual space for accounts of fundamental structure? If the extant conceptual space exhausts all possible views, Fazang's view must be incoherent in some way. But there are two good reasons to resist this dour conclusion. The first reason is that Fazang offers a variety of metaphors for his view, and these metaphors seem amenable to perfectly coherent analyses. (Such analyses form the substance of this book.) The second reason is that the range of views familiar to contemporary analytic metaphysics shares a presumption that Fazang has good reason to reject. This second reason, if cogent, suggests that the extant conceptual space for accounts of fundamental structure is incomplete.

Accounts of fundamental structure familiar from contemporary analytic metaphysics presume that relations of metaphysical priority are rigid (or determinate). They presume, in other words, that one individual is metaphysically prior to another in one situation only if it is prior to that same other in all situations. This presumption entails that there is at most one fundamental structure of the world. For example, if Oppenheim and Putnam's view is correct, elementary particles are the fundamental constituents of the world and there is no situation in which composites are metaphysically prior to the elementary particles from which they are built.

The presumption that metaphysical priority relations are rigid also has a significant historical pedigree. It appears in Buddhist traditions—in Abhidharmic conceptions of *dharmas* as self-natured and perhaps also in Nāgārjuna's arguments about the emptiness of *dharmas*. The same presumption permeates Greek and Abrahamic philosophical traditions. For example, from the Greek tradition, it appears in Plato's contention that the task of metaphysics is to carve nature at its joints.[31] It also appears in Aristotle's assumption that there is a kind of predication—*saying of*—that functions to designate the fixed essences of individual substances.[32] Similarly, in the Abrahamic tradition, the assumption

---

[31] *Phaedrus* 265e; Nehamas and Woodruff 1997, 542.
[32] *Categories* 1a20–b9; Ackrill 1984, 2–3.

222 METAPHORS FOR INTERDEPENDENCE

appears in the contention from *Genesis A* that God makes the world by forming kinds and separating them into distinct places.[33]

Fazang's metaphysics rejects the presumption that relations of metaphysical priority are rigid. For Fazang, every *dharma* in the realm of Samantabhadra has one aspect whereby it is metaphysically prior to others and another aspect whereby those same others are prior to it. When one *dharma* is prior to another, the one exists and has power while the other is empty and lacks power. So cognizing a *dharma* as metaphysically prior to others is correct when conceptualizing the *dharma* as existing and having power, but the same cognition is incorrect when conceptualizing the *dharma* as empty and lacking power. Because Fazang maintains that all *dharmas* are existent and empty as well as powerful and powerless, he allows for multiple correct but competing conceptions of how *dharmas* relate to each other in the realm of Samantabhadra. Whether one *dharma* is metaphysically prior to another thereby varies with the aspects of the *dharma* to which conceptual cognition attends.[34]

9.3.3. An Analogy from Music Theory

The notion of variable metaphysical priority relations is foreign to contemporary analytic metaphysics. For the sake of better envisioning what it means to allow that metaphysical priority relations are variable rather than rigid, consider an analogy from music theory.[35]

Music theorists divide musical sounds into distinct notes. They represent these notes with letters, where the letters range from A to G and where special symbols indicate that the note is flat (as with B♭ for B-flat) or sharp (as with C# for C-sharp). Music theorists also group subsets of notes together into chromatic scales. Each scale is an ordered arrangement of notes, and music theorists assign to each note in a scale a scale degree. (Degrees are useful for indicating musical chords.) Music theorists have names for each category of scale degree: tonic, supertonic, mediant, subdominant, dominant, submediant, and leading. The first note of each scale is the tonic for that scale, and other notes in the scale have their degree by virtue of their relation to the tonic.

Consider, then, an analogy between metaphysics and music.[36] For the sake of simplicity, restrict attention to the following notes: A, B, C#, D, E, F, G#. These

---

[33] Van Wolde 2017.

[34] For an interpretation that treats Fazang's rejection of rigid metaphysical priority relations as evidence that Fazang endorses a holistic approach to causation (in contrast to an analytic approach), see Nichols and Jones 2023, 107–10.

[35] For additional explanation of variable metaphysical priority relations, see Jones 2023a.

[36] Inspiration for the analogy between metaphysics and music derives from LaFave 2018, 13.

Table 9.1 Variability of Scale Degrees

Scale Degree	D Major Scale	B Minor Scale
tonic	D	B
supertonic	E	C#
mediant	F#	D
subdominant	G	E
dominant	A	F#
submediant	B	G
leading	C#	A

notes appear in two scales, but their relations to each other—their scale degree—varies across these scales. For example, D is tonic and B is submediant in the D Major Scale, but B is tonic and D is mediant in the B Minor Scale. (See Table 9.1.)

Let each of the notes in Table 9.1 be akin to a kind of *dharma*, and let the relation whereby one note is tonic to other notes be akin to *dharmas* of one kind being metaphysically prior to *dharmas* of other kinds. Then tonic notes are akin to foundational *dharmas*, and the variability of scale degree (from music theory) is akin to variability of metaphysical priority relations among *dharmas* (in Fazang's metaphysics). For example, the note D has one aspect whereby it is tonic relative to others but another aspect whereby it receives its degree by virtue of its relation to the note B. In the same way, for Fazang each kind of *dharma* has one aspect whereby it exists with power and another aspect whereby it is empty and powerless by virtue of receiving its causal efficacy from *dharmas* of some other kind. Insofar as scales with exactly the same notes are akin to fundamental structures among exactly the same *dharmas*, the way in which music theory allows for distinct but equally "correct" scales is akin to the way in which Fazang allows for distinct but equally correct fundamental structures.

9.3.4. Insights from Jizang

Some justification for conceptualizing the fundamental structure of the world as variable rather than rigid derives from two insights by the Chinese monk Jizang 吉藏 (549–623).[37] Jizang's first insight, borrowed from the Indian Madhyamaka tradition of Buddhism, is that all *dharmas* are empty of self-nature.[38] His second

---

[37] For evidence of Jizang's impact upon Fazang's philosophy, see Kamata 1965, 134–43, 325–31.
[38] See T25.1509.294b18-25; Chödrön 2001, 1752.

insight is that any *dharma* with a rigid ground for its causal efficacy is thereby self-natured.[39] (The ground of a *dharma*'s causal efficacy is that which puts the *dharma* into action, and a rigid ground puts the *dharma* into action in all situations.) These two insights entail that no *dharma* has a rigid ground for its causal efficacy.

1. All *dharmas* are empty of self-nature.
2. Any *dharma* with a rigid ground for its causal efficacy is self-natured.
3. Therefore, no *dharma* has a rigid ground for its causal efficacy.

The first premise of this argument is Jizang's first insight. The second premise is his second insight. Because every ground for the causal efficacy of a *dharma* is either rigid or variable, the premises jointly entail that, for any *dharma*, the ground for the causal efficacy of that *dharma* is variable, functioning as ground in some but not all situations. This variability is precisely the kind of variation that occurs in Fazang's metaphysics, with each *dharma* (insofar as it is chief and thereby has power) functioning as ground for the causal efficacy of all others and each *dharma* (insofar as it is attendant and thereby lacks power) not functioning as ground for the causal efficacy of anything.

9.3.5. Henology

Because Fazang's metaphysics denies that relations of metaphysical priority are rigid, it motivates re-envisioning the contemporary notion of *fundamental* structure—and, in particular, it motivates allowing that fundamental structure might vary across changes in situation or context. But inquiry into fundamental structure is not the only dominant kind of inquiry in contemporary analytic metaphysics. Ontological inquiries are also dominant.[40] Fazang's metaphysics motivates reconsidering whether ontology is a primary task of metaphysics. It does so by treating metaphysics as an inquiry in which concerns about henology dominate concerns about ontology.

Etienne Gilson (1884–1978), a French philosopher working in the Catholic Thomistic tradition, coined the term "henology"—"(h)énologie" in French, deriving from the Greek *to hen* (τὸ ἕν) meaning *that which is one*—to distinguish a metaphysics of the One from a metaphysics of being.

In a metaphysics of being, such as Christian metaphysics, for instance, each and every lower grade of reality owes its own being to the fact that the

---

[39] See Ho 2014, 405–10.
[40] See Schaffer 2009, 347; Hofweber 2016.

first principle itself *is*. In a metaphysics of the One, however, it is a general rule that the lower grades of reality are only because their first principle itself is not. In order to give something, a cause is bound to be above it, for if the superior already had that which it causes, it could not *cause* it, it would *be* it.[41]

Gilson interprets a variety of metaphysical views as henological rather than ontological—views from the Neoplatonists Plotinus (204/5–270) and Proclus (412–485) as well as views from Christian theologians such as Pseudo-Dionysius the Areopagite (5th–6th century) and Meister Eckhart (1260–1328). Others extend this list to include the Pure Land Buddhist thought of Hōnen 法然 (1133–1212) and bhakti theory from the Indian philosophical tradition.[42] These views are henological, in Gilson's sense, because they maintain that there is one source for all that exists and that this source itself lacks existence. This distinguishes henology from ontology—the study of what exists—because ontological views presume that any source of existence also exists.[43]

Some scholarship replaces Gilson's restrictive definition of henology with a more liberal one. For example, Richardson defines henology as the study and theory of unity.[44] Similarly, Crager attributes henological views to Aristotle because Aristotle investigates different ways of being one.[45] On this more liberal conception, henology is the study of the relation between one and many, and ontology—named for the Greek *to on* (τὸ ὄν), meaning *that which is*—is the study of what exists or has being. So conceptualized, henology and ontology differ by virtue of their distinctive subject matter rather than by virtue of presumptions about sources of existence. Henological inquiries examine the unity of that which is one and how that which is one relates to that which is many. Ontological inquiries, by contrast, examine commitments about and conceptions of what there is.

The restrictive and liberal distinctions between henology and ontology are useful for contextualizing Fazang's metaphysical vision. Fazang's analyses for the metaphors of Indra's net, counting coins, and the building are primarily henological rather than ontological.[46] His analyses proceed with minimal

---

[41] Gilson 1952, 23.
[42] Taguchi 2009, Butler 2018.
[43] See Wyller 1997, 10–1.
[44] Richardson 1967, 2.
[45] Crager 2018.
[46] This agrees with Liu's remark that "'mutual determination' and 'interpenetration' have meaning only so long as they are used to describe dharmas as they exist in the phenomenal realm . . . where consideration of the ontological status of dharmas is left aside for the time being and attention is concentrated on the examination of the relations of dharmas as they appear to us" (Liu 1979, 444).

226   METAPHORS FOR INTERDEPENDENCE

ontological commitments. Fazang assumes that there are many *dharmas*, that every *dharma* has the aspects of existing with power and being empty without power, and that some *dharmas* compose wholes. Components of Fazang's metaphors model these assumptions. Jewels and building materials model *dharmas*. Reflecting and being reflected model existing with power and being empty without power. The building models wholes. But Fazang's analyses do not aim to explain his ontological commitments, and they do not bother themselves with particulars about the kinds of *dharmas* there are. Instead, Fazang uses the metaphors to explain his henological commitments. Indra's net models the relation between one *dharma* and many others. Counting coins models the variability and multiplicity of the relation between one *dharma* and many others. The building models the relation between one *dharma* and many others when the one and many compose a whole. In each case, one is the source of many by virtue of acting as chief to others, and one unifies many by virtue of also acting as attendant to others.

Fazang's metaphors help to explain his contentions about mutual identity and mutual inclusion because Fazang's relations of identity and inclusion are fundamentally henological. Identity and inclusion are relations between one and many others. Hence, Fazang's metaphysical vision is henological in the liberal sense of that term. One and many, related as mutually identical and mutually inclusive, transcend the dichotomy between existence and non-existence—not, however, by virtue of being neither existent nor inexistent, but instead by virtue of having the inseparable aspects of both existing and being empty. Hence, Fazang's vision is also henological in the restrictive sense of that term.

Because Fazang's metaphysics is more henological than ontological, it prioritizes inquiry into how one relates to many. It also prioritizes inquiry into what is required for a henological source to have or lack existence. Central to Fazang's vision is the contention that all *dharmas* have two inseparable aspects. Each *dharma* has an aspect whereby it acts as chief to others, existing with power and thereby lending causal efficacy to other *dharmas*. Each *dharma* also has an aspect whereby it acts as attendant to others, being empty and powerless and thereby indebted to others for causal efficacy. Because these aspects are inseparable, and because all *dharmas* are mutually identical and mutually inclusive, each of the many to which one *dharma* relates as source also relates as source to that one *dharma*. Hence, for Fazang, being a henological source is aspectual rather than determinate. Being a henological source does not preclude having a henological source—and indeed, being a henological source does not preclude having many other henological sources. Further, because the aspects of existing and being empty are inseparable, every henological source has one aspect whereby it is empty rather than existent and another aspect whereby it is existent rather than empty. Hence, for Fazang, lack of existence for henological sources is also aspectual rather than determinate. Being a henological source involves lacking existence (or being empty), but it also involves—in a different aspect—being existent.

9.4. Soteriological Justification

According to Cook, Fazang's metaphysical vision has its source in advanced meditation (Skt. *samādhi*), and in particular in the meditation "in which the newly enlightened Buddha beheld the entire universe as one living organism of identical and interdependent parts."[47] But no meditative insight is likely to provide the kind of technical specifics that Fazang uses to articulate his vision. Moreover, even if meditative insight reveals that the fundamental structure of the world is variable rather than rigid, and even if it inclines theoreticians to prioritize henology over ontology, a pressing question remains. Is there any good reason to suppose that Fazang's metaphysical vision is correct? Answering this question requires first determining what would count as good reason for supposing that a metaphysical vision is correct. Here there is abundant room for reasonable disagreement.

9.4.1. Standards of Justification

Given the analytic orientation of this book, and because this book aims to engage a growing interest in Fazang's metaphysics among contemporary analytic metaphysicians, it is appropriate to adopt standards of justification from contemporary analytic metaphysics. Even here reasonable disagreement remains. Rather than engage in prolonged and ongoing debate about appropriate standards of justification, consider one prominent view of those standards. The quotation that follows pithily captures the relevant view.

> The distinctive nature of the philosophical project comes from the fact that the style of theorizing involved uses inference to the best explanation to draw conclusions from a mix of (defeasible) ordinary judgments, a priori suppositions, and empirical results from natural science and psychology. We can think of such theorizing as modeling the true nature of the world.[48]

---

[47] Cook 1977, 73.
[48] Paul 2012, 222.

228 METAPHORS FOR INTERDEPENDENCE

On this view, there is good reason to endorse a metaphysical contention when three conditions are satisfied. The first is that the contention is the conclusion of some argument. The second is that the premises of the argument are justified by some mix of *a priori* supposition (perhaps as conceptual truths), empirical results from rigorous scientific inquiry, and popular intuition. The third is that the presumed truth of the premises provides strong reason for considering the concluding contention to be likely true.

The preceding view about standards of justification in metaphysics presumes that it is possible to correctly cognize reality through the mediation of concepts. Arguments are collections of declarations, and any such declaration is conceptual. If conceptual cognition of reality precludes correctness, every metaphysical contention for which there is an argument is incorrect, and so the preceding standards of justification entail that there is no good reason to endorse any metaphysical contention. Fortunately, Fazang allows that it is possible to correctly cognize reality through the mediation of concepts. This cognition is, for Fazang, cognition of the *dharma*-realm of dependent arising—or, equivalently, cognition of *dharmas* in the realm of Samantabhadra. So even if the preceding standards of justification are inappropriate for some Buddhists, at least they are not obviously inappropriate for Fazang.

9.4.2. A Strategy for Fazang

Fazang hints at a strategy for justifying his metaphysical vision in his *Commentary on Awakening Mahāyāna Faith*. The hint occurs in Fazang's commentary to a passage about the *dharma*-body (Skt. *dharmakāya*; Ch. *fǎshēn* 法身).

> The dharma body pervades everywhere and the forms in which it appears have no boundaries. It is capable of revealing at will the countless bodhisattvas, the countless recompense bodies [that bodhisattvas receive as reward for their good work], and the countless ornamentations of the worlds of the ten directions. Each is differentiated yet none impedes the others for they have no boundaries.[49]

The *dharma*-body is the body of teachings that express truth. This body manifests in many forms. Some are oral instructions. Others are written documents. Still others are performative interactions. Some teachings of the *dharma*-body might seem to contradict others.[50] *Awakening Mahāyāna Faith* maintains that, despite

[49] Jorgensen et al. 2019, 108.
[50] See Gregory 1983, 231–3.

this appearance, no teaching of the *dharma*-body contradicts another. Fazang explains why in his commentary on the passage.

> Because the enlightened mind is unobstructed and pervades everywhere, the forms that manifest also completely harmonize freely and without obstruction.[51]

The enlightened mind (Ch. *zhēn xīn* 真心) lacks obstruction because it is free from ignorance and attachment.[52] Free from ignorance and attachment, the enlightened mind adjusts its teaching to suit audience and circumstance. Because there is no boundary or limit for its context-sensitivity, the enlightened mind pervades everywhere—it is able to express truth in all contexts. Because all of the different teachings of the *dharma*-body are fit for their context, all express truth. Because all teachings of the *dharma*-body express truth, there is no conflict or obstruction among the teachings. Because there is no conflict among the teachings, the teachings completely harmonize (Ch. *yuán róng* 圓融) with each other.

9.4.3. A Preliminary Argument

Fazang's argument for why the many teachings of the *dharma*-body harmonize with each other is not, by itself, an argument for why the many *dharmas* of the *dharma*-realm—the realm of Samantabhadra—make and include each other. But mutual identity and mutual inclusion secure a kind of harmony among *dharmas*. Fazang also conceptualizes the realm of Samantabhadra as free from ignorance and attachment. This hints at some connection between the nature of the realm of Samantabhadra and the relation between *dharmas* within that realm.

Consider, then, a preliminary argument for Fazang's metaphysical vision.[53]

1. No constituent within the realm of Samantabhadra obstructs another.
2. Hence, if one constituent within the realm of Samantabhadra does not arise, no other arises either.
3. One has power to cause another to arise if, when the one does not arise, the other also does not arise.[54]

---

[51] T44.1846.276a20-1. For an alternative translation, see Vorenkamp 2004, 257.

[52] For further discussion of ignorance and attachment as sources of obstruction, see Muller 2014.

[53] This argument improves upon a prior effort in Jones 2023b, 137–8. For an effort to explain why Fazang provides no explicit argument for his metaphysical vision, see Nichols and Jones 2023, 113–5.

[54] The third statement in the preliminary argument for Fazang's metaphysical vision is equivalent to the principle named *Power* in Chapter 4.2.

230 METAPHORS FOR INTERDEPENDENCE

4. Therefore, each constituent within the realm of Samantabhadra has power to cause all others to arise.

An obstruction (Skt. *āvarana*; Ch. *zhàng* 障) is that which hinders or impedes the arising or attaining of another. For example, ignorance is an obstruction to wisdom, and attachment is an obstruction to *nirvāṇa*.[55] Fazang conceptualizes the realm of Samantabhadra as a realm cognizable without ignorance or attachment. This conception supports an *a priori* supposition, namely, that the realm of Samantabhadra is free from ignorance and attachment. General Buddhist soteriology—a soteriology that, for Chinese Buddhists at least, has strong empirical support—supports an accompanying empirical contention, namely, that ignorance and attachment are the sources of all obstructions.[56] This empirical claim, and the preceding *a priori* supposition, entail that there are no obstructions in the realm of Samantabhadra. Because an obstruction just is that which obstructs another, it follows that no constituent within the realm of Samantabhadra obstructs another. This is the first statement in the preliminary argument for Fazang's metaphysical vision.

The second statement in the preliminary argument for Fazang's metaphysical vision—that no constituent within the realm of Samantabhadra arises unless all arise—is a conceptual consequence of the first statement. Because an obstruction is that which hinders or impedes the arising or attaining of another, for one to obstruct another is just for the other to arise upon the cessation of the one. Schematically, for any x and y,

x obstructs $y := _{df}$ if x ceases, then y arises.

For example, wisdom arises upon the cessation of ignorance. This is what it means for ignorance to obstruct wisdom. If, in the realm of Samantabhadra, nothing obstructs another, it follows that none arise unless all arise.[57]

The third statement in the preliminary argument for Fazang's metaphysical vision—that one has power to cause another to arise if, when the one does not arise, the other also does not arise—derives from the standard Buddhist formula for dependent arising. This formula is that one arises in dependence upon

---

[55] See Muller 2014. See also Vorenkamp 2004, reciting T44.1846.268b18-27.
[56] See Muller 2014.
[57] Here is a more abstract argument for the inference from *none obstructs another* to *all cease if any cease*. Consider two *dharmas*, d_1 and d_2, from the realm of Samantabhadra. Suppose, without loss of generality, that d_1 does not obstruct d_2. Then, from the definition for the obstruction relation, it is not the case that d_2 arises if d_1 ceases. This entails, by some elementary logical reasoning, that d_2 does not arise if d_1 ceases. Because arising and cessation are contraries, it follows that d_2 does not arise if d_1 does not arise. Hence, when one does not obstruct another, the other does not arise if the one does not arise. More generally, when nothing obstructs another, none arise unless each arise.

another just in case the one does not exist without the other.[58] This formula supports an *a priori* supposition, namely, that arising in dependence upon another coincides with the other having power to cause the arising. This supposition is equivalent to the third statement in the preliminary argument for Fazang's metaphysical vision.

The conclusion of the preliminary argument for Fazang's metaphysical vision follows directly from the second and third statements in that argument. The overall argument itself fairly well satisfies standards of justification from contemporary analytic metaphysics. Each premise is justified through a mix of *a priori* supposition and empirical contention. The *a priori* suppositions are truths from Fazang's conceptual framework. The empirical contention derives from Buddhist soteriology. Although Buddhist soteriology is not what many would consider to be a natural or psychological science (by contemporary scientific standards), the empirical contention has fair claim to being based upon long-standing religious practice that is sensitive to empirical outcomes.

The conclusion of the preliminary argument does not demonstrate that the constituents of the realm of Samantabhadra are identical with and included within each other. But these are straightforward corollaries. For Fazang, one includes another if the one has power to cause whatever effects the other projects.[59] Because the constituents of the realm of Samantabhadra are ephemeral, their arising coincides with the enacting of whatever effects they project. So causing something to arise just is causing it to enact whatever effects it projects. Because each constituent of the realm of Samantabhadra has power to cause all others to arise, it follows that each includes all others. For Fazang, one includes another only if the other is identical with the one. Because each constituent of the realm of Samantabhadra includes all others, it follows that each is identical with all others.

9.4.4. Contemplating *Dharmas* as Free

The preceding justification for Fazang's metaphysical vision is only preliminary. More can be done to locate the relevant considerations from Buddhist soteriology. More also can be done to clarify the empirical basis for those considerations. Even so, the argument has at least two virtues. Because it fairly satisfies standards of justification from contemporary analytic metaphysics, it should be intelligible to analytic metaphysicians willing to explore Fazang's

---

[58] See Anālayo 2021a.

[59] For some qualifications to this condition for inclusion, refer to Chapter 3.5.3. (The qualifications are that the one and the other should be numerically distinct and belong to different kinds.) I omit the qualifications here for the sake of readability.

232 METAPHORS FOR INTERDEPENDENCE

conceptual framework. The argument also coheres with the connection Fazang makes between mutual identity and freedom from obstruction.

Fazang connects mutual identity to freedom from obstruction through a contemplation that he names "all *dharmas* being mutually identical and free" (Ch. *zhū fǎ xiāngjí zìzai* 諸法相即自在). Fazang presents this contemplation using a metaphor of a golden lion in *Treatise on the Golden Lion*. The presentation focuses on the mutual identity of a lion's various organs.

> The eyes are the ears. The ears are the nose. The nose is the tongue. The tongue is the skin. All of the organs are mutually identical. The body does not prevent the free establishment [of the organs] without hindrance and without obstruction.[60]

A more abstract presentation of the same contemplation appears in Fazang's *Treatise on the Five Teachings of Huayan*.

> Third, the meaning of all *dharmas* being freely identified with each other. . . . One is identical with all and all are identical with one. Complete harmony, free and without obstruction, is established.[61]

Three aspects of Fazang's contemplation are especially noteworthy. The first is the connection between mutual identity and free establishment. When one organ or *dharma* is identical with another, the other establishes—or brings about—the one. That which establishes is prior to that which is established, and priority is an asymmetric relation. Hence, when one is identical with another, the other is prior to the one and the one is not prior to the other.

This consequence seems to establish a fixed priority relation between that which establishes and that which is established. Fazang's comment about establishment being free makes explicit that this is not so. Mutually identical organs and *dharmas* have two aspects—one whereby they exist with power, another whereby they are empty and powerless. So any organ or *dharma* established by another is free to establish that other. Although an organ or a *dharma* is established by others insofar as it is empty and powerless, its aspect of existing with power frees it to establish others. This aspect of Fazang's contemplation confirms that Fazang conceptualizes the world's fundamental structure as variable rather than fixed.[62] It is an artifact of conceptualizing *dharmas* as nominal existents rather than real existents.

---

[60] T45.1880.665b21-3. Because skin is the organ for touch (Skt. *sparśana*), I translate 身 as *skin* rather than *body*. For an alternative translation, see Chang 1971, 228.

[61] T45.1866.505a26-8. For alternative translations, see Cook 1970, 498; Unno et al. 188-9.

[62] Oh endorses a similar interpretation, characterizing Fazang's metaphysics as "relationistic" with respect to fundamental structure. See Oh 1979, 88-9.

The second noteworthy aspect of Fazang's contemplation is the connection between mutual identity and harmony. Justification for this connection derives from Fazang's theory of six characteristics. According to this theory, when many make a common whole, they harmonize together (Ch. *hé tóng* 和同). In his analysis for the building metaphor, Fazang associates this harmonizing together with the characteristic of identity.[63] In his analysis for the golden lion metaphor, he associates it with the characteristic of integration—but he conceptualizes integration as the lion's organs harmoniously uniting (Ch. *hé huì* 合會) to make the lion.[64] The difference in naming is insignificant because both characteristics are corollaries to Fazang's doctrine of mutual identity. This aspect of Fazang's contemplation supports the third noteworthy aspect.

The third noteworthy aspect of Fazang's contemplation is the connection between mutual identity and freedom from obstruction. In his analysis for the building metaphor, Fazang clarifies that the building's parts harmonize together by virtue of not opposing (Ch. *xiāng wéi* 相違) each other.[65] When many harmonize by virtue of their mutual identity, they are mutually responsive (Ch. *hù yìng* 互應).[66] Freedom from opposition is necessary for mutual responsiveness. For example, according to Chapter 4A9 of *Mengzi* 孟子, Jie 桀 and Zhou 紂—kings responsible for the demise of the Xia 夏 and Shang 商 dynasties, respectively— ruled in ways that caused opposition among their subjects because they lost the hearts of the people, and they lost the hearts of the people because their leadership was tyrannical and debaucherous rather than responsive to the desires of the people. Because obstructions are a kind of opposition, it follows that mutual responsiveness suffices for freedom from obstruction.

Fazang's contemplation of all *dharmas* being mutually identical and free shows that mutually identical *dharmas* lack obstruction among themselves. Insofar as lack of obstruction among *dharmas* in the realm of Samantabhadra also suffices for their mutual identity, Fazang's vision for the realm of Samantabhadra translates the content of *nirvāṇic* cognition into the domain of metaphysics. *Nirvāṇic* cognition is free from obstruction. So, too, is the realm of Samantabhadra. Each being who achieves *nirvāṇic* cognition establishes the *dharma*-body—the body of true teachings.

> The word 'mind' designates mind without obstruction. All Buddhas realize this and thereby establish the *dharma*-body.[67]

---

[63] T45.1866.508b7-8.

[64] T45.1881.670b9.

[65] T45.1866.508b8-9.

[66] For paradigmatic examples of mutually responsive collections, and for a discussion of the relation between mutual responsiveness and the principle of sympathetic resonance (Ch. *gǎn yìng* 感應), see Sharf 2002, 82–6.

[67] T45.1876.640a25-6. For an alternative translation, see Cleary 1983, 166.

234 METAPHORS FOR INTERDEPENDENCE

So, too, does each *dharma* in the realm of Samantabhadra establish all other *dharmas*.

9.5. Is Fazang's Metaphysics Syncretistic?

Scholars of Chinese Buddhism tend to characterize Buddhism in China as syncretic—a mixture, merging, or fusion of views that seem to be competitors rather than companions. Ching, for example, takes this characterization to be obvious, asserting that "Chinese Buddhism is obviously a product of syncretism."[68] Because Fazang is a Chinese Buddhist, it is tempting to infer that his metaphysics is also syncretistic. But there are good reasons to resist this inference.

9.5.1. The Syncretic Interpretation

Because Fazang incorporates elements from many prior Buddhist traditions into his own metaphysics, scholars tend to characterize Fazang's metaphysics as syncretistic. For example, according to Cook, Fazang's metaphysics is syncretistic because "it drew together all the diverse strands of Buddhism and rewove them into the one Dharma which Buddhism is supposed to be."[69] Cook elaborates on this weaving metaphor elsewhere, claiming that Fazang—and others in the early Huayan tradition—saw his mission as "reassembl[ing] all the apparently separate, diverse threads of Buddhist thought and weav[ing] them into a seamless whole."[70] Liu offers a similar characterization, claiming that although teachings from the Madhyamaka and Yogācāra traditions of Indian Buddhism have different conceptual foundations and historical backgrounds, Fazang insists on their compatibility because of "his predilection for syncretism."[71]

9.5.2. Against Syncretism

Despite these precedents, there are good reasons to resist characterizing Fazang's metaphysics as syncretistic. The first reason concerns the meaningfulness of syncretism as a category. The notion of a syncretistic metaphysics (or culture, or religion) lacks analytic precision. If syncretism is a matter of harmonizing conflicting or incompatible ideas, then no metaphysical system is syncretistic,

[68] Ching 1993, 205.
[69] Cook 1979, 367.
[70] Cook 1977, 25–6.
[71] Liu 1981, 30.

because harmonizing incompatible ideas is conceptually impossible.[72] If syncretism is a matter of blending ideas that are merely different (and so not genuinely in conflict), then all metaphysical systems are syncretistic by virtue of having historical antecedents.[73] Because, on either precisification, the category of syncretism does not distinguish Fazang's metaphysics from any other metaphysical system, characterizing his metaphysics as syncretistic is uninformative.

The second reason to resist characterizing Fazang's metaphysics as syncretistic concerns the aptness of the characterization. Set aside the issue of informativeness. Each of Fazang's metaphors—Indra's net, counting coins, the building—has some precursor in prior Buddhist tradition. So, too, do his conceptual insights. From Nāgārjuna and the Indian Madhyamaka tradition, Fazang borrows the insight that conditionality is utterly pervasive. From Vasubandhu and the Indian Sarvāstivāda tradition, he borrows the insight that conditioned things have multiple aspects. From Jizang, he borrows the insight that contraries are provisional rather than determinate. From the broader Buddhist tradition, he borrows the insight that variability among aspects can conceptualize provisionality.

If these borrowings are akin to different threads or strands of Buddhism, and if syncretism is a matter of weaving many strands into a single fabric, there is some sense in which Fazang's metaphysics is syncretistic. This is why Cook characterizes Fazang's metaphysics as syncretistic. But the characterization is not apt. It does not fit Fazang's conception of his contribution to Buddhism. The reason is that, from Fazang's perspective, the insights from prior Buddhist traditions are parts of one harmonious strand.[74] There is nothing for his metaphysics to unify, and there are no conflicts for his metaphysics to reconcile, because the many different Buddhist teachings are parts of the one true teaching.[75]

9.5.3. Weaving and Crocheting

The fundamental problem with characterizing Fazang's metaphysics as syncretistic is the presumption that Fazang encounters insights from his predecessors as somehow disunified. This presumption is why Cook models Fazang's metaphysics as a seamless fabric woven from diverse strands. But Fazang does not

---

[72] Baird 1971, 147–8.

[73] Baird 1971, 146–7.

[74] See T44.1846.276a20-1; Vorenkamp 2004, 257. In *Treatise on the Five Teachings of Huayan*, Fazang maintains that differences among teachings from various Buddhist traditions fit together perfectly (T45.1866.481b3-4; Cook 1970, 172; Unno et al. 2023, 59). Because of this coherence, Fazang characterizes the many and diverse Buddhist teachings as a great net for rescuing sentient beings from *saṃsāra* (T45.1866.482b14-7; Cook 1970, 186; Unno et al. 2023, 65).

[75] See also Baird 1971, 148–51.

share the presumption. For Fazang, the insights from his predecessors are parts of the one harmonious strand that is the one true teaching.

Modeling Fazang's metaphysics as a woven fabric is inapt, because weaving requires multiple strands. Weaving makes fabric by wrapping one set of yarn (the warp) around a loom and pulling another set of yarn (the weft) back and forth across the width of the first. Repetition of this pulling creates a grid that holds together the warp and the weft. Because weaving requires the prior separation of weft from warp, and because Fazang conceptualizes his metaphysics as arising from one harmonious strand, Fazang's metaphysics is not akin to a woven fabric.

A better model for Fazang's metaphysics likens it to a crocheted fabric— and, in particular, to a fabric crocheted by planned pooling. Like weaving, crochet is a technique for transforming yarn into fabric. Unlike woven fabric, crocheted fabric arises from a single strand of yarn.[76] The technique involves using a single-hooked needle to make a series of stitches in one strand of yarn. Planned pooling is a crochet technique that uses variegated yarn—many-colored yarn dyed so that its colors repeat in fairly regular sequence—to create fabrics with colorful patterns. Planning pooling involves varying the gauge (or tension) of stitches to control the placement of colors in the fabric. When done well and with properly variegated yarn, planned gauge variations allow patterns to emerge from areas (pools) of same-colored stitches.

For those who might be unfamiliar with planned pooling (or crochet more generally), Figure 9.2 depicts two patterns that emerge from one skein of yarn.

The skein is visible in the center of Figure 9.2. It is one continuous strand of yarn. The yarn is dyed so that its color shifts gradually from white, through various shades of increasingly dark gray, into black, and then back again to white. This sequence of colors repeats in a regular pattern for the entire skein. The top of Figure 9.2 shows a striped pattern that emerges by crocheting the yarn in accordance with one plan. The bottom of Figure 9.2 shows a plaid pattern that emerges by crocheting the same yarn (from the same skein) in accordance with a different plan.[77] The difference in the two patterns arises from different crochet plans rather than different strands of yarn: changing the number of stitches per row (and making other skillful adjustments to the gauge of each stitch) changes the pattern from one to the other.

---

[76] For a brief history of crochet, see Karp 2018.

[77] For other examples of planned pooling, see Bird 2017. I thank Holly Jones for sharing her knowledge of crochet and planned pooling. I also thank her for crocheting the patterns that appear in Figure 9.2.

Figure 9.2 Planned Pooling. The same skein of yarn (middle) gives rise to a striped pattern (top) and a plaid pattern (bottom).
Image created by the author.

Suppose, following Fazang, that insights from different Buddhist traditions arise from a single thread—namely, the one true teaching. Then the insights from Fazang's predecessors are akin to colors in one skein of variegated yarn. Fazang's integration of these different insights into a systematic metaphysics is akin to pooling colors from the skein of variegated yarn. Fazang's reliance upon insights about interdependence from the *Flower Adornment Sūtra* is akin to the selection of a specific plan for pooling colors. His adaptation of insights from his predecessors is akin to the creative decisions—arising from skill-based intuitions for how to vary the gauge of each stitch—necessary for making a crochet plan work.[78] Because of these parallels, the coherence of Fazang's metaphysics is akin to a pattern that emerges from planned pooling of colors. This is why Fazang's metaphysics is more akin to a crocheted fabric than a woven one.

9.6. Revisiting Soteriology

Fazang's metaphysical vision is complex and provocative. Explaining this vision—or, at least, explaining the part that concerns the *dharma*-realm of dependent arising—has taken nearly the entirety of this book. But, as Chapter 1 notes, Fazang's metaphysics serves a broader soteriological purpose. Prior chapters have hinted at how Fazang's metaphysics helps to satisfy this purpose. Chapter 7, for example, explains how Fazang's coin-counting metaphor is a proxy for a kind of breathing meditation. Because explaining the full soteriological significance of Fazang's metaphysics is a book-length project in itself, I conclude with some suggestions for how that explanation might go. The suggestions derive from the observation that Fazang's metaphysics implicitly endorses a principle of tolerance.

9.6.1. Tolerance as Soteriological

Recent metaphysical inquiry associates the principle of tolerance with the anti-metaphysical project of Rudolf Carnap (1891–1970). Carnap's principle of tolerance directs philosophers to arrive at conventions rather than set up prohibitions.[79] For Carnap, conventions are better or worse for various practical contexts, but none is correct apart from a particular context. Insofar as metaphysical inquiry aims for views that are correct apart from any particular context or across all contexts, Carnap's principle of tolerance directs philosophers away from metaphysics.

Although Fazang does not articulate anything like Carnap's principle of tolerance, there is something quite tolerant about his metaphysical vision. This

---

[78] For detailed substantiation of the claim that Fazang constructs his metaphysics from creative exegesis of *Flower Adornment Sūtra*, see Lin 2016.

[79] Carnap 1937, 51.

tolerance concerns soteriological, rather than theoretical, practicality. For those attached to the existence of particular *dharmas* or collections thereof, Fazang's vision directs attention to the emptiness of *dharmas*. For those attached to emptiness, it directs attention to existence. For those attached to the powerful causality of *dharmas*, Fazang's vision directs attention to their powerless conditionality. For those attached to powerless conditionality, it directs attention to powerful causality. For those attached to a particular henological source, Fazang's vision directs attention to the variable indeterminacy of sources. For those attached to indeterminacy, it directs attention to the correctness of different variations. By redirecting attention in these ways, Fazang's vision serves as a vehicle for overcoming attachment.[80]

Fazang's metaphysical vision fosters a tolerance that extends from the domain of cognition to the domain of action. Cognizing self and others as mutually identical and mutually inclusive renders incoherent any intention to preserve one's self against others or subjugate the powers of others to one's own domain of control. When one is identical with others, the one becomes what it is only by virtue of others. Because the one is empty of self-nature, nothing it does can remove its vulnerability to others. Hence, if each is identical with all others, the only way for one to preserve itself against others is to control absolutely everything. Similarly, when each includes all others, none has within itself the power to bring about its distinctive effects. For example, even if gold projects monetary value, owning the gold does not guarantee having wealth. Because others include the gold, the gold lacks power to cause wealth and so owning the gold is not owning the cause of wealth. If each includes all others, the only way to control the causes of desirable objects is to control absolutely everything. Insofar as the intention to control everything is incoherent, Fazang's vision serves as a vehicle for revealing that efforts for self-preservation and other-domination are inherently delusional.

9.6.2. Overcoming Attachment

Fazang's tolerant vision makes his metaphors more than explanatory models of metaphysical reality. The metaphors, and Fazang's analyses for them, explain his vision. Because this vision facilitates overcoming attachment, and because delusion ceases when attachment ceases, Fazang's metaphors are also tools for

---

[80] There is a similar kind of tolerance at work in Fazang's approach to categorizing and classifying Buddhist views and doctrines (Ch. *pànjiào* 判教). See, for example, Gimello 1976a, which frames tolerance in doctrinal classification as a preference for "disciplined kataphasis" over "exclusive apophasis" (Gimello 1976a, 119). For application of Gimello's idea to the Huayan tradition, see Gregory 1983. For a review of more specific details from Fazang's approach to doctrinal classification, see Liu 1981, 18–29.

conceptualizing reality without fear of delusion. A stanza from "Peaceful Dreams of Wandering in Late Spring: A Poem of One Hundred Rhymes," by the poet Bai Juyi 白居易) (772–846), pithily intimates a similar role for metaphor and serves as a fitting end for this book.

Awakening's arousal depends on metaphor, delusion's grip comes from empowering the limited.[81]
覺悟因傍喻，迷執由當局。

Bai's poem is written to console his friend, Yuan Zhen 元稹 (799–831). Yuan had a difficult professional career. Because his superiors did not appreciate his cleverness, he had been demoted and sent to wander, suffering, through distant regions.[82]

Bai's advice to Yuan is twofold. Bai's first piece of advice is that Yuan's suffering arises from "empowering the limited" (Ch. *dāng jú* 傍喻), from his personal attachment toward the negative attitudes of his superiors. Bai's second piece of advice is that Yuan can overcome this attachment by studying religious discourses and meditating upon their instructions.[83]

Religious discourses often convey their teachings through metaphor. For Bai, studying and meditating upon these metaphors arouses awakening, and awakening puts an end to personal attachment. So, too, for Fazang. Fazang's metaphors are models for the realm of Samantabhadra. Studying and meditating upon these metaphors is a pathway to achieving insight into the interdependence of everything within this realm.

---

[81] Bai's poem is notoriously obscure and difficult to translate. Levy offers an alternative: "Aroused awareness depends on insight; // delusion's grip comes from authority" (Levy 1971, 97). Li offers another: "Aroused awareness depends on objective insight; // Delusion's grip comes from personal involvement" (Li 2020, 107). I translate 傍喻 as "empowering the limited," because the context of the poem indicates that Bai thinks his friend is suffering by virtue of his sense of self—a sense that views the self as limited and separate from others. I translate 喻 as "metaphor" rather than "insight" for two reasons. The first is that Bai's poem itself is littered with metaphors that give life to Bai's religious insights. The second is that, if Yuan were to follow Bai's advice to study religious discourses, he would encounter many metaphors designed to arouse insight. Translating 喻 as "insight" obscures these important roles for metaphor by focusing on outcome rather than procedure. Translating 喻 as "metaphor" emphasizes that Bai intends his poem to give direction to Yuan and not merely encourage Yuan to focus on a better outcome.

[82] Levy 1971, 96–7.

[83] See Levy 1971, 97.

References

Canonical Works

Amoghavajra 不空 (不空金剛). *Dhāraṇī for Adorning the Bodhi Site* (*Bodhimaṇḍalalakṣālaṁ kāranāmadhāraṇī*; *Pútí cháng zhuāngyán tuóluóní jīng* 菩提場莊嚴陀羅尼經). T, volume 19, number 1008.

Bai Juyi 白居易. "Peaceful Dreams of Wandering in Late Spring: A Poem of One Hundred Rhymes" (*Hé mèng yóuchūn shī yībǎi yùn* 和梦游春诗一百韵). In *Complete Tang Dynasty Poetry* (*Quán táng shī* 全唐诗), volume (*Juǎn* 卷) 437. Cited as reprinted in Sturgeon 2011. Available online at https://ctext.org/text.pl?node=191871.

Buddhabhadra 佛馱跋陀羅. *The Great Expansive Buddha Avataṃsaka-sūtra* (*Mahāvaipulya Buddha Avataṃsaka-sūtra*; *Dàfāngguǎng Fó huáyán jīng* 大方廣佛華嚴經). T, volume 9, number 278.

Buddhayaśas 佛陀耶舍, and Zhu Fonian 竺佛念. *Longer Āgama-sūtra* (*Cháng āhán jīng* 長阿含經). T, volume 1, number 1.

Chengguan 澄觀. *Mysterious Mirror of the Dharma-Realm of Huayan* (*Huáyán fǎjiè xuánjìng* 華嚴法界玄鏡). T, volume 45, number 1883.

Ch'oe Ch'iwŏn 崔致遠. *Biography of the Preceptor Fazang, the Late Venerable Translator and Abbot of the Great Jianfu Monastery of the Tang* (*Tang Tae ch'ŏnboksa kosaju pŏn'gyŏng Taedŏk Pŏpchang hwasang chŏn* 唐大薦福寺故寺主翻經大德法藏和尚傳). T, volume 50, number 2054.

Daoxuan 道宣. *Continued Biographies of Eminent Monks* (*Xù gāosēng zhuán* 續高僧傳). T, volume 50, number 2060.

Dharmayaśas 曇摩耶舍, and Dharmagupta 曇摩崛多, trans. *Treatise of Abhidharma [Preached by] Śāriputra* (*Śāriputra-abhidharma[-śāstra]*; *Shelifu apitan lun* 舍利弗阿毘曇論). T, volume 28, number 1548.

Dushun 杜順. *Cessation and Contemplation in the Five Teachings of Huayan* (*Huáyán wǔjiào zhǐguàn fǎmén* 華嚴五教止觀法門). T, volume 45, number 1867.

Fazang 法藏. *Biographies and Records of the Flower Ornament Discourse* (*Huáyán jīng zhuànjì* 華嚴經傳記). T, volume 51, number 2073.

Fazang 法藏. *Commentary on Awakening Mahāyāna Faith* (*Dàshèng qìxìn lún yìjì* 大乘起信論義記). T, volume 44, number 1846.

Fazang 法藏. *Commentary on the Flower Adornment Sūtra* (*Huáyán jīng zhǐguī* 華嚴經旨歸). T, volume 45, number 1871.

Fazang 法藏. *Commentary on the Laṅkāvatāra Sūtra* (*Rùléng jiāxīn xuányì* 入楞伽心玄義). T, volume 39, number 1790.

Fazang 法藏. *Commentary on the Non-Duality of the Dharma-Realm in Mahāyāna* (*Dàshèng fǎjiè wú chābié lún shū* 大乘法界無差別論疏). T, volume 44, number 1838.

Fazang 法藏. *Commentary on the Twelve Gate Treatise* (*Shí èr mén lún zōngzhì yì jì* 十二門論宗致義記). T, volume 42, number 1826.

Fazang 法藏. *Contemplations on Exhausting Delusion and Returning to the Source by Cultivating the Mysteries of Huayan* (*Xiū Huáyán àozhǐ wàngjìn huányuán guàn* 修華嚴奧旨妄盡還源觀). T, volume 45, number 1876.

Fazang 法藏. *Essay on the Three Treasures* (*Huáyán jīng míng fǎ pǐn nèi lì sānbǎo zhāng* 華嚴經明法品內立三寶章). T, volume 45, number 1874.

Fazang 法藏. *Introduction to the Golden Lion Seal of the Flower Adornment Sūtra* (*Huáyán jīng jīn shīzi zhāng zhù* 華嚴經金師子章註). T, volume 45, number 1881.

242 REFERENCES

Fazang 法藏. *Investigating the Mysteries of the Flower Adornment Sūtra* (*Huáyán jīng tànxuán jì* 華嚴經探玄記). T, volume 35, number 1733.

Fazang 法藏. *Record of Freely Wandering Mind in the Dharma-Realm of Huayan* (*Huáyán yóuxīn fǎjiè jì* 華嚴遊心法界記). T, volume 45, number 1877.

Fazang 法藏. *Treatise on the Divisions within the One Vehicle Doctrine of Huayan* (*Huáyán yīshèng jiàoyì fēnqí zhāng* 華嚴一乘教義分齊章). Also known as *Treatise on the Five Teachings of Huayan* (*Huáyán wǔjiào zhāng* 華嚴五教章). T, volume 45, number 1866.

Fazang 法藏. *Treatise on the Golden Lion* (*Jīn shīzǐ zhāng* 金師子章). T, volume 45, number 1880.

Guṇabhadra 求那跋陀羅. *Connected Scriptures* (*Saṃyukta Āgama*; *Zá āhán jīng* 雜阿含經). T, volume 2, number 99.

Harivarman 訶梨跋摩. *Treatise on Accomplishing Reality* (**Tattvasiddhi-śāstra* or *Satyasiddhi-śāstra*; *Chéng shí lún* 成實論). Translated by Kumārajīva 鳩摩羅什. T, volume 32, number 1646.

Hōtan Sōshun 鳳潭僧濬. *Commentary on Treatise on the Five Teachings of Huayan for Assisting the Tradition and Aiding the Truth* (*Kegon ichijō kyōbunki fushū kyōshin shō* 華嚴一乘嚴分記輔宗匡眞鈔). T, volume 73, number 2344.

Huiyuan 慧遠. *Chapters on the Meaning of Mahāyāna* (*Dàshèng yì zhāng* 大乘義章). T, volume 44, number 1851.

Kumārajīva 鳩摩羅什. *Lotus Sūtra of Wondrous Dharma* (*Miàofǎ liánhuá jīng* 妙法蓮華經). T, volume 9, number 262.

Kumārajīva 鳩摩羅什. *Sūtra on the Concentration of Sitting Meditation* (*Zuòchán sānmèi jīng* 坐禪三昧經). T, volume 15, number 614.

Nāgārjuna. *Commentary on the Great Perfection of Wisdom* (*Dà zhìdù lún* 大智度論). Translated by Kumārajīva 鳩摩羅什. T, volume 25, number 1509.

Nāgārjuna. *Twelve Gate Treatise* (*Shí èr mén lún* 十二門論). Translated by Kumārajīva 鳩摩羅什. T, volume 30, number 1568.

P'yowon 表員. *Questions and Answers on the Essentials of the Textual Meaning of the Flower Adornment Sūtra* (*Hwaŏm-gyŏng Munŭi Yogyŏl Mundap* 華嚴經文義要決問答). X, volume 8, number 237.

Paramārtha 真諦. *Compendium of Mahāyāna* (*Mahāyānasaṃgraha*; *Shè dàshèng lún* 攝大乘論). Attributed to Asaṅga 無著. T, volume 31, number 1593.

Piṅgala (Blue Eyes) 青目. *Middle Treatise* (*Zhōng lún* 中論). Translated by Kumārajīva 鳩摩羅什. T, volume 30, number 1564.

Prajña 般若. *The Great Expansive Buddha Avataṃsaka-sūtra* (**Mahāvaipulya Buddha Avataṃsaka-sūtra*; *Dàfāngguǎng Fó huáyán jīng* 大方廣佛華嚴經). T, volume 10, number 293.

Saṃghabhadra. *Abhidharma Treatise Conforming to the Correct Logic* (**Abhidharma-nyāyānusāra-śāstra*; *Āpídámó shùn zhēnglǐ lùn* 阿毘達磨順正理論). Translated by Xuanzang 玄奘. T, volume 29, number 1562.

Saṃghadeva, Gautama 瞿曇僧伽提婆. *Middle Length Sūtras* (*Zhōng āhán jīng* 中阿含經). T, volume 1, number 26.

Saṃghadeva, Gautama 瞿曇僧伽提婆. *Numerical Sūtras* (*Ekottara Āgama*; *Zēngyī āhán jīng* 增壹阿含經). T, volume 2, number 125.

Śikṣānanda 實叉難陀. *The Great Expansive Buddha Avataṃsaka-sūtra* (**Mahāvaipulya Buddha Avataṃsaka-sūtra*; *Dàfāngguǎng Fó huáyán jīng* 大方廣佛華嚴經). T, volume 10, number 279.

Sūtra on the Monk Nāgasena (*Milindapañha* or **Nāgasena-bhikṣu-sūtra*; *Nāxiān bǐqiū jīng* 那先比丘經). Translator unknown. T, volume 32, number 1670B.

Vasubandhu. *Treatise on the Compendium of Mahāyāna* (*Mahāyānasaṅgrahabhāṣya*; *Shè dàshèng lún shì* 攝大乘論釋). Translated by Xuanzang 玄奘. T, volume 31, number 1597.

Vasubandhu. *Treatise on the Ten Stages* (*Daśabhūmikasūtra-śāstra*; *Shí dì jīng lún* 十地經論). Translated by Bodhiruci 菩提流支. T, volume 26, number 1522.

Xuanzang 玄奘. *Greater Compendium of Abhidharma* (*Abhidharma Mahāvibhāṣā Śāstra*; *Āpídámó dàpípóshā lún* 阿毘達磨大毘婆沙論). T, volume 27, number 1545.

Xuanzang 玄奘. *Treatise on Foundations of Yogic Practice* (*Yogâcārabhūmi-śāstra*; *Yúqié shīdì lùn* 瑜伽師地論). Attributed to Maitreya 彌勒菩薩. T, volume 30, number 1579.

Xuanzang 玄奘. *Treatise on the Demonstration of Consciousness-Only* (*Chéng wéishí lún* 成唯識論). T, volume 31, number 1585.

Yijing 義淨. *Root Monastic Code of the Mūlasarvāstivādins* (*Gēnběn shuō yīqièyǒu bù* 根本說一切有部). T, volume 24, number 1450.

Zhanran Jingxi 湛然荊溪. *Commentary of the Profound Meaning of the Lotus Sūtra* (*Fǎhuá xuányì shìqiān* 法華玄義釋籤). T, volume 33, number 1717.

Zhiyan 智儼. *Record on Fathoming the Mysteries of Huayan* (*Huáyán sōuxuán jì* 華嚴搜玄記). T, volume 35, number 1732.

Zhiyan 智儼. *Ten Mysterious Gates of the Unitary Vehicle of Huayan* (*Huáyán yīchéng shíxuán mén* 華嚴一乘十玄門). T, volume 45, number 1868.

Zhiyi 智顗. *Great Cessation and Contemplation* (*Móhē zhǐ guàn* 摩訶止觀). T, volume 46, number 1911.

Zhiyi 智顗. *Six Wondrous Dharma Gates* (*Liù miào fǎmén* 六妙法門). T, volume 46, number 1917.

Zhiyi 智顗. *Subtle Meaning of the Lotus Sūtra* (*Miào fǎ lián huá jīng xuán yì* 妙法蓮華經玄義). T, volume 33, number 1716.

Non-Canonical Works

Ackrill, J.L. 1984. "Categories." In *The Complete Works of Aristotle: The Revised Oxford Translation, Volume 1*, edited by Jonathan Barnes, pp. 2–27. Princeton, NJ: Princeton University Press.

Amatayakul, Supakwadee. 2023. "Khema of Great Wisdom from India *Circa* 563 BCE–483 BCE." In *Women Philosophers from Non-Western Traditions: The First Four Thousand Years*, edited by Mary Ellen Waithe and Therese Boos Dykeman, pp. 103–114. Chaim: Springer Nature Switzerland AG.

Ames, Roger T. 2003. *Confucian Role Ethics: A Vocabulary*. Honolulu: University of Hawai'i Press.

Anālayo, Bhikkhu. 2009. "The Lion's Roar in Early Buddhism—A Study based on the *Ekottarika-āgama* Parallel to the *Cūḷasīhanāda-sutta*." *Chung-Hwa Buddhist Journal* 22: pp. 3–24.

Anālayo, Bhikkhu. 2012. "The Chinese Parallels to the *Dhammacakkappavattana-sutta* (1)." *Journal of the Oxford Centre for Buddhist Studies* 3: pp. 12–46.

Anālayo, Bhikkhu. 2015. *Saṃyukta-āgama Studies*. Taipei: Dharma Drum Publishing Corporation.

Anālayo, Bhikkhu. 2021a. "Dependent Arising and Interdependence." *Mindfulness* 12: pp. 1094–1102.

Anālayo, Bhikkhu. 2021b. *The Scripture on the Monk Nāgasena: A Chinese Counterpart to the Milindapañha*. Moraga, CA: BDK America, Inc.

Bacon, Andrew. 2020. "Logical Combinatorialism." *Philosophical Review* 129 (4): pp. 537–589.

Bachynski, Kathleen. 2010. "'Le Vain Bastiment': Human Systems and Philosophy in Montaigne's *Apologie de Raimond Sebond*." *The Romanic Review* 101 (4): pp. 619–637.

Baird, Robert D. 1971. *Category Formation and the History of Religions*. The Hague: Mouton & Co.

Barnes, Jonathan. 1991. *The Complete Works of Aristotle: The Revised Oxford Translation*. Princeton, NJ: Princeton University Press.

Barnhill, David L. 1990. "Indra's Net as Food Chain: Gary Snyder's Ecological Vision." *Ten Directions* 11 (1): pp. 20–29.

Bass, Jules, and Arthur Rankin, Jr. 1979. *Jack Frost*. Rankin/Bass Productions.

Baxter, Donald L.M. 2017. "Self-Differing, Aspects, and Leibniz's Law." *Noûs* 52 (4): pp. 900–920.

244 REFERENCES

Benická, Jana. 2002. "Concepts of 'Levels' of Discernment of *Reality* in Different Schools of Chinese Mahāyāna Buddhism." *Asian and African Studies* 11 (2): pp. 169–184.

Benn, James A. 1998. "Where Text Meets Flesh: Burning the Body as an Apocryphal Practice in Chinese Buddhism." *History of Religions* 37 (4): pp. 295–322.

Bennett, Karen. 2017. *Making Things Up*. New York: Oxford University Press.

Berkowitz, Alan J. 1995. "Account of the Buddhist Thaumaturge Baozhi." In *Buddhism in Practice*, edited by Donald S. Lopez, Jr., pp. 578–585. Princeton, NJ: Princeton University Press.

Bingenheimer, Marcus, Bhikkhu Anālayo, and Roderick S. Bucknell. 2013. *The Madhyama Āgama (Middle-Length Discourses), Volume I*. Moraga, CA: BDK America.

Birch, Jonathan. 2019. "Joint Know-How." *Philosophical Studies* 176 (12): pp. 3329–3352.

Bird, Marly. 2017. *Yarn Pooling Made Easy: Techniques for Using Variegated Yarn for Planned Patterns*. Little Rock, AR: Leisure Arts, Inc.

Bliss, Ricki, and Graham Priest. 2017. "Metaphysical Dependence, East and West." In *Buddhist Philosophy: A Comparative Approach*, edited by Steven M. Emmanuel, pp. 63–85. Malden, MA: John Wiley & Sons, Inc.

Bliss, Ricki, and Graham Priest. 2018. "The Geography of Fundamentality: An Overview." In *Reality and its Structure: Essays in Fundamentality*, edited by Ricki Bliss and Graham Priest, pp. 1–33. New York: Oxford University Press.

Bocking, Brian Christopher. 1984. *An Annotated Translation of the Chung-lun, with Nāgārjuna's Middle Stanzas, a Basic Text of Chinese Buddhism, Volume II*. Ph.D. Dissertation, The University of Leeds.

Bodhi, Bhikkhu. 2000. *The Connected Discourses of the Buddha: A New Translation of the Saṃyutta Nikāya*. Boston: Wisdom Publications.

Bodhi, Bhikkhu. 2012. *The Numerical Discourses of the Buddha: A New Translation of the Aṅguttara Nikāya*. Boston: Wisdom Publications.

Bokenkamp, Stephen R. 1989. "Chinese Metaphor Again: Reading—and Understanding—Imagery in the Chinese Poetic Tradition." *Journal of the American Oriental Society* 109 (2): pp. 211–221.

Bradshaw, David. 2004. *Aristotle East and West: Metaphysics and the Division of Christendom*. New York: Cambridge University Press.

Butler, Edward P. 2018. "Bhakti and Henadology." *Journal of Dharma Studies* 1 (1): pp. 147–161.

Canton, Barry, Anna Labno, and Drew Endy. 2008. "Refinement and Standardization of Synthetic Biological Parts and Devices." *Nature Biotechnology* 26: pp. 787–793.

Cao Jin. 2018. "The Chinese Way of Minting: Comparative Perspectives on Coin Production before Mechanisation." In *Southwest China in Regional and Global Perspectives (c. 1600–1911)*, edited by Jin Cao and Ulrich Theobald, pp. 184–223. Leiden: Brill.

Capra, Fritjof. 1975. *The Tao of Physics: An Exploration of the Parallels between Modern Physics and Eastern Mysticism*. Boulder, CO: Shambhala.

Carnap, Rudolf. 1937. *The Logical Syntax of Language*. London: Kegan Paul.

Carpenter, Amber D. 2014. *Indian Buddhist Philosophy*. New York: Routledge.

Carter, John Ross. 1976. "Traditional Definitions of the Term 'Dhamma.'" *Philosophy East and West* 26 (3): pp. 329–337.

Chang, Ae Soon (Venerable Kye Hwan). 2012. "Contemplation of Mutual Identity Theory in Chinese Buddhism." *International Journal of Buddhist Thought & Culture* 18: pp. 25–46.

Chang, Garma C.C. 1971. *The Buddhist Teaching of Totality: The Philosophy of Hwa Yen Buddhism*. University Park: The Pennsylvania State University Press.

Che, Chan Ngan 陳雁姿. 2013. 《十地經論》的六相詮釋方法與意義 [《*Shí dì jīng lún*》 *De liùxiāng quánshì fāngfǎ yú yìyì*, The Hermeneutic Methodology and Significance of the Six Characteristics in the Daśabhūmikasūtra-śāstra]. 第一屆慈宗國際學術論壇議程 *Dìyī jiè cízōng guójì xuéshù lùntán yìchéng*: pp. 496–505.

REFERENCES 245

Chen, Jinhua. 2002. "An Alternative View of the Meditation Tradition in China: Meditation in the Life and Works of Daoxuan (596–667)." *T'oung Pao* 88 (4/5): pp. 332–395.

Chen, Jinhua. 2007. *Philosopher, Practitioner, Politician: The Many Lives of Fazang (643–712).* Boston: Brill.

Cheng, Hsüeh-li. 1982. "Causality as Soteriology: An Analysis of the Central Philosophy of Buddhism." *Journal of Chinese Philosophy* 9: pp. 423–440.

Ching, Julia. 1993. *Chinese Religions.* London: Macmillan.

Chödrön, Gelongma Karma Migme. 2001. *The Treatise on the Great Perfection of Wisdom by Nāgārjuna (Mahāprajñāpāramitāśāstra).* Pleasant Bay, NS: Karma Changchub Ling. English translation of Lamotte 1944–1981. Available online at https://www.wisdomlib.org/buddhism/book/maha-prajnaparamita-sastra.

Choong, Mun-keat. 2010. *Annotated Translation of Sutras from the Chinese Samyuktagama Relevant to Early Buddhist Teachings on Emptiness and the Middle Way.* 2nd revised, ed. Songhkla: International Buddhist College.

Cleary, Thomas. 1983. *Entry into the Inconceivable: An Introduction to Hua-yen Buddhism.* Honolulu: University of Hawai'i Press.

Cleary, Thomas. 1993. *The Flower Ornament Scripture: A Translation of the Avatamsaka Sutra.* Boston: Shambala Publications.

Cohen, S. Marc. 2013. "Accidental Beings in Aristotle's Ontology." In *Reason and Analysis in Ancient Greek Philosophy: Essays in Honor of David Keyt,* edited by Georgios Anagnostopoulos and Fred D. Miller, Jr., pp. 231–242. New York: Springer.

Cook, Francis H. 1970. *Fa-tsang's Treatise on the Five Doctrines: An Annotated Translation.* Ph.D. Dissertation, University of Wisconsin.

Cook, Francis. 1977. *Hua-yen Buddhism: The Jewel Net of Indra.* University Park: Pennsylvania State University Press.

Cook, Francis. 1979. "Causation in the Chinese Hua-yen Tradition." *Journal of Chinese Philosophy* 6 (4): pp. 367–385.

Cook, Francis H. 1999. *Three Texts on Consciousness Only.* Berkeley, CA: Numata Center for Buddhist Translation and Research.

Copp, Paul. 2014. *The Body Incantatory: Spells and the Ritual Imagination in Medieval Chinese Buddhism.* New York: Columbia University Press.

Cotnoir, A.J. 2017. "Mutual Indwelling." *Faith and Philosophy* 34 (2): pp. 123–151.

Cowling, David. 1998. *Building the Text: Architecture as Metaphor in Late Medieval and Early Modern France.* New York: Oxford University Press.

Cox, Collett. 1995. *Disputed Dharmas: Early Buddhist Theories on Existence—An Annotated Translation of the Section on Factors Dissociated from Thought from Saṅghabhadra's Nyāyān usāra.* Tokyo: The International Institute for Buddhist Studies.

Cox, Collett. 2004. "From Category to Ontology: The Changing Role of 'Dharma' in Sarvāstivāda Abhidharma." *Journal of Indian Philosophy* 32 (5/6): pp. 543–597.

Crager, Adam. 2018. "Three Ones and Aristotle's *Metaphysics*." *Metaphysics* 1 (1): pp. 110–134.

Craver, Carl F., and Lindley Darden. 2013. *In Search of Mechanisms: Discoveries across the Life Sciences.* Chicago: University of Chicago Press.

Defoort, Carine. 1997. "Causation in Chinese Philosophy." In *A Companion to World Philosophies,* edited by Eliot Deutsch and Ron Bontekoe, pp. 165–173. Malden, MA: Blackwell Publishers, Inc.

Dhammajoti, K.L. 2008. "The Sixteen-mode Mindfulness of Breathing." *Journal of the Centre for Buddhist Studies, Sri Lanka* 6: pp. 251–288.

Dhammajoti, Kuala Lumpur 法光. 2015. *Sarvāstivāda Abhidharma.* Hong Kong: The Buddha-Dharma Centre of Hong Kong.

Dharmamitra, Bhikshu. 2009. *The Six Dharma Gates to the Sublime: A Classic Meditation Manual on Traditional Indian Buddhist Meditation.* Seattle: Kalavinka Press.

Dharmamitra, Bhikshu. 2022. *The Flower Adornment Sutra: An Annotated Translation of The Avataṃsaka Sutra.* 3 volumes. Seattle: Kalavinka Press.

246 REFERENCES

Di Giacomo, Francesco. 2021. "Early Theoretical Chemistry: Plato's Chemistry in Timaeus." *Foundations of Chemistry* 23: pp. 17–30.

Dor, Galia. 2013. "The Chinese Gate: A Unique Voice for Inner Transformation." *Journal of Daoist Studies* 6: pp. 1–28.

Duncan, Michael, Kristie Miller, and James Norton. 2018. "Ditching Determination and Dependence: Or, How to Wear the Crazy Trousers." *Synthese* 198 (1): pp. 395–418.

Elstein, David. 2014. "Fazang, The Rafter Dialogue." In *Readings in Later Chinese Philosophy: Han Dynasty to the 20th Century*, edited by Justin Tiwald and Bryan W. Van Norden, pp. 80–85. Indianapolis: Hackett.

Engle, Artemus B. 2009. *The Inner Science of Buddhist Practice: Vasubandhu's Summary of the Five Heaps with Commentary by Sthirmati*. Ithaca, NY: Snow Lion Publications.

Ettlinger, Nancy. 2007. "Precarity Unbound." *Alternatives: Global, Local, Political* 32 (3): pp. 319–340.

Fan Wen-li 范文麗. 2019. "寂護的因果論 [Śāntarakṣita on Causation]." *Xuánzàng fóxué yánjiū* 玄奘佛學研究 [*Hsuan Chang Journal of Buddhist Studies*] 31: pp. 95–127.

Fang, Alex Chengyu, and François Thierry. 2016. "Chinese Charms and the Iconographic Language of Good Luck and Heavenly Protection." In *The Language and Iconography of Chinese Charms: Deciphering a Past Belief System*, edited by Alex Changyu Fang and François Thierry, pp. 1–30. Singapore: Springer.

Fang Litian 方立天. 1991. 法藏 [*Fazang*]. Taibei: Dongda tushu gongsi.

Fardin, M.A. 2014. "On the Rheology of Cats." *Rheology Bulletin* 83 (2): pp. 16–30.

Fausböll, Viggo. 1880. *The Jātakatthavannana, Volume 1*. Translated by T.W. Rhys Davis. London: Trubner & Co.

Findlay, Scott D., and Paul Thagard. 2012. "How Parts Make Up Wholes." *Frontiers in Physiology* 3: pp. 455.1–10.

Fink, Charles K. 2015. "Clinging to Nothing: The Phenomenology and Metaphysics of Upādāna in Early Buddhism." *Asian Philosophy* 25 (1): pp. 15–33.

Forte, Antonino. 2000. *A Jewel in Indra's Net: The Letter Sent by Fazang in China to Ŭisang in Korea*. Kyoto: Italian School of East Asian Studies.

Fox, Alan. 2013. "The Huayan Metaphysics of Totality." In *A Companion to Buddhist Philosophy*, edited by Steven M. Emmanuel, pp. 180–189. Malden, MA: John Wiley & Sons, Inc.

Fox, Alan. 2015. "The Practice of Huayan Buddhism." In *Chinese Buddhism: Past, Present, and Future (Hànchuán Fójiào yánjiū de guòqù xiànzài wèilái huìyì lùnwénjí* 《漢傳佛教研究的過去現在未來》會議論文集), edited by Xie Daning 謝大寧, pp. 259–285. Yilan 宜蘭: Foguang University Center for Buddhist Studies (Fóguāng dàxué Fójiào yánjiū zhōngxīn 佛光大學佛教研究中心).

Frankel, Lois. 1986. "Mutual Causation, Simultaneity and Event Description." *Philosophical Studies* 49 (3): pp. 361–372.

Frost, Gloria. 2022. *Aquinas on Efficient Causation and Causal Powers*. New York: Cambridge University Press.

Fu Xinian. 2017. *Traditional Chinese Architecture: Twelve Essays*. Princeton, NJ: Princeton University Press.

Fuller, Paul. 2005. *The Notion of Diṭṭhi in Theravāda Buddhism*. New York: RoutledgeCurzon.

Fung, Yiu-ming. 2020. "Sameness (*Tong* 同) and Difference (*Yi* 異)." In *Dao Companion to Chinese Philosophy of Logic*, edited by Yiu-ming Fung, pp. 213–231. Cham, Switzerland: Springer.

Garfield, Jay L. 1995. *The Fundamental Wisdom of the Middle Way: Nāgārjuna's Mūlamadhyamakakārikā*. New York: Oxford University Press.

Garfield, Jay L. 2006. "Reductionism and Fictionalism: Comments on Siderits' *Personal Identity and Buddhist Philosophy*." *APA Newsletter on Asian and Asian-American Philosophers and Philosophies* 6 (1): pp. 1–7.

Garfield, Jay L. 2015. *Engaging Buddhism: Why It Matters to Philosophy*. New York: Oxford University Press.

Geen, Jonathan. 2007. "Knowledge of Brahman as a Solution to Fear in the Śatapatha Brāhmaṇa/Bṛhadāraṇyaka Upaniṣad." *Journal of Indian Philosophy* 35 (1): pp. 33–102.

Geng, Ji-peng. 2016. "Coin Charms Featuring Gods and Spirits during the Song and Jin Dynasties." In *The Language and Iconography of Chinese Charms: Deciphering a Past Belief System*, edited by Alex Changyu Fang and François Thierry, pp. 83–104. Singapore: Springer.

Giddings, William J. 2017. "Liberating the Whole World: Sudhana's Meeting with Samantanetra from the *Sūtra of the Entry into the Realm of Reality*." In *Buddhism and Medicine: An Anthology of Primary Sources*, edited by C. Pierce Selguero, pp. 92–102. New York: Columbia University Press.

Gilbert, Scott F., Jan Sapp, and Alfred I. Tauber. 2012. "A Symbiotic View of Life: We Have Never Been Individuals." *The Quarterly Review of Biology* 87 (4): pp. 325–341.

Gilson, Erinn C. 2014. *The Ethics of Vulnerability: A Feminist Analysis of Social Life and Practice*. New York: Routledge.

Gilson, Etienne. 1952. *Being and Some Philosophers*. Toronto: Pontifical Institute of Mediaeval Studies.

Gimello, Robert M. 1976a. "Apophatic and Kataphatic Discourse in Mahāyāna: A Chinese View." *Philosophy East and West* 26 (2): pp. 117–136.

Gimello, Robert Michael. 1976b. *Chih-yen (智儼, 602–688) and the Foundations of Hua-yen (華嚴) Buddhism*. Ph.D. Dissertation, Columbia University.

Girard, Frédéric. 2012. "*The Treatise on the Golden Lion* Attributed to Fazang in China and Japan." In *Avataṃsaka Buddhism in East Asia: Origins and Adaptation of a Visual Culture*, edited by Robert Gimello, Frédéric Girard, and Imre Hamar, pp. 307–338. Wiesbaden: Harrassowitz Verlag.

Gold, Jonathan C. 2007. "Yogācāra Strategies against Realism: Appearances (*ākṛti*) and Metaphors (*upacāra*)." *Religion Compass* 1 (1): pp. 131–147.

Gold, Jonathan C. 2015. *Paving the Great Way: Vasubandhu's Unifying Buddhist Philosophy*. New York: Columbia University Press.

Goodman, Charles. 2004. "The Treasury of Metaphysics and the Physical World." *Philosophical Quarterly* 54 (216): pp. 389–401.

Goudriaan, Teun. 1978. *Maya: Divine and Human*. Delhi: Motilal Banarsidass.

Gregory, Peter N. 1983. "Chinese Buddhist Hermeneutics: The Case of Hua-yen." *Journal of the American Academy of Religion* 51 (2): pp. 231–249.

Gregory, Peter N. 1991. *Tsung-Mi and the Sinification of Buddhism*. Honolulu: University of Hawaii Press.

Gregory, Peter N. 1993. "What Happened to the 'Perfect Teaching'? Another Look at Hua-yen Buddhist Hermeneutics." In *Buddhist Hermeneutics*, edited by Donald S. Lopez, Jr., pp. 207–230. Delhi: Motilal Bonarsidass Publishers.

Gregory, Peter N. 2005. "The Sutra of Perfect Enlightenment." In *Apocryphal Scriptures*, edited by Bukkyō Dendō Kyōka, pp. 47–113. Moraga, CA: BDK America.

Griffith, Ralph T.H. 1889. *The Hymns of the Rigveda: Translated with a Popular Commentary, Volume 1*. Benares: E.J. Lazarus and Co.

Griffith, Ralph T.H. 1896. *The Hymns of the Atharvaveda, Volume 2, Part 2*. Benares: E.J. Lazarus and Co.

Guenther, Herbert V. 1957. *Philosophy and Psychology in the Abhidharma*. Lucknow: Pioneer Press.

Guo Xiu-nian 郭秀年. 2018. *The Background of the Idea of "Inseparability" (xiangji 相即) according to Zhiyi and Fazang* [Zhìyǐ yú Fǎzàng "xiāngjí" sīxiǎng yuānyuán yánjiū 智顗與法藏「相即」思想淵源研究]. Ph.D. Dissertation, Huafan University 華梵大學.

Haiming, Wen. 2011. "A Reconstruction of Zhuang Zi's Metaphysical View of Dao from the Heavenly Axis Perspective." *Contemporary Chinese Thought* 43 (1): pp. 78–92.

Hall, Ardelia Ripley. 1935. "The Early Significance of Chinese Mirrors." *Journal of the American Oriental Society* 55 (2): pp. 182–189.

248 REFERENCES

Hamar, Imre. 2007. "The History of the *Buddhāvataṃsaka-sūtra*: Shorter and Larger Texts." *Reflecting Mirrors: Perspectives on Huayan Buddhism*, edited by Imre Hamar, pp. 139–167. Wiesbaden: Harrassowitz Verlag.

Hamar, Imre. 2014a. "Huayan Explorations of the Realm of Reality." In *The Wiley Companion to East Asian and Inner Asian Buddhism*, edited by Mario Poceski, pp. 145–165. Malden, MA: John Wiley & Sons, Inc.

Hamar, Imre. 2014b. "The Metaphor of the Painter in the *Avataṃsaka-sūtra* and Its Chinese Interpretations." *Studia Orientalia Slovaca* 13 (2): pp. 175–198.

Hamar, Imre. 2023. "The Huayan Understanding of One-mind and Buddhist Practice on the Basis of the Awakening of Faith." *Távol-Keleti Tanulmányok* [*Journal of East Asian Cultures*] 15 (2): pp. 41–58.

Han, Jaehee. 2020. *The Sky as a Mahāyāna Symbol of Emptiness and Generous Fullness: A Study and Translation of the Gaganagañjaparipṛcchā, Volume 2.* Ph.D. Dissertation, University of Oslo.

Harvey, Peter. 1995. *The Selfless Mind: Personality, Consciousness and Nirvāṇa in Early Buddhism.* New York: RoutledgeCurzon.

Harvey, Peter. 2013. "Dukkha, Non-Self, and the Teaching on the Four 'Noble Truths.'" In *A Companion to Buddhist Philosophy*, edited by Steven M. Emmanuel, pp. 26–45. Oxford: Wiley-Blackwell.

He Fan. 2019. "Difference to One: A Nuanced Early Chinese Account of *Tong*." *Asian Philosophy* 29 (2): pp. 116–127.

Heldke, Lisa. 2018. "It's Chomping All the Way Down: Toward an Ontology of the Human Individual." *The Monist* 101: pp. 247–260.

Hesse, Hermann. 2003. *Siddhartha: An Indian Tale.* New York: Penguin Books.

Hino, Taidō 日野泰道. 1953. "A Historical Consideration of the Sixfold Nature Theory of Huayan" [*Kegon ni okeru rokusōsetsu no shisōshiteki kōsatsu* 華嚴に於ける六相説の思想史的考察]. 印度学仏教学研究 *Indogaku Bukkyōgaku kenkyū* 1 (2): pp. 410–411.

Ho, Chien-hsing. 2014. "The Way of Nonacquisition: Jizang's Philosophy of Ontic Indeterminacy." In *A Distant Mirror: Articulating Indic Ideas in Sixth and Seventh Century Chinese Buddhism*, edited by Chen-kuo Lin and Michael Radich, pp. 397–418. Hamburg: Hamburg University Press.

Ho, Chien-hsing. 2020. "Ontic Indeterminacy: Chinese Madhyamaka in the Contemporary Context." *Australasian Journal of Philosophy* 98 (3): pp. 419–433.

Ho, Chiew Hui. 2018. "Samantabhadra: Iconographical Transformations and Ritual Identities." *International Journal of Buddhist Thought & Culture* 28 (2): pp. 147–176.

Hoffman-Kolss, Vera. 2021. "Intrinsic/Extrinsic." In *The Routledge Handbook of Properties*, edited by A.R.J. Fisher and Anna-Sofia Maurin, pp. 92–102. New York: Routledge.

Hofweber, Thomas. 2016. *Ontology and the Ambitions of Metaphysics.* New York: Oxford University Press.

Holder, John J. 2006. *Early Buddhist Discourses.* Indianapolis: Hackett Publishing Company.

Holst, Mirja Annalena. 2021. "'To Be Is To Inter-Be': Thich Naht Hanh on Interdependent Arising." *Journal of World Philosophies* 6: pp. 17–30.

Hong, Hao. 2019. "The Metaphysics of *Dao* in Wang Bi's Interpretation of *Laozi*." *Dao* 18: pp. 219–240.

Hopkins, Jeffrey. 1996. *Meditation on Emptiness.* Boston: Wisdom Publications.

Hota, Kashinath. 1998–1999. "Dharma as a Property." *Bulletin of the Deccan College Post-Graduate and Research Institute* 58/59: pp. 279–287.

Hsien, Heng. 1980. *The Great Means Expansive Buddha Flower Adornment Sutra.* Talmage: Buddhist Text Translation Society. Translated from T, volume 9, number 278.

Hsing-kong. 1995. "The Translation of the Term 'Samskara' in the Chinese Buddhist Literature." 佛教與中國文化國際學術會議論文集 (上輯) [*Proceedings of the International Conference on Buddhism and Chinese Culture (Part One)*]: pp. 285–302.

Hsu, Chien Yuan. 2007. *The Eight-Negations of Pratityasamutpada in Mulamadhyamakakarika*. M.A. Thesis, University of Calgary.

Huang, Chun-chieh. 1995. "Historical Thinking in Classical Confucianism: Historical Argumentation from the Three Dynasties." In *Time and Space in Chinese Culture*, edited by Chun-chieh Huang and Erik Zürcher, pp. 72–85. New York: E.J. Brill.

Hung, Jenny. 2020. "Is Dharma-nature Identical to Ignorance? A Study of '*Ji* 即' in Early Tiantai Buddhism." *Asian Philosophy* 30 (4): pp. 307–323.

Hwang, Soonil. 2006. *Metaphor and Literalism in Buddhism: The Doctrinal History of Nirvāṇa*. New York: Routledge.

Ichimura, Shohei. 2015. *The Canonical Book of the Buddha's Lengthy Discourses, Volume I*. Moraga, CA: BDK America, Inc.

Ireland, John D. 1997. *The Udāna: Inspired Utterances of the Buddha & The Itivuttaka: The Buddha's Sayings*. Kandy, Sri Lanka: Buddhist Publication Society.

Ishii Kōsei 石井 公成. 2003. "Kegonshū no kangyō bunken ni mieru zenshū hihan Kainō no sanka hōmon ni ryūi shite" 華厳宗の観行文献に見える禅宗批判－慧能の三科法門に留意して [Criticism against Zen sect in the Meditation Document of Huayan School with Focus on Huineng's Three Categories]. *Matsugaoka bunko kenkyū nenpō* 松ヶ岡文庫研究年報 [*Matsugaoka Library Annual Research Report*] 17: pp. 47–62.

Jammer, Max. 2006. *Concepts of Simultaneity: From Antiquity to Einstein and Beyond*. Baltimore: The Johns Hopkins University Press.

Jennings, Carolyn Dicey. 2022. *Attention and Mental Control*. New York: Cambridge University Press.

Jiang, Tao. 2001. "The Problematic of Whole-Part and the Horizon of the Enlightened in Huayan Buddhism." *Journal of Chinese Philosophy* 28 (4): pp. 457–475.

Jin Tao 金濤. 2013a. "初唐文人作品中的援儒入佛以及佛教漢化之思想背景：以二諦論與李師政《內德論》為中心之探討 [The Confucian Reading of Buddhist Teaching: Two Truths, Li Shizheng and the Intellectual Milieu of Buddhism in the Early Tang]." *Xuánzàng fóxué yánjiū* 玄奘佛學研究 [*Hsuan Chang Journal of Buddhist Studies*] 19: pp. 113–146.

Jin Tao. 2013b. "What It Means to Interpret: A Standard Formulation and Its Implicit Corollaries in Chinese Buddhism." *Philosophy East and West* 63 (2): pp. 153–175.

Jin Young-you 진영유. 2009. "「화엄경」에 나타난 불타관 [A View on Buddhakāyas in the Avataṃsaka Sūtra]." 불교사상과 문화 제 [*Buddhist Thought and Culture*] 1: pp. 43–83.

Johnston, Ian. 2010. *The Mozi: A Complete Translation*. New York: Columbia University Press/ Hong Kong: The Chinese University Press.

Jones, Nicholaos. 2018a. "Huayan Numismatics as Metaphysics: Explicating Fazang's Coin-Counting Metaphor." *Philosophy East and West* 68 (4): pp. 1155–1177.

Jones, Nicholaos. 2018b. "The Metaphysics of Identity in Fazang's *Huayan Wujiao Zhang*: The Inexhaustible Freedom of Dependent Origination." In *Dao Companion to Chinese Buddhist Philosophy*, edited by Youru Wang and Sandra A. Wawrytko, pp. 295–323. Dordrecht: Springer.

Jones, Nicholaos. 2019. "The Architecture of Fazang's Six Characteristics." *British Journal for the History of Philosophy* 27 (3): pp. 468–491.

Jones, Nicholaos. 2020. "An Account of Generous Action and Esteem in Pāli Buddhism." *International Journal of Buddhist Thought & Culture* 30 (2): 195–225.

Jones, Nicholaos. 2021. "Mereological Composition in Analytic and Buddhist Perspective." *Journal of the American Philosophical Association* 7 (2): pp. 173–194.

Jones, Nicholaos. 2022. "Interpreting Interdependence in Fazang's Metaphysics." *The Journal of East Asian Philosophy* 2: pp. 35–52.

Jones, Nicholaos. 2023a. "Metaphysical Foundationalism, Heterarchical Structure, and Huayan Interdependence." *Asian Journal of Philosophy* 2: article 65.

Jones, Nicholaos. 2023b. "Soteriological Mereology in the Pāli Discourses, Buddhaghosa, and Huayan Buddhism." *Dao* 22: pp. 117–143.

Jones, Nicholaos. 2025. "Prolegomenon for Fazang's *Essay on the Golden Lion.*" *British Journal for the History of Philosophy* 33 (1): pp. 48–63.

Jorgensen, John, Dan Lusthaus, John Makeham, and Mark Strange. 2019. *Treatise on Awakening Mahāyāna Faith.* New York: Oxford University Press.

Kahn, David. 2017. "LEGO˚, Impermanence, and Buddhism." In *LEGO˚ and Philosophy: Constructing Reality Brick by Brick*, edited by Roy T. Cook and Sondra Bacharach, pp. 185–196. Hoboken, NJ: Wiley Blackwell.

Kamata, Shigeo 鎌田茂雄. 1965. *Chūgoku kegon shisōshi no kenkyū* 中国華厳思想の研究 [*A Study of Chinese Huayan Buddhism*]. Tokyo: Tōkyō daigaku shuppankai.

Kamtekar, Rachana. 2024. "Causal Pluralism in Vasubandhu and Plato." In *Crossing the Stream, Leaving the Cave: Buddhist-Platonist Philosophical Inquiries*, edited by Amber D. Carpenter and Pierre-Julien Harter, pp. 73–95. New York: Oxford University Press.

Kang, Li. 2024. "The Relative Identity of All Objects: Tiantai Buddhism Meets Analytic Metaphysics." *Ergo* 11: article 44.

Kantor, Hans-Rudolf. 2006. "Ontological Indeterminacy and Its Soteriological Relevance: An Assessment of Mou Zongsan's (1909–1995) Interpretation of Zhiyi's (538–597) Tiantai Buddhism." *Philosophy East and West* 56 (1): pp. 16–68.

Kantor, Hans-Rudolf. 2024. "Tiantai's Reception and Critique of the Laozi and Zhuangzi." *Religions* 15 (1): article 20.

Kaplan, Stephen. 1990. "A Holographic Alternative to a Traditional Yogācāra Simile: An Analysis of Vasubandhu's Trisvabhāva Doctrine." *The Eastern Buddhist* 23 (1): pp. 56–78.

Kapstein, Matthew. 1988. "Mereological Considerations in Vasubandhu's 'Proof of Idealism.'" *Idealistic Studies* 18 (1): pp. 32–54.

Karp, Cary. 2018. "Defining Crochet." *Textile History* 49 (2): pp. 208–223.

Karunadasa, Y. 2019. *The Theravāda Abhidhamma: Inquiry into the Nature of Conditioned Reality.* Somerville, MA: Wisdom Publications.

Kasulis, Thomas P. 2009. "Helping Western Readers Understand Japanese Philosophy." In *Frontiers in Japanese Philosophy 6: Confluences and Cross-Currents*, ed. Raquel Bouso and James W. Heisig, pp. 215–236. Nagoya: Nanzan Institute for Religion & Culture.

Kasulis, Thomas P. 2018. *Engaging Japanese Philosophy: A Short History.* Honolulu: University of Hawai'i Press.

Kawamura, Leslie S. 1964. *A Study of the Triṃśikā-Vijñapti-Bhāṣya.* M.A. Thesis, Kyoto University.

Kazama Toshio 風間敏夫. 1962. "On the Conception of Ātman in the Brāhmaṇa." *Journal of Indian and Buddhist Studies* [*Indogaku Bukkyōgaku Kenkyū* 印度學佛教學研究] 10 (1): pp. 363–359.

Keenan, John P. 2003. *The Summary of the Great Vehicle by Bodhisattva Asaṅga*, Revised Second Edition. Berkeley, CA: Numata Center for Buddhist Translation and Research.

Kellner, Birgit. 2014. "Changing Frames in Buddhist Thought: The Concept of Ākāra in Abhidharma and Buddhist Epistemological Analysis." *Journal of Indian Philosophy* 42 (2/3): pp. 275–295.

Kim, Jaegwon. 1998. *Mind in a Physical World: An Essay on the Mind-Body Problem and Mental Causation.* Cambridge, MA: The MIT Press.

Kim, Kyung-nam 金京南. 2007. "Interpretation of the Six Characteristics in the Dasabhumi-vyakhyana (DBhV): Focusing on vivarta and samvarta' [十地経論』の六相解釈 -- 成相・壊相を中心として]." 印度學佛教學 研究 *Yìndù xué Fójiào xué yánjiū* 55 (3): pp. 945–942.

Kim, Young-ho. 1990. *Tao-sheng's Commentary on the Lotus Sūtra: A Study and Translation.* Albany, NY: SUNY Press.

King, Martin Luther Jr. 1986. "The Ethical Demands for Integration." In *A Testament of Hope: The Essential Writings and Speeches of Martin Luther King, Jr.*, ed. James Melvin Washington, pp. 117–125. New York: HarperCollins.

King, Martin Luther Jr. 1992. "The Chief Characteristics and Doctrines of Mahayana Buddhism." In *The Papers of Martin Luther King, Jr. Volume I: Called to Serve, January 1929–June 1951*, ed. Clayborne Carson, Ralph Luker, and Penny A. Russell, pp. 313–327. Berkeley: University of California Press.

Kiyotaka, Kimura. 1977. *A History of Chinese Huayan Thought [Shoki chugoku kegon shiso no kenkyu]*. Tokyo: Shunjasha.

Koh, Seunghak. 2015. "The Huayan Philosophers Fazang and Li Tongxuan on the 'Six Marks' and the 'Sphere of Edification.'" *The Eastern Buddhist* 46 (2): pp. 1–18.

Koh, Seunghak 고승학. 2019. "A Huayan View of the Infinite Regress [무한소급에 대한 화엄의 입장]." *Journal of the Society of Philosophical Studies [Cheolhag-yeongu 철학연구]* 127: pp. 11–31.

Koh, Seunghak. 2024. "Interpretation of the Method of Counting Ten in the East Asian Tradition of Huayan Scholasticism." *International Journal of Buddhist Thought & Culture* 34 (1): pp. 169–203.

Kronen, John, and Jacob Tuttle. 2011. "Composite Substances as True Wholes: Toward a Modified Nyāya-Vaiśeṣika Theory of Composite Substances." *Canadian Journal of Philosophy* 41 (2): pp. 289–316.

Kubo, Tsugunari, and Akira Yuyama. 2007. *The Lotus Sutra (Taishō Volume 9, Number 262): Translated from the Chinese of Kumārajiva*. Berkley, CA: Numata Center for Buddhist Translation and Research.

LaFave, Kenneth. 2018. *The Sound of Ontology: Music as a Model for Metaphysics*. Lanham, MD: Lexington Books.

Lai, Whalen. 1977. "Chinese Buddhist Causation Theories: An Analysis of the Sinitic Mahāyāna Understanding of *Pratitya-samutpāda*." *Philosophy East and West* 27 (3): pp. 241–264.

Lamotte, Étienne. 1944–1981. *Le Traite de la Grande Vertu de Sagesse de Nāgārjuna (Mahāprajñāpāramitāśāstra) [The Treatise on the Great Perfection of Wisdom by Nāgārjuna]*, Tome I–V. Louvain: Publications de l'Institut Orientaliste de Louvain.

Ledderose, Lothar. 2000. *Ten Thousand Things: Module and Mass Production in Chinese Art*. Princeton, NJ: Princeton University Press.

Levy, Howard S. 1971. *Translations from Po Chü-i's Collected Works, Volume 1: The Old Style Poems*. New York: Paragon Book Reprint Corp.

Li, Qiancheng. 2020. *Transmutations of Desire: Literature and Religion in Late Imperial China*. Hong Kong: The Chinese University of Hong Kong Press.

Lička, Lukáš. 2019. "What Is in the Mirror? The Metaphysics of Mirror Images in Albert the Great and Peter Auriol." In *The Senses and the History of Philosophy*, edited by Brian Glenney and José Filipe Silva, pp. 131–148. New York: Routledge.

Liefke, Lena, and Jörg Plassen. 2016. "Some New Light on an Old Authorship Problem in Huayan Studies: The Relation between T.1867 and T.1877 from a Text-Critical and Linguistic Perspective." *Bochumer Jahrbuch zur Ostasienforschung* 39: pp. 103–136.

Lin, Chen-kuo. 2016. "*Svalakṣaṇa* (Particular) and *Sāmānyalakṣaṇa* (Universal) in Abhidharma and Chinese Yogācāra Buddhism." In *Text, History, and Philosophy: Abhidharma across Buddhist Scholastic Traditions*, edited by Bart Dessein and Weijen Teng, pp. 375–395. Leiden: Brill.

Lin, Weiyu. 2021. *Exegesis-Philosophy Interplay: Introduction to Fazang's 法藏 (643–712) Commentary on the Huayan jing 華嚴經 (60 juans) [Skt. Avataṃsaka Sūtra; Flower Garland Sūtra]—the Huayan jing tanxuan ji 華嚴經探玄記 [Record of Investigating the Mystery of the Huayan jing]*. M.A. Thesis, The University of British Columbia.

Liu, Ming-wood. 1979. *The Teaching of Fa-tsang: An Examination of Buddhist Metaphysics*. Ph.D. Dissertation, University of California, Los Angeles.

Liu Ming-wood 廖明活. 1981. "The P'an-chiao System of the Hua-yen School in Chinese Buddhism." *T'oung Pao* 67 (1/2): pp. 10–47.

252 REFERENCES

Liu, Ming-wood. 1982a. "The Harmonious Universe of Fa-tsang and Leibniz: A Comparative Study." *Philosophy East and West* 32 (1): pp. 61–76.

Liu, Ming-wood. 1982b. "The Three-Nature Doctrine and Its Interpretation in Hua-yen Buddhism." *T'oung Pao* 68 (4/5): pp. 181–220.

Liu, Ming-wood. 1994. *Madhyamaka Thought in China*. New York: E.J. Brill.

Liu, Ming-wood. 2003. "Fazang (Fa-tsang)." In *Encyclopedia of Chinese Philosophy*, edited by Anthony Cua, pp. 252–257. New York: Routledge.

Liu Ning 刘宁, and Yancheng Zhang 张晏诚 (executive producers). 2018. 香蜜沉沉烬如霜 [*Ashes of Love*]. Chongqing Broadcasting Group (重庆广播电视集团) and Jiangsu Broadcasting Corporation (江苏省广播电视总台).

Mace, Sonya Rhie. 2020. "Clearing the Course: Folio 348 of the Nepalese *Gaṇḍavyūha-sūtra* in the Cleveland Museum of Art." *Religions* 11(4): article 183.

Macy, Joanna. 1991. *Mutual Causality in Buddhism and General Systems Theory: The Dharma of Natural Systems*. Albany: State University of New York Press.

Manné, Joy. 1996. "Sīhanāda—The Lion's Roar: Or What the Buddha Was Supposed to Be Willing to Defend in Debate." *Buddhist Studies Review* 13 (1): pp. 7–36.

Marmodoro, Anna. 2010. *The Metaphysics of Powers: Their Grounding and their Manifestations*. New York: Routledge.

Matilal, B.K. 1977. "Ontological Problems in Nyāya, Buddhism, and Jainism: A Comparative Analysis." *Journal of Indian Philosophy* 5 (1/2): pp. 91–105.

McBride, Richard D. II. 2005. "Dhāraṇī and Spells in Medieval Sinitic Buddhism." *Journal of the International Association of Buddhist Studies* 28 (1): pp. 85–114.

McBride, Richard D. II. 2012a. "Questions and Answers on the Essentials of the Textual Meaning of the Avataṃsaka-Sūtra." In *Hwaŏm II: Selected Works*, edited by Richard D. McBride II, pp. 75–268. Seoul: Jogye Order of Korean Buddhism.

McBride, Richard D. II. 2012b. "Self-Diagram Symbolizing the Dharma Realm of the One Vehicle of the Avataṃsaka." In *Hwaŏm I: The Mainstream Tradition*, edited by Richard D. McBride II, pp. 99–186. Seoul: Jogye Order of Korean Buddhism.

Mellamphy, Dan. 1988. "Fragmentality (Thinking the Fragment)." *Dalhousie French Studies* 45: pp. 83–98.

Milburn, Olivia. 2010. *The Glory of Yue: An Annotated Translation of the Yuejue shu*. Boston: Brill.

Morganti, Matteo. 2014. "Metaphysical Infinitism and the Regress of Being." *Metaphilosophy* 45 (2): pp. 232–244.

Muller, A. Charles. 2014. "A Pivotal Text for the Definition of the Two Hindrances in East Asia: Huiyuan's 'Erzhang yi' Chapter." In *A Distant Mirror: Articulating Indic Ideas in Sixth and Seventh Century Chinese Buddhism*, edited by Chen-kuo Lin and Michael Radich, pp. 214–270. Hamburg: Hamburg University Press.

Muller, A. Charles. 2016. "The Emergence of Essence-Function (*ti-yong*) 體用 Hermeneutics in the Sinification of Indian Buddhism: An Overview." *Bulgyohaglibyu* 불교학리뷰 [*Critical Review for Buddhist Studies*] 19 (6): pp. 111–152.

Muller, A. Charles. 2022. *Digital Dictionary of Buddhism*. Edition of November 30, 2022. http://www.buddhism-dict.net/ddb/.

Mun, Chan Ju. 2002. *The History of Doctrinal Classification in Chinese Buddhism: A Study of the Panjiao Systems*. Ph.D. Dissertation, University of Wisconsin—Madison.

Murcott, Susan. 2006. *First Buddhist Women: Poems and Stories of Awakening*. Berkeley, CA: Parallax Press.

Nakamura Hajime 中村元. 1989. *Iwanami Dictionary of Buddhism* [*Iwanami Bukkyō jiten* 岩波仏教辞典]. Tokyo: Iwanami Shoten.

Nakasone, Ronald Yukio. 1980. *The Huan-yüan-kuan: A Study of the Hua-yen Interpretation of Pratītyasamutpāda*. Ph.D. Dissertation, University of Wisconsin.

Nakasone, Ronald Y. 2022. *Mapping the Pathways of Huayan Buddhist Thought: Its Origin, Unfolding, and Relevance*. New York: Peter Lang.

Ñāṇamoli, Bhikkhu. 2010. *The Path of Purification (Visuddhimagga)*. Kandhi: Buddhist Publication Society.

Ñāṇamoli, Bhikkhu, and Bhikkhu Bodhi. 1995. *The Middle Length Discourses of the Buddha: A New Translation of the Majjhima Nikāya*. Boston: Wisdom Publications, 1995.

Needham, Joseph. 1971. *Science and Civilization in China. Volume 4: Physics and Physical Technology. Part III: Civil Engineering and Nautics*. New York: Cambridge University Press.

Nehemas, Alexander, and Paul Woodruff. 1997. "Phaedrus." In *Plato: Complete Works*, edited by John M. Cooper, pp. 506–556. Indianapolis: Hackett Publishing Company.

Nhất Hạnh, Thích. 2017. *The Art of Living*. London: Penguin.

Nichols, Ryan, and Nicholaos Jones. 2023. "Holistic Cognitive Style, Chinese Culture, and the Sinification of Buddhism." *Res Philosophica* 100 (1): pp. 93–120.

Obert, Mathias. 2000. *Sinndeutung Und Zeitlichkeit - Zur Hermeneutik Des Huayan-Buddhismus*. Hamburg: Felix Meiner Verlag.

Oddie, Graham. 2001. "Axiological Atomism." *Australasian Journal of Philosophy* 79 (3): pp. 313–332.

Oh, Kang-Nam. 1979. "*Dharmadhātu*: An Introduction to Hua-yen Buddhism." *The Eastern Buddhist* 12 (2): pp. 72–91.

Ohnuma, Reiko. 2000. "The Story of Rūpāvatī: A Female Past Birth of the Buddha." *Journal of the International Association of Buddhist Studies* 23 (1): pp. 103–146.

Ohnuma, Reiko. 2004. "Rūpyāvatī Gives Away Her Breasts." In *Buddhist Scriptures*, edited by Donald S. Lopez, Jr., pp. 159–172. New York: Penguin Books.

Olivelle, Patrick. 1998. *The Early Upaniṣads: Annotated Text and Translation*. New York: Oxford University Press.

Oppenheim, Paul, and Hilary Putnam. 1958. "Unity of Science as a Working Hypothesis." *Minnesota Studies in the Philosophy of Science* 2: pp. 3–36.

Owens, Alex. 2022. *Inventing Indra's Net: The Modern Construction of an Ancient Metaphor*. Ph.D. Dissertation, Lancaster University.

Park, Boram 박보람. 2016. "A Study of the Changes of the Six Characteristics Theory (六相說) from Daśabhūmikasūtra to the Dilun school" [육상설은 어떻게 변해 왔는가?: [십지경]부터 지론종까지를 대상으로Yugsangseol-eun eotteohge byeonhae wassneunga?: [sibjigyeong]buteo jilonjongkkajileul daesang-eulo]. 불교학연구 *Bul Gyo Hak Yeongu* 47: pp. 1–28.

Park, Boram. 2018. "Authorship Attribution in Huayan Texts by Machine Learning Using N-gram and SVM." *International Journal of Buddhist Thought & Culture* 28 (2): pp. 69–86.

Park, Jin Y. 2008. *Buddhism and Postmodernity: Zen, Huayan, and the Possibility of Buddhist Postmodern Ethics*. New York: Lexington Books.

Paul, L.A. 2012. "Building the World from Its Fundamental Constituents." *Philosophical Studies* 158: pp. 221–25.

Pesala, Bhikku. 2001. *The Debate of King Milinda*. Alperton, UK: Association for Insight Meditation.

Ping, Yanhong. 2023. "A New Exploration of the Dharma Lineage of Fazang (法藏): The Third Patriarch of the Huayan School." *Religions* 14 (9): article 1200.

Plassen, Jörg. 2007. "Some Remarks on the Authorship of the *Ilsŭng pŏpkyedo*." In *Reflecting Mirrors: Perspectives on Huayan Buddhism*, edited by Imre Hamar, pp. 261–280. Wiesbaden: Harrassowitz Verlag.

Plassen, Jörg. 2012. "From Terms to Schemata: Some Prefatory Remarks on a Complementary Approach to Wŏnhyo's Practice." *Buddhist Studies* [불교연구 *Pulgyo yŏn'gu*] 36: pp. 109–134.

Plassen, Jörg. 2020. "Some Remarks on Influences from Silla in Some Works Commonly Ascribed to Du Shun 杜順, Focusing on *Huayan fajie guanmen* 華嚴法界觀門." *The Review of Korean Studies* 23 (1): pp. 35–54.

Plassen, Jörg. 2023. "Is All-Unity a Possibility in Mahāyāna Thought? Some Musings Centering on Huayan Expositions of the Net of Indra." In *God or the Divine? Religious Transcendence beyond Monism and Theism, between Personality and Impersonality*, edited by Bernhard Nitsche and Marcus Schmücker, pp. 133–147. Berlin: Walter de Gruyter GmbH.

Priest, Graham. 2014. *One: Being an Investigation into the Unity of Reality and of Its Parts, including the Singular Object Which Is Nothingness*. New York: Oxford University Press.

Priest, Graham. 2015. "The Net of Indra." In *The Moon Points Back*, edited by Koji Tanaka, Yasuo Deguchi, Jay L. Garfield, and Graham Priest, pp. 113–127. New York: Oxford University Press.

Priest, Graham. 2018a. "Buddhist Dependence." In *Reality and its Structure: Essays in Fundamentality*, edited by Ricki Bliss and Graham Priest, pp. 126–139. New York: Oxford University Press.

Priest, Graham. 2018b. *The Fifth Corner of Four: An Essay on Buddhist Metaphysics and the Catuṣkoṭi*. New York: Oxford University Press.

Priest, Graham. 2022. "Causation in Buddhist Philosophy." In *From Electrons to Elephants and Elections: Exploring the Role of Context and Content*, edited by Shyam Wuppuluri and Ian Stewart, pp. 99–116. Cham, Switzerland: Springer.

Pruden, Leo M. 1991. *Abhidharmakośabhāṣyam of Vasubandhu*, by Louis de La Valée Poussin. Berkeley: Asian Humanities Press.

Pruitt, William. 1998. *The Commentary on the Verses of the Therīs (Therīgāthā-Aṭṭhakathā, Paramatthadīpanī VI) by Acariya Dhammapāla*. Oxford: Pali Translation Society.

Purdy, Daniel. 2011. *On the Ruins of Babel: Architectural Metaphor in German Thought*. New York: Cornell University Press.

Qian Zhongshu 錢鍾書. 1998. *Limited Views: Essays on Ideas and Letters*, translated by Ronald Egan. Cambridge, MA: Harvard University Press.

Qing, Fa. 2016. "Counting the Breath in Kumārajīva's Meditation Texts." *Journal of the International Association of Buddhist Universities* 9 (2): pp. 68–80.

Que, Ze-li, Zhe-rui Li, Xiao-lan Zhang, Zi-ye Yuan, and Biao Pan. 2017. "Traditional Wooden Buildings in China." In *Wood in Civil Engineering*, edited by Concu Giovanna, pp. 197–221. Rijeka: InTech.

Ratié, Isabelle. 2017. "An Indian Debate on Optical Reflections and Its Metaphysical Implications: Śaiv Nondualism and the Mirror of Consciousness." In *Indian Epistemology and Metaphysics*, edited by Joerg Tuske, pp. 207–240. New York: Bloomsbury.

Reat, N. Ross. 1993. *The Śālistamba Sūtra*. Delhi: Motilal Banarsidass Publishers.

Repetti, Rick. 2017. *Buddhist Perspectives on Free Will: Agentless Agency?* New York: Routledge.

Restivo, Sal P. 1978. "Parallels and Paradoxes in Modern Physics and Eastern Mysticism: I—A Critical Reconnaissance." *Social Studies of Science* 8 (2): pp. 143–181.

Richardson, Herbert W. 1967. "A Philosophy of Unity." *Harvard Theological Review* 60 (1): pp. 1–38.

Robins, Dan. 2000. "Mass Nouns and Count Nouns in Classical Chinese." *Early China* 25: pp. 147–184.

Ronkin, Noa. 2005. *Early Buddhist Metaphysics: The Making of a Philosophical Tradition*. New York: RoutledgeCurzon.

Rowe, Christopher. 2015. *Plato: Theaetetus and Sophist*. New York: Cambridge University Press.

Ryle, Gilbert. 2009. *The Concept of Mind*. New York: Routledge.

Salvucci, Emiliano. 2016. "Microbiome, Holobiont, and the Net of Life." *Critical Reviews in Microbiology* 42 (3): pp. 485–494.

Sangpo, Gelong Lodrö. 2012. *Abhidharmakośa-Bhāṣya of Vasubandhu: The Treasury of the Abhidharma and its (Auto) Commentary*. Delhi: Motilal Banadsidass Publishers.

Sastri, N. Aiyaswami. 1978. *Satyasiddhiśāstra of Harivarman, Volume II*. Baroda, India: Oriental Institute.

Schaffer, Jonathan. 2009. "On What Grounds What." In *Metametaphysics: New Essays on the Foundations of Ontology*, edited by David J. Chalmers, David Manley, and Ryan Wasserman, pp. 374–383. New York: Oxford University Press.

Scheimer, Lou (executive producer). 1983–1985. *He-Man and the Masters of the Universe*. Filmation Associates and Mattel.

Sen, Tansen. 2014. "Relic Worship at the Famen Temple and the Buddhist World of the Tang Dynasty." In *Secrets of the Fallen Pagoda: Treasures from Famen Temple and the Tang Court*, edited by Eugene Y. Wang, Tansen Sen, Wang Sen, Alan Chong, Kan Shuyi, Pedro Moura Carvalho, Libby Lai-Pik Chan, and Conan Cheong, pp. 24–49. Honolulu: University of Hawai'i Press.

Seok, Gil-am 석길암. 2005. 화엄의 상즉상입설, 그 의미와 구조 - 數十錢法의 전개와 관련하여 [The Meaning and Structure of Mutual-Identity and Mutual-Entering (相卽相入) in Huayan Buddhism, Centered on the Developments of the Metaphor of Counting Coins]. 불교학연구 [*Korean Journal of Buddhist Studies*] 10: pp. 5–28.

Sharf, Robert H. 2002. *Coming to Terms with Chinese Buddhism: A Reading of the Treasure Store Treatise*. Honolulu: University of Hawaii Press.

Shen, Hsueh-man. 2012. "Between One and Many: Multiples, Multiplication and the Huayan Metaphysics." *Proceedings of the British Academy* 181: pp. 205–258.

Shoppa, Clayton. 2016. "Relative Unity in an Undone World: Paraconsistence and the Meaning of Being." *The Review of Metaphysics* 69: pp. 787–809.

Sider, Theodore. 2012. *Writing the Book of the World*. New York: Oxford University Press.

Siderits, Mark. 2007. *Buddhism as Philosophy: An Introduction*. Indianapolis: Hackett Publishing Company.

Siderits, Mark. 2013. "Causation, 'Humean' Causation and Emptiness." *Journal of Indian Philosophy* 42 (4): pp. 433–439.

Siderits, Mark, and Shoryu Katsura. 2013. *Nāgārjuna's Middle Way: Mūlamadhyamakakārikā*. Boston: Wisdom Publications.

Smithers, Stuart Waynne. 1992. *The Vedic Idea of the Soul*. Ph.D. Dissertation, Columbia University.

Spackman, John. 2020. "Nonconceptual Cognition in Yogācāra and Madhyamaka Thought." In *Buddhist Philosophy of Consciousness: Tradition and Dialogue*, edited by Mark Siderits, Ching Keng, and John Spackman, pp. 62–88. Boston: Brill Rodopi.

Stacey, Peter. 2011. "The Sovereign Person in Senecan Political Theory." *Republics of Letters: A Journal for the Study of Knowledge, Politics, and the Arts* 2 (2): pp. 15–73.

Steenhagen, Martin. 2017. "False Reflections." *Philosophical Studies* 174 (5): pp. 1227–1242.

Steinhardt, Nancy S. 2002. "Introduction." In *Chinese Architecture*, edited by Nancy S. Steinhardt, pp. 1–10. New Haven, CT: Yale University Press.

Stewart, Donald. 1971. "Metaphor and Paraphrase." *Philosophy and Rhetoric* 4 (2): pp. 111–123.

Strange, Steven K. 2004. "The Stoics on the Voluntariness of the Passions." In *Stoicism: Traditions & Transformations*, edited by Steven K. Strange and Jack Zupko, pp. 32–51. New York: Cambridge University Press.

Sturgeon, Donald. 2011. *Chinese Text Project*. http://ctext.org.

Sun, Chuang. 2011. "Measurement and Analysis of the Ancient Chinese Timber-Frame Building." In *Proceedings of CIPA Symposium 23*, n.p. Prague: CIPA Heritage Documentation.

Swanson, Paul L. 2018. *Clear Serenity, Quiet Insight: T'ien-t'ai Chih-i's Mo-ho chih-kuan*. Honolulu. University of Hawai'i Press.

Taguchi, Shingeri. 2009. "From Henological Reduction to a Phenomenology of the 'Name': A Reinterpretation of Japanese Pure Land Thought." In *Frontiers of Japanese Philosophy 4: Facing the 21st Century*, edited by Lam Wing-keung and Cheung Ching-yuen, pp. 51–64. Nagoya: Nanzan Institute for Religion & Culture.

Takakusu Junjirō. 1956. *The Essentials of Buddhist Philosophy*. Bombay: Ashgate Publishing House.

Tanaka, Kenneth K. 1985. "Simultaneous Relation (*Sahabhū-hetu*): A Study in Buddhist Theory of Causation." *Journal of the International Association of Buddhist Studies* 8 (1): pp. 91–111.

256 REFERENCES

Tanner, Jeremy. 2018. "Visual Art and Historical Representation in Ancient Greece and China." In *Ancient Greece and China Compared*, edited by G.E.R. Lloyd, pp. 189–233. New York: Cambridge University Press.

Thagard, Paul, and Craig Beam. 2004. "Epistemological Metaphors and the Nature of Philosophy." *Metaphilosophy* 35 (4): pp. 504–516.

Thanissaro, Bhikku 2008. *The Shape of Suffering: A Study of Dependent Co-Arising*. Valley Center, CA: Metta Forest Monastery.

Thapar, Romila. 1994. "Sacrifice, Surplus, and the Soul." *History of Religions* 33 (4): pp. 305–324.

Thompson, Naomi. 2016. "Metaphysical Interdependence." In *Reality Making*, edited by Mark Jago, pp. 38–56. New York: Oxford University Press.

Thurman, Robert A.F. 1980. "Voidnesses and Totalities: Madhyamika and Hua-yen." In *Studies in History of Buddhism: Papers Presented at the International Conference on the History of Buddhism at the University of Wisconsin*, Madison, Wisconsin, USA, August 19–21, 1976, edited by A.K. Narain, pp. 343–348. Delhi: BR Publishing Corp.

Travagnin, Stefania. 2018. "Reception History and Limits of Interpretation: The Belgian Étienne Lamotte, Japanese Buddhologists, the Chinese Monk 印順 and the Formation of a Global 'Da zhidu lun 大智度論 Scholarship.'" *Hualin International Journal of Buddhist Studies* 1 (1): pp. 248–277.

Tucci, Guiseppe. 1934. "The Ratnāvalī of Nāgārjuna." *Journal of the Royal Asiatic Society* 66 (2): pp. 307–325.

Turner, Jason. 2014. "Donald Baxter's Composition as Identity." In *Composition as Identity*, edited by A.J. Cotnoir and Donald L.M. Baxter, pp. 225–243. New York: Oxford University Press.

Ujike, Kakusho. 1983. "On the Penetration of Dharmakāya and Dharmadeśanā—Based on the Different Ideas of Dhāraṇī and Tathāgatagarbha." *Journal of Indian and Buddhist Studies* (*Indogaku Bukkyogaku Kenkyu*) 32 (1): pp. 558–552.

Unno, Taitetsu. 1978. "Review of *Hua-yen Buddhism: The Jewel Net of Indra*. By Francis Cook." *The Journal of Asian Studies* 38 (1): pp. 163–165.

Unno, Taitetsu, Mark Unno, and Monica E. McLellan. 2023. *Treatise on Doctrinal Distinctions of the Huayan One Vehicle (Taishō Volume 45, Number 1866)*. Moraga, CA: BDK America, Inc.

Vallicella, William F. 2002. "Relations, Monism, and the Vindication of Bradley's Regress." *Dialectica* 56 (1): pp. 3–35.

Van Norden, Bryan W. 2014. "Fazang, 'Essay on the Golden Lion.'" In *Readings in Later Chinese Philosophy: Han Dynasty to the 20th Century*, edited by Justin Tiwald and Bryan W. Van Norden, pp 86–91. Indianapolis: Hackett Publishing Company.

Van Norden, Bryan W., and Nicholaos Jones. 2019. "Huayan Buddhism." *Stanford Encyclopedia of Philosophy* (November 2019). https://plato.stanford.edu/entries/buddhism-huayan/.

Van Wolde, Ellen. 2017. "Separation and Creation in Genesis 1 and Psalm 104, A Continuation of the Discussion of the Verb ברא." *Vetus Testamentum* 67 (4): pp. 611–647.

Vorenkamp, Dirck. 2004. *An English Translation of Fa-tsang's Commentary on the Awakening of Faith*. Lewiston, NY: E. Mellen Press.

Wallace, Megan. 2011. "Composition as Identity: Part 2." *Philosophy Compass* 6 (11): pp. 817–827.

Walshe, Maurice. 1995. *The Long Discourses of the Buddha: A Translation of the Dīgha Nikāya*. Boston: Wisdom Publications.

Wang, Yueqing, Qinggang Bao, and Guoxing Guan. 2020. *History of Chinese Philosophy Through Its Key Terms*, translated by Shuchen Xiang. Singapore: Springer/Nanjing University Press.

Warder, A.K. 1971. "Dharmas and Data." *Journal of Indian Philosophy* 1 (3): pp. 272–295.

Wayman, Alex. 1957. "The Meaning of Unwisdom (Avidya)." *Philosophy East and West* 7 (1/2): pp. 21–25.

Wayman, Alex. 1974. "The Mirror as a Pan-Buddhist Metaphor-Simile." *History of Religions* 13 (4): pp. 251–269.

Wei Daoru. 2007. "A Fundamental Feature of the Huayan Philosophy." In *Reflecting Mirrors: Perspectives on Huayan Buddhism*, edited by Imre Hamar, pp. 189–194. Wiesbaden: Harrassowitz Verlag.

Westerhoff, Jan. 2009. *Nāgārjuna's Madhyamaka: A Philosophical Introduction.* New York: Oxford University Press.

Westerhoff, Jan. 2018. *The Golden Age of Indian Buddhist Philosophy.* New York: Oxford University Press.

Wickstrom, Daniel (ヴィットストローム, ダニエル). 2017. "A Study of Xianshou Fazang: Fazang's Biography and Its Problems" (賢首大師法蔵の研究: 法蔵の伝記とその問題). *Ryukoku University Bulletin of the Graduate School of Letters* (龍谷大学大学院文学研究科紀要) 39 (33): pp. 12–20.

Wilkinson, Endymion. 2013. *Chinese History: A Manual.* Cambridge, MA: Harvard University Asia Center.

Wilkinson, W.H. 1895. "Chinese Origin of Playing Cards." *American Anthropologist* A8 (1): 61–78.

Williams, Paul M. 1981. "On Abhidharma Ontology." *Journal of Indian Philosophy* 9 (3): pp. 227–257.

Williams, Paul. 2000. "Response to Mark Siderits' Review." *Philosophy East and West* 50 (3): pp. 424–453.

Wright, Dale S. 1982. "The Significance of Paradoxical Language in Hua-yen Buddhism." *Philosophy East and West* 32 (3): pp. 325–338.

Wut, Tai Shing. 2013. "Investigating the Meaning of Dharma '*Fa*' (法): With Chinese *Saṃyuktāgama* as the Subject." In *New Perspectives on the Research of Chinese Culture*, edited by Pei-kai Cheng and Ka Wai Fan, pp. 77–97. New York: Springer.

Wyller, Egil A. 1997. "The Discipline of Henology: A Synopsis." In *Henologische Perspektiven II: Zu Ehren Egil A. Wyllers*, edited by Tore Frost, pp. 5–12. Amsterdam: Rodopi.

Xiong, Ye. 2024. "*Treatise of the Golden Lion*: An Exploration of the Doctrine of the Infinite Dependent Arising of Dharmadhātu." *Religions* 15 (4): article 482.

Yamabe, Nobuyoshi, and Fumihiko Sueki. 2009. *The Sutra on the Concentration of Sitting Meditation.* Moraga, CA: BDK America, Inc.

Younger, Paul. 1969. "The Concept of Duḥkha and the Indian Religious Tradition." *Journal of the American Academy of Religion* 37 (2): pp. 141–152.

Yu, Jimmy. 2022. *Reimagining Chan Buddhism: Sheng Yen and the Creation of the Dharma Drum Lineage of Chan.* New York: Routledge.

Zacchetti, Stefano. 2021. *The Da zhidu lun* 大智度論 *(*Mahāprajñāpāramitopadeśa) and the History of the Larger Prajñāpāramitā.* Bochum/Freiburg: projekt verlag.

Zhao, Fei. 2016. *A Study of the Usages and Meanings of Ākāra in Abhidharma.* M.A. Thesis, University of Washington.

Ziporyn, Brook. 2003. "Li (Principle, Coherence) in Chinese Buddhism." *Journal of Chinese Philosophy* 30 (3–4): pp. 501–524.

Ziporyn, Brook. 2010. "Tiantai Buddhist Conceptions of 'The Nature' (*Xing*) and Its Relation to the Mind." *Journal of Chinese Philosophy* 37 (3): pp. 493–512.

Ziporyn, Brook. 2013. *Beyond Oneness and Difference: Li* 理 *and Coherence in Chinese Buddhist Thought and Its Antecedents.* Albany: State University of New York Press.

Ziporyn, Brook A. 2016. *Emptiness and Omnipresence: An Essential Introduction to Tiantai Buddhism.* Bloomington: Indiana University Press.

Ziporyn, Brook. 2018. "The *Ti-Yong* 體用 Model and Its Discontents: Models of Ambiguous Priority in Chinese Buddhism and Zhu Xi's Neo-Confucianism." In *The Buddhist Roots of Zhu Xi's Philosophical Thought*, edited by John Makeham, pp. 193–276. New York: Oxford University Press.

Ziporyn, Brook A. 2020. *Zhuangzi: The Complete Writings.* Indianapolis: Hackett Publishing.

Index

For the benefit of digital users, indexed terms that span two pages (e.g., 52–53) may, on occasion, appear on only one of those pages.

Abhidharma
  on aspects, 83–84
  on foundationalism, 220
  on independence, 37
  on indeterminacy, 44
  on mutuality, 193–95
  on real existence, 49, 60, 73
activity
  and aspect, 86
  of *dharmas*, 46, 47, 197–98
  and directionality, 46–47, 50
  of mind, 106–7
  and power, 88, 104
  of wholes, 192, 196–97
aggregate, 40–41, 64, 128, 188–89. *See also*
  composites
appearance of existence, 61–62, 87–88, 92, 163,
  184, 212
Aquinas, 53
Aristotle
  and henology, 225
  on power, 52–53
  on substance, 41n.12, 113n.4, 221–22
Asaṅga, 103, 153
aspect
  and attention, 93, 136, 207, 212
  definitions of, 82–83
  gradings of, 90–92, 122, 131, 136, 174,
  225–27
  pairings of, 89–90, 122, 123, 132, 136, 147–
  48, 174, 222
  parameterizing of, 87–89, 122, 125,
  223, 232
asymmetry
  and attention, 136
  and causality, 73
  and coherentism, 123, 220–21
  as a constraint, 80, 99, 214
  and counting, 141, 147
  and priority, 207, 214, 219–21, 232
ātman, 24–25, 25n.23, 30
attachment
  definition of, 25–26

freedom from, 30, 34, 97, 103, 174–75, 205–6,
  212, 238–39
  manifestations of, 26, 27–29, 32, 103, 105,
  181–82, 230
  Zhuangzi and, 109n.51
attendant. *See* chief-attendant heuristic
attention
  and attachment, 27–28, 97, 109n.51, 238–39
  and causal overdetermination, 101, 105,
  133–34, 136
  focusing of, 93–94, 95–96, 98–99, 104, 136,
  154, 207
  and mind, 102, 106–7, 130–31, 155
  and mutuality, 97–98, 101–2, 107, 125, 137
  shifting of, 94–97, 99, 105, 108–9, 173, 212
Avataṃsaka Sūtra. See Flower Adornment Sūtra

Baozhi, 94
Bhīṣmottaranirghoṣa, 38
bodhisattva, 30, 35, 36, 103, 118, 131, 187, 228
body
  as composite, 11, 25, 40, 181
  different (*see* different body)
  and mutuality, 106n.48
  same (*see* same body)
  and *saṃsāra*, 19–20, 29
breathing, 77–78, 152, 153, 155
Buddhaghosa
  and metaphor of creeper vines, 217n.21
  and metaphor of traveler, 193–94, 195
  on mutuality, 65–66, 193–94
  on real existents, 195
buildings
  architecture of, 14–15, 177–81
  Daosheng on buildings, 182
  as fabrication, 4, 182, 183
  Nāgārjuna on, 183–84
  Nāgasena on, 182–83
  and no-self, 181
  and *saṃsāra*, 182
  and six characteristics, 186
  and unity, 61, 183, 188, 207–8, 225–26
  Zhiyan on, 185

260 INDEX

Capra, F., 9–10
cards, 65–66, 80, 88–89, 91–92, 98–99, 107–8
Carnap, R., 238
causal exclusion, 78, 79, 100, 135–36
causal overdetermination, 77, 81, 133–34, 135, 136
chanting, 171
characteristic, 4, 26, 41, 86, 205
    determinate, 42–43, 44–45, 47, 60–61, 62–63, 97, 200–1
    general, 41–42, 86, 186, 211–12
    indeterminate, 43, 59, 199–200
    specific, 41–42, 46, 51, 105, 109, 114–15, 205–6
    See also six characteristics
chariot, 3–4, 48, 58, 83, 94, 116, 198
Chengguan
    and Indra's net, 111n.1
    and interdependence, 107n.50
    on metaphor, 129n.54
chief-attendant heuristic
    and attention, 96, 97–98, 101, 104–5, 106–7, 207, 222
    and coherentism, 123, 220–21
    definition of, 91
    and henology, 226–27
    and Indra's net, 112, 121, 122, 130–31, 174, 206
    and unity, 176
cognition, 26, 48, 59
    conceptual, 34, 36, 102, 103–4, 202, 205, 211, 216
    correct, 103, 109, 136, 217, 222, 228, 233
    delusional, 19–20, 25–26, 28–29
    erroneous, 62n.66, 105, 202
    nonconceptual, 34, 103, 216–17
coherentism
    and fundamental structure, 9–10, 219–20
    and Indra's net, 122–23, 129n.52
    and mutuality, 123, 220–21
coins, 32n.36, 148–52, 169, 170–71, 207, 225–26
Commentary on Awakening Mahāyāna Faith, 2, 103, 228–29, 230n.55, 235n.74
compassion, 33–34, 117
composites
    and attachment, 181
    and conditionality, 25, 40–41, 48–49, 177, 219, 221
    and indeterminacy, 44
    as nominal existents, 48–49, 181
    See also aggregate
conflict. See obstruction
consciousness
    and contact, 177

as dharma, 41–42, 46, 85
discriminating, 28–29, 65, 102, 162–63
Nāgārjuna on, 183–84
Nāgasena on, 182–83
and self, 77–78
Vasubandhu on, 54
See also mind
Contemplations on Exhausting Delusion, 28, 30, 31, 33, 35n.44, 119–20, 121, 233
conventions, 58–59, 161, 164n.38, 238
Cook, F.
    on causality, 71, 144n.9, 145n.11
    on coins, 148
    on emptiness, 70, 209, 211–12
    on identity, 11–12
    on inclusion, 10–11, 69–71
    on organicism, 15–16, 69, 227
    on power, 70–71
    on syncretism, 234
    on wholes, 11–12, 69–71, 189n.39, 190n.41, 192n.48
cooperation, 144n.9, 177, 178, 194–95
counting
    and attention, 94, 137, 171
    of breaths, 152–53, 154
    of coins, 152, 169, 170
    and directionality, 141, 157, 158, 174
    and emptiness, 162–63
    and gateways, 142, 145, 146–47, 170–71, 173–74, 207
    as incantation, 171
    kinds of, 138–39
    as meditation, 163
    and mind, 155, 162, 163
    as rotational, 158–59
Cox, C., 37n.1, 41–42n.14, 46n.35, 48n.37, 48n.38
crochet, 236

Dao, 109n.51, 193
Daosheng, 182
Daoxuan, 152
dependent arising, 14–15, 87, 109
    and conditionality, 20–21, 90
    dharma-realm of, 110, 118, 205
    teaching of, 67, 72–73, 203, 209–10, 230–31
determinacy
    and characteristics, 42–43, 44–45, 47, 60–61, 62–63, 97, 200–1
    and identity, 56–57
    and power, 51
    and real existence, 49, 52, 61, 62, 106–7, 195, 200–1, 202

INDEX 261

dharma
  and activity, 46, 47, 50–51, 55
  and characteristics, 41, 114–15, 205
  definition of, 41, 64, 118
  and emptiness, 59, 60–61, 64–65, 90, 205–6
  examples of, 40, 46–47, 84, 85
  and existence, 59–62
  as nominal existents, 49, 52, 59, 60–61, 205–6
  and power, 51, 53–54, 78–79, 106–7, 205–6
  and projection, 46–47, 50, 205–6
  as real existents, 49
dharma-body, 228–29, 233
Dharmaguptaka, 182
diamond, 43–44, 48
difference, 145, 186, 190–91, 203, 208
different body, 138–39, 144–45
  Fazang on counting and, 140–41, 142–43,
    159, 207
  Fazang on identity and, 165–66
  Fazang on inclusion and, 139, 159–61
  Zhiyan on counting and, 164, 185
  Zhiyan on identity and, 166
  Zhiyan on inclusion and, 164, 168
discrimination, 28–29, 65, 102, 162–63
disintegration, 186, 198–99, 200–1, 203, 208–9
disposition, 12, 46–47, 52, 53–54, 62–63, 64, 114, 198
doctrinal classification, 7, 239n.80
duḥkha, 22–23, 28, 29, 34, 82–83
Dushun, 17, 123–24
  and perspectivity, 125, 132
  on reflections, 126, 127
  on skillful means, 125–26, 129–30, 133

emptiness
  and coherentism, 123
  Cook on, 70–71, 209, 211–12
  Fazang on, 85, 87, 97, 165
  in *Flower Adornment Sūtra*, 159–62
  Jizang on, 223–24
  Liu on, 71–72
  meaning of, 48, 59, 61, 88, 113, 200
  Nāgārjuna on, 183–84, 210–11
  Nhất Hạnh on, 9
  in relation to existence, 61–62, 86, 91, 92, 97–
    98, 167, 222, 225–27
  of self, 181
  of self-nature, 184, 210, 223–24
  Zhiyi on, 155–56
entering, 7, 35, 36, 37, 38–39, 106, 142
  and power, 54, 55, 74, 76, 89, 91, 98, 198–99
  and reflections, 124–25, 133, 172–73
  See also inclusion
evanescence, 21–22, 41–42, 154

existence
  as apparent, 61–62, 87–88, 92, 163, 184, 212
  meaning of, 59–60
  as nominal (*see* nominal existence)
  as real (*see* real existence)
  in relation to emptiness, 61–62, 86, 91, 92,
    97–98, 167, 222, 225–27

fire
  Aquinas on, 53
  as *dharma*, 25, 40, 41–42, 46–47, 129, 198–99
  and evanescence, 22
  Nāgārjuna on, 212–13
  Plato on, 219
  and *saṃsāra*, 29
  Zhiyi on, 56–57
Flower Adornment Sūtra, 2n.10
  metaphors in, 15, 55n.54, 116, 120, 162–63
  metaphysics in, 35–36, 37, 40, 52, 106, 162, 187
  soteriology in, 29, 34–35, 120
  Sudhana in, 38–39, 104n.46, 120
foundationalism, 4, 219–20
four noble truths, 82–83
Fox, A., 10n.30, 73, 82n.2
freedom
  of *dharmas*, 22, 106, 112, 215, 216, 229, 231–34
  of mind, 29–30, 33, 34, 37–38, 86, 103, 109,
    205–6
  of self, 24, 27n.27
Frost, J., 32n.36
fundamentality
  and ontology, 3–4, 6, 9–10, 105, 121, 132,
    206–7, 219–20
  and priority, 218–20, 224
  and rigidity, 221–24, 227, 232

Garfield, J., 59n.59, 74–75, 201n.70, 213n.16,
    214n.17
gateway, 45, 140–41, 142, 155, 168–69, 173, 207,
    215–17
generosity, 35, 117
gentleness, 32–34, 35, 36
Gilson, Etienne, 224–25
Gimello, R., 10, 187n.29, 239n.80
gods, 4, 35, 37–38, 55n.53, 193, 221–22
Gold, J., 37n.2, 46n.34, 54n.52, 106n.49
golden lion, 2–3, 4–5, 9, 11, 232, 233
gradation
  and attention, 96, 97–98
  as chief-attendant, 91
  as manifest-hidden, 92
  Sarvāstivāda on, 90
Gregory, P., 10, 107n.50, 208, 228n.50, 239n.80

262   INDEX

Hamar, I., 2n.10, 12n.40, 55n.54, 102n.42
Harivarman, 44, 164n.38
harmony
    and breathing, 155
    and mutuality, 36, 71–72, 84, 229, 232
    and teachings, 229, 234–36
    as virtue, 32–34, 35
    and wholes, 12, 146n.12, 189–90, 191, 233
He-Man, 198–99
henology, 224–25
hologram, 73, 191
honesty, 33–34
Hōtan Sōshun, 157
Huiyuan, 187n.32
hypostatization, 210–11

identity (characteristic of), 186, 188–90, 192,
        196–97, 203, 204, 208
identity (relation of)
    and asymmetry, 80, 106–7, 123, 206–7, 214,
        216–17, 220–21, 232
    and attention, 96, 97–98, 101–2
    Cook on, 11–12, 69–70, 227
    definition of, 56–58, 63, 64–65, 86, 192
    and emptiness, 86, 88, 96, 113–14, 115, 165–
        68, 206, 214
    Fazang on, 85, 97, 106, 165, 166–67, 215, 232
    in Flower Adornment Sūtra, 35, 37–38
    and golden lion, 2–3, 9, 12, 232
    and inclusion, 57, 231
    Ŭisangon, 169
    and wholes, 58–59, 195, 196, 197–98, 208–9
    Zhanran on, 199
    Zhiyan on, 166, 167, 185
    Zhiyi on, 56–57, 199–200
ignorance
    definition of, 25–26, 84
    freedom from, 28–30, 34, 36, 97, 102, 103–4,
        182–83
    manifestations of, 26, 27–29, 32, 103, 181–82,
        230
    Zhanran on, 199
impermanence (see evanescence)
incantation, 127n.44, 169, 171
inclusion
    and asymmetry, 76–77, 80, 99, 123, 125, 214,
        220–21
    and attention, 96, 98, 101–2, 104–5
    Cook on, 10–11, 69–71
    definition of, 54, 58n.58, 63, 64–65, 86
    Fazang on, 74, 75–76, 78–79, 85, 98, 139
    Flower Adornment Sūtra on, 35–36, 37
    and golden lion, 2–3, 11
    and identity, 57, 231

    and indeterminacy, 55, 206
    and Indra's net, 72–73, 112
    Nhất Hạnh on, 9
    and power, 55, 57, 75, 79, 88, 96, 98
    and projection, 54, 55, 57, 196–97, 206, 231
    Ŭisang on, 170–71
    and wholes, 58–59, 146–47
    Zhiyan on, 130, 164, 168
indeterminacy
    and characteristics, 43, 59, 199–200
    of diamond, 43–44
    and inclusion, 55, 201
    and nominal existence, 52, 61, 114–15, 202
    and power, 51, 52, 53–54, 58–59, 62, 205–6
Indra, 43, 116–17, 118, 215, 216
infinitism, 219–21
integration, 14, 186, 196–98, 201, 233
Investigating the Mysteries of the Flower
        Adornment Sūtra, 2, 75–76, 78, 104n.46,
        187

jewels, 33, 36, 120
    as dharmas, 118–19, 121–22, 206–7
    Dushun on, 124–26
    of Indra's net, 110–11, 121, 123, 134–36
    Zhiyan on, 130–32
Jizang, 164n.38, 223–24

Kantor, H., 44n.24, 45n.31
Kasulis, T., 73n.20, 191n.45
Khemā, 24
King, M.L. Jr., 9
Koh, S., 49n.40, 157n.32
Kumārajīva, 182
    on characteristics, 41–42
    on counting, 154–55

Lai, W., 72–73
Laozi, 142n.4
LEGO® model of reality, 3–6, 218–19
Liu, M.-w.
    on causality, 71–72
    on coins, 148–49
    on ontology, 225n.46
    on six characteristics, 187n.27
    on teachings, 7n.22, 234, 239n.80
    on three natures, 104n.46
    on Tiantai, 44n.24, 56n.56
lute, 25

Maitreya, 120, 153
making
    and conditionality, 20, 195
    definition of, 56, 192

and identity, 12, 56–57, 64–65, 97–98, 113, 165, 203, 206
and inclusion, 146, 161–62
and painting, 55–56
and wholes, 176, 178, 180–81, 189–90, 193, 199, 200, 204
Mañjuśrī, 103, 104n.45
realm of, 103, 104, 105–6, 216–18
meaning, 85–86. *See also* aspect
meditation, 6n.19, 7, 104, 152, 154, 163, 227
Mengzi, 233
Mīmāṃsā, 126–27
mind
and aspect, 84–85
and attention, 93–94, 102, 106–7, 152, 155–56
well-directed, 29–30, 205–6, 229, 233
mirror, 1–2, 119, 126–30
Mozi, 145–46
mutuality condition, 65, 193–94, 195, 207–8

Nāgārjuna
on buildings, 183–84
and characteristics, 41–42, 113–14
and conditionality, 37, 40
and emptiness, 59, 209, 210–11, 212, 221–22
on fire and fuel, 212–13
and power, 52–53
on reflections, 128
Nāgasena, 182–83
Nakasone, R., 10n.32, 45n.27
Nhất Hạnh, 9
nihilism, 212
nirvāṇa, 29–30, 31, 34–35, 120, 155, 162–63, 183, 230
no-self, 25, 27, 181
nominal existence
and determinacy, 49, 52, 59, 61, 115
meaning of, 48, 60–61, 62–63, 88, 202
non-duality, 75, 76, 86, 132, 144
Nyāya, 41n.12, 126–27

obstruction, 229, 234–35
ocean, 31, 117, 199–200
One Mind, 102n.42
ontology, 64, 202, 218, 225–26
opposition, 45, 186, 189–90, 211, 212, 233
overdetermination. *See* causal overdetermination

P'yowon, 149n.19, 170n.52, 212n.14
Paramārtha, 45n.27
parents, 1, 19–20, 22–23, 31, 32, 113–14, 115–16
Park, J., 6n.19, 10n.32, 82n.2
particularity, 186, 196, 203, 208

parts, 4, 145–46
additive, 191, 193, 194, 195
of building, 177, 179, 181
of chariot, 58
Cook on, 11–12
of golden lion, 3, 11, 12
holistic, 191, 193
and unity, 188–89, 191, 192, 196, 204, 208
perspectivality
and Indra's net, 125, 130–31, 207
and power, 82n.2
Piṅgala, 211
Plassen, J., 6n.19, 34n.40, 111n.1, 124n.37, 169n.47
Plato, 50n.42, 219, 221–22
power
and activity, 88, 104
as complete, 64–65, 74–75, 79, 93, 96, 98, 145, 146–47 (*see also* power, as total)
as determinate, 51
as indeterminate, 51, 52, 53–54, 58–59, 62, 205–6
as partial, 68, 194–95
and projection, 51–52, 195, 198, 205–6, 239
as total, 192n.48 (*see also* power, as complete)
Priest, G., 10n.31, 73, 107n.50, 122n.32, 220n.30
principle, 8, 12n.40, 33, 107n.50, 198, 211
priority
and asymmetry, 207, 214, 219–21, 232
and causation, 71, 131, 217
conditions for, 213, 214, 216–17, 232
among *dharmas* and characteristics, 114
and fundamentality, 218–20, 224
and identity, 206–7, 214, 220–21, 232
and rigidity, 221–22, 224
projection
and causation, 49–51, 52–54, 197–98
definition of, 46–47
and determinacy, 47, 62–63
and identity, 57, 203
and inclusion, 54, 55, 57, 196–97, 206, 231
and power, 51–52, 195, 198, 205–6, 239
and reflection, 126–27

real existence
and determinacy, 49, 52, 61, 62, 106–7, 195, 200–1, 202
meaning of, 47–48, 60
reflections
Dushun on, 126, 127
Fazang on, 111, 132–33, 206
Mīmāṃsā and Nyāya on, 126–27
and moon, 15
Nāgārjuna on, 128
Vasubandhu on, 128–29
Zhiyan on, 130, 132
Zhiyi on, 156

264 INDEX

regress, 49, 62–63
responsiveness, 144, 145–47, 176, 185, 233
root-branch heuristic, 139, 143n.5, 144
  for coins, 150–51
  for counting, 139, 140–41, 143, 145, 161,
    163–64, 165, 171
  and substance-function heuristic, 87, 132
Rūpāvatī, 19, 30–31, 33, 35

Samantabhadra, 104
  realm of, 104, 105–6, 109, 110, 118, 202, 203,
    229–30
Samantanetra, 40
same body, 138–39, 145–46
  Fazang on counting and, 140–41, 144, 146–
    47, 153
  Fazang on identity and, 166–67, 185, 215
  Fazang on inclusion and, 146, 161–62
  and unity, 146, 173–74, 176, 204
  Zhiyan on inclusion and, 168
Saṃghabhadra
  on projection, 46
  on real existence, 48, 60
saṃsāra, 28–29, 30–31, 32, 103, 104, 117, 181–
  82, 202
Sanlun, 44, 59
Sarvāstivāda
  on aspects, 83–84, 90
  on characteristics, 41–42n.14
  on dharmas, 90, 219–20
  on projection, 46
  on truth, 164n.38
self. See ātman
self-nature, 48, 205–6, 213, 221–22
sequentiality
  and evanescence, 22
  Fazang on, 75–76, 93, 97, 101–2, 133–34, 215–16
  and ranking, 45
simultaneity
  Fazang on, 79, 215–16
  in standard interpretation, 65, 70–71, 73, 74–
    75, 99, 105, 106–7
sincerity, 33–34
six characteristics, 186–87, 202, 208, 233
six meanings of cause, 211–12
soteriology, 7–8, 12, 20, 25–26, 34–35, 41–
  42n.14, 230, 238
Sthiramati, 93–97
substance, 41, 64, 113–14, 205, 219, 221–22
substance-function heuristic, 87
  Dushun's use of, 125
  Fazang's use of, 87–88, 89, 96, 133, 144–45,
    147–48, 165–66, 174

Zhiyan's use of, 132, 133
suchness, 103, 105–6
Sudhana, 38–39, 104n.45, 120
support
  for characteristics, 41, 43n.21, 46
  conditions for buildings, 14–15, 61, 177–78,
    179, 180, 183, 200–1
  conditions for effects, 50, 52, 54, 55, 129,
    177–78, 180–81, 206–7
  conditions for saṃsāra, 29, 181–82
  and mutuality, 193, 206–8
svabhāva. See self-nature

three natures, 104n.46
Tiantai
  and emptiness, 59
  and identity, 199–200
  and indeterminacy, 44, 45
trees
  and coins, 149–50
  and root-branch heuristic, 143, 144
  and substance-function heuristic, 132
  and three natures, 104
tripod, 65, 193
truth, 28–29, 82–83, 86, 117–19, 131, 164n.38,
  202–3, 228–29

Ŭisang, 162, 169–72
unity
  and buildings, 61, 183, 188, 207–8, 225–26
  and chief-attendant heuristic, 176
  and parts, 60, 188–89, 191, 192, 196, 204, 208
  and same body, 146, 173–74, 176, 204
  strategies for explaining, 188–90, 191, 192,
    194, 195, 204, 225

Vairocana, 120
Vaiśeṣika, 41n.12, 219–20
Vasubandhu
  on aspects, 84–85
  on counting, 94, 152
  on dharmas, 46n.34, 52, 54
  on reflections, 128–29
virtue, 32–34, 35, 36
Vritra, 116–17
vulnerability, 19–20, 21, 25, 26–27, 30, 181, 239

Wang Bi, 193
water
  as dharma, 25, 40, 44, 47, 50, 129
  etymology for, 118–19
  and Indra, 116–17, 118
  and nirvāṇa, 31

Plato on, 219
Tiantai on, 199–200
and virtue, 33
Wei D., 56n.55, 74n.23
Westerhoff, J., 42n.18, 48n.38, 114n.5
wholeness, 186, 191, 192–93, 194–95, 196–97,
204, 208–9
wholes
Buddhaghosa on, 177–78, 193–94
Cook on, 11–12, 69–71, 189n.39, 190n.41,
192n.48
as imaginary, 201
Nāgārjuna on, 184
Nāgasena on, 183
as nominal existents, 202, 219, 225–26
in relation to parts, 58–59, 173–74, 180–81,
189–90, 191, 196–97, 198, 208
and same body, 146–47, 174–75, 176, 185,
215
as unified, 145–46, 185–86, 188–89, 191,
192–93, 194–95, 204, 233
Zhuangzi on, 184
See also six characteristics
wisdom, 7, 24, 33–34, 35, 60–61, 103, 230
Wu, Empress, 1–2

Xuanzang, 45n.27, 46

Yogācāra
and attention, 93–94
and causality, 45n.27
and characteristics, 41–42n.14
and cognition, 56
and counting, 152–53
and projection, 46
and wholes, 201

Zhanran Jingxi, 199–200
Zhiyan, 1, 10, 123–24, 162
on causality, 45n.27
on counting, 163–69
on Indra's net, 130–32
on mutual identity, 184–85
on reflections, 130, 132
Zhiyi
on counting, 155–56
on indeterminacy, 45, 56–57, 199–200
on reflections, 156
Zhuangzi, 109n.51, 142n.4, 184
Ziporyn, B., 44n.24, 45n.31, 81n.1, 87n.25,
102n.41, 200n.65